HAWKE'S
GREEN BERET
SURVIVAL
MANUAL

ESSE~~NTIAL STRATEGIES FOR~~

SHELTER A~~...~~ FIRE,
TOOLS AND~~...~~ N AND
SIGNALIN~~...~~ OGY,

AND ~~GETTING OUT ALIVE~~

MYKEL HAWKE
CAPTAIN IN THE U.S. ARMY SPECIAL FORCES AND DIRECTOR, HAWKE BRAND & SCHOOL

Skyhorse Publishing

First Skyhorse Publishing edition copyright © 2021 by Mykel Hawke

Skyhorse Publishing books may be purchased in bulk at special discounts for sales promotion, corporate gifts, fund-raising, or educational purposes. Special editions can also be created to specifications. For details, contact the Special Sales Department, Skyhorse Publishing, 307 West 36th Street, 11th Floor, New York, NY 10018 or info@skyhorsepublishing.com.

Skyhorse® and Skyhorse Publishing® are registered trademarks of Skyhorse Publishing, Inc.®, a Delaware corporation.

Visit our website at www.skyhorsepublishing.com.

10 9 8 7 6 5 4 3 2 1

Library of Congress Cataloging-in-Publication Data is available on file.

Cover design by Kai Texel

Print ISBN: 978-1-5107-6308-1
Ebook ISBN: 978-1-5107-6334-0

Printed in the United States of America

DEDICATION AND ACKNOWLEDGMENTS

I'd like to dedicate this book to:

The Past: My fathers Earl, Pete and the others no longer with us, who gave the ultimate sacrifice.
The Present: My wife Ruth; brothers, Jay, Steve, Russ, Zach, Rick, David, Randy, Chris; and those family and friends who stick by through thick and thin.
The Future: My sons Anthony, Nicholas, and Gabriel, and the youth who will carry the torch when our flame has gone out.

I'D LIKE TO GIVE SPECIAL THANKS TO:

My mother, Patricia, she was a true survivor. My sisters Naomi and Michelle and their families: loyal survivors. My in-laws: Tom (for his personal editing) and Elaine, Joe and Georgia—generous and sharing, they survive through life's troubles. Thanks Mamasan and RIP- Papasan, Mama Hoo, Papa Hoo, and Yedidia the Teacher. The men with whom I served, who risked much, gave much, and asked little. The Great Spirit, who guided me in the dark times and blessed me, even when I didn't know it.

Other thanks along the Survival Trail:

Norman the Blood, Ken the last, Owlie & his Son Jon, Beth the Mother, Karl of Aikido, Jim the Author, Mike the Commander, Jake the Recruiter, OB of Africa, Ranger Ryan, General Davis, and Greg and Jay of Books.
And finally, I thank Greg Jones at Running Press, who had the vision and the belief to make this book possible and Jay Cassell of Skyhorse Publishing, who had the vision to keep running with it.

Table of Contents

Foreword

If you think about it, and you won't have to think for very long, you'll see that the term "survival situation" is redundant. If you're in a situation it's a survival situation.

One thing I've run into a lot lately, particularly among women, is a quest for the feeling of safety. To me the feeling of safety is an illusion of safety, but in actuality the only place safety exists is in the grave. If you're dead, nothing worse is going to happen. Life is tough for everybody, but it's deadly for the complacent.

Americans live in comparative safety. I live in Southern California, where we have a much better chance of surviving an earthquake than people in Guatemala. In the area where I live we're surrounded by woods, and the place could go up in an hour, starting from any time at all. So, we might be isolated by an earthquake or roasted by a forest fire. Am I afraid? No. Am I concerned? You betcha. We have a first aid kit, thirty gallons of water, enough gas in the car to get out of Dodge, and a bunch of other sensible stuff.

Do I feel safe? No. Are we safe? No. Are we relatively safe, and are we prepared? Uh huh.

Mykel Hawke has written a really valuable book here, and not only because it's packed with surefire survival techniques. It has some of those, but mostly it's about attitude, and I believe that attitude is necessary for all of life, not just extreme situations. What it's about is awareness, preparedness, and being ready to take every aspect of your situation back to zero, to look at everything around you for threats and tools. It's about being calm when all about you are losing their minds. It's about looking at things as they are, and not how you wish they were or how you fear they are.

A few years back I was getting ready for a flight to Texas from Kennedy in New York. The flight was delayed for an hour. My companion, who was a real dish, and moreover in the movie business, stomped her little foot and said, "This is unacceptable!"

Imagine, humanity longs to be able to fly for the entire 5,000 year history of our "civilization" and this one hour delay is "unacceptable." This is not the attitude to take into a survival situation.

Actually my companion was just playing the role of "Cherokee American Princess." She could ride and she could shoot. Other than the fact that she'd probably be wearing heels and an Armani suit, there's no one I'd rather be thrown into a real survival situation with.

But I digress.

Point is, you need the survival attitude for every aspect of life. They're all survival situations to one degree or another. What we call "survival situations" are sudden, unexpected survival situations, such as being downed in the arctic or the desert, having your safari overtaken by a civil war in some third-world hellhole.

But your home is a survival situation, your car, your job, a day in the park. Every one of those has potential threats that you'd be better off to be aware of and prepared for, better off to keep a cool head and an open mind.

That's what my friend Hawke is about. Read this book carefully. The journey will be fun on one level, and instructive on another. If it makes you one-tenth more aware it may well have been the best investment you ever made.

—Jim Morris

Preface

A bit of background before we begin. . . .

I was born a po' boy in Kentucky. My Pa was a soldier and my Maw was a waitress and we didn't have squat. That's it.

We lived like lots of soldiers' families in the 1960s, especially the young ones like my folks: very, very poor. We literally had outhouses and well water. But hey, it wasn't bad. And like a lot of families during the '60s when the free love and wartime mentalities separated the nation, my folks split up when I was young. So most of my childhood was spent living all over the Southeast with many different friends and relatives, whoever could take me in for a while.

What this meant was a lot of poverty and lot of hardship for my family, and a lot of time for me to try to escape all of that and explore the world away from all the troubles at home, whether it was in the country woods or the city—areas not safe for the general public, let alone a child.

Now, much of the time, I'd be with my mother, back and forth in between spells with relatives, boyfriends, neighbors, sitters, and other friends or co-workers. My mother and father were both good-hearted people, but both had a rough childhood themselves and so, as very young parents, there were a lot of things they could've done better.

Many times, we had electricity or gas or heat or water cut off, or were evicted from our home. We lived in shacks, cars, and trailers with no utilities. We even lived one winter in a house under construction with nothing working, no doors or windows, buckets to catch the rain in the bedroom that only had one bed that we all slept in under one car blanket in all our clothes that we'd then wear to school the next day and all week.

So, many days I spent trying to scrounge food for my brothers and sisters since I was the eldest and the adult(s) were often nowhere to be found. Sometimes we'd have gas and water—shoot, if we only had flour, I'd make flat bread—and sometimes, I'd just go steal some food from the local store.

Can't count how many times they caught and kicked me out of stores, haha! But when they found out what and why I was stealing, they'd usually just let me go.

Now, I could speak a lot about falling in with wrong crowd and all that, but that is another story. The key in that part of my growing up was that I had a lot of near-death experiences, from car crashes to shootings, stabbings and a whole lot more. In all that, I developed an approach to life that comes down to this: Never Quit.

But what really set me on the path to cultivating a deep interest—and eventually, expertise—in survival, was the winter my mother went away.

I was 14; it was late fall in Virginia. I had started working at eight years old, doing yard work for folks around the neighborhood, then paperboy, dishwasher, and grocery bagger, before a great job came along. A friend was working for his stepfather doing high-water-pressure washing of trucks. They got a contract out in the country to use their water to clean the paint off a building and it was short notice; the money was good, so I left that day.

Now, I wasn't in school, and I'd often be gone days at a time. I'd tell my Maw I was at a friend's and that would be fine by her as she'd have one less mouth to feed. So, it wasn't too big a deal when I didn't show up for a few days, but this job was two weeks, and it coincided with a time when she was evicted and had run out of options in Virginia. She got an invite from a friend to move to Texas, and she took it, leaving with my li'l bro and my two sisters, and without me.

Since we never had a phone, there was no way for her to reach me. When I eventually did return home, full of joy at the proper money I had earned, it was nighttime. It wasn't unusual for the doors to be locked so I broke in. I went for the lights and the power was off; again, not too unusual, but when I called out and got that hollow echo of an empty house, I knew something was wrong.

I slept on the cold floor and, come daylight, I saw the house had been vacated and there was a note on the kitchen counter for me. Something to the effect of, "Dear Myke, I had to go to Texas. Sorry. Love, Ma." And with that, I was on the streets. Winter was coming on hard and I had nowhere to go, but at least I had some money in my pocket.

I exhausted the good will of my friend's parents after a couple of weeks, and there were no more regular homes and couches available to me, so I took to the streets in search of food, water, shelter, and warmth.

It was during this winter, when I had nothing, that I became a student of and believer in survival. Not that I knew it at the time; I was too busy trying to survive and being angry at my circumstance, in between bouts of sadness as well. I didn't like it, but I could understand my friend's inability to help me. I learned I could rely on no one but myself. On the whole I guess I did alright; heck, I survived.

I slept in dumpsters and hallways, broke into cars, homes, and offices—anything I could find. I found food in trash cans and behind grocery stores, ate lots of ketchup and mustard from fast food places, drank water from mall water fountains, took baths in public toilets, found heat in the form of homemade fires and the old fave: the heat cranked out from the refrigerator units behind grocery stores. I had to keep slapping rats that were trying to nibble on my head, but the need for heat made them only a small nuisance.

Spring came and I got a real break with a job at a grocery store, saved up enough money, and soon ran into my mother's number-one fallback guy, Earl (R.I.P.), and he took me in.

From there, it's just a story like many others—joining the service and growing up.

What I will say is that many men in the Elite Forces are just regular guys with a little extra drive. Some come from a background that pushed them a little harder; some come from the stock of being a little more gifted. But most are just regular folks who wanted something they believed in, tried, didn't quit, and they made it. That's all.

When it comes to career military pursuits, some try to be the best at what they do. For example, one man might get into hand-to-hand fighting and become expert. Some focus on the shooting, or scuba, or skydiving, or other such skills. For me, the thing that always held my interest was basic outdoor survival. So, whenever we deployed, that's what I was interested in and developed. And over time, it became my area of expertise.

As to military background, my service started in the U.S. Army in 1982 and I've seen service in Active Duty, in the Reserves, in the National Guard, and later as a defense contractor operator and manager. I spent time in the Cavalry and Rangers before joining Special Forces. I qualified as a Special Forces Communicator, Intelligence Operator, and Medical Specialist attaining the enlisted rank of Sergeant First Class before being Commissioned as an Officer in the Medical Branch. After 9/11 I was activated to report for the Special Forces Officer course, almost 20 years after first joining the Army. Upon completing this Detachment Commander course and all Officer Advanced courses required until reaching Lieutenant Colonel rank, I served in the Global War on Terror both abroad and at home. All told, my accumulated experience was gained in African, Asian, Latin American, Eastern European, and Middle Eastern theaters seeing combat in eight conflicts including over 80 actual engagements. An "engagement" in my experience was defined as folks actually shooting at me, unlike the current trend of counting a trip to the market as a "combat" mission. What it all means is that I gained a lot of real experience all over the globe under high threat—very risky and very real threats to my life with death a real, constant possibility.

As it was then, so it is now: I still have a job and family to tend, so you won't catch me traipsing off to live a life in the Alaskan wilderness for a year at a time. I find that to be a luxury only afforded to people with lots of money or lots of time. And that's not most of us. So I learn, do, and share what I can as I can in hopes that it will be useful for other folks like me: not the extremely rich or just plain extreme, but regular folk who have an interest in but not a consuming lifestyle in survival.

And my brand of survival could not be called "fancy camping," nor is it an interesting academic pursuit of lost traditions and ancient primitive practices. It surely isn't like some of the survival shows on TV these days that teach crazy stuff that might be able to be done by someone when things are extremely bad, but isn't the best thing for most, most of the time. For most, doing some of those TV drama-survival acts will get you killed. And finally, my survival teaching isn't some extension of all those military survival books out there, talking about techniques geared towards soldiers and the kit they have issued and available at all times. Heck, if you have even just a parachute kit for survival, you pretty much have everything you need.

Nope, this book is about a fusion of all these things. Using some real experience both from study and living, with some military aspects like the discipline and drive, with some good old fashioned common sense and, most importantly, the one thing we all have—the "will to live" no matter what it takes, to draw from everything around you to make it out alive and get home safe.

That's what I hope to instill in anyone who reads this book—the belief that you will survive, and the knowledge that will help you to survive. I want you to believe that just because you don't have all the goodies and supplies, or the training and experience, doesn't mean you won't or can't make it; it only means it will not be as easy and you'll have to try harder. But that's ok, because lesson one is the most important lesson of all: NEVER QUIT!

Introduction

The Hawke Teaching Methodology

When it comes to learning, I am not a natural genius or gifted with a high IQ. What I do, and do very well, is work smarter, not harder. More times than not, this actually serves better than having big brains, as those who do often know too much and perhaps think too much.

Within my company, Hawke Brand and School, we train civilians in the skills of survival with a focus on medicine, mental and physical fitness, self-protection, food, water, shelter, navigation, and basically how to get out of simulated survival scenarios alive and well. These scenarios can border on the extreme, but our teaching methodology always remains simple: provide the most useful information and skills, and do so in a way that our students will be able to comprehend and apply the knowledge quickly and accurately.

When it comes to teaching, I try to reduce everything down to its simplest components. Then I place those components in order of their importance or sequence. I reduce these key concepts to one word each, then I use the first letter of each word to give me an acronym. Each word within the acronym reminds me of a phrase, and each phrase helps me to remember what I need to do or know. This method helps me retain complex information without feeling overwhelmed, and enables me to act effectively without becoming subdued due to the sheer volume of information.

An example is the common term "ABC" as it applies to basic first aid—Airway, Breathing, and Circulation. I, however, jumble the acronym to "CAB" for Circulation, *then* Airway, *then* Breathing, since most folks in dire situations are suffering from wounds and bleeding more than airway issues. Also, we can go a minute without air and be fine, but we can bleed out in a minute and be dead. So, I remember CAB, and if I don't tend to these elements in that order, the victim will be catching a CAB—to the afterlife. I'll expand on this lesson inside the book.

For now, another quick example of my teaching methodology is the "K.I.S.S." principle: Keep It Simple, Stupid! That's exactly what I always try to do, and encourage you to do the same when in a survival situation.

So in this book I will normally reduce everything down to one word. Those will lead to other words, then other phrases, then other concepts and ideas. In this way, you will have a mental survival kit containing the smallest, lightest things with the most uses.

You might also notice as you go along that I stay away from using names. I don't say use this tree or that plant as you never know where you are going to be. I don't give a rat's butt what a thing is called by scientists or other experts. What I do care about is universal principles. There are always exceptions, but for most things there are general rules that will serve you well. For example, it's not important to know the scientific or common name of every hard wood—if I can't stick my thumbnail into it, it's a hard wood. If I can, then it's a soft wood. I will then use it according to my needs. If a wood is light and floats, maybe I'll use it for a boat. If it's hard and tough, maybe I'll use it as a weapon handle or tool.

I suggest, as you go about learning, that you ask questions of folks wherever you are. Don't mind so much what they call something, but rather note how it looks, feels, smells, etc. Then note its purpose and uses, as food, medicine, tool, or poison. And then give it your own name. This is how you'll retain it best, and be most likely to recall it when necessary and apply as required. For example, I don't recall the name for a plant; instead, I'll name it the medicine plant, like the "tummy ache leaf" or the "fever root" or the "roof-tile leaf," etc. This way, I'll be able to identify a familiar plant and associate it with its purpose. After all, that's all I really need—to see it and to use it.

With all my subjects, I teach that you should try to know about 10 options. Master one, be very good at two more, have tried three more, and be familiar with four more after that. If you have about 10 options for food, water, fire, and shelter, and master at least one in each category, you will be able to do whatever you need with the one you master and the other nine will serve you in various situations should circumstances change or preclude you from doing the ones you know best.

So, these are the basic things that everyone should learn, know, and be able to do with nothing but your bare hands, the clothes on your back, and your knowledge:

FIRE: Know how to make fire in at least one way with sticks only.

SHELTER: Know how to make one type of shelter from scratch that stops wind, rain, cold, and predators with no tools to assist you.

WATER: Know how to get water with no tools in at least one way, in the primary area where you live, work, and travel.

FOOD: Know how to make at least one simple trap or snare very well, and/or at least one fishing technique, with nothing but what's around you.

PLANTS: Know at least three plants that are edible, nutritious, filling, plentiful, and easily identifiable in the area where you live, work, and travel. Learn them by their leaves, stalks/stems, and roots as all three are part of the plant, might have use, and will confirm identity of the plants. Take into account the seasons when they grow and soils where they grow, and any relative plants that are around that might lead you to them. Also know at least three plants that are medicinal in some significant way and that are easily identified, readily available, and most useful based on your needs.

WEAPONS, TOOLS, INSTRUMENTS: Know how to make at least one weapon that can defend your life or take an animal's. Know how to make at least one tool that can assist you in improving your quality of life.

When you finish this book, don't put it down. March right out with it into the woods or whatever your environment is, right now, today, or as soon as possible. Do this at least once, if never again, for the sake of your future survival and for those whom you care to return to should you ever become separated. Do it for life.

Finally, know that this book will NOT save your life. Let's just set the record straight right up front. This book will give you some vital information that will serve you in a difficult time. But at the end of the day, should this hardship come your way, there you'll be and then . . . YOU will save you. That's all I have to say on that.

Happy Survivalin'!

WARNING: If you are a survival expert or outdoor professional, this book is not for you! (Although you may learn something useful which you may have considered beneath your skill set.)

This book is for every housewife, businessman, weekend adventurer, and any other person who is exactly the opposite of the typical tested survivalist. It's for anyone who may one day find themselves in a dire position between life and death, where survival comes down to will and certain skills that you may not otherwise have. And my primary goal is to impart to you both the supreme importance of developing your natural will to survive, while also providing you with enough simple skills to make it happen.

As for me, I didn't ask for this and didn't necessarily want to ever be in the position where survival was my only option. But it came to me, and I learned from it. And now, I feel it'd be wrong of me not to share what I've learned. And that is the simple fact that anyone can survive even the harshest circumstance; they need only choose to do so. The rest is simply details that will help along the way. This book is meant to provide the simplest means to that end—everything you really need to know to survive, and nothing else.

The Psychology of Survival

I t happens to thousands of people every year, and it could just as easily happen to you. Your airplane goes down in the wilderness; or the train you're riding derails miles from the nearest junction; or your car breaks down in the desert; or you get lost while hiking in the woods; or a snowstorm strands you in the mountains unprepared . . . the possibilities are endless.

In any case, you may survive the initial trauma event only to quickly realize that you are now in a terrible, dangerous predicament. It's possible that everyone who was with you has died, including your spouse, child, or friend; or maybe some have also survived. It's likely that you or others have sustained bad injuries; injuries that would make you vomit to look at. You may find that you have little-to-no resources available—no food or water, no tools, no communication device, and no clue where you are or how to get to someplace safe. But the biggest question of all is whether or not you will be able to handle the reality of the situation in your head and heart: **Do you have the *will* to survive?**

This book is for anyone who would hope to be prepared should they find themselves in such dire straits. The general survival situation I talk about inside this book is the kind that no one chooses to place themselves into—in other words, this is not for hikers or mountaineers or skilled outdoorsmen. And the information and skills I provide are meant to be grasped and applied by anyone. By far the most important factor in anyone's survival in these cases is not only the topic of this first chapter, but it is something that anyone can develop and carry with them at all times. That is, a strong psychology for survival—the will to live.

Now I am not the smartest, strongest, toughest, baddest fella in the land. But I am the most dedicated to the commitment that I will fight death in all its forms; I will cheat it every chance I get; I will take every advantage I can get away with; and I will never, ever, EVER give up. Even if I should perish, I vow that my very cells will never quit and will fight even as the maggots eat my flesh, grow into flies, get consumed by birds and so on up the food chain until my cells make it back to civilization and home to those I love. It is my mission and my purpose to face down my fears and to fight for my survival with every fiber of my being. I will do everything and anything it takes to stay alive and to keep going with every ounce of my physical and spiritual energy, and I will do this until I get back home and into the hearts of the ones I love.

I am telling you right now that this is the single most important lesson in this book: NEVER QUIT!

No matter what your circumstance, the most important aspect of survival is psychology. This, ironically, is the easiest and simultaneously most difficult part to teach, because it is the only thing that absolutely must come from within. As a survival expert and teacher, I can open doors to your own survival psychology, and I might even find a trigger to release a trap and allow some crucial part of you out, but at the end of the day, this is the one thing that you must find within yourself, and you must allow it to take control in the worst of situations. Most of my survival courses, since they are usually with regular folk and not woodsmen, take the form of helping students to find this key element within themselves—the "will" to survive. All of the other skills and knowledge I teach are useless without it.

As we'll discuss in this chapter, there are several elements you need to develop a strong psychology of survival—get prepared by learning and practicing the skills and knowledge offered here; build confidence that you'll always make it; learn to face the negatives; always use your head and your heart; know the reasons why you must survive; and, of course, NEVER QUIT!

PREPARATION AT FORT LIVING ROOM

The general rules of life clearly state that if you're ready for something, it won't happen; and if you ain't ready, it sure will happen! This phenomenon is sometimes called "Murphy's Law" (or "Sod's Law" in the UK) and I have found that it also translates perfectly into "Hawke's Law of Survival." So when I travel, I always have a little chuckle to myself thinking, "If this plane goes down and anyone survives, it probably won't be me, but rather someone who wouldn't even know how to use half my travel survival kit, providing they even thought to look for it, haha!" I'll be the dead guy with all the handy stuff on his body, so search me well if you happen to be on my flight!

Okay, this gives you a feel for my sense of humor. You'll see that I apply it throughout the book, and heck, throughout my life for that matter. You'd be surprised at how a sense of humor can benefit you in the worst of situations. Look at it like this: it'd be pretty funny to survive a plane crash or boat sinking, and then die from lack of food or water! But look at the upside—either way, if you die fast, there's no suffering; if you die of starvation or exposure, well, at least you had time to make peace with your maker. You see, either way and in all things, I suggest you always look for the positive, and don't dwell on the negative any more than you need to in order to identify it and learn not to repeat whatever caused it. If something you're doing or thinking ain't fixing or improving your situation, it's wasting your time. And the clock is always ticking towards your death, so don't squander one moment in unproductive depression or self-pity or any of the other things that only serve to drain your energy without benefit.

Now, don't get me wrong: of course you should take some time—after you've done all you can to handle the immediate disaster and are having a well-deserved and well-timed break—to give things a think, even have a cry. This is healthy if controlled, and even necessary for your psyche. We must mourn if we experienced loss, and usually with a survival situation, there is loss. Make peace with that concept. And accept the possibility that more anguish may be on the way—otherwise, you will fear it, and fear will beat you down faster than anything and spread like a virus. It will consume you in a heartbeat and even spread to others very quickly if you're in a group.

That is why combat commanders cannot tolerate fear in the ranks. I have literally seen an entire battalion running in fear, to the point they attacked *my* troops in mad panic when we came to assist. Fear is *that* dangerous, and you should view FEAR as your worst enemy in any survival situation. The way we as commanders manage it, is to keep the troops busy and productive. All that apparent "busywork" that soldiers always seem to be doing has a purpose—commanders are making sure the men don't have time for fear to set in. You should do the same.

You see, most fear is a result of ignorance; it's a fear of the unknown. By sitting down in Fort Living Room, right now, learning techniques and gaining confidence in your knowledge of what to do, you are putting yourself in a better position to handle a survival situation when you're in a real hurt box. So, good on ya'!

Now, reading and thinking about it is better than nothing, but nothing is better than hands-on experience when it comes to the survival arts. So GET PREPARED by reading this book, trying many of the skills and techniques within, getting good at the ones that feel most natural to you, and practicing them every once in a while. This will give you the hard skills and confidence that will keep you prepared for anything. And that is the number-one way to fight fear—to know what to do.

I will refer to psychological and even spiritual concepts as we go. Some might not see this as befitting a down-and-dirty guide to survival. But let me dispel this myth right up front. In all my years of training and fighting, I have learned one thing is always true—human spirit is what counts the most when all else is equal and all else fails. It is what one believes in, including one's self, which makes the difference between those who make it and those who don't.

In fact, many of my best fighters have been fat old guys or scrawny runt guys or lanky big guys who were flat-out brave in firefights and other dangerous situations. They used their heads and hearts to complement their skills. The only men I ever relieved for cowardice under fire, happened to be young, fit guys. The lesson to me was the reinforcement of that old adage, "You can't judge a book by its cover." I've seen more pretty-boy body-builders quit and more fat, skinny, short, tall, old, and young guys make it—always based on their heart and mind first and foremost. In a nutshell, attitude is everything.

No matter whether you are a man, woman, child, old, young, fit, or even disabled—I don't give a rat's butt, frankly—you can make it as long as you work on your basics, know what you want to live for, and never quit. Heart, Mind, and Skills (in that order!) vanquish fear. This is the key to survival.

So you didn't grow up as an Eagle Scout. So what? Get over it! I ain't a billionaire either, but I eat every day. And in a survival situation, even without tons of skills and experience, you can make do with a few basics and some common sense. The most important skill you can have and develop is simply good old-fashioned common sense. And before we get into what it takes to be prepared, let's talk for a moment about *not* being prepared. As in Murphy's Law of combat, you'll likely find yourself in a survival situation right on the day you decide to go to the store to buy a bunch of survival stuff, haha!

Ultimately you need to be mentally prepared for the harsh realities of surviving. Death is real and a real possibility always. One of the big things I teach in all my survival classes is that it ain't a game; it ain't TV or a movie; it's real, and lots of folks bite the dust simply because they don't comprehend this. It's no joke, and it sure ain't camping. The key is, if you find yourself in a bad situation and you have nothing:

You lock it in your head right now that you will survive, you will not quit, and even if they find your dead body, there will be no mistake that you were fighting the fight right to the end!

When you have nothing, this commitment is all you have, and, more times than not, this can actually be enough. My combat base camp has been overrun by the enemy a few times, and I've been in a lot of firefights, and there were days I could see the bad guys all around and the bullets were whizzing. At times I could even see some of them smiling, they have been that close, and I just knew in those moments that this was it, I would not see the end of this day, and like so many bodies I had looked upon, I wondered how they'd look upon mine. But despite all this, I kept on with my job and my mission, whether it was moving or rescuing or what have you.

You don't stop to think and let the fear get a grip, you just keep driving on and never quit. Keeping a grip on one's courage has carried countless many through almost certain death in battle, and so it can serve you, too, in the battle for survival. I cannot repeat or stress enough the mantra: NEVER QUIT!

Of course the survival situation is quite a different reality than that of the combat soldier. However, the potential end result is the same. Dead is dead. And it is in this way that the psychology of survival is applicable both to soldiers and survivors.

TOOLS & TOYS

Obviously, most survival scenarios happen instantly and without warning, so it's unlikely that you will have any tools at all on your person to help you through. Or is it?

I always carry at least a minimal "survival kit" most places I go. I'll discuss these in detail in Chapter 10. But for now, let's look at some of the most practical survival tools—or "toys" as we sometimes call 'em—you should consider carrying whenever you travel.

COMMUNICATIONS

First and foremost is communications. Let's face it, the best way outta trouble is the most direct and easiest—pick up the bat phone and call for the rescue limo service.

SATELLITE PHONES. Sat phones are the best thing to have when travelling above or across great expanses of wilderness. They're not much bigger than a modern cellular phone. So, get a sat phone if you're into flying, boating, or doing anything where you're in remote areas on a regular basis. Heck, even if you're going somewhere remote on a one-time basis, it's good to borrow or otherwise get your hands on one. It could mean all the difference in the world should the unimaginable befall you. They're not as expensive as one might think, but the usage rates can be. Of course, when it comes to life saving, it's best to spend a bit if needed. Like all items in your survival kit, play with it and make sure you know how to work it *before* you go. It's also smart to know how to do it in the dark. Get into the closet or slap on a blindfold and practice. Sounds crazy, I know, but it works. Also, think about trauma, and protect it with a solid, waterproof, shock-resistant case.

CELL PHONES. I go with a service provider that covers the whole globe. I can get a signal in any major town anywhere in the world without switching service or falling off the radar. However, out in the hinterlands, I have found my major provider lacking. A good back-up plan is to either have a world phone and buy a local sim card in the area of your travels for a few bucks, or just buy a cheapo local phone as soon as you hit the ground in any country. Again, just being able to make commo might save your life. But do yourself a favor when you buy these phones or sim cards: take a second to ask how to dial for help. Even better, I line up three medical evacuation companies capable of air or sea rescue in the area and have three hospitals lined up with the best level of care for trauma and disease just in case, whenever I travel. And finally, while you're doing your area study, look into who are the official SAR (Search and Rescue) folks in that neck of the woods. Good to know, better to make contact in case.

RADIOS. If I'm going to be somewhere for a while, and can carry extra gear, I always have an HF (High Frequency) radio. These can broadcast around the world with very little power and no license, and they operate in almost any weather. Now, there are some tricks to frequencies and antennas, wave theory and propagation, etc., that throw people off. But it's not as tricky as one might think to master the basics. They're worth their weight in gold if you are going to operate somewhere remote. So, plan these into your supply list and get familiar with them. Much more on this later.

Next are the hand-held radios. There are some good ones now that combine GPS with radio and even help you find the other radios near you if you're in a team on "walkie-talkies." These are great, but at best, they have a two-mile range. The marine band radios for sea only have about a five-mile range. So, while handy for daily operations, it's not really something to bank on in a survival situation.

SIGNALS

There are all kinds of laser lights, strobes, beacons, transponders, flares, etc. on the market these days. It's good to get something for daytime and night-time signaling. There's even a nifty watch that has a beacon transponder built into it. The key when it comes to signals is to do some research and find the ones best suited for your needs. I always look for size and weight first. The reason is simple: if it's too big and bulky, it becomes cumbersome and eventually gets left behind. Murphy's' Law of Combat states: "The day you leave it behind, even after years of carrying it without use, will be the very day you need it most." So, with that rule in mind, I try to carry every-thing all the time and that is why I go for size and weight as priority criteria. Always test these devices before you leave home.

KNIVES, TOOLS, AND OTHER GIZMOS

Everything you can get, and carry, is good. And anything is always better than nothing. But make it count. There are lots of products out there that I've bought and tried and found either to be wholly lacking or downright worthless! Much to my chagrin and surprise in some cases. So, I always like to experiment with new things, and first thing after I buy them, I actually try them. Don't make the mistake of keeping it in the wrapper and thinking that's the best way to keep it new and ready. Check it out.

I once bought a really cool fire starter, this impregnated-wax product. In the old days, we'd take cotton balls soaked in Vaseline and put them in foil, then in a Ziploc baggie, and this made a good fire starter material for rainy days when you didn't have a lighter or match. So, I thought, great, someone finally made a commercial version of it. I bought it, tucked it in my emergency rucksack and forgot all about it. A few months later I got tasked to do a TV show and we went to start a fire (the fire wasn't part of the show, just cooking up some bugs and roots) so I tried the fire wax. Not only did it not work, I had to use other methods to start the fire, and after a few hours of cooking and eating and filming, when I put the fire out and went to sterilize the area, the dang thing was still there, completely intact, un-melted and not worth a darn. How bad would that have sucked if my life depended on it?

So, try new things, but TRY them after you buy them and before you need them!

And remember: keep it light. If you are stranded in a survival situation and have to walk out, that might make all the difference in the world. We used to joke in Special Forces that we had 100 pounds of lightweight stuff. But guess what, it was still 100 pounds of weight in our rucksack, which we affectionately called, "the life-sucking tick." *Think light.*

That's all I'm going to go into at this point for gadgets and gizmos.

As for knives and tools, for every pro there is a con. A big knife is great for whacking down trees to make a shelter, a raft, a sled, etc. But, they not only make it really hard to do small stuff like make snares and traps, they can actually be dangerous.

The same goes for knives that are too small. These are great for most jobs around the camp for surviving, but they sure make it hard to build a shelter. Try for a middle ground. But knives are for another chapter, too. Just want to address the, ahem, "point" that they are a gadget to be considered. I have many different kinds to choose to carry. Some for when I'm in a suit, some for when I travel by air, some for when I do medical or communications work, some for when I go into heavy bush, or just field camping. I even have a specific one for when I walk the streets of London, as they have very strict laws about what you can carry. I learned about this the hard way when I was almost arrested for a one-inch locking-blade knife.

The number-one tool in survival is the knife. Always carry one or have one available and/or accessible. And learn a few ways to make or improvise different knives. Whatever the size or quality—and quality is important when it comes to blades—I always make sure that one principle holds true for all of them, and that is that I have one!

THE POSITIVITY OF NEGATIVES

Most folks will tell you that personality is the most important trait. Looks, smarts, strength, skills—all these are important, and contribute, but when it's all said and done, personality is what matters most, as it is an outward observable manifestation of one's attitude towards life and those in their life. So, it is in life, it is in death.

Your attitude towards your newfound survival situation—really, your potential demise and death—is going to be the dominant internal factor determining your mission success or failure. It will get you through more things than you can imagine.

But the external factors—the elements of your circumstance—will always vary. In this book, and in real survival situations, I refer to these as the *Negatives*. The negatives are part of your reality. There are always negatives in life, and rarely are they so immediate and significant as when one is truly surviving, facing the potential for death. So, I will always address the negatives, but note that I address them first, and then the positives. I do this for a reason. You must always face the negatives, and that means to acknowledge them, identify them, define them, and find ways to deal with them. You cannot negate or mitigate the negatives if you do not address them. Basically, you must confront your demons. No one can or will do it for you. To ignore or pretend they're not there, to wish or hope they'll go away, is to do nothing more than open the door and wait for them to do all that you fear. So, face your fears, stare them right in the eye, and smile, saying, "Ahh, I know you're there, and can get me, but not yet, not yet!" Then you count your positives—or in other words, your options—and take what seems to be the best of them at the time.

This is a key component of my survival philosophy—working effectively within your reality. I've seen people freeze in the face of fear and death. Very rarely has this served any good that I have observed. Both in street fights and in trauma when I worked as a paramedic, I have seen people freeze in some way, not willing to open their eyes. Although their eyes were wide open, they simply did not want to accept what was happening right in front of them and they froze.

You must not fall into this trap. The best and easiest way is to do *some*thing, almost *anything*, and it will snap you out of the shock and horror that beset you in the first place. When there is no one around to pimp slap you back to reality, you must do it yourself. Action is the answer.

I call this approach the "positivity of negatives." Look for all the negatives you can find, and then figure out the best ways around them. When you do, you feel better because you have a plan, you have considered the negatives, you are aware of them, and you know what they mean or could mean. But now that you have calculated them and factored them into your plan, you've effectively neutralized your negatives! How's that for survival algebra.

In essence, I am a "yes man." I want to hear and see all the "no's" and ask why and how? When I find out "why" I can't do this or that, I then look for and find out "how" I can get to "yes." In fact there can be only one answer: *yes* I can survive, *yes* I will survive, *yes* I will try and do and go until I need not do any longer, *yes*, this I can do and will. *Yes!*

Okay, the rest of the book will get more into basic stuff for those who don't care to wax philosophical on the subject. I don't sweat that too much, as everyone who has been and anyone who will be in a real survival situation, will find themselves touching the esoteric anyway; even if they are reluctant to indulge me here and now, they will later.

One of Murphy's/Sod's Laws is that there are no Atheists in foxholes. That means, when you're in battle and bullets are flying, folks who do not believe in God or some spiritual entity by any name, tend to find themselves making prayers to someone or something when it looks like death is an imminent potentiality. And the same holds true for those surviving: all of a sudden, you figure out what matters to you most and what you believe in, if you hadn't before. I've seen it happen plenty of times, so I don't fret it when folks say to me, "Hawke, shut up about the philosophy; tell me how to survive." Even though I *am* telling them the most important thing, I shut my trap, smile, and start talking about something else. . . . They'll see.

MURPHY'S LAWS OF COMBAT AND HAWKE'S LAWS OF SURVIVAL

Let me share with you a few of Murphy's Laws of Combat, as they're extremely relevant to Hawke's Laws of Survival. For you vets, these will remind you of the tickle you got the first time you learned them in practice. For those of you not familiar with them, they will give you a great insight into the realities of survival, since survival really is combat between you and nature, a fight to live. And nature is always stronger, you never defeat her, you only overcome her challenges. Respecting the laws of combat is tantamount to respecting the laws of nature. You will be better off for it in both instances.

MURPHY'S LAWS OF COMBAT (JUST A FEW, AS THERE ARE MANY)

- If it's stupid but it works, it ain't stupid
- No plan ever survives first contact with the enemy
- The enemy attacks on two occasions—when he's ready, and when you're not
- No inspection-ready unit ever passed in combat, and no combat-ready unit ever passed inspection
- When you are short everything but enemy, you are in combat
- When the battle is going your way, you're in an ambush or trap

HAWKE'S LAWS OF SURVIVAL (FOR STARTERS . . .)

- Never quit
- Everything you plan and pack, will be lost in the event that causes the survival scenario
- Survival situations happen to those who haven't studied, or have but aren't ready
- The best-trained, most-equipped survivalist will be the first one killed in the crash
- The person least likely to survive will be the one left to face surviving
- When you lack everything but misery, you are surviving
- When you think you got it all handled, you're in the biggest trouble

INSTRUCTORS & INSTRUCTION

The first rule about instructors and instruction is that no one owns the market on survival. It is innate in every living thing on the planet. Man has been doing this as long as we have existed, and it is inherent within each of us. Remember that.

Do not be misled by any claims to mastery of survival by anyone. Most people who teach survival have never been in a situation in which they had to survive or die. And most folks who have overcome a survival situation either never studied survival before, or, after their ordeal, never wanted any more to do with it.

I teach my style, which is simple and basic. Hawke Survival is for when you have nothing but a knife, the clothes on your back, your wits, and heart. (And if you don't have a knife, you make one!) That is what I learned in those hard winters on the streets as a kid with no money, and I enhanced that education with much army and Special Forces training later. All the goodies are good, but what if you don't have them? Then what? That's what this book is all about: "Then what?!"

In all my hands-on survival training, I combine the techniques and methods and devices I've learned to impart the most practical information, along with my own influence and experience.

The U.S. Air Force (USAF) has a great survival school. Since pilots have always flown across borders and risked being shot down, survival training has pretty much been a part of their preparation from the early days. But know this—their instructors start off as kids like any other military enlistee. No one is a born expert. These men and women go to a course, and then presto, they are instructors. Granted, if they get into their work and do it long enough, they become pretty good. But, USAF teaches a very different type of survival designed for pilots, with military survival items, and that makes a huge difference. So, if you want to learn how to use lots of gadgets and travel with a vest full of military kit, this is great training. The premise is that a pilot need only survive until rescue, as most of the time his location and the time of his downing is known precisely. In short, a one- to three-day time frame is the key component of the USAF survival school mentality.

The U.S. Special Forces (SF) is a bit different, in that they mostly use seasoned folks to teach their courses. (The British Special Air Service (SAS) and a few others fall into this category as well.) Some of their instructors are retired SF men who practice their trade as a passionate hobby when not instructors, so their practical skills are as sharp as their teaching skills.

The basic SF course was set up by a famous SF survivor and escapee, Nick Rowe, who spent five years as a POW in Vietnam. The focus of the course is geared toward actually living and operating behind enemy lines for extended periods, often with no gear, as an escapee, which is very different from USAF training for pilots who would have a vest full of the best government-issued survival stuff available.

Many of the early Army SF S.E.R.E (Survival, Escape, Resistance, and Evasion) instructors were POWs or escapees from internment camps during the cold wars. Many retired from active duty at the school and continued to teach long afterwards as civilians. This gives the graduates of USSF SERE school some distinct advantages in survival skills. But again, it is only a school, with limits on time and instruction. Like learning combatives, you can get a lot out of 30 days of training, but unless it is practiced and applied, it is just another course, just theory.

However, it should be pointed out that despite my obvious bias towards SF survival training, the SF training still often had instructors who only knew their own specific area of survival, and did not know many other elements. Furthermore, just because a man went through survival school, does not make him a true expert on the matter. It just means he's been through a pretty good course to give him some skills in case he ever needs it, yet most never do and therefore they cannot give you any idea of the reality of survival situations since they don't know it themselves.

But in all Special Operations Forces (or SOF, a blanket name covering any unconventional force, and often mistaken for SPECIAL FORCES which is the unique elite force specializing in unconventional/guerrilla warfare) there are people who take an interest in a specific skill set and seek to develop that niche. Some focus on shooting or sniping; some get into scuba and underwater training; some concentrate on alpine or arctic knowledge; others specialize in skydiving; some become world class martial artists.

It is in this way that I took an interest in survival training. Because I had lived it as a kid, always scrounging and improvising to procure food, clothing, and shelter, this topic became my natural area of interest. And one thing I learned very quickly was that because we travel so much, to so many different locations on too short notice most of the time, it's virtually impossible to really develop an in-depth knowledge of all the factors in all areas—for example, which plants are poisonous, edible, and medicinal in every region of the world. In fact, one could spend a lifetime studying and earning multiple degrees in plant life and still make a fatal mistake and eat the wrong thing. So, it became apparent to me early on, that what was needed was a set of UNIVERSAL SURVIVAL PRINCIPLES that I could take with me anywhere and apply in any circumstances. This was to become the foundation of my core survival techniques.

Besides SOF trainers, there are many civilian instructors out there teaching great stuff. One of the advantages of a civilian instructor is that they usually have only one thing to focus on—teaching, learning, practicing survival. Most military folks do not have that luxury; they have other jobs and missions that require most of their attention and skills. But they have to learn and master to one degree or another, survival, as a potential reality in their occupation. Civilians need only to do one thing. Often in SF we went to a civilian to learn a particular skill, as he or she might have been the best mountain biker or alpine skier in the world, as that's all they do. And often that civilian might have grown up in that specific area, know it inside and out, might even be a native or local tribesman and that's great, especially if that's where you want to learn your survival craft as that's likely the only place you'll use it. In these cases, I highly recommend going to local talent for local knowledge.

ECOLOGICAL FOOTPRINT

Another element I constantly encounter in the comparison of the civilian instructors to military instructors is the consideration of the land and animals. First off, many civilian courses teach to pack food, and otherwise eat roots, plants, nuts, and berries—now that's all fine and good. But it takes an immense amount of knowledge to know which ones to eat in the first place, and it actually takes a ton of effort to attain these things, too.

The military teaches specifically to kill and eat animals. To kill takes some skill and work, but actually, far less than finding and digging up the edible roots. Some plants can't be eaten, or else. But most animals can be eaten. Also, some roots need to be boiled to get out the toxins. (Do you know which ones? You'd better!) Most meat can be eaten raw if eaten right away. Finally, the fat and protein of the animal will give you more bang for the buck than any root, fruit, plant, nut, or berry when it comes to nourishment for surviving. And so, we kill to live.

I am constantly surprised by the number of people who have never killed for their own food. Even though they are meat eaters at home, they flat refused to kill, like they are somehow better than that or above it. Let me tell you right now, survival is the great equalizer in that rich or poor, smart or not, if you don't do what you have to do, you won't live.

Unfortunately many civilian survival classes skip this piece of training, and that is a shame. If there is no killing, you are merely camping!

Another difference is that many civilian classes teach you how to pitch your tent and set up your sleeping bag. Now, I love my "wubby," a.k.a. the army poncho liner, our equivalent to a lightweight sleeping bag, but more on that later. For now, I will say this, if you have a tent and bag, you're camping! Survival is when you don't have these things. How do you make a shelter or a blanket from the cold and wet environment? Bottom line, you chop a tree or kill some plants. Survival is brutal, make no mistakes about it. Like war, it is a fight to the death; something must die for you to live. Many civilian courses disapprove of this element of survival training, and do not want to harm the environment. And I agree, to a degree. I was raised with many Native American ideals, and to live with nature is one of them. But I also know that man has always taken what nature has had to offer and used it for his needs. It is seen as a gift as long as it is respectfully done. Only take what is needed, and always being humble and thankful. But, cut a tree or kill an animal to survive nonetheless, this is the only way.

One superior element of SF survival training is that it teaches you to live off the land, specifically behind enemy lines where you may have to do so for long periods of time. We are schooled and constantly tested to understand one thing: we are there for the duration. If that war goes on for ten years and we can't get out and they can't get to us, we must be prepared to settle in for the long haul. If we do get out, most likely it will be by walking a mighty long way—like across the country, a few countries, or even a continent. What it means is that we learn to ration, to be constantly aware of surroundings, and to live behind the lines with trackers and dogs looking for us. So we live "small," leaving as little a footprint as possible for them to track and find us as we know what awaits us if we're caught.

However, such eco-minded survival—leaving no trace—is not for this book, and not for the lay person to consider when in a real survival situation. In that case, you want to leave as big a mark on the ground (or at sea) that you can, so that ground or air rescuers can see your mark. Heck, make it so that even a satellite will find you if it passes overhead!

What it all means is this: when I encounter people who don't want to chop a small tree for their shelter in the cold, or they don't want to kill a small mammal for their meal, then I hand them a pencil and paper. I ask them, "Who is the most important person alive on this planet that you love and care for?" Then I tell them to write this letter:

> "Dear Jonnie/Janie,
> I love you very much, but I love this tree or this critter more than you, so, I refuse to kill it. Therefore, I will lay down here and die. But know that I love you, very much, just not as much as this rabbit or bush."

They always chop or kill after that. . . .

So these are all the factors to consider when you are deciding what survival class and teacher you want to train with. One area where the military instructors tend to be a lot better is exactly the opposite of the localized instructors—they must be prepared to deploy and operate anywhere in the world, so they train to survive likewise. No one else does this, simply because they don't need to do so.

Now, I'm not taking anything from anyone. What I am saying is that learning survival is the same as learning a martial art—you must learn what the differences are, then find the right art for you and the right instructor for that art. Consider that when choosing to further your education in survival. And no matter what you study, with whom, where, when, or how, the most important thing is to get out and do it. Go to your yard, do it in your house, go camping, pull off the roadside, anything—just go and do is the key.

SHOULD I STAY OR SHOULD I GO

The second key decision you will have to make after a tragic event leaves you in a survival situation is: Should I stay or should I go? (The first, of course, is: "Do I want to live, or am I gonna give up right now because it's all just too much." By now, you know the answer to that question. Hint: NEVER QUIT!

Before you can start considering food, water, fire, shelter, and other necessities, you must first assess your immediate circumstances. If your life is in peril, you must remedy that condition. If someone else is in peril, too, and you assess that you can get them and yourself out at the same time, then do not hesitate to snatch them up and scoot. However, if you've got a snapped arm, and they've got double broken legs, then it's not heroism but rather foolishness to try and pull them and you out, if the plane is about to go over a cliff, for example. In the first moments, it's all about heartbeat assessments and split-second decisions. Many folks can and will second-guess themselves later, but that is for then, not now. If you're a fitness stud and conditions are right, go for the heroism. If you're hungover, or sick, or otherwise weak, and you just know you can't get them too, then get yourself out—otherwise, there is just one more dead person and that would be a tragic waste as you might have saved ten people later if you had lived. Now if your child or lover is in danger, and you'd rather not live without them, what the heck, go for it—do all you can to save them regardless of your position or the situation. Either way, your problems will be solved.

But once you have yourself and others out of immediate harm's way, and you've treated yourself and others—as FIRST AID is the real first priority of survival—then you make the decision to STAY where you are and wait for help, or GO, evacuating the immediate area and looking for ways out.

This decision will determine everything that follows. What to bring, what to leave, what to use now, what to ration; these are all answered based on this one key decision—to stay or to go.

Now sometimes you won't even have an option. If your ship sinks, you're pretty much stranded right where it sunk unless you have a lifeboat. But without it, you're stuck at the mercy of the seas, currents, winds, and other elements at play. In these cases, you just start working on improving your situation, seeking refuse, debris, other survivors, etc.

But when it is an option to stay or go, the general thinking is most of the time it is better to stay put. Especially nowadays when most aircraft, sea vessels, and other forms of transport are tied into radio, satellite, and navigation systems that tell others back in civilization where that transport is and where it isn't, when it should have reported in, and when it didn't make its last required communications.

For these reasons, most of the time, the right answer is to stay put. Even when you are alone in a broken down vehicle or at a campsite, these things have a larger footprint than a lone individual walking around by themselves. This means it will be easier for someone to find you if you are lost or stranded. Staying put near a crash site will highly increase the chances of being found and ultimately surviving.

In these cases, figure out what the priorities are. In most cases, water will be the very first priority, but, if you're in a harsh environment, shelter might be the top priority. And if very cold or wet, fire might be more immediately important than water. But in all cases, make water a priority and when not number one, keep in mind that it is always a close number two unless you happen to have plenty of it on hand.

Of course, there will be situations in which you will come to realize that your best chances of survival will be to pack up and start walking. In some cases, the place you're at will be so inhospitable that extended survival there doesn't seem likely. In other cases, you may do all you can to survive for several days or even weeks at the scene of the disaster while hoping that rescuers are on the way, and then finally decide that no one is coming to save you, in which case you would have to seriously consider making a plan and heading out to find your own rescue.

Whether you stay or go, the priorities of survival remain the same. The constants are: **shelter, water, food, and fire**. Their order is variable, but these factors are not. Remember the acronym: S.W.F.F. In other words, you need to think and act "SWiFFly" in all things survival.

We'll discuss these things in detail in each specific chapter. For now, it is enough to know that you must make a decision early on to stay or to go. The rest of your dramatic story will unfold and be told as you go from that fork in the road.

REASON TO SURVIVE

Let's go back once again to very first question you will have to answer when facing death: "Do I want to live? Do I have what it takes to do whatever it takes to make it out of here alive?"

In fact, you will probably find yourself asking that question more than just once, until you either die or get rescued. As I said before, survival ain't a TV show. It's real, just as your potential death is extremely real. And the challenges you will face in a survival scenario—mentally, physically, and spiritually—are greater than anything you could ever imagine. That's exactly why you need to draw on things from within yourself that trump every one of the obstacles you will come across.

Mentally, picture your spouse back at home. Picture your child, your parents, your siblings, all the people you love. Make a pact with them that you will do everything in your power and then some to keep yourself alive and get home to them safely. Draw energy and strength and commitment from them. Though you may be in the darkest place imaginable, they can be a beacon to keep you going.

Physically, trust your body to take on all you ask of it and more. The human body—and especially the mind/body connection—is capable of accomplishing vastly more than the average person imagines. As I've said before, some of the most successful soldiers I've seen have been of the fat, skinny, too tall, or too short variety. But they fought with all their heart and got more out of their bodies than could be expected. There will be plenty of moments during your ordeal in which you think you've reached the end. Ignore those thoughts and push through it—and don't be surprised when your body actually delivers what you ask it to do. When you feel pain or you're extremely tired or starving or dehydrated or generally depleted physically—and you just want to stop and sit down, or lay down and go no further—tell yourself: "Keep Going!" Your body will respond, you *will* keep going around each new obstacle until, hopefully, you turn a corner and find rescue.

Spiritually, some pray to their God for help. Others speak to something like the Native Americans' "Great Spirit." Others simply ask Mother Earth for protection. And some start to pray to God even if they never have before.

Whatever your beliefs, now is a good time to tap into them and use them for support as you work your way through the ordeal. Throughout time people have reported gaining amazing advantage through mysterious powers. Now, I'm not going to preach about God or the spirit world, but in a survival situation, I'm all for someone going to God or gods or spirits or what have you for help, strength, and the power to go on.

Whatever it takes for you to keep trying to make it, works for me and should work for you. Use your innate powers of the physical, mental, and spiritual in every way you can to drive home to yourself the number one point of survival: NEVER QUIT!

PLAN MAN VERSUS *SEMPER GUMBY*

Always make a plan, no matter what. It gives you (and others, if present) a starting point. It helps you to keep focused and on-track when things happen to confuse or interrupt your efforts.

But remember Murphy's Law: No plan survives first contact with the enemy. The same is true for you in a survival situation. Rarely will anything you plan work out just the way you think or envision. In fact, it is best to plan on having numerous changes in the plan!

What I have found—and this helps me when I get frustrated or thwarted in my endeavors—is that when things aren't going my way, it is often because I need to stop, step back, re-think it, and find a better way or solution. If I'm working too hard, usually it means I'm doing it wrong.

Secondly, I've seen over time that when things don't go according to my plan, it usually ends up turning out far better than I could have ever hoped by revising the plan on the fly and doing what I need to do in the moment. So when things don't go right, I try not to get too upset and don't take it to heart; I simply back up, give myself and the situation some space and time, and things just work themselves out.

So, the bottom line is to always make a plan, and have a plan, but to never expect that plan to work out exactly the way you expect. Do your best and do all you can, rest and relax when you must, and things will be alright. There is nothing more you can do than all you can do, then, let go and be flexible.

You probably know the famous 1960s claymation cartoon called *Gumby*. And you probably didn't know that the name became part of an oft-chanted exclamation by U.S. Marines whenever a plan changed, which was nearly always in war time: "*Semper Gumby!*" This makes sense, as their motto is *Semper Fidelis*, or shortened to Semper Fi, which means "Always Faithful" in Latin. So, in the humorous way of soldiers, always with a bit of bite, *Semper Gumby* means "Always Flexible," just like Gumby since he's made of clay and can be stretched into anything one can imagine.

So, make a plan, but always remember, "*Semper Gumby!*" And when it comes to initial decisions and moves, remember the acronym "D.A.P.R. S.o.G." In other words, "Dapper before SOGgy." This relates to four elements:

DANGER: Get out of harm's way, and get others out of harm's way if you safely can.

ASSISTANCE: Provide first aid to yourself and others.

PRIORITIZE: Assess the situation and prioritize the SWFF constants (shelter, water, fire, food).

REALITY: Decide to stay or go.

Ration and plan for the long haul, no matter what your circumstances and decisions, as it is the case more times than not that folks are stranded far longer than they ever anticipate. Whether you opt to stay at the site or make a move, rationing is the smart move.

ANCIENT CHINESE WISDOM: EXPECTATION IS THE SOURCE OF ALL UNHAPPINESS

I have one more thing to say along the lines of the "foo-foo" philosophy of survival according to Hawke. And it's about expectation.

Some people expect people to give them things, like they are owed by the world for no other reason than being born. Some people expect people to sacrifice for them without reciprocation. They expect that even if everyone else dies, they will get out. Some call these people winners, but I call them takers.

Some people expect to have to share, they expect to have to lose something just because it is the way and it happens. They even expect to die in some cases. Some folks call these people losers, but I call them givers.

These are very critical points to understand about humans if you find yourself in any survival situation with people other than yourself. "G&T." That's the quick label to help you figure out who's who and how they'll likely jump in a pinch. Givers and Takers are who you'll be with—know the difference.

Again, there are no easy answers, not black or white or grey and shades in between. Both have their merits and faults. The key is to recognize them in others and yourself and work with these natural traits, not against them. That is to go against nature, and the number one Hawke principle of survival is to accept the ways and go with the flow of nature.

One of the fundamental keys to your survival is to not expect anything.

Do not expect to be rescued; you will only be let down, disheartened, and disillusioned if it doesn't come to pass. Do not expect to have any creature comforts; you will only become angry, frustrated, and fatigued when you don't have them. Do not expect that anything will go right or go your way or be easy; you will only lose interest, drive, and motivation at every corner when they don't.

Expect nothing. Expect no one to do anything for you. Expect no one to find you. Expect not to live. This is your reality. You must accept this and live in this very moment this way. To expect to get out and walk away is to fear the opposite if it happens. To fear is to freeze, and to freeze can be the very thing that causes what you fear to happen.

The point of this Asian concept is to live right here, right now, in this present moment.

If you see a poisonous snake, do not expect it to pass you by without striking, but rather see it for what it is at that very moment—a potentially deadly threat to your life in that exact instant. Then, look at it for what it is—simply an animal with a purpose, to weed out the weak animals in its environment, and to survive itself. Its intention is merely to live, the same as yours. It does so by killing, same as you will need to do.

Simply living in the moment without expectation allows you not to fear but to see the potential to make the most of the situation and maximize its potential. Without fear of death or expectation of being left alone, you merely strike the animal and make it a meal. You'll never know if it was going to strike you or not. You don't live in the past or future of "what ifs", you only live in the here and now, without expectation, only action or inaction.

Expectation is different than hope. Hope for everything. Believe in yourself. Dream of your return to better times, see it and envision a happy ending. Do this in the slow moments, or the quiet, cold, wet, or hot moments when you can do nothing else but think. But then, when that time has passed and it's time to work or move, put those thoughts away and hold no expectations of their fruition. Keep all of these alive and within you, and nurture them every day and re-kindle them when doused, so as to never let them fade and pass. BUT DO NOT EXPECT.

As the ancient Chinese wisdom says, expectation is the source of all unhappiness. It is true. It is a false seed that will not bear fruit. Do not plant it; do not let it take root. Rip it out if it does begin to grow in you, and do this with a vengeance.

Expect nothing. Hope for everything.

REMEMBER: Choose Life; Kill to Live; be DAPR before SoGgy; think SWFFly; and above all, NEVER QUIT!

This is all I have to say on Survival Psychology. Now let's do stuff!

Shelter

E asiest first is the rule for shelters.

Look around you and make what you have work for you. If you have a broken down vehicle, aircraft, sea vessel, or any wreckage or building debris, use it.

Be very aware that building a shelter takes time, and a good one takes some work and therefore energy—especially to make it windproof and waterproof. If you are lucky enough to have all that sorted out for you, or if you're in such a pleasant climate that you can do without, then maybe you would consider not even making a shelter. Forget that! In the best of conditions, I still recommend using something for cover. Weather can change quickly, night temperatures may be very different than daytime temperatures, and most of all, you never know what critters and creepy crawlers are about.

Just don't risk it.

And don't fool yourself by thinking you're tough and try to suck it up and go without a shelter. I read in a book once where a guy slept in the snow, so I tried sleeping out in the cold one night without anything but my clothes. . . . I was sick with a cold for a week, ha!

Thinking you're tough is foolish thinking. Preserve your health and energy like a precious jewel. It is your life savings at this point, and it just might be what saves you. Guard it in all you do, and let common sense and concern for unnecessary risk be a major factor in all your decision-making criteria.

So, first use what you have. If you don't have a ready-made shelter, use what is readily available in your surroundings to make the easiest thing first. Of course, the situation dictates. If you need to keep dry from the rain or heat or snow, cold, and wind, then do what you need, but just past the minimum is what I recommend the first night. You will have plenty of other things to do.

THE TIME FACTOR Give yourself at least one hour to make a minimal shelter if you have good stuff around you. If there's not much around, give yourself two hours. Shelters take time to build. Build time into your plan. If it's early morning, great, you have time; if it's afternoon or evening, move shelter higher on the priority list. Even if you have something for shelter already, get in it and test it before dark. I've had great shelters in cars, dumpsters, hallways, caves, and in bushes, but at times still had a bad night of sleep because I was too confident in a particular shelter, and little things like a few holes or lumps caused me more grief than I bargained for.

I have also taken all day to make a very good shelter, but only after I had food and water sorted out. In some shelters I have slept as good as I ever have in any bed anywhere. In these I took the time to get it off the ground and protect it well from wind and rain and critters, and made sure that I was well padded and covered while inside. With every shelter, be sure to gather lots of cushion for sleeping and lots of leaves and foliage to cover yourself for warmth.

But on Day One, you need only to create a shelter that's just good enough. Otherwise, hydrate, eat, keep dry, tend wounds, make fire, make tools, make signals, or do anything productive if there is plenty of daylight once you've made the shelter.

OTHERWISE, SLEEP! Sleep as much and as long as you can the first night. You have likely just gone through hell. You are more tired than you know, and scared, afraid of the uncertainty of your situation. This is normal. Everyone is concerned when they are not in control. But you can control yourself.

Start by getting rest, or "recovery." It is necessary for your machine, your body, to have down time to recover its strength and maintain its health. Do not underestimate the power of sleep to do this, and do not neglect it as a mandatory part of your planning in all phases.

It is a fact that airborne troops who parachute into a tactical scenario are often at just fifty percent of their fighting capacity when they arrive, as compared to ground troops who were transported by other means. This is because the airborne troops went through hours of strenuous preparation and then a stressful jump where risk of death is real for every jumper, every time (I personally have broken my back and neck, dislocated my femur, and cracked ankles during jumps). And that adrenaline surge takes a tremendous toll on your mental and physical reserves of energy.

The kind of event that leads to a survival situation is also usually an adrenaline surge. So your energy stores must be replenished, and the only way to do that is through sleep.

I know it doesn't sound like tough-guy thinking, but sleep is imperative to your survival.

If you're fatigued, you'll likely pass out until daylight wakes you; if not, you'll likely find the first night to be the longest, and that works on people's heads. Just remember: the first night is the roughest, and odds are good that the rest won't be like that. So, do not let yourself become demoralized during the next day, and instead, focus on remedying the situation by making your shelter good enough to ensure you get a good night's sleep the second night. The whole world will seem better to you after that.

STAY OR GO? After you've rested you can make a more informed decision to stay or go. If you decide to go, then having spent too much time on a shelter would have been a waste of time and energy, and one that could cost you dearly later. This is another reason why you should only make a just-better-than-needed shelter for the first night.

Also, even if you do decide to stay at your location, you might find your actual shelter site might not be the best one available in your immediate vicinity. You might be in an opening to the prevailing winds, or be open to a trickle of water if the rains pour.

So, SCOUT! If you're staying put, scout around and see what you have available. I call it shelter shopping. If I can find me some super digs that are already dug, I am all about being lazy. I've only ever found one great cave—that is, that a critter hadn't already made home. But I've found lots of natural holes, indentures, or concave pieces of terrain suitable for building up into a nice low-level hooch. And I've found many nicely leaning trees, large-rooted trees, and well-placed boulders, all good for turning into a nice shelter.

If you decide you need to go, as you walk, always be on the lookout for a good deal, that bargain shelter waiting for you to pay a visit.

I have cut a long trip short simply to exploit a nice target of opportunity when it comes to shelters. If you're making a movement, you have no real idea how long you'll be going. I always plan for a long time, so I get my head around the fact that "I'm here . . . until I'm not." So when I see Nature offering a nice natural place for shelter, I accept her courteous offering graciously. Like in POW survival, it's all about small victories. Every little break Mother Nature gives you, bask in it and enjoy.

Bottom line, the function of a shelter is to protect you from the elements when necessary, and to protect you while vulnerable during sleep. Its quality level will affect your sleep, which in turn will affect all your decisions, judgement, and reaction time.

CONSIDERATIONS FOR SHELTERS

THE BASICS. First of all, let me say that there is no exact "right way" to build a survival shelter. You will be making your shelter out of the materials available to you, and so each shelter you build will look different. However, there *are* basic principles that you should know and practice that will enable you to make fine protective shelters in practically any environment, regardless of what tools or resources you may or may not have. Some terms describing the most basic shelters include A-frame (a stick frame shaped like the letter "A"), tepee (shaped like a common Native American tepee and made from sticks and foliage), and lean-to (basically, a wall of sticks built on a leaning angle to protect from elements). You can also burrow out a shelter, make a shelter from rocks or logs, dig into snow, and so on. Let's get into the details.

BOX OF ROCKS. That is, do not be as dumb as a box of rocks and sleep on rocks! They're too hard and will cause body parts to fall asleep resulting in aches and pains that may wake you or cause pain the next day. They're also too cold, and will zap your energy and you'll wake up fatigued. Be careful in the desert, as rocks feel warm by day but by night get very cold. It's also wise not to sleep *under* rocks, either. I've seen big rocks fall for no reason, like they waited a million years just to fall when I was around. And critters like to get in there under low-hanging rocks, sometimes the dangerous kind.

GET OFF THE GROUND. The first rule in all cases, really, is to get off the ground. I always look to the trees for shelter first when I need shelter fast. It gets me off the ground and keeps me safe from most things—flash floods, mean beasties, and bad bugs. No shelter is perfect, and there is always risk of something like a snake or insect, but rarely is this more likely in a tree than on the ground.

In a worst-case scenario where you have no tools or little time, simply find two good branches—one to sit on, straddle, or otherwise hold you up, with another one close enough to wedge yourself in so you won't fall out. And then let the rest of your body lean against the base of the tree. I call this "airplane sleeping." You're high up, and you can almost sleep, but not quite, like in the economy seats on airplanes.

But it will get you off the ground, provide you some shelter (if it's bushy enough, and not too windy or rainy), and it is safer than nothing unless you're so high that a fall would be harmful or fatal. In any case, it's wise to use a belt or shoe strings or an extra item of clothing to "tie in" so you don't fall completely. For one example, you can tie your arms or legs together and, if you should fall, the tug will hold you up while you quickly respond. It's up to you to picture and figure out the best way to tie yourself into the trees that you choose; I'm just giving you the basic principles.

IMMEDIATE ACTION DRILLS. I always rehearse my "immediate action drills," or IADs, before I go to sleep. If in a tree, I practice a few times, preferably before dark, by reaching and seeing where I'd grab if I fell this way or that. So if something happens or gives way, my response will be rehearsed enough that I'll react appropriately and immediately, even from a dead sleep.

I practice IADs if sleeping on the ground, or in a cave or rock shelter, or anywhere for that matter. I imagine what could happen, make a plan, rehearse it in my head, and practice it if it's something that requires a physical response. It's a good starting point for any exigency.

I also always have some sort of weapon for defense, whether it's a stick or rock or something else, and I rehearse reaching for it and using it, so that if I'm disturbed from slumber, something is going to get a strong and painful response.

So, tie in and rehearse IADs before going to sleep.

BUILDING A TREE SHELTER. When picking a tree or trees, I first look to see if it is easy in and out, or in this case up or down. All things considered, I try to find an easily climbable tree with a nice fork of two very strong branches so I can lay some other branches between them as a platform—and now I have a pretty good start point for a shelter. It helps to lash these branches down before building up on them. I also look for a nice third branch as my roof center-piece, above. The height of your shelter off the ground will be dictated by the trees you find, but ideally you'll be at least shoulder height, and not so high that a fall would be fatal.

If I'm among trees that are simply too big, too high, or just not right for a shelter, I look for groves of smaller trees, ideally three or four close enough together that I can, again, lay some other small log-like branches across their branch joints near the base to give me a platform off the ground.

Think of these strong branches laid across as your bed frame. Try to make them as level as possible. Using the trees' forks in this way will save you from having to make and apply lashings, which is especially handy if you don't have any.

Also, don't be self-restricting in your preconceived ideas about how things should look. If you can't make a square bed like back home, maybe because you only have 3 trees close together, then make a triangular bed and sleep curled up. Or if you have many trees, like five or six, but they can be linked together by your branch poles, then make that situation work.

Getting yourself off the ground and on a fairly flat platform upon which you can rest safely is the key. Outside of those two criteria, there are no limits to what you might make and no number of drawings can cover all the possibilities.

Once I build my bed frame, whatever its shape, I lay more branches in between and parallel to the outer structure. Think of these as the slats for the bed frame. Then I put down lots of soft bushy stuff for my mattress, actually about two-feet thick since much of the green stuff will mat down as I sleep on it and none of the slats I laid will be exactly flat and smooth.

platform of sticks built between
lower boughs of three trees

Tree shelter

I then fashion a roof in the same manner. Use the higher-up branches to lay slats and cover, if available, and if not, you can make a pyramid roof by angling long loose branches starting from the four corners of your platform and connecting at the center point above. Leave the open side away from the wind direction as best you can, and stack as much foliage as possible on the roof as the more there is, the less chance of wind and rain getting in.

The main concepts for the tree shelter are that it's off the ground, you have a strong platform, and there's a decent overhead cover. A lot of times it will end up looking just like a bird's nest, but these things are easy to build, require nothing but the trees around you, and they'll protect you and help you sleep well. The only thing is that they do take time, so make time.

SWAMP BED. A swamp bed is sorta like the tree shelter, except instead of using standing trees as the "legs" that hold your platform, you create the legs by hammering three or four logs into the ground and then creating a platform frame on those. Many survival books encourage you to build these, but I'm here to tell you now, that is a nice fiction. Unless you have incredible tools or amazing strength to drive the log-legs into the ground, they will give and sway sideways until you end up on the ground—exactly where you don't want to be. You will also be more depleted from all the effort needed to make it in the first place.

GROUND-BASED SHELTER. Let's say you don't have trees nearby, or they're so huge or tiny that they won't work for shelter purposes. No problem! The ground is where most mammals live, and so can you. Just get comfortable with the idea and apply common sense to your situation.

So, we're on the ground, but we're not. We want to get ourselves as separated as we can from the ground. If we have to find logs, rocks, piles of vegetation, even a stack of flat cacti can be used (make sure you tamp down the spikes if your boots are solid and the spikes aren't too long and hard!). After you've laid down your sticks or logs or rocks, soften the base by covering it with sand or topsoil or more vegetation.

There are no limits to what you might find and use; the key is to look at everything around you as a resource and see it not for what it is and what

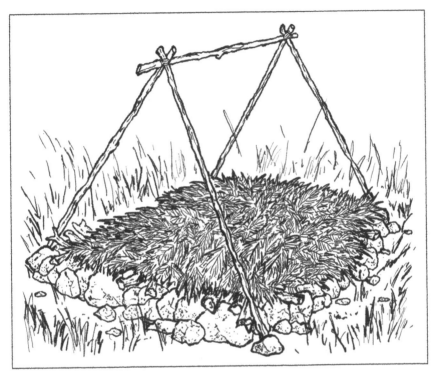

Ground-based shelter

you know of it, but for what you need and how it can be made to serve your purpose. Survival situations are all about imagination and creative problem solving. This is why I find it one of the best ways to teach leadership and family counselling as it forces you to search for new and different ways to solve common problems.

Once you've got the platform laid out, start to fashion walls and a roof—IF you have the time, energy, and materials available. (You can just sleep right on the ground platform if necessary.) Again, many survival sources instruct you to build a classic "A-frame" structure, which is all well and good. In reality, anything you can come up with that makes sense in your surroundings, works. Now, the A-frame is simple to make. Start by angling two long branches from the ground up (about three to five feet apart), meeting at a center point a few feet off the ground, and lash them together, creating what looks like the letter "A." This is the front end of the frame where you get in. Then make another "A" for the back of the shelter. Then lash one end of a long thick stick to the top of one A, and the other end to the top of the other A, and you've got the basic structure. Then lay many sticks on an angle from this top beam down to the ground on either side, and cover with as much foliage as you can find.

Remember that you can also use existing trees, rocks, ledges, and anything else to help create walls and a roof above your platform—just make sure you SCOUT the area and make best use of all resources available.

A-frame shelter

Once you've got the platform and walls/roof set, if you're in a cool climate, fill your hooch to overflow with leaves and burrow into them; it's kinda like a big comforter blanket, and will do much to keep you warm and make you feel cozier. If you're in a really hot spot, try to give yourself more space in your hooch for air flow, like a higher roof or wider walls or edges, so the breeze can get in and you don't trap your own heat.

ON, NOT IN. *On* the ground is typically better than *In* the ground for numerous reasons. First, if it rains, you likely won't be flooded out. Second, creepy crawlies just naturally seem to find holes in the ground, and you don't wanna wake up with bug bites or worse. Next, the ground is colder and more wet if you dig into it, not usually a plus for the survivor. And finally, the biggest factor—it takes hard work and energy to dig into the ground! Ask any infantryman who has had to dig a trench, only to pick up and move out shortly thereafter. And without a decent tool, this can be a very tasking endeavor. So, unless you have the tools, time, strength, and necessity, it is better to go on the ground. But of course, there are exceptions.

IN, NOT ON. If it is excruciatingly hot or cold, try to get into the ground. Usually in such environments the ground tends to be very hard, so look for the soft spots.

If you are in a desert area that is all sand dunes, you're in a bad place. Be exceedingly frugal with all energy and make conservative decisions. The key is to save water, so, dig into the sand to get to a little cooler spot and then use something to shade you from the sun. Even if you have to get naked to use the clothes on your back as the layer that separates you from the sun, do it. Make a small hole, lay your clothes across it and put more sand on the edges to hold them in place, then get into the hole and rest by day and work or move by night.

In a non-sand-dune desert environment that is also extremely hot by day and cold by night, dig in. Fortunately, most deserts have a rich variety of terrain. So, again, scout about, find an area that is more sandy or soft and dig in there. Always try to use a tool if you can to prevent scratches and small injuries which could lead to infection easily and quickly.

In cold environs, like mountains or forest, look for areas covered in snow to dig a cave. Do so right away—as heat will surely cook you, cold will quickly freeze you. Get out of it. Just digging into the snow and burrowing in will be surprisingly warmer than the outside air around you. Also try to put something between you and the snow; as your body warms it, you'll get moist if not in waterproof clothes. When all else fails, at least keep your torso dry and head warm.

If there isn't enough snow to burrow into, but there is some, then try to fashion it into some form of shelter, like an igloo or a couple walls with sticks and branches on top. I've found igloos are hard to make without a snow shovel to cut nice blocks. But you can make large snowballs, place them as you would bricks, and then fill in the holes and gaps with snow and pack it in. I find a pyramid shape works best because, as you stack your walls, each one a little closer in, the last row of snowballs will make your roof.

But again, this takes time and, without gloves, it can be very difficult. So, weigh out the time and energy expenditure with the value added you expect. If planning to hold tight for a spell in the cold, it might be worth cold hands the first day while the strength is good to make a snow hooch.

Again, the point here is if you don't have a shelter or something to make a shelter with, and it's really cold, don't stay on the ground—get into it. It will give more warmth as it reduces your exposure to wind and precipitation. In the worst-case scenario, just scrape a burrow into the snow, lay in it, and cover up. This will buy you some time to rest and regroup. Then decide if you need to build up or move out.

TIME TO ACT. It sounds hateful, but when you're really surviving, everything is out to kill you. Remember that in all things. Always take a moment to think and question before you take an action. What could go wrong? Can I do this in a better way? Do I really need to do this at all, or are there other options? When you have time, take time!

Now, if you don't have time, then make a decision and go hot! Often in urgent circumstances, where time is not an option, *some* decision is better than *no* decision. I cannot tell you how many times in operations I have seen a person die unnecessarily because someone couldn't figure out whether to start an IV, apply a tourniquet, or dress a wound. Sometimes, because people are in shock, afraid, or busy trying to call for a medic, they simply don't apply common sense and reach down and plug the hole to stop the bleeding, then do whatever else needs to be done. And in survival, the same thing applies—more times than not, *inaction* to an immediate need will cause more harm or loss than a *poor action*, but action nonetheless. In other words, you might spill a lot of water by trying to catch a falling bucket, for example, but you will lose *all* the water if you don't try to reach for it.

THINK ABOUT "SITTING." This is another handy acronym that relates to survival shelters, and it makes sense since "sitting" is something you'll be doing a lot of inside it—sitting, thinking, working, planning, doing, and making things.

"S" is for "shelter." Always find, build, and use one based on your environment.

"I" is for "improvise." Use wreckage if available, and improvise all other materials from what's around you.

"T" is for "trees." Always look to trees for shelter, whether as a quick sleep spot, as a frame with two or three trunks, or in a cluster.

"N" is for "nature." Use all that Nature provides, including caves, holes, logs, fallen trees, ditches boulders, foliage, dirt, rocks, and so on.

"G" is for "ground." Make a platform on the ground at least, as a last resort, and go underground in extremes.

Now let's look at typical survival shelters in specific environments.

JUNGLE

The best types of shelters are the store-bought kind that are a combination of a hammock, rain fly roof, and mosquito net. There are great lightweight ones available on the market. Of course, if you're in an unplanned survival situation, you won't have this. But if you're travelling into, over, or through a jungle region, it's good to pack one of these in case. The concept is that these set the standard for you to strive for as you go about improvising your own shelter in the jungle environment.

Tents simply are not a good idea in real jungle as it's hard to find a clear, level, dry place to put one down. Any rain or critters pose more of a hazard to tent shelters as well. Best to think hammock and get off the ground.

But when it comes to jungle survival, I find old-fashioned is best. I go for the jungle trio "HiPiN" (Hammock, Poncho, Net)—and I prefer these to be separate units. For hammocks, I prefer the old-fashioned U.S. Army jungle hammock. Not because it's the best; in fact, I often get a snag or button caught in the netting during the night. But I prefer them for their multipurpose utility. I can make them into a rucksack for carrying things or a litter for a wounded person or a trap for animals or a net for larger fish. They just make a good generic tool for a lot of uses. But I mostly use them as a bed, as opposed to the "survival" nets which can be used for everything *and* a bed, but they don't make the best bed, as they're not primarily a bed. Best to have a true bed that can also do other things, than to have a multipurpose tool that serves as a bed secondarily.

I also like my rain fly to be separate. Again, I prefer the U.S. Army poncho. The reason is the same as with the hammock: I can use it as a poncho for shelter against wind, rain, and sun; I can make a raft or a huge watercatcher with it; I can use it to smoke meat; and any number of other uses.

The general rule in survival packing and planning is to get the most use for the least weight and space.

Most of the expensive specialty items that are designed for one specific thing offer less practicality when surviving, as the basic day-to-day needs of a human require many implements to fulfill. Therefore, your best tools are those you can rely on to handle a variety of jobs.

If I'm going to take the time to buy, pack, and carry stuff, I want to make sure I really get all I can out of it. And so it goes with my mosquito net. I like a separate mosquito net as I can use it in so many ways. Besides being a must-have item for sleeping, it can be used as a bird trap or a fish net. Sometimes you can get enough tiny minnows in them to make a nice simple meal all by itself.

Sometimes it's so sweltering hot and humid, that poncho is just a huge heat retainer. If it's not pouring rain, I'll skip the poncho and just spread the skeeter net and have a bug-free slightly cooler jungle night's sleep. Let's say it's late, dark, and I'm too tired to build the three-part jungle hooch of poncho, hammock, and net. Then I will use the net as insulation, the poncho as a blanket to protect from rain and bugs, and the rolled-up hammock as a pillow—I've had many decent nights' sleep this way.

JUNGLE SHELTER WITHOUT GEAR. Now if you don't have any gear, it gets back to the beginning on shelters—take to the trees.

The **swamp bed** comes to mind here. But the smart way is the easiest way that works. Don't bother with the classic method of making a swamp bed described above. Instead, take three smaller sticks/logs about one-foot long each, hold them in a bundle, and tie them with cordage (shoe string, ripped cuffs off your pants, natural material, whatever is available) and make one lash and a granny knot. When securely fastened, open the sticks like a tripod and place them down on the ground. Make four tripods and you got a swamp bed stand that you can take with you. These will set on the ground sturdily, no force needed, and they're easy to adjust as well. Once the four tripods are down, lay two long "poles" (branch, limb, thin log, etc.) lengthwise onto the tops of the tripods, and two shorter poles as your width, and then lay slats, and then lay foliage to lay on and under.

Swamp bed

As for the lashings needed to put this all together, if you have no manmade cordage available, find some flexible vines, or pliant young sapling branches, or tough longer roots of small trees or plants, and wrap them into bundles; these should hold as a temporary lashing. It all takes a bit of feeling it out, but that's what it takes. Some getting used to your environment, opening your mind to your new surroundings, and taking in what is available to you and seeing how you can make it do your will.

If you have nothing, and it's dark, or you're zapped of energy, you can always grab a few large-leafed plants and make a sort of blanket over yourself while leaning against the dry side of a tree. Try to find a tree that rises on a bit of an angle, and always look above for loose branches that may fall. Be sure and lay a lot of foliage underneath you for that ever-important elevation, and you'll make it through the night.

THE BENEFITS OF BAMBOO. Of all the great materials the jungle offers with which to build impressive structures, bamboo has to be the all-time best thing growing out there in nature—always be on the lookout for it. Not only can you make a bed or shelter from bamboo, you can also make utensils, weapons, canteens, pots, pans, cups, and more—heck, you can even EAT it! In short, you can do almost anything with bamboo. It's even great for starting fires. So, if you find a clump of bamboo growing, it's a good idea to consider making a home nearby as you'll have plenty of supplies in the store for building.

One of the coolest uses of bamboo is to make a rain-gutter roof. To do this, split a number of bamboo shafts in half, and lay them all tightly together with the curved part facing up. The shafts should be vertical to the ground; not horizontal. Then lay other halves on top so that one edge is sitting in the groove of the upward facing pieces on either side. This make a wonderful waterproof roof in that most of the rain is blocked by the bamboo and then caught in the upward facing cups of the first row, allowing the water to run down to the edge.

It's important to make the roof plenty long so that the rain falls off the edge far enough away from you. I prefer a lean-to type roof as they're faster and easier to build. I make it at least two feet more around the edges than I need, and have it sloping downward in whatever I think is the best direction to block the rain.

If it's rainy season, and you'll be holing up for awhile at your site, best to make an A-frame roof with your bamboo, and lay one long fat piece of

Bamboo roof with gutter

bamboo across the top to keep the rain from coming down the middle. You should also consider improvising a gutter to channel rain away from you and into some water-holding vessel. Even if it's just a hole you scraped out with a stick and then line with leaves to make a reservoir, it's a good way to save water and energy.

Bottom line in the jungle: you need to get off the floor, mind the bugs, and do all you can to stay dry. Think of these things when it comes to shelter building.

DESERT

The desert is a funny place. It can be scorching hot or downright freezing, even snowing.

There can be long periods of drought, and then a sudden flash flood. So, the first thing to do in the desert is to get rid of any preconceived notions of what it is or isn't. The desert can kill you quick if you're sloppy or disrespectful.

Most likely, you won't have a poncho or parachute or anything else besides the clothes on your back. Every time I've been in the desert, I've had virtually nothing and it is a real challenge to get shelter in pure desert without a cover of some sort.

Start by looking at what is available. There will likely be some sort of physical terrain that will give you shade for a period of the day—find it and use it. In the middle of the day when the sun is at its blazing hottest, if you can't find any natural cover, then sit down, take off your clothes and use them to create a shade above yourself. If you can find or make a hole or depression to get into, and then use your clothes as a cover above you, all the better. The key is to not leave your flesh exposed. Sunburn is fast, painful, and potentially deadly in the desert, and the resulting blisters only serve to suck even more water out of your circulatory system.

But when you do have a tarp of some form, use it as a shelter during daytime. Place it a few feet above you to allow more heat to radiate off of it. If you have two covers, use one as the sun shield higher up, and the other a few inches under it to create a space that will trap heat while you remain remarkably cool underneath. However, this can be difficult if you don't have enough workable lashings and poles to keep your cover in place. So, operate on the principle of simplicity and simply get one cover high up. That will do you just right.

Desert shelter

At night in the desert, expect the temperature to drop dramatically. If your overall plan includes trying to walk toward safety wherever it may be, then you may consider doing your travelling at night to avoid the crippling heat of the day. If you need to sleep at night, then be sure to scout a good location long before dark, and to gather the materials that will keep you warm. Small caves, the underside of rock ledges, thick brush, and other natural formations can serve as cover or shelter. In the desert, if you have nothing else, a rock ledge with a small fire can provide enough warmth and safety to get you through the night.

ARCTIC

When you're in the Arctic, or any sub-zero climate for that matter, the first order of business is to get out of the cold as soon as possible. As far as priorities go, water, fire, food, and all but immediate life-saving first aid, all come second to seeking shelter and getting out of the cold. Every moment you

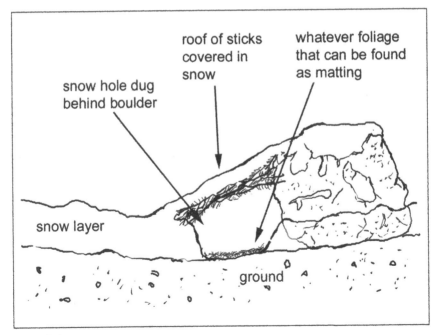

Snow shelter

spend exposed reduces your physical and mental capacities, which leads to poor decisions and, ultimately, quick and final breakdown.

If you can find a field or cluster of rocks, seek shelter in them. There will likely be good pockets of space between the snow and rocks, and they'll block the wind better than trees can. If there are no such rock resources, get into the trees. Often there is space under the snow-covered tree boughs that make for a really nice, ready-made snow den. If the snow isn't deep enough, then use the tree as temporary shelter for breaks from the wind as you build up a snow or debris wall.

Debris includes anything and everything around you that you can simply grab, drag, pull up, break off, and gather around yourself to fashion a rudimentary shelter. It ain't pretty, no two ever look alike, and they're not ideal shelters as they don't completely protect you from wind, rain, sun, and critters. But the very notion of having even a rudimentary shelter is extremely comforting, and psychologically, that mental security blanket can go a long way in reinforcing your will to live. But even debris shelters take a lot of time and energy to make, so plan on the time to make even this simplest of shelters.

The simplest and quickest technique of getting out of the cold in an arctic or snow-covered area is simply to dig into the snow and cover up. This will buy you time while you think about your next moves. Also, it is remarkably warmer inside a snow cave—even a small one that you quickly dig out—than you might imagine.

Ultimately, anytime you are stuck in a sub-zero environment, trying to stay and wait might not be your best option unless you have materials to sustain yourself for a long wait or you are fairly confident that a search party will be looking for you. Without resources, merely waiting alone can do you in. So, without resources or imminent rescue, quick shelters and quick movements are your keys to survival.

SEASHORE/ISLAND

The seashore is a relatively easy environment for survival. You can pretty much get all you need in most cases on the seashore. I call this easy living.

Unless you're stuck on a tiny islet with zero growth, you can usually fashion a decent shelter when on or near a beach. There is always debris floating up on the shore that can be used to make an elevated shelter. Combined with a small burrow and your clothing as a cover, this will suffice to keep you out of the elements of sun.

Whether you choose to build a swamp bed or an A-frame shelter or some such thing, always first look above your chosen location to ensure that nothing is above you that might fall on you, such as coconuts, loose branches, rocks, etc. Coconuts are especially dangerous, ironically, as they are also lifesavers when in such a locale since they provide water and food. I've seen them just drop at any time and an unexpected number of folks die every year just from coconuts falling on their head!

Also study the ground near your potential shelter location. Look for grooves in the ground that could have been made by flash streams of water. Also search for signs of animal life in the immediate area, such as tracks, holes, nests, or droppings, and if there are many such signs, find a different place to put down. Another consideration in selecting a location is tidal movement—check the shoreline for signs of recent tidal activity, and notice whether the tide is moving in or out, and determine if it will soon cover the area you are considering for a shelter.

One good thing about seashore survival is that the leaves and branches often found near beaches are great for making a shelter. The best leaves for making a shelter are the ones that require the least amount of work to use. For this, I prefer "elephant ears," which look exactly as the term implies. If they are not around, I'll reach for palm fronds or any other large-leafed plants. Round palm fronds work well just as they are; other elongated fronds work better if split down the middle. All require a stick structure with slats, such as a lean-to, tepee, A-frame, etc. to build upon. If you have time, weave the leaves into the slats for extra sturdiness and weather protection. When there is no time to do so, simply lay enough slats to hold the leaves without falling through, and then lay a few more slats over all the leaves to give them security in bad weather.

In the simplest of terms, find the right location, make a frame, lay the fattest leaves, anchor them, and rest. If you're going to be in such an

Leaves woven into slats

environment for weeks or longer, you will have plenty of time and materials to construct a very fine shelter.

WOODLANDS

The type of shelter you can create in woodlands is relatively more sturdy as the environment produces stronger resources. In most woodlands there are many branches on the ground that still retain a lot of their original sturdiness and, unlike equally sized branches in the tropics, they have not been corroded by the fast-decaying tropical climate. Also, the vegetation in woodlands is easier to deal with than jungles, as it doesn't grow as thick. Another helpful aspect of woodland survival is there isn't a real need to get off the ground; therefore the logistics are quite simple. Just lean some sticks together in an A-frame or teepee structure, or construct a basic lean-to, or use a tree as a lean-to, and start stacking pine boughs, various leaves, soil, and/or other resources, and you're sorted.

If it's still daylight after you've made your shelter, perform a quick "sun-spot check." Just lie inside your shelter and look up, and if you can see any sunlight, that's an area that will be susceptible for rain to come in—so quickly fill those spots in with more debris. You can also do a similar leak-check by building a small, safe fire in your hooch and look for smoke leaks coming out. With the smoke-check technique, you'll have the added benefit of repelling bugs.

Woodland shelter

MOUNTAINS

Mountain-area shelters are about the same as the woodlands, except you might incorporate boulders as walls against which you can fashion your lean-to. You may also find clusters of boulders to be your walls and you'll just need to make a roof and fill in any gaps in your walls with brush and branches.

If there are no boulders to work with, there will likely be plenty of stones or rocks you can stack to make a good wall. Another technique is to make a shape of stones—square, circular, or triangular—simply piled one or two high. Then use them as a form against which you can wedge your sticks and make a nice little shelter.

Stone and stick tepee shelter

Often a fallen tree or log can be found in the mountains, and these make a nice starter structure for a shelter, or even a good self-contained temporary shelter if you're wounded or too ill or depleted to make a shelter in time. Just pull up some soil or debris for coverage and get as comfortable as possible.

In fact, whenever you're building a shelter, make use of all your effort.

What I mean is, when you dig up dirt or break apart sticks or rip up leaves, there will be debris from that activity. Use that debris! Put it to use by forming it into a small wall around your shelter, or as an insulator to keep out bugs, or as a stopgap to prevent leaks of water and wind, or as a small rain ditch around any ground shelter. The basic idea is to use all resources available in your situation, and to maximize all your efforts.

Another trick to handling rain is to tie a piece of string where it is entering and angle it so the water will be diverted away from you. Or, for the edges of a roof or the top joint of an A-frame, have your foliage overlap a good six inches or more so that the rain is dispersed long before it gets to the joint and then flows down the side walls instead of dripping into the middle of your home. If despite all that, it still rains into your hooch, dig a little channel and direct it out the door and sleep on the opposite side. You've got nothing better to do but home improvement in these cases, or conduct personal hygiene and take a bath instead!

SWAMP

The swamp can be pretty tough going. If you get stranded there, be prepared for a mental battle as it can be very intimidating as you're frequently submerged, which reduces your body temperature and softens the skin which increases exposure to damage and infection. Also, swamps are often filled with gators and snakes. However, like the jungle, mountains, or island settings, one can survive there a long time—unlike the desert and arctic. But the chances of being found in a swamp are extremely slim unless a plane wreck left a good imprint in the ground. Even then, the marsh usually just swallows these up and the traces of a wreck are very hard to find for rescuers. So, staying in the swamp is not a real good plan. What that means here is that you don't really want to spend a lot of time making a shelter here. Therefore, swamp shelters should be the minimum needed to get through the night, and then you should continue moving by day unless you're ill or injured.

The ultimate rule of swamp shelters is to seek high ground. Often you'll find small patches of drier, harder ground to make a shelter on. It's still good to get off the ground and even if it is harder, it will often moisten very quickly as you work around your site and turn into quite a muddy mess. If you can get off the ground, take extra care and time to stack a very high pile of grass and padding to keep you dry at the top.

I've spent days in knee- to waist-deep water, and it isn't fun. In these cases, start early and make a swamp bed. Forget the method of driving poles into the ground, and instead tie into some trees. The ground here is often so wet and sloppy, it's pure foolishness to try making a platform of sticks stabbed into the boggy ground.

Again, like the nest platform described earlier, chop or break some strong branches, lay them into the forks formed by branches of a closely grouped set of standing tree branches, and build a platform to get you up out of the water. Hang everything off the trees around you to dry while you rest, and do all you can to keep yourself dry as well.

Once you have a platform constructed to hold you up and get you out of the water, try to fashion a roof over your structure in case it rains. But if

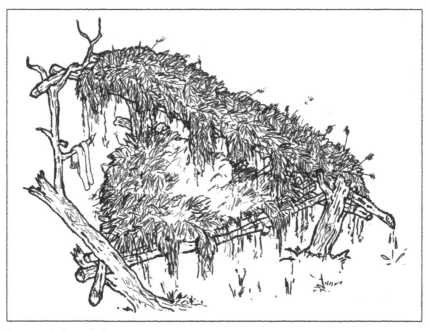

Swamp platform shelter

you don't think it necessary, don't spend the time on a roof. The platform alone will take longer than you think. Again, the key is that you won't be staying long and therefore, it's more like a roadside motel instead of a nice vacation resort. Just get dry, get rest, and then get moving.

URBAN

Some may ask, why bother even covering urban survival in this book? And I'll explain. If a war breaks out or a *coup d'état* occurs, or there's a natural disaster, you may find yourself in a city with no way out and not wanting to be found. In this sense, it actually is important to teach and learn about surviving in an urban environment.

The first priority tends to be shelter in terms of staying hidden from anyone who might be a threat. Warehouses, abandoned buildings or vehicles, particularly trucks and trailers, are good places. Containers and dumpsters can be if they're not in a highly populated area. The main thing is to be sheltered from harm by remaining unseen.

A significant factor here will be time. If unfriendly people will be looking for you, you don't have time and so you must make a movement. Or if you don't think anyone is coming to your rescue, you don't have time and must make a movement. Either way, you may have to move around often and find various shelters until you can make a movement out of the urban environment and start living off the land.

There are a few key elements to consider for urban shelters:
How much space it gives you to loiter and rest during daylight, as you'll likely be making any movements at night.

Does a shelter offer an escape route, or would it become a death trap if the entrance was blocked?

Are you able to eat, drink, and utilize the latrine, if there is one, without compromise?

The fact is you won't be constructing anything, but rather, you'll be exploiting objects based on availability and isolation. We've all seen hobos and homeless folks turn boxes into homes, and newspapers into beds, and the tools of their trade is good stuff in urban survival.

Also, think about all the places to hide in plain sight. Overpasses, railroads, bushes in the middle of a highway exit ramp, even sewers and under houses are good places to hole up for the day. I have slept in every one of these at one point or another, and it's amazing to me how many people simply don't look at what's right in front of them. You can even sleep in the row of bushes outside of a mall or corporate building as everyone is so busy there during the day, they never think to suspect someone might be hiding in the bushes in broad daylight right in the public view.

Sewers are rough and smell, but they have the advantage of being overlooked by most, and you can discreetly track what's going on around you, and often you'll have an egress route.

The other thing I have learned, having been discovered in a few hide sites, is that dogs and kids will always find you. When we would build a hide site to overlook a drug field, for example, the exact places we seek to make a hidey hole are the same things kids look for to play in. Likewise, if you're close enough to people, you'll be close enough for their pets, and pets are always sniffing around for places to defecate or urinate.

I've had two dogs, one teenager, and one adult use the latrine right next to my hole over the years, and it never ceases to amaze me how that works. Think about this if you ever find yourself in an urban survival situation and need a place to hide. Better to go right *in* public than *near* public.

In plain sight, will serve you right; public too near, much to fear.

Two of the most important factors for urban improvised shelters are to always have an egress or escape route, and to set up early-warning alarm systems by placing bottles or twigs or leaves or gravel around your sleeping area. This way, if anyone happens to walk near you, they will make a crunch or other noise to wake you. At that point you have to decide whether to utilize your egress, or freeze and wait. Often the sound will distract them, too, and they'll be less inclined to notice you.

3

Water

I like to break down the basics of water into a few simple rules.

1. Keep it in you.
2. Get it in you and keep it flowing in.
3. If you have it, ration it. If not, prioritize the gettin' of it.
4. Scan around for water sources such as flows, holes, cracks, and traps.
5. Use plants, animals, bugs, and birds before working for it yourself.
6. Scout hard before walking long; look hard before digging. Never dig too deep, and consider digging more than one hole.
7. Combine digging, plants, and other options and tricks when there is no obvious answer.
8. Use all your wits when you have nothing else to go on.
9. Break all the rules when all else fails.

WHAT YOU REALLY NEED, AND HOW TO USE IT

Everyone starts off by saying a lot about what you need. I'm gonna start by talking about what you don't need.

You don't need as much as you think and you certainly don't need as much as you drink back home. Whether you're a health nut who drinks gallons a day or you're horrible about water and only drink sodas, humans can survive with a lot less water than ideal. In fact, we have mostly lived throughout history at a very low level of hydration, yet, we're still here. So we don't need as much as is modern conventional wisdom, so get those standards outta your head now. However, you must get *some* fluids in you or the harsh fact is that you will die.

People have about five liters of blood in their body. The heart pushes this amount from any start point to the same finish point in one minute. About 60–100 beats per minute, about 12–16 breaths per minute.

Each minute, you lose a certain amount of fluid just by breathing and living, and on each pass, organs and tissue take a little water out of the bloodstream to maintain their functioning.

On average about one liter of water can be lost each day, just by lying there and breathing.

Add to that any complications such as high heat, high humidity, extreme cold making the body work harder to stay warm, loss of blood through trauma, less than optimal functioning and therefore inefficient use of water in the body already due to illness or fatigue, which is to be expected in the stress of any survival scenario, and it is easy to see how dehydration can set in very quickly.

The human body starts to lose effectiveness with a simple decrease of only ½ liter of blood volume since the average total body composition is about 60% water. A mere loss of only 2% causes overall performance to deteriorate. A 4% loss leads to muscle capacity decreasing; 6% leads to heat exhaustion; 8% leads to hallucinations; and loss of 10% of body fluid can cause circulatory collapse, stroke, and death.

Most people do not drink enough water daily to begin with, so they are already operating at a deficit when the survival scenario commences.

What all this means is, unless you happen to have plenty of water, then water needs to be one of your very first priorities. Right after life-saving first aid and shelter, water is right there or else survival won't be happening.

Do not become complacent because it is too hot or cold, etc. You must be very aggressive in your pursuit of water while you can, or you'll quickly be out of the game and done for. This is no joke and cannot be emphasized enough. Heat stroke and dehydration can jump your bones before you even know it and then it's game over.

Let's look at what happens when you don't have water so you'll know what to be looking for and how to track your progress and status. However

. . . I want you to remember to take all this in, and then throw it out. You'll see what I mean shortly.

THE FIRST SIGNS AND SYMPTOMS OF DEHYDRATION:
- Thirst
- Headache
- Decreased urinary output
- Dark strong-smelling urine, pain
- Light-headedness, dizziness, or fainting when standing up from sitting or squatting (Postural Hypotension)

MORE ADVANCED STAGES OF DEHYDRATION:
- Lack of tears if crying
- Rapidly fatigued (Lethargy)
- Constipation and loss of appetite
- Rapid heart rate (Tachycardia)
- Elevated body temperature
- Nausea and vomiting
- Tingling in the limbs (Paresthesia)
- Skin may become shrivelled and wrinkly; pinching it may reveal reduced elasticity (Turgor)
- Visual disturbances, hallucinations, delirium, unconsciousness and death.

You should be aware of these things so that you will know what they mean if you experience them when survivin'. Don't get caught up in the moment and forget to pay attention to your machine—You!

For example, if you're working hard to get a shelter set up before nightfall and you notice that you feel light-headed when you stand up, then take a swig of water if you've got it. That's the only reason why I teach these symptoms. They are not meant to be a countdown to death as many other books would say. I believe in the power of the mind and if you believe you can go longer, do more, and outlast the checklist, then that is what you will do. I call this, knowing your enemy. Doesn't mean you have to let him beat you, you just need to respect him and fight!

So, know the signs and symptoms of dehydration as a check system for yourself, but do not get discouraged by any doctrine that states you only have so long to live or can't make it without a certain amount of water. Human beings have survived weeks without water. They have drunk urine and lived. They have drunk sea water and lived. They have lost tremendous amounts of blood from trauma or electrolytes from disease and diarrhea and still lived; and so can you!

Ideally, one would drink 500ml every hour when it's hot or when doing strenuous exercise or very laborious work. That's one of the standard individual drinking water bottle sizes. It works out to about 10 hours of work a day, drinking 5 liters of water total, which is completely replenishing the full amount of blood volume. This is an ideal.

The reality is that we lose about 3–4 liters of water a day and we get most of that back every day, about 20% from our food and the other from the thirst generated by the food we ate and then slaked by quenching that thirst.

However, in extreme circumstances, if you can get just one 500ml bottle's worth of fluid in you each day you can survive. Even if you only get 100ml, that is something, and can help keep you hanging in there.

Whether you get this from your environment, from cacti or fish eyes or frozen ice or another source, or from what small amounts of water you have already that you're rationing, then your approximate number of survival days is roughly equal to the number of 500ml life-giving water infusions you have or can make available.

That is, provided one is not ill or injured, and is working with their environment in as smart a manner as possible, and the daily physical workload isn't much more than standing and walking. If you can give your body minimal work each day, there is a very good chance your machine, while unhappy, will continue to drive on and serve you.

Using what you have—and keeping it inside you—is the key to success, when you don't have enough water. So, working smarter is the way ahead. If it's hot, work by night if there is enough illumination from the moon. If not, then work at dawn and dusk, but rest in the middle of the day.

If you're in the cold, hole up and rest at night, and work during the day.

Keep dry if it's cold, and pace your work the best you can so you don't sweat. You try to pace yourself in all survival situations so that you don't rush and make mistakes, but also so you don't sweat and lose water.

Sweat happens when you push the machine and it needs to cool down. It's a mechanism that allows the body to push hard and still keep cool. But when sweat is precious life-water draining your very chance of survival drop by drop, try to work at a comfortable pace so that the work is still being accomplished but the sweat is not wasted. Best to keep it in you is the golden rule.

When it comes to hardcore immediate survival, food is simply not an important issue initially so forget about it, but make water one of your almighty priorities. Even if you have plenty, keep it if you can find other water and make it safe to consume. Make safekeeping what you *do have* a priority as well, since one never knows when circumstances might change. A large reservoir could break in a storm and then feast turns to famine overnight.

HOW MUCH TIME YOU HAVE

Now here are the harsh facts. If you're seriously dehydrated, diseased, have terrible diarrhea, have lost lots of blood, had been partying hard the night before you got stuck in this situation and have a bad hangover, and you're in the middle of the desert in the summer time . . . realistically, you only have about 24 hours to live.

If you're ok in all the above categories but you're still in the desert in summer, without water, you realistically only have about three days.

And in an ideal situation, with some water and some know-how, in the desert in summer, you might have about seven days.

These are your approximate timelines for survival in a desert region. They basically apply in the sea as well, since that is also one of the harshest environments to survive without water. They don't really apply to the arctic as you can eat the snow. Everyone says not to do so, but that is crap. The reason they say not to is because it reduces your core temperature, which is true. But if you have dry clothes and a shelter and can basically maintain warmth, without a fire, then there is no reason to die of dehydration when surrounded by good water in the form of snow.

Now, these are only approximations to help you make the best strategies for how you work, build a shelter, and maneuver yourself in your environment. If you factor these in, and operate accordingly, you can extend these timelines indefinitely.

Knowing you only have seven days in the desert with a small amount of water, will help dictate to you if you need to risk a movement or if you can afford to hold and wait for rescue. But all the hope and willpower in the world will not change the fact that you will need some water sooner or later, so plan on getting it or using what you have to get you out.

FIRST PRIORITY IN FINDING WATER

The first place to start looking is where you are and in what you have.

Is there water around you? Look for a river, stream, lake, creek, pond, water fountain, fish tank, toilet, flower pot, kettle, water tank on the roof of a building, and anywhere around you naturally or manmade.

Next, look at the environment's indirect potential water sources: snow, ice, rain, fog, morning dew, puddles, etc.

If nothing directly or indirectly water-producing is available, start by looking right where you are as many folks end up in a survival situation while in transit on some form of transportation. Is there any water in your craft, vessel, or vehicle? Look first in all the obvious places—storage spaces, emergency compartments, maybe things that were left behind or stowed away and forgotten.

Then do the unsavory task of searching bodies and personal effects of anyone who might not have made it. Look at everything that you can from the perspective that it might hold water or some other form of fluid that you can use for hydration.

When all the immediate ideas do not produce or stop producing, start to think outside the box. Look in the engine compartment of the vehicle—is there a water reservoir or anything that can be used as a source of water? The key is look everywhere as you might even find it in places you couldn't imagine . . . sometimes, you get lucky.

If your natural and manmade resources are lacking, it's time to start looking at the alternatives and techniques that can get you water without

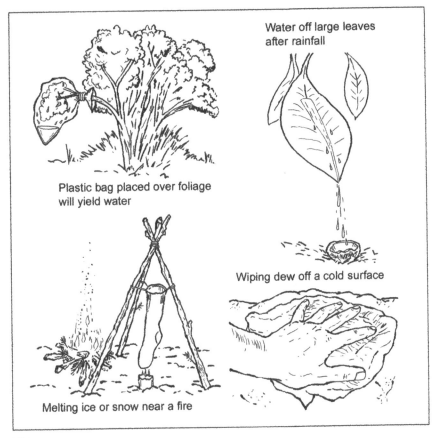

Water off large leaves after rainfall

Plastic bag placed over foliage will yield water

Wiping dew off a cold surface

Melting ice or snow near a fire

Water sources

digging. The reason for avoiding the digging if you can is that you will burn energy and therefore water doing the digging, and you might not find any water or might not get enough to replace what you've lost.

So, the next step is to start looking at the environment for anything that might serve as a catchment for water. Rock crevices , holes, cracks, plants with pockets or pools of water that might be trapped at joints, the base of stalks, the splits in trees, or anything around you that may contain small pools of water. Look everywhere! And when you find any water, act quickly to prepare it for drinking.

MAKING WATER SAFE TO CONSUME

There are many ways to make water safe to drink, and water from any unknown source, natural or manmade, should be made safe to drink ALWAYS.

Of course, if there is simply no way to make found water safe, and you can find no other source, then the choice is simple: drink it and *maybe* die, or don't drink it and *surely* die.

The real nastiest water-borne bugs are called *giardia lamblia*, which cause *giardiasis*, or basically, real bad diarrhea. And the other most significant cause of water-borne disease is the meaner and harder to kill bug called *cryptosporidium*. Falling victim to either of these or other bacteria by drinking untreated water can cause a world of pain, and the inevitable weakening of your body can start you down a slippery slope to, that's right, your death. So take water purifying seriously and, for the most part, never drink untreated water in the wild.

BOIL IT. The best way to make sure your water is 100% safe is to boil the heck out of it for 10 minutes. This is what most books and experts say, and that's groovy *if* you happen to have enough firewood for sustaining the fire that long. It's also time consuming, as it takes a while to get the fire going, boil the water, drain it and/or let it cool so you can drink it, and then, really, it's time to begin again.

So, ideally, do 10 minutes of boiling if you have a pot and fuel. If you have less tinder or time, drop it down to 5 minutes, unless it's really muddy, dirty water.

If scant fuel is available, a full one minute at a rolling boil will do the trick most of the time and, in fact, this is all I ever do. But in a real bind for a heat source, just get it hot enough to hit a boil and most likely it will be ok, but it will be safer than before anyway.

Note: At higher elevations, double the minimum boil time to at least two minutes.

TREAT IT WITH CHEMICALS. Ideally, one can use any of the multitude of fancy chemical tablets and liquids out there that are designed to make the water safe to drink—that is, if these are available when you find yourself surviving. The medical fact is that many bacteria are in water and they are fairly easy to kill with some heat or chemicals. But some other organisms are not so easily killed.

However, the survivor rarely has access to these store-bought chemicals specifically marketed to kill bacteria in water, so let's look at some improvised ways to treat water chemically.

Bleach is great as it's found all over the world and it's easy to use. There are many formulas out there for how much to use, but I try to keep everything simple and use the "P for Plenty" formula as long as it's safe. Basically, a spoonful per gallon won't hurt you.

RULE FOR ADDING BLEACH TO CLEANSE WATER:

- 1 drop of 10% strength for a liter
- 10 drops of 1% strength per liter
- 5 drops of 10% strength for a gallon
- 10 drops of 1% strength for a gallon

Double all amounts above if the water is especially dirty. Add the bleach, shake vigorously, let set for 15–30 minutes, then drink up. Most people drink some chlorine in their tap water every day, so it is safe.

Bleach will kill a lot, and though it won't kill all giardia, it sure will put a hurt on it and if it's all you got, go hot.

Iodine is also a great way to treat your drinking water. The thing is that it takes longer, so allow it to sit about 30 minutes to do its work, or double that time it if it's very cold.

This is why I keep liquid iodine drops in my first aid kit. It not only can treat a minor cut when you don't have water to wash it out, but it also doubles as a way to treat water and make it safer to drink.

Most Tincture of Iodine comes in a dark glass bottle of 2% strength. You need to place a few drops into your water and shake, then let stand for 30 minutes before consuming.

RULE FOR CLEANSING WATER WITH 2%-STRENGTH IODINE:

- 2 drops per 1 liter
- 10 drops per gallon

There are other chemicals available for this purpose, but these two are by far the safest, most commonly used, and most commonly found out and about.

FILTER IT. There are many store-bought filters which can be used and should be used whenever possible and available. Usually they are not handy, and some sort of filtration method is better than nothing to get rid of at least the big bugs and other debris. There are various methods to filter water.

Layers of material can best filter water. Try to use a couple of socks, pant legs, a few scarves tied to a tripod of sticks—anything to form a set of shelves through which to flow the water. Or use anything else you may have or can find, such as a gallon jug with the bottom cut off and turned upside down with the lid off to filter it through.

Once you have your shelves set (if you can only make one layer of shelf, so be it), then use whatever natural materials you have available to filter the water through; think of a charcoal filter.

You can use sand, loam, rocks, dirt, charcoal from your fire, or other such materials to filter your water. The key here is to use the biggest stuff at the top and make layers down to the finest stuff at the bottom. Also be sure to use your finest cloth at the bottom to keep the smallest particles from draining into your container.

If you have a lot of water, like a stream, it's good to run the water though this a few

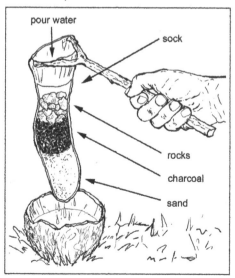

pour water

sock

rocks

charcoal

sand

Water filter

times to drain out and dilute any particles, bad flavors, or odors. I usually run some water through three times to get the actual filter ready for action.

This method of filtering will not kill or remove giardia, but it will make the water smell and taste better and reduce the overall bacteria load.

STRAIN IT. When you really have nothing, and you can't afford to be cutting up your clothes to make a temporary filter for what amounts to just about a luxury item anyway, sometimes it's just best to use Mother Nature as your strainer.

Dig a hole near the water source and let that hole fill in. Then drink up. You might feel a bit like a dog lapping from a bowl, but it does work, and I've been lucky enough to not get sick doing it this way, so there must be something to it.

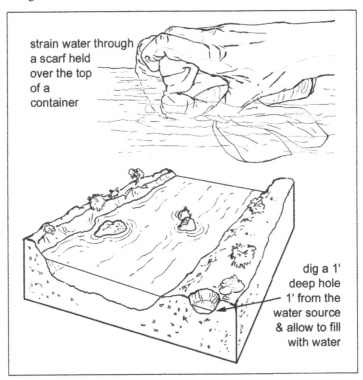

strain water through a scarf held over the top of a container

dig a 1' deep hole 1' from the water source & allow to fill with water

Water-straining techniques

Find a good place where you can access safely, since you'll have to get on your hands and knees to dig and to drink. Make sure you have a clear area of view for your dig spot, so you're not exposed to predators or dangerous critters like snakes. I recommend setting up about one foot or so from the river or pond to dig your hole.

Dig about one foot deep, and wait and watch as the water seeps in. It ain't the best, but it will reduce potential bacteria load, and it works best if you can find a nice-looking piece of soil. The one thing to remember is that this is natural! Humans have been drinking from rivers and streams forever, so, this is not that bad. As always, mindset is everything.

SUN IT. When you have no way to boil, layer, filter, or otherwise treat your water, you can let the sun do the work for you. That is, if you have sun. The light from the sun comes in the form of UV rays, and can actually help you to make your water safe.

If you have a clear plastic bottle, this is ideal, but anything that is clear can be used, even a Ziploc bag or piece of plastic. Ideally, you only want to use about four inches of water, as any more than that makes it harder for the UV rays to penetrate that far, so it takes longer.

The concept is simple. Take the water you have, and filter it as best you can to get the sun-blocking particles out. Put the water in the cleanest, clear plastic or glass container you have, nearly fill it, shake it well to oxygenate it, then top it off so that no air space is left.

Then, leave it in the sun for as long as you can. Lay it on something black or hot like a dark rock or metal surface to help increase the heat. The hotter it gets, the better. The longer in the sun it remains, the better.

BASIC GUIDELINES FOR SUNNING WATER:

- On a hot day, the water can get over 120 degrees (the target temp) in about an hour
- If it's sunny and warm but not hot, it will take about six hours
- If it's not that hot, but bright and sunny, it can take 12 hours, or all day
- If it's consistently cloudy, then let it sit for two full days

The one problem with this technique is that the bacteria will build back up, unlike when you boil water which makes it safe for storage for awhile. So, in all sun conditions, it's best to set your bottle(s) out in the morning and drink the water when the time is right. In other words, you pretty much have to drink what you treat each day.

But the bottom line, you can make your water safer to drink just by putting it in the sun. As a last resort for sunning water, even a bucket or other container with the water exposed to the sun can do some good; just sip the water off the top after it's been exposed for a period of time.

JUST DEW IT. A great simple way to get some water is to collect dew in the morning hour. The simplest method here is to use all the clothing you have and wipe it all over the grass, plants, and foliage on trees. Just walk through the thick fields of grass at the first light of the morning with scarves and t-shirts tied around your ankles to catch all the dew, then squeeze the water into your mouth or container. Make sure you do this first thing in the morning, as dew will quickly evaporate in the morning sun.

WORST-CASE SCENARIO: ENEMA In medicine, when faced with severe cases of dehydration and when IV access is not available, a method for consuming water that has been around a long time is to use an enema. Obviously it's not an ideal method, but if you have water and you know it's not clean, but it's all you have and you have none of the other methods of cleaning it, you will have to sort this out to get it in you.

Typically, you'll need a tube of some sort, some lubrication, and a container you can use to squeeze the water into the rectum. If none of these specific things are available, you have to manage to find your own way based on what is available.

The key things to note here are to try and keep everything as clean as possible before and after; use lubrication if available; don't insert the tubing too deeply, a couple inches is okay; don't force too much in, 500ml to 1liter max; try to keep it in as long as possible, from 5–30 minutes (not as easy as you may think).

This method allows water to be absorbed, and the amount of time is necessary because the rectum only efficiently absorbs approximately 15% of fluids from feces at its last point before departure.

Remember, this method will cause an urge to defecate, especially if you're moving around. Try to refrain, or plan your activities accordingly to allow some time to lounge afterwards. Also, try not to do this more than twice a day as it tends to cause some unpleasant side effects, though none are enough of a concern to not give or receive an enema water injection if you or another is severely dehydrated and dying, and all that is available is unclean water through the back door.

KEYS TO FINDING WATER

Water is usually not hard to find if it's available. The secret is to use your wits and look around thoroughly, using all your senses.

Can you hear it running? Can you smell it? Sometimes you can smell rain coming, or smell a pond or stream if you're downwind and paying attention. Look at the flow of the land, and key in on all things sloping downward that might lead to water. Look at the terrain and think about where water might be naturally occurring in that environment. Draw on your experiences from parks, gardens, local forests, or any similar environment you've been in before.

If all else fails, try to get to a high point for a better vantage point—climb a tree, walk up a small hill, or climb a bit up a mountainside to see if the enhanced viewing position will show you the way to water. But take care to conserve your energy in these endeavors.

If you can't get to a better position to scout, stay on the lookout in your immediate environs. Keep your sense of smell and sound open to water at all times. Also, scan your horizon. Even if surrounded by trees in the jungle or the forests, often you'll see gaps in the tree tops which tell you there might be a pond, stream, path, or just a simple open field which might be good for collecting dew or making a solar still, etc.

Bottom line: Always look at the environment and pay attention, it will tell you many things.

PLANTS. All kinds of plants can help you find water and tell you when it's bad. If you find what looks like a stagnant pool, look for the plant life—if it's void of any, steer clear. If plants are thriving there, chances are good the water is ok. It still needs to be treated if possible, but in the worst case, it's potable. Often stagnant-looking pools are not potable. Sometimes, what looks like a stagnant pool actually isn't. To find out, drop a small leaf or some light debris that will float, and many times you'll actually see a slight flow as the leaf moves—this may mean that the pool is a surface break from an underground spring. Otherwise, take note of the surrounding plant life as an indicator to a pool's potability.

ANIMALS. They can help you find a source of water in that most animals are as dependent on water as humans are. This general rule doesn't apply so much to the meat eaters as they get some fluids from their prey, but they do need to drink after a kill, so, they aren't to be discounted. If you see a predator, take note of its direction of travel and also if it has recently killed and eaten (look for blood). If it just finished dinner, it might just be going toward a water hole to top off.

Look for game trails. Like with people, these will likely lead to a home or a hole. If you find such trails coming together, you're likely headed in the right direction. At times, I've gotten on my hands and knees and followed these trails for hundreds of meters through thick shrubbery to find small streams.

Finally, look for animal feces as a sign for water nearby.

Most animals need water regularly, and so they drink every day, usually at morning and evening. So, this is the best time to take note of your surroundings, study what is going on, and look for the critters to talk to you. They can show you the way to their favorite drinking spot, and yours.

Note that reptiles are not good indicators for water, however you *can* squeeze some juice out of them if you can catch them. BUT, do use the reptiles as a way to train your eye. . . . Specifically, you should always be on the lookout for snakes in terms of self-defense, as you do NOT want to get bit by a venomous snake in the wild. So, whenever you're moving about and looking for snakes to avoid, also train your eye to look at every crack and crevice and shadow to see if there are any places where water might be contained from a previous rain or an underground source. I have seen small puddles of water in rock depressions that remain shaded throughout the day even though there had been no rain in a week.

HUMANS. If there are or have been humans residing in the area, their past activities can also help you find water, in that all human-made trails lead to water or a village. Find a trail, stay on it, and you are nearly there!

INSECTS. Bugs can be a pain in the neck, but they can also help you find water. Flies tend to always stay within a short distance of water, normally 100–200 meters. Bees generally stay within five miles of a water source. Ants tend to form lines leading to water catchments likes trees or plants. Mosquitoes often breed in or around water. And there are countless other insect species that can be found near, or on their way to, water.

BIRDS. If you are on land, and you see small grain-eating birds (as opposed to predatory birds) flying in the morning or evening, they are often heading to or from a water source. Especially if they are flying fast and low in a general direction as a group, then they are headed for water. If they are moving in short sort of hops from tree to tree, they have just likely come from a water hole. However, birds of prey get their water from their prey as do fish-eating water birds, and hence, they are not good indicators for water being near.

CLOUDS. These can sometimes help you to find water as well. The very obvious and ominous, heavy-looking, low-hanging black clouds say rain is coming. If the winds are medium to high, chances are good that you're about to have a drink. So, when it does rain, *stop everything* and *use everything* to catch all the water you can.

Take off your clothes and get a wash (hygiene is still important when you're surviving, but more on that later). Use your clothes to catch water and wring it into a container or your mouth if you have nothing else. Make a hole if you don't have any leaves or poncho or tarp or cups or jugs. Catch, drink, and repeat as long as it's pouring down. Enjoy!

If you're out to sea or in a remote place like the desert, clouds can indicate a possible water source if they are hovering in the same area for a long time.

HOW TO FIND WATER IN SPECIFIC ECOSYSTEMS

DESERT

The desert is the classic worst-case scenario for survival. However, most deserts are not barren wastelands of pure sand, as many people may wrongly believe. Very few places are like that, and those that are mean certain death without water or rescue in a very short time.

Know this first: Most deserts do have plenty of life, and all life depends on water. The key is to know where to look and what to use.

SCOUT. First, follow the basic rules for locating water: scan the area, look for low-lying areas where water would converge and collect if it were flowing. Follow the natural lines of the terrain for the lowest points. Then look and see if there are plants and, if so, notice how green and healthy they appear. The greener the plant life, the more plentiful the water.

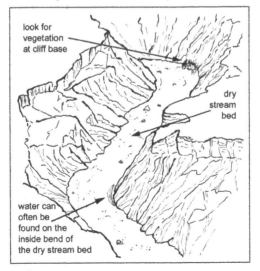

Finding water sources

If you do find these low points with greenery, they are likely in some dry stream bed. Look for water first just to see if it's sitting there on the surface, then look at any walls of the gullies to see if there is some seepage of water on the face of the rocks.

If there is no open source, or no obviously wet or moist areas, then look for the bends in the dry river bed. The outsides of these bends will be where the water would have been the most recently, as it would have lasted there longest. Therefore, you might find some water there if you dig a bit.

But before you start digging, take a good look. If it looks bone dry, chances are there isn't any water there. So, calculate how much time, energy, and water you have on and in you, *before* you start prospectin' for water in the desert. Save the digging until you're sure, or you're desperate.

If the ground looks a bit moist, find the lowest point and dig about one foot down to start. If you dig two feet down and don't hit water, chances are, you're not gonna find any in that location. But don't give up yet; come back and check your holes later, maybe some water will have seeped in.

COLLECT DEW. If you find there is morning dew, first try to collect it off plants and grass if there are any about with dew on them. Then try flipping over some rocks to see if the cold air from the night had condensed as the sun rose and heated them; this will at least give you a bit of a wetness for your tongue. Every little bit counts, so you need to try all these methods at all times.

Alternatively, you can try to make your own dew. Dig a hole about two feet around and about one foot deep, line it with a small piece of plastic (if you don't have plastic, use desert plants like the flat cacti that can keep moisture partially retained), and lay some rocks in the hole overnight. Make sure you wipe the rocks free of all dirt, debris, and sand first. In the morning, the rocks in the hole will have collected more dew than the surrounding exposed rocks, and you should at least get to lick a little off them.

CACTI AND PLANT LIFE. The cactus is a good source of moisture in the desert. Notice I said moisture, not water. You have to chop them off and cut off the outside if they are the flat cacti; or if you've got barrel cacti, lop the top and chop up the insides. In both cases, get past the spikes and get the clean pulp into your mouth. The flat cacti are slimy, the barrel cacti are spongy, but they both will give you moisture. Suck out all the juice you can and spit out the pulp . . . but don't just throw it away, use that stuff for your solar still (see below).

The prickly pear is a nice fruit that grows on the tops of the flat cactus. They are tricky to de-skin as their spines are much finer than the cactus itself, but they are a deliciously sweet thing. I don't count them as a good source of water due to their sugar content, but if you're down to suckin' cacti, suck them too.

The big agave plants that are common in most deserts sometimes have water trapped at the base of their meaty and pointy leaves, although these things are strong and the water is hard to get to. Again, a sip of water is not to be turned down wherever you can find it. Check most plants for such deposits.

MAKE A SOLAR STILL. Save all the ejected pre-sucked cacti bits and pieces and then use them to make a solar still. The solar still is one of the best friends of anyone surviving. The only catch is, without a poncho, tarp, or some sort of plastic, you can't make one. If you have none of these to begin with, always keep your eyes open for them as you make your way around. Unfortunately in this day and age (though fortunately for survivors in such situations), you can find human trash and debris in every corner of the planet, including all kinds of plastics, containers, and so on.

The concept of making a solar still is simple. Dig a hole about 1–2 feet deep minimum, or a bit deeper if you can do so without putting yourself in jeopardy by sweating too much. Make the hole as wide as your tarp, poncho, or plastic sheet will cover completely. In essence, you want a cone-shaped hole dug into the ground.

Then place a bunch of vegetation, spit-out cacti, bad water, even urine, and anything green in the hole. Now, place a cup or something to catch water in the center of the hole. Lay you tarp over the hole and use rocks or sand to secure its edges on the surface above the hole so that it's as air tight as possible. Then place a nice-sized, smooth, and as round a rock as you can find in the middle of the tarp outside the hole. This rock should force the tarp to droop slightly down into the hole above the water catch that's inside.

Now, here's how it works. The heat from the desert sun will draw all the moisture from all your materials inside the hole, and it will condense on the inside of the tarp. Then, gravity from the rock that's on the outside of your tarp will cause the water to trickle downward and drop into your cup. If you happen to have a bit of tube, you can use it like a straw to suck the water out without messing up your still. If not, just raise the tarp gently, get the cup, drink it all, place it back, and then re-seal your still to keep it working. Make as many of these stills as you have time and supplies.

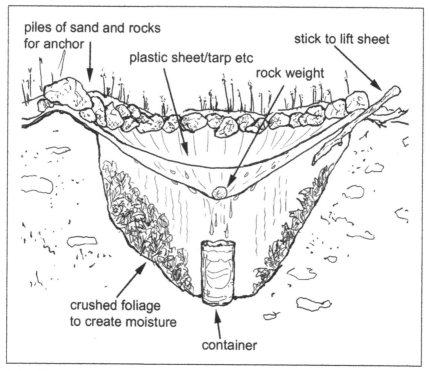

Solar still

Now, back to what goes into the hole. Chuck all your spat-out cacti in there. And add any leafy green stuff you can find, just don't let it touch the edges of the poncho—keep it flat, and step on the plants a bit to bruise and crush them and get them oozing and leaking any moisture they have. Then, take a nice long urination into the hole all around and on the vegetation (any impurities from the urine will be distilled in the solar process).

Be aware that a solar still won't fix you for the day, hydration wise. Usually, I get maybe 200–300 ml of water, or about maybe half a normal bottle of drinking water. But in the harsh desert, that is a wonderful amount to have. So make stills and use them.

If you have an abundance of plastic bags, you can try the evaporation method of placing the bag around as much foliage and vegetation as you can and tie it off on one end and place a small pebble in a corner to weigh it down so all the water converges there. You can poke a hole in it and drink that water, or, if bags are sparse, untie it carefully to keep as much water as you can in the corner, then tilt it and drink that way. I find in the desert, there is a tendency for the plants to poke holes in the bag as everything is sharp and pointy.

Note that in most other environments, this method produces more water than in the desert—typically a small cup of water in a few hours, depending on how leafy the plants and how hot it gets. If I have a handful of bags, I will tie them over many branches at once and it really produces a good quantity of water. The trick is to find leaves that appear light and green and not too thick or dark, and certainly not any that ooze white stuff if you break them. The water will be greenish in color, but it is fine. Don't leave the bags on too long as the leaves will start to wilt and make the water less tasteful.

The bottom line for desert drinking: cracks, crevices, cacti, and solar stills are your best bet for desert hydration.

ARCTIC

The arctic environment has plenty of water in the form of snow and ice, but its form can kill you if you're not careful because consuming ice or snow will decrease your core body temperature, which will cause your body to shiver more to stay warm, which in turn will cause further dehydration. This is why it is strongly advisable to always melt snow or ice with fire before consuming it in water form.

However, I say that if you have absolutely no means to melt the snow or ice, it is better to take small amounts and let it melt slowly in your mouth than to sit there looking at all that frozen water and die of dehydration.

The key to all this survival stuff is to know fact from fiction, and law from life!

Yes, eating a lot of snow will eventually do you in. But, if you're nearly done in already, refusing to take in some icy cold water because some book or expert said not to, is just like laying down to die. Remember, the expert wrote about what one should do *in general* while sitting at a desk, not in a life-or-death situation.

Likewise, many experts simply will not advise you to eat snow in ANY situation because they fear lawsuits and litigation from people who either applied these concepts poorly, or who were going to die anyway because they got in a bad situation, and yet someone wants to profit or to take action against the helplessness of losing a loved one to a survival situation—there will always be someone saying "what if?".

But that does not change the outcome of the person on the ground. You either have options that you can try when all else fails, no matter how extreme, or you don't have the options or refuse to take them.

Rules for Hydrating in Arctic Regions:

Snow and ice should be melted and boiled before drinking.

The best and most effective way to melt it is in a pot over a fire.

If you have no pot, wrap a ball of ice or snow in a t-shirt or other material, hang near fire and let it drip into a container.

If you have no cloth or pot or cup, try heating a rock in the fire and then melting snow or ice with it. First, dig a small hole and pack the inside walls of it tightly. Then drop in a soft pile of snow, and drop the heated rock on it. Once the snow has melted, quickly and safely remove the rock and sip out all the water.

If you need to draw water from sea ice, use the blue stuff—the bluer the better as it has less salt.

Make a hard-packed snowball and place it on a stick like a big marsh-mallow over a fire, but first have something to catch the water as it drips. If you don't have a catch, clean the stick as well as you can, and then let the water from the melting snowball drip down the stick into your mouth.

AT SEA

The sea is one of the most desolate places for finding drinking water.

If you don't have a fresh store of water, or a desalinization kit or a reverse-osmosis pump, you're starting off with a serious challenge. This is a case in which you might consider drinking urine or seawater (see below).

Otherwise, the best source of water when surviving at sea will come from the atmosphere. If it rains, drink all you can, catch all you can, store all you can, for as long as you can. You don't know how long it will be before you are rescued, make landfall, or get another rain. Catch and use any and all precipitation sent your way very judiciously. If you have fog, then use all the cloth you can to capture that and squeeze its moisture into a container or your mouth. Don't let any fresh water go by un-drunk!

If you have the equipment and some sort of vessel or float, you can try to make a solar still. Obviously this is impossible if you're simply floating in the water trying to survive.

You can also get some juice and hydration from fish. I have found their eyeballs to have very little water, and taste extremely salty. Not to mention, it is very viscous. So, while it does provide some fluid, do not think of it like small sips of water, but rather as a jelly water. But take it if you can get it.

Also, the spines of fish retain some water, but again, it's very hard to get to without losing a lot, especially if you don't have a sharp knife. I have not managed to master the art without getting other fish bits and juices in my mouth, which does detract a bit from the fresh water with its salt and meat, but there is some fresh water there to be had.

In addition, you either have to catch a lot of small fish or a few very large ones to get any real source of fluid for sustenance from them. The risk of trying to catch fish that are too big when surviving is injury to you or your craft, energy expended, and frankly, unless you have a large crew to feed, most of it will spoil too quickly for you to eat. That's if you had the tackle to catch the big fish in the first place. You're best off to stick with small fish.

SEASHORE

The seashore can be a very formidable place to find water indeed. If you're stranded on a small island with no dune break, then try to drop back past the highest water mark you can see and start digging a hole there. If there is vegetation, that is a good sign, as usually plants won't grow where the tide reaches.

If there are dunes, then drop back behind the first row of dunes and start digging.

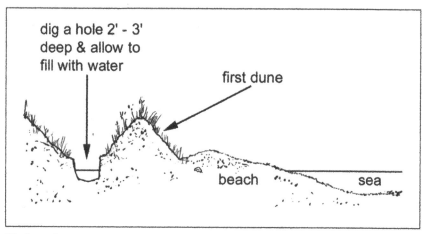

dig a hole 2' - 3'
deep & allow to
fill with water

first dune

beach   sea

Dig for water

In both cases, the holes you dig will fill with water and this water will be safe enough to drink. It takes some work, as the holes need to be a bit deeper than the freshwater filter holes discussed earlier. Be prepared to dig a 2- to 3-foot-deep hole, and just as wide as the sand tends to fall back in. The upside is that digging sand is a lot easier than digging dirt.

Once these holes fill, if you want to make the water a bit safer to drink, get a fire going, heat up some cleaned rocks, and place them in your pool of filtered sea water. That will hopefully bring that water to a boil or, at least, a hot steamy temperature so that the water will be just that much safer to drink.

The key is to do all that you can first, and then do what you must! In the worst-case scenario when your initial holes produce no water, go back as far as you can from the shoreline and dig even deeper, then wait for the hole to fill. The good news is that there should be plenty of water, so your sweat equity will be rewarded and replenished.

Also, often the seashore in the tropics will have coconuts. The coconut is a great source of water and food. The greener the nut, the better the water; the browner the nut, the more meat and white milk which will cause diarrhea if too much is drunk. But if that's the first nut you crack, drink up. There are likely more green ones around, so go for them next and don't drink more than one white-milk coconut a day if you can help it.

A word of caution: a coconut is a truly tough nut to crack without a blade. The best method I have seen is to shave down to the nut with a shell or rock, then use the outer shell as a way to hold the nut up so you can crack into it without spilling the juices everywhere. This is tricky, so be extremely careful that you do not injure your fingers or any other body part.

A final way to make water potable if on the shore without a pot, is to make a fire, dig a hole, let it fill in with water, and drop hot rocks from the fire into the hole and drink!

When push comes to shove and your water resources are extremely low, you may be tempted to drink from the bountiful sea water. Of course, sea water is extremely salty and drinking any good amount of it will lead to certain death. But with everything else, if it becomes your last resort, take it.

Hawke's Rules for Drinking Sea Water:

Don't do it unless you are sure you will die from dehydration; wait until it's absolutely desperate, and you realize there is no hope for finding water via fish, rain, or other means.

Start early if you know it's inevitable. If you are in the middle of the ocean and have no water at all, and there's no real hope of immediate rescue, your start point is after your first 24 hours without water.

Don't wait until it's too late, as you may start to go crazy from delirium caused by dehydration, and the salt will push you over the edge.

Dilute it if you can with any good water you may have, or take sips here and there in between rinses or swallows of your fresh water.

If you have the materials and are on a small vessel or floating device, make a solar still (as described above). Scoop some seawater into a container, place a smaller cup or catch in the middle of the container (you may need to place something in it to hold it down), then cover the container tightly with plastic or similar material, and place a weight on top of the cover to sink it slightly into the container. Any condensation that collects on the inside of the cover and drips into the cup will be fresh water.

Never, ever drink more than a few gulps of seawater at a time, and then never more than approximately a cup over a 24-hour period.

Ration small amounts of fresh water and space out the timing of consumption.

The bottom line is that drinking salt water from the sea is a bad thing, and shouldn't be done. But it *can* be done and should *only* be done when death seems very probable.

JUNGLE

The jungle is one of my personal favorite regions for surviving, especially because of the abundance of water sources. Not only do you often have rain, and usually plenty of water in the form of rivers and streams, but there are many plants that offer a source of water if you know what to look for. A key element here is to always take the time to ask locals, whenever possible, about what plants are good for water. If you don't have the luxury of getting local knowledge, rely on the basic concepts and information provided here.

WATER VINE. There are many vines in the jungle. Not all provide water, but most do. It takes a bit of practice at first to identify them. Usually their bark is a bit lighter and fluffier than the non-water vines, and when you tap them, they sound more hollow than the white sap–producing varieties. To get to the water, cut HIGH then LOW. They suck the water up from the ground at the first cut (called "capillary action") so that if you cut low first,

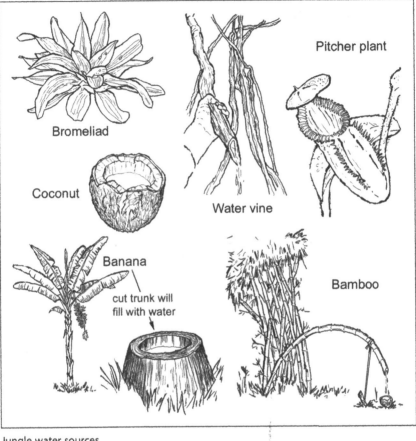

Jungle water sources

the water will be sucked up already by the time you cut high and you'll have less water to drink.

Hold the vine like a long canteen and let the water drain into your mouth. If you can get your fill and also have a container, fill up on all the water from vines you can find. The water tastes great, it's safe, and the vines are easy to cut. Without a knife, try to break it open high with a heavy stick, then break it low with your hands and/or with leverage over a branch and drink it that way.

BANANA (OR PLANTAIN) PLANTS. This is a wonderful plant to find. It can be felled right across the base just like chopping a head of cabbage in half, and then, watch it fill. The water is good, though it's strong-tasting at first and mellows after a few bowlfuls. This plant will also generate water for awhile, so you might even camp there for a day or two if you find one.

FIG TREE. It can give up a lot of water but needs to be tapped into. Use a piece of pipe, or tube, or some small bamboo fashioned into a tube, then cut a hole into the tree and wedge the tube in and let the water drain, but make a reservoir catch for it.

PALMS. Nipa, Buri, Coconut, and Sugar. You can get water from many of these fruits, and even the little ones will yield a nice lemonade-flavored water. As well, you can draw water from the tree itself. Best to use the small ones 12 feet high or smaller so you can reach the top, chop it off, and keep it bent over so it will "bleed" water for you. This can be a repeated a few times to stimulate more sweet water production.

LEAVES. Bromeliads, Pitcher Plants, Elephant Ears, et al. Bromeliads are what I call "tree celery." They are sometimes called air plants, because they seemingly grow in the air (some take root in pockets on a tree, like where a branch broke off; others grow in the soil that settled where a tree fell). Not only do these plants have a sort of lettuce quality in that they are smooth, but they're also crisp like celery and they trap water in the joints. Also, their leaves can be chewed like the white base of celery, and a good amount of tasty water will come from them. I usually eat the base anyway after I suck the water from it.

The elephant ears or any other big leaves should catch your attention for two reasons.

First, they might have some water trapped in them or at their base. Of course, you should look at all plants as you walk through the jungle for the types of leaves that might have water caught in them which you can drink.

Also, these large leaves make excellent devices for catching rain water. I have surrounded my base camp with these rolled cone shapes and then wedged into every tree branch around my hooch so they could catch and fill up with water during the typical jungle torrential downpour.

BAMBOO. As stated before for different reasons (i.e., shelter building), bamboo is a gift from the gods in respect to water, as well. The green bamboo can be bent over and the top cut off to produce water; the older, browner ones usually have water trapped inside their segments. Tap or shake them and listen for the water swishing and splashing. If you hear that, cut a little notch at the base and drain the water. Usually, you can do this with each segment above and below as bamboo shoots are compartmentalized.

PITCHER PLANT. This Southeast Asian plant looks just like a pitcher of water. It's usually filled with dead bugs and what not, but if you can boil or treat the water, it's a nice find.

BAOBAB TREE. Found in Africa and Australia, the baobab holds large amounts of water in its trunk and is a true gift if you happen across one. They're easy to identify as they're super fat and funky looking.

TRAVELER'S TREE. This native of Madagascar has leaves with a cup at the base that catches and holds water. These are niceties, but not really worth planning for.

ROOTS. Roots are, to my way of thinking, a similar fallacy to mushrooms as a survival food. Just as mushroom identification is tricky even for experts— and deadly when it goes wrong—the same is true for roots unless you know very well the plant you're looking at and can take the time to dig up the root and beat it to a pulpy mush. Like mushrooms, roots can be very toxic since they hold concentrated amounts of water if they have it, or dangerous toxins if they don't hold water. Basically, leave roots alone unless you know exactly what you're digging up.

MOUNTAINS

Finding water in the mountains can be a challenge, but there is often one distinct advantage in that you have better visibility than, say, the jungle or forest. With that vision of what surrounds you, it greatly increases your chances of finding water. Look for all things and land sloping down, but don't drop down just yet until you're certain you see a source of water. Stay on the high ground, preferably the ridge line, so you can look both ways on your hunt for water. If the weather is too rough to walk the ridgeline, drop on the safe side of the wind, but every kilometer or so, go back to the ridge top and look over the other side, both behind and ahead of your direction of travel.

Once you have spotted water, *then and only then*, start dropping down and mind how you go so you don't end up in a false valley and have to make another water-draining ascent before you can get to the true valley with your spotted water source.

I have seen a very fit man drop and do the "flopping fish" for lack of water after having to do one extra, unplanned ascent to the ridge line.

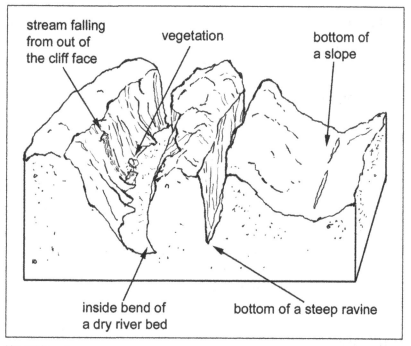

Mountain water sources

If there is snow in the mountains, refer to the ARCTIC section on water above.

Remember this: walls and cliffs are the best secrets for looking for water in mountainous areas. If you spot any of these, and the trek to them is within reason and your ability, try to scope them out. Often these breaks in the integrity of the mountain range will have a leak from some small underground spring as it pushes through the mountain. It might only be a wet little trickle, but you can lick that trickle all day long!

FOREST

Finding water in the forest usually isn't too difficult, but sometimes you can come upon a long stretch of land before you do find a water source. So, refer to the top portion of this chapter—i.e., scope your surroundings and follow the land to where it looks like it would naturally produce water. If all else fails, dig, but dig wisely.

Find the lowest point you can in what looks like the nicest ravine you can find. Usually, the higher and steeper the two hills are that create the ravine, the better the chances are of finding water. And, just like in the desert, find the greenest, wettest, lowest point you can and dig a hole 1- to 2-feet deep maximum. Give it awhile and see if any water seeps in. If not, try the condensation method described above using a poncho (or natural materials like leaves) to cover the hole, so your effort in digging it doesn't go to waste, then keep looking. Now, if you're hunting for little trickles of water, the opposite holds true—a good, long, wide slope of a hill basically means more surface area to catch water and channel it down, so if you see a great expanse of field sloping down, try walking to the bottom of it.

I do not teach a lot of technical stuff like names of plants and trees and that sort of thing. Occasionally, it is very helpful to know a bit of technical information. For instance, know what a willow tree looks like and remember that these are always near water. Cottonwoods share that quality. Further, be ever aware that underground springs are all over in the forest, so anytime you step on some soggy soil, you're likely there. So look for these darker patches of soil as you walk through the forests.

SWAMP

Swamps are just plain filled with water, but that doesn't necessarily mean that your problems are solved. The problem is making that water safe to drink. Fires can be a challenge to make in the swamp, especially if you're in proper mangrove-type swamps. So the strategies here are much like in the jungle—i.e. dig a filter hole, use your clothes and charcoal/sand if you can find some, and in the worst case, scoop up some water into a shallow container and let the sun work on it for the day, then sip the top water off at night. It's not ideal, but it'll make you feel like you've attempted to make it as safe as possible.

URBAN

Surviving in a city that's under siege from a natural or manmade disaster is an often overlooked aspect of surviving, but one I am particularly fond of teaching. I'd like to just touch on some things to consider if you find yourself in a town during a black out, or in a city during a coup or some natural disaster, and water is simply cut off and there are no measures being taken to get water to people.

In these cases, it is good to look for water near you and to start early. Areas to consider include parks, golf courses, drainage ditches, rooftop reservoirs, water cans in gardens, water hoses with water left inside, city water fountains found in parks, amusement parks, aquariums, farms or zoos or anywhere animals may be kept, and so on.

These examples are just to get your mind thinking now, before anything terrible happens that thrusts you into such a situation. Do you know where the water sources are near your home, your work, and the routes to and from the places you go? Plan now to be prepared later.

LAST RESORTS

Yes, you can drink urine! Now that I have your attention. . . . The rules for urine drinking are pretty straightforward: drink it as soon after you urinate as possible; the first time you urinate is usually fine to drink; and you can drink the second pass in dire circumstances.

After the second pass, chances are that you won't be urinating again anyway if there is no more fluid going in. There simply won't be any fluid left to be passed. It will go by breathing, sweat, etc.

FACT: Urine drinking has been around for literally thousands of years. It has been considered a medicinal practice for health by nearly every major culture at one point or another through time, since ancient China, India, the Egyptians, Greeks, and Aztecs, in a practice called urotherapy. Even in modern times, there have been bars where people actually pay to drink urine. So, contrary to survival manuals by both the U.S. Army and the British SAS, you *can* drink urine safely, if done correctly.

MYTH: You will *not* die or get sick if you drink urine. It is not poisonous. It is actually sterile the moment it leaves your body, and only contact with the air allows for bacteria to grow.

This is why you shouldn't urinate and then store it for later. As for technique, I recommend to let a little out first to clean the urethra of any residual bacteria before filling your container with the rest.

YES, YOU CAN GET WATER FROM FECES. Like drinking urine, this practice should never be a first choice for anyone. In fact, one needs to be pretty desperate to try it. I personally have not tried it, but I'm not saying I wouldn't under certain circumstances. I can only evaluate it against my own medical knowledge, military training, and my personal and professional experience in survivalin'.

Let's look at some facts to consider when this is your last option, and see if it passes the common-sense test.

First, I know for a scientific medical fact that feces is not sterile and is heavily laden with bacteria as well as parasites.

Second, I know for a biological fact that the bladder must be sterile for a person to be healthy, which makes urine clean. On the other hand, the anal cavity faces direct exposure to the external environment making it inherently less hygienic than the bladder, and therefore, feces is less clean than urine.

Now, if you're down to your last resort, you can't find water anywhere, and you stumble upon some fresh animal feces, such as that of an elephant, you do not want to eat the feces. Rather, squeeze out all the liquid you can.

Make a filter with a shirt to squeeze it through or, in a pinch, just squeeze the stuff and let the fluid drip into your mouth.

If you do get to this point, make sure the feces is fresh—in other words, see it come from the elephant. Of course, if you do see elephants, know that they are often near water, and consider trying to find that water if you still have energy left. They are not hard to track. However, they can range long distances between water stops, and so they might not be near water at all. So if your life is at stake and elephant dung is all you have, go for it.

I know that indigenous bushmen have done this for eons, and some professional trackers and rangers have learned this as well. But I would surmise from my experience in Africa as a soldier and a medic, that these bushman probably had the same parasites as the elephants and, like many Africans, have learned to live with their parasite load, whereas the rest of us have not.

But the bottom line, I'd rather drink dung juice and live to treat the parasites later. So, I'm not recommending this practice, and I think 99% of the time, there would be no call for it, but if you happen to be near a defecating elephant in Africa during the dry season, then it might be poo juice for you!

That's all I got to say about that.

ALCOHOL AND CIGARETTES. In general it is better to not drink alcohol or smoke cigarettes when you don't have water. It is a medical fact that both of these will only serve to dehydrate you even more. However, in combat, a little drink helps to take the edge off a bad day and the loss of a comrade, and a smoke helps when a drink isn't an option. The same principle holds true when in a real survival situation. If you have a bottle of booze or a pack of smokes on hand, and things look very bleak, I speak in direct contradiction to all the accepted norms on this issue. I believe that if you are craving a cig or a sip, and that little reprieve will make you feel better mentally, then I say go for it. I don't recommend smoking a pack or downing a bottle, but I do say that the psychological benefit of having that little respite from the misery and suffering can do so much to renew your morale. The psychological advantage from this type of small indulgence can be the very thing that reinvigorates one's will to live, and in fact can be the very thing that determines if one survives or not.

TALKING POINT. They say talking uses up body fluids, as well, and it is true. When water is scarce, try not to speak, and try to breathe through your nose. If you're in the heat of the desert drying up, likely you won't want to talk to your buddy anyway, but if you do speak, it might actually give one of you an idea heretofore not considered and might save your lives.

Humans need hope. We all need a break now and then. When things are tough, a small pleasure can work miracles for the soul and re-instill hope where there was only despair. So, know that smoke and booze or a chat with your survival partner might very well be your death knell, but they might also be your salvation. Only you can decide at that critical moment, but I say, live until you die.

Fire

Fire is one of the key elements in any survival situation. It provides warmth, light, and heat for cooking. It can sterilize knives for first aid and help you make cooking utensils. It boils water clean. It protects you against predators. You can use it to signal. Obviously, fire is a major necessity in the wild.

LIGHTERS

I hate rubbing sticks together. I don't smoke, but I live with a lighter on my person at all times. If I'm travelling and must pass security without a lighter, I carry a magnifying glass and magnesium bar—but more on that later.

First and foremost, always have a lighter! Stash them all over your rucksack, house, vehicle, and on your person whether you're in or around wilderness or on the streets of a city.

Now, there are lots of different types of lighters. You might think it's worth it to have those expensive wind-proof kinds, especially if you spend time up on mountains or in generally open areas. And they're not bad for some purposes. But in fact, the jet-propulsion of the flame can blow out your fledgling fire. And typically, no matter where you are, you should seek out a sheltered area to start your fire, so you won't need the wind-proof kind. Besides, they're expensive.

Disposable lighters are great, cheap, and easy to come by. Even after the fuel runs out, you can get a spark out of them, which is still good for getting a fire going in a pinch. And now you can get tiny-sized ones which are great for stashing everywhere.

Sometimes, though, you need a lighter for actual "light." In these cases, Zippos really earn their keep. A Zippo can be lit and set down and used as a lamp. I've even used it in tight times as a mini stove or just a little fireplace when I had nothing; the Zippo just sat there and burned and gave me comfort as a little fire, a little light, a little heat, and that made all the difference. Of course, if you're unsure of your time frame and don't have copious amounts of fuel, be sure to conserve the fuel as much as possible.

You can also refill Zippos. And when you're away from civilization, you can use other fuels like moonshine alcohol, alcohol in first-aid kits, vehicle fuel, or what have you to refill a Zippo.

CAUTION: Some fuels are dangerous as they have fumes and vapors that will create a nice little fireball when ignited, so, before you load up your Zippo with an alternative to lighter fuel, give a test light of a small puddle. If it gives off a great ball of flame when sparked, it's likely too combustible to use in your lighter. In these cases, just load it in a container and carry it, with the Zippo for the spark. But when the liquid fuel source candidate just gives a nice, smooth burn, then it's usually safe to top off your Zippo. The general rule with fuel, as with anything in survival situations, is always to use common sense and to look before you leap.

TIP: A crucial good habit is to test all gear in your survival kit regularly. It doesn't need to be daily, but it should be looked at, played with, and tried out every once in a while.

TIP: *Always* carry a lighter. Everything else that follows in this chapter is what you have to do because you **didn't** carry a lighter. There are a million reasons to carry one at all times, and not one reason not to do so.

HOW TO MAKE FIRE

The million reasons you should carry a lighter—or some other means of ignition—refer to the minimum number of strokes you will need to get a fire going when you have to resort to rubbing sticks together!

That's right, rubbing sticks together to make fire can be done, but it is extremely hard work, even after you perfect your technique. It is very time consuming and, therefore, can take a toll on both your physical *and* mental well being. If you know and accept this going in, you'll be able to withstand the doubt and frustration that may otherwise cause you to give up. And what is the most important thing about survival?

NEVER GIVE UP!

HARD WOOD VS. SOFT WOOD

Before we get into the various preparations and techniques, let's have a look at the kind of woods you may consider.

Most survival books—in fact, every one I have read—state that for starting fires, you use a hard wood against a soft wood.

I have found this not to be true.

Both the British SAS and U.S. Army manuals, and indeed in all the most popular survival books, promote the hard-wood-on-soft-wood theory. Now it might be a hard-wood spindle or a soft-wood base, etc., depending on the technique being applied, but they all speak to using contrasting woods.

But I have found, when it comes to rubbing sticks together to make fire, is that **two soft woods work best**.

Now there are lots of experts gettin' all excited right about now after reading this. So, let's talk about hard and soft woods and I'll explain.

First and foremost, remember, I don't claim to be an expert; I just have expertise. I'm a regular "Joe" who just happens to have tried lots of stuff, regularly enough to have a good handle on what works and what doesn't. In fact and to be honest, I don't know all the names for all the woods. (But then again, you probably don't either.) I do know that some woods classified as hard woods are soft, and some softwood classifications are actually very hard. So, let's look at what is a hard and a soft wood.

Try the "nail test." If you can stick your thumbnail into a wood and leave a dent, it's a soft wood. If not, it's a hard wood. It's that simple. I don't care what its name or scientific designation is, and neither will you when you're freezing in the wild alone.

Now, rubbing any two sticks together long enough and hard enough will get you some friction and some heat. Also, if you're starting with green trees and saplings, you might as well be starting fire with water; you're going to be there a while. We're operating under the premise that you, the reader, have been endowed with the basic level of common sense and therefore understand, you need to start with some dry wood.

The best place to get the dry wood is not from the standing trees, they're often green and not helpful. Likewise, unless you're in a very dry place, you don't want wood off the ground. The best kind is that which is either in the bushes or on a broken, but still hanging tree branch, or in some other way, still as dry as you can find about.

Next, you don't want something so soft it will crumble, either. What you're looking for is some wood that will be strong enough to hold up to the pressure you're going to apply to it, but also, not so hard that it will take a team of people a week to get it to heat up.

What I have found to be the very best for fast fire starting is yucca. If you know what that is, let that be your standard. The reason I bring it up is because the bamboo saw is a well-tested and universally known fire-by-friction starting method. And ironically, it is bamboo on bamboo, so no hard wood against hard wood issues and guess what, it's neither a soft or hard wood, it's actually a grass!

So, I too have found that a moderately hard piece of softwood against another piece of the same thing is the best way to go. Think of balsa wood as an example. When it's thinly sliced, it's very fragile, but when in a solid piece, it's still light, but sturdy. The real secret here is the friction-to-flame ratio.

If the wood is softer, it'll give way to more friction, and the more friction, the quicker the flame comes. But any way you work it, it will be work.

PREPARATION

Now let's look at the things you need to consider before attempting to start your fire.

LOCATION

First, choose your location wisely.

Here are the key factors regarding location:

Find a spot away from wind, rain, other elements, and harm's way (e.g., under snow-covered tree branches).

Give yourself enough area to work around the fire—cooking, sleeping, drying clothes, etc.

Pick a generally dry spot, and clear away combustible materials from the surrounding ground surface.

Lay some sticks, logs, leaves, rocks, etc. on the ground so your fire is elevated to allow a slight amount of air/oxygen under it, as well as to keep it off the moist ground, which tends to zap a fledgling fire.

Look for soil, rocks, logs, snow, etc. to create a wall around your fire area.

STARTER MATERIALS

Once you've found an ideal location, begin to gather up a good supply of starter materials—tinder, kindling, and fuel.

Tinder is the smallest material, and includes all the little fragile things you can find and grind into a powder—think furry, fuzzy, light, and fluffy material.

Kindling is anything slightly larger than tinder, and includes small branches and twigs not much bigger than a match or birthday candle.

Fuel refers to everything larger that will combust and grow into your full-on fire. You should collect fuel of various sizes, starting with 3-to-6 stacks of wood branches that are just bigger than a twig, and then work your way up to a large pile of wrist- or ankle-sized logs.

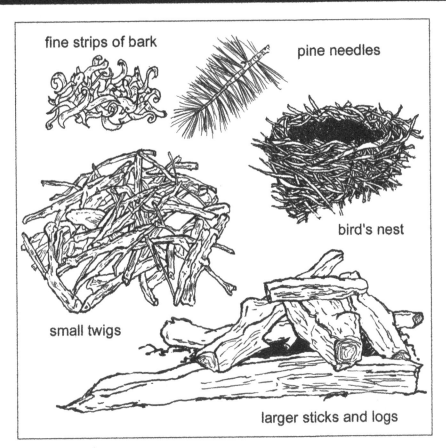

fine strips of bark

pine needles

bird's nest

small twigs

larger sticks and logs

Tinder, kindling and fuel

TINDER. After getting the initial ember from friction, combustion, heat, or another energy source, tinder is what makes the bridge from spark to flame.

There are many cool-guy techniques out there, but the basic idea is to get the driest, fluffiest little poof ball you can from whatever is around you for your tinder. I've seen pocket lint, a lock of hair, toilet paper, leaves, bark, and much more, all used to make a **tinder ball**. You can take strips of bark and dried leaves, mix it with whatever other manmade materials you can supplement with, and then rub them together and mix them up in your hand and try to make a nice little fluffy ball. Take all the powder and scraps that might have dropped and sprinkle them back into the mix. Once you have a nice wad of fibrous material, spread it a little so as to make a little ball. Then make a dent in that ball and form it into a nest. Then take all the loose powder and shavings and droppings from your friction formation and sprinkle it back into the middle of your nest. You now have a new home for your baby coal, a chariot to transport the coal to its new tepee home.

One of the best all-around sources for tinder one can find in nature is actually a bird's nest. Birds usually take from all the light and fluffy things in the environment exactly as one needs to make a fire. If you look around, you'll often find one; I've even found them in the desert when I was looking to start a fire.

Another way to get tinder is to look for the tinder fungus. Scan around trees; there is sometimes a black-looking mucky wad that looks like sap has oozed out of a tree and turned dark. But if you look closer, it's actually a fungus growing in some damaged area of tree bark. If you break it off and it's red-brown inside, it's tinder fungus and makes for a great way to start a fire.

There is a false tinder fungus, as well, so be wary. This one looks like a clam on the side of the tree. It is striped and grayish looking. Not as good as the true tinder fungus, but in a pinch, it will do.

Also, in dry environments, if you can find dung that is so dry that it's pure powdery white, you can crush this up and the dust helps to get a fire started.

In many areas, you can take the loose bark off trees and rub it together into a small pile of dust and flakes that will catch a spark easily.

If everything is wet, look for the slanted trees and take the bark on the underside, peel it off, and underneath the outermost layers you'll find dry bark that you can crush into a fine tinder.

If you can only find hard woods, look for the dry bark under the slanted trees. Cut a piece of bark off and then scrape it to make shavings. This makes an excellent source of tinder, and is often my first choice. Scrapings make flat little curly-cue pieces of wood that catch easy and burn in a circle, and so, the flame is warming the wood before it burns it and does a really nice job of keeping air circulating while preserving heat.

Now sometimes you need a little cheater helper. For me, I find pine resin does just the trick. Pine resin makes a good food and glue, but it also burns very well. This fuel source is called "lighter knot" or "fat lighter." Often a fallen pine tree will have a lot of resin that will have oozed and concentrated in the stump. (This resin is often found in stumps where trees have been felled, and if you're near felled trees, you're likely close enough to civilization to walk out!) Pine resin is usually orange or yellowish. This stuff will burn even in rain. I have used this to start fires in the rain, and it's a real life saver, so always look for it while gathering fire materials. If you have good weather, save it for the wet days.

Another great tinder in nature is the ever-useful cat tails. Not only can you eat these, but if you scrape the brown heads you'll get lots of fluff, and this stuff catches pretty easily. Even if the cat tail has been in the rain, the fluffy stuff is still dry.

Of course, leaves and needles are great as long as they are dry and brittle brown. Crush up some of the leaves into a powder and they'll catch the ember pretty quickly. Also, some types of dry moss will catch as well, but they don't burn long or well. There are other plants, depending on your location, such as the milkweed, that if you bust open a pod, you'll find lots of hairs that are good tinder. If you don't know one plant from another, try manipulating some to see what's inside.

The key to finding tinder is to look through "tinder glasses"—simply look at everything around you for its fire-catching potential. This is such an important part of making a fire, and such effort will go into creating the initial heat that you need for success.

KINDLING. Kindling are the transition linking logs from twigs to sticks. Kindling is to baby food what tinder is to mother's milk. Kindling materials should always start from toothpick size, then up to pencil size, then finger size, then wrist size, then ankle sized.

Everything above that in size is just a big fat log, also known as fuel. The most basic rule for fire making is simple—use dry stuff. So try and gather your kindling from tree branches that are dead and brittle. Try not to use ones that are lying on the ground, as those tend to be moist. And don't use any live branches, as they're green and most definitely moist.

You *can* burn green stuff once you have a good fire going; technically, the hot fire will dry out the green stuff before burning it. However, these make a lot of noise and smoke. And smoke might be what you want for signalling, but we'll discuss that later.

FUEL. The term pretty much says it all: if it burns strong, it's fuel. If you can burn it, do it. One of the funny things I see all the time with students is their perceived need to make a huge fire. I've seen them burn their boots, their bags, their tents, and themselves all because they just couldn't stop throwing logs on the fire. Ironically, it is always the same type of folk who didn't gather up enough fire wood to see them through the night in the first place so that they end up waking up at 4 a.m., when it always seems to get the coldest, with no light and no heat and no logs to rekindle with. And since they aren't allowed flashlights in my outdoors courses, they sit there and hover over their embers until dawn.

So, plan your fuel supplies out and use them sensibly. Some people make small fires and sit real close, while some make big fires and stand far back.

Now there might be times when you want a huge fire, again, maybe to signal for help or to make a lot of coals for cooking or to make a coal bed to sleep warm through the night. In these cases, burn on! But mostly, go easy; you don't need a huge fire, and gathering materials itself can be hard work that depletes energy.

THE TEPEE METHOD

I find the "tepee method" is the best way to prepare your tinder, kindling, and fuel to start your fire. There really isn't any need to know the pyramid or log cabin methods, etc. All the rest of the so-called techniques are just flashy ways to get the same basic thing done.

Start by using a bunch of kindling to make a small "tepee" shape—about 1–2 feet tall—that rests on a bed of sticks and tinder. Leave an opening in the tepee for access to the empty space inside. Then take your soft tinder nest and place it right next to that opening.

Once you've generated your tiny coal ember, transport that ember on a small piece of bark or leaf onto the tinder nest (which should be very close by). With the coal atop the tinder nest, begin to gently breathe air onto it, bringing it from a smoldering coal to a beautiful ember and into a fantastic little flame!

Then, place the flaming nest through the opening in the tepee and onto the bed of tinder inside, and continue to nurture it with gentle breaths as it catches the twigs of the tepee on fire. Once the tepee twigs begin to catch fire, gently lay one piece of kindling after another onto the tepee, slowly reinforcing the walls of it as each layer is consumed by your new hungry off-spring of flame. After a few minutes, you'll have a nice little fire and a giant feeling of warmth inside you.

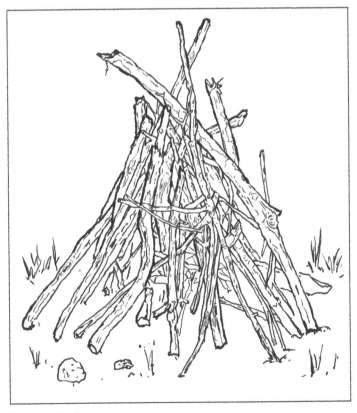

Tepee method

At this point, stay calm and do not rush the process. I have seen more fires killed at this critical juncture by people who are so excited that they over-stack their fire too quickly and crush it. The end result is no fire and a crushed morale, which takes a good bit of mental CPR to get back to that point.

Since you've done all the preparation beforehand, there is no need to rush and panic, no need for excessive moving around finding and breaking sticks. It's all there and you are ready, so enjoy the show and watch it grow.

Now, let's talk about some of the techniques of fire making, or more pointedly, "ember making." Some are very basic; some are really far out there. But as in everything else regarding survival, there are no hard fast rules other than what you can imagine; there are only principles by which you should be guided.

OTHER PREPARATIONS

Here are a few ways to make sure your fire survives the conditions, and you get the most out of it for your purposes.

FIRE PIT. There are a few types of fire pits. The main two I suggest using—besides the simplest form of fire pit—are the Dakota pit and the Cross pit.

The Dakota pit is made by digging two adjacent holes a couple feet apart and connecting them with a tunnel. This is helpful in areas with high winds, or when you have less fuel, or when you don't want to be seen. Start your fire above the hole using methods described above, then move it into one of the holes which should already be filled with kindling and fuel. The tunnel and empty connecting hole maintain air flow to keep the fire going.

The cross pit is just a big "X" dug into the ground so that the wind can still feed your fire while the center of the X lowers the fire so it's not blown all over by the wind.

Most of the time, however, you'll want to make a really simple fire pit. This is done by scraping out a circle of dirt with a stick, rocks, your feet or hands. Make it about six-inches deep in the middle and sloping up to ground level on the edges, and about 12–24 inches around. This pit will let more heat get to you at ground level. If you build on flat ground, use rocks

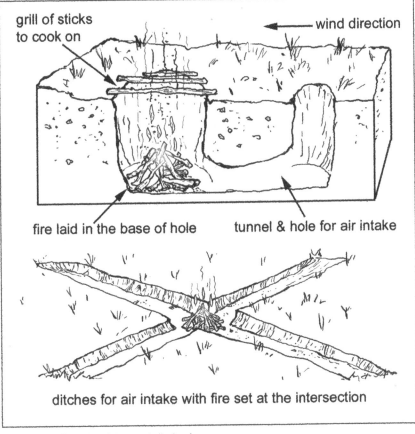

grill of sticks to cook on

wind direction

fire laid in the base of hole

tunnel & hole for air intake

ditches for air intake with fire set at the intersection

Dakota pit (above) and Cross pit (below)

to either contain the fire or give you something to cook on. But leave a gap in the rocks facing you to allow heat to reach you directly. If you dig too deep, the heat will not be reflected at you but rather straight up.

In all cases, put leaves or logs or twigs down under the fire, as it's better to have the fire start on drier material and it allows that little bit of air in there which aids your cause.

FIRE WALL. This is a really great supplement to get the most out of your fire. Whether you're sleeping in the open on the ground or in a shelter, it's good to make a wall of some fashion on the opposite side of the fire. This will reflect more heat and light your way and deflect more wind and cold as well. It also keeps the smoke flow down so your face doesn't get smoked out—and you always want to avoid any drain on your physical condition, such as smoke in your eyes.

You can make a fire wall with sticks and logs, dirt, rocks, a tarp or other manmade materials if you have any. The concept is simple—just fashion a wall about a foot behind the fire, extending a couple feet to either side of the fire, and at least three feet high. Make sure it's as wind-proof as you can make it, often by packing the holes with dirt. The specifics of what you build will be dictated by time, terrain, and need. But do give consideration to a fire wall and do use one whenever possible. It's simple, easy, works and makes a world of difference. And in survival, it's all about the little victories that get you through.

Fire walls

FIRE BED. If you've managed to get a good fire going, but it's freezing and you ain't got a sleeping bag or a very good shelter, then you need yourself a fire bed. But in order to make one, you have to prepare long before the 2 a.m. freeze-out.

Make a big fire by day so you get lots of coals. Dig out an area about the size of your body, but only about six inches deep. When you're ready to sleep, spread your coals evenly inside the hole, and cover them with about three inches of dirt. Depending on the amount of coal and size of the coals, you might need a bit more or less dirt between you and the coals—you'll know either way, haha! And the amount of coals will determine how long they last and keep you warm. Keep your main fire going throughout the night, as well.

Again, this is a supplement for the very cold environment. It takes a lot of work and you might be better off just making a better shelter or sleeping close to your fire and keeping it going throughout the night. However in extreme conditions, this is something to consider.

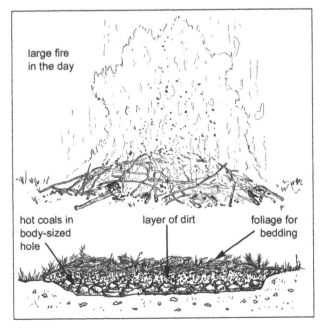

Fire bed

FIRE-STARTING TECHNIQUES

Once you've made all preparations including choosing a wise location, gathering your materials, and building a fire wall, it's time to start rubbing sticks! First of all, there are many variations on how to start fire with sticks. Each one requires a lot of hard work, many require special accessories, and most require a refined technique. But these are all variables. **Fuel**, **Air**, and **Heat** are the constants. Think: **FAHre**.

You can have gas, wood, paper, or anything that burns as a fuel. You've got to have air, not too much to blow it out, especially at the delicate starting stages, but enough for the fuel to combust. And finally, you'll need heat. This might be the spark from a lighter or battery. It might be from a lens of a glass, or it might be from heat generated by friction. In most cases, when you're caught in the wilderness with no tools or resources, it comes down to friction, usually in the manner of rubbing sticks together.

Beside the tried-and-true methods, I will mention a few of the more fascinating techniques, inasmuch as it opens the mind of the modern city dweller. It is important to consider various ways for doing something, which is vital to survival over long periods of time, for those who have had neither time, reason, nor inclination to do so with anything other than modern, readily available means of a "flick and a flame."

Before you ever find yourself out there surviving, it's good to consider how this universal problem has been solved by other primitive cultures around the world for countless centuries.

FIRE PLOW

The fire plow is the best way to start a fire when you have nothing. Now, I'd say it's the worst way, in that it requires the most work. However, for a true survival situation—when you have no tools whatsoever—then grabbing two sticks in your environment and using the fire plow technique is the way to make it happen.

The fire plow requires one "plow stick" about the thickness of a broom handle and about a foot long. You also need a "base board," which should be about 2- to 3-feet long and about 2 inches thick. You'll need to use a rock or other object to scrape a running rut or groove into the top face of the base board through which the plow stick will be rubbed back and forth. The technique is not complicated, but it is hard work and hard to master.

First, find a comfortable kneeling position that allows you to hold the base steady either on the ground, in your lap, or wedged into your waist or tummy and the ground at an angle. Then hold your plow stick with both hands, begin rubbing it quickly back and forth into the rut of the base log and begin to develop some friction. I find that keeping the base flat with my foot helps a lot once I have a good groove made. The concept and goal is to rub the plow stick quickly, with force, and with high friction into the base log until it produces heated shavings that eventually become ignited and a coal is generated. Then you use that coal to light your gathered tinder.

It's important to find the right angle of pushing down. If your plow stick is pointed too sharply down, you risk digging a hole through your base board. If your plow stick's angle is too close to parallel with the base log, the area of friction is too dispersed and there's no chance for a coal to develop. So, the essential element is to get the right angle to develop friction, then heat, then smoke, then a coal on the end of your plow stick's runway. Be prepared: this takes time.

Fire plow

If your sticks build up too much slickness or get shiny, then there's less friction, so sprinkle a little sand or dry dirt in the base log's groove to roughen it up, or scrape it with something like a rock and get the friction increased. It is hard work, I can't say that enough. It'll make you sweat, make you tired and winded, and even get your muscles fatigued. It just might take hours or days, but you'll eventually get the hang of it, so never quit. And even if you rub and rub for hours without getting fire, you'll be breaking in your base log and plow stick to the process, and when you pick them up to try again later they'll be more apt to get you a coal.

Ideally, you'll do this a few times for fun, practice, and exercise before you need it. If you do find yourself in a survival situation, hopefully you'll find or make time to start working on this before you need it. I should point out here that once you know how to do this, and have refined your technique as well as developed your sense of which types of wood work best, this *can be done* in 15–30 minutes given good environmental factors. And once you have your materials broken in, they can often get you a fire in only about five minutes. Of course, if you're completely new to this and in a survival situation for the first time, it could take you an hour or more of constant work to get a spark.

HAND DRILL

Another one of the primitive friction methods for when you have nothing is the hand drill. This is basically the same thing as the fire plow, but the difference is that your friction is pinpointed onto a particular spot on the base, as opposed to a long groove, and the friction is created by quickly spinning the stick on that point instead of rubbing it lengthwise.

You'll need to make a notch in your wood base, and I find this no easy task without a knife. Not to mention, unless you happen to find some really nice, smooth, thin sticks, without a knife to whittle it down and make it smooth, this technique is not suitable as it requires some modifications to the base and spindle that simply can't be done without an implement of some sort. If you can improvise a knife with a sharp rock or other found object, that will help you create a good enough notch in the base that will focus the friction, and also to smooth out the spindle stick to make it easier to work with.

Find a good piece of base wood that's flat on top, and make a little notch in the middle of the flat surface that tapers down to a small hole that you can lay some tinder directly under. Then place your long spindle into the hole and sit down comfortably. Press your hands together with the top of the spindle between them, and rub them together briskly as if you're warming them up. At the same time, apply pressure downwards to create friction and heat. Your palms will slip down toward the base pretty quickly, so when they get to the bottom, hang onto your stick with one hand while holding pressure downward, quickly bring the other hand to the top of the spindle and keep pushing downward, and then bring the bottom hand up and resume the motion. Keep the spindle spinning back and forth and driving down the whole time to keep up friction. If your spindle is not smooth, this activity will not feel good on your hands and will tear them up something fierce. So take the time to smooth out your spindle before starting.

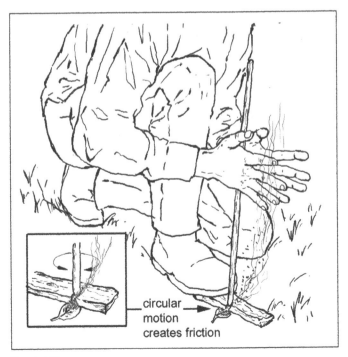

circular motion creates friction

Hand drill

If you don't have the strength to do the fire plow method, this works well as it will accomplish the same effect. Again, getting the coal embers to drop into the bundle of tinder below, will give you what you need to start your fire. At the end of the day, the fire plow and the hand drill are the most truly primitive ways to start a fire with just two sticks. It is good to try both. Master one and you'll always be comforted with the knowledge that you can make a fire if needed, and that can make all the difference between living and dying.

FIRE BOW DRILL

Now, **if** you have a knife and string, then the bow drill method is far better on your back and hands and muscles than most of the other methods.

Materials Needed:

- One flat base board (think of a wooden cutting board) that's about an inch or so thick and made of dry, sturdy wood.
- One spindle stick, also about an inch thick and straight, that you will use to spin rapidly to create friction. This should be dry, sturdy wood about 12 inches in length.
- One wooden block to press down on top of the spindle. This should be a couple inches thick and wide, and should fit into your closed hand, though it can vary; just understand that the purpose of this block is to protect your hand when you're pressing down on the spindle.
- One spindle handle, or bow. This should be about an inch thick, two feet long, green/fresh wood so that it's strong yet flexible, and not brittle or easily breakable. It needs to be strong and thick enough to take your weight as you put downward pressure on the spindle.
- One long, sturdy string (when necessary, even a 6-inch piece will do).

First, carve a round indentation with your blade tip on the top face of your base board, less than an inch from either long end. Also carve the tip of your spindle to a blunt point in order to fit into the indenture. Prepare the wooden block by carving a shallow round groove in its face into which the top of the spindle can be held in place as you press down on it. Then cut a "V" notch on the underside edge of the base board directly below the indent—you want to remove most of the wood here, leaving about a quarter inch of the board's thickness below the indentation above. When you're making these cuts, place the board on something like a sheet of bark or leaves to catch and hold the dust that results; it's that dust with your bit of tinder that will catch and give you a coal.

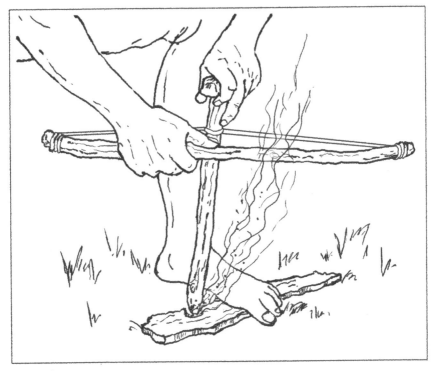

Bow drill

Use whatever string you have—almost any thickness will do, but a sturdy boot string will usually do the trick if it's thick and not made of synthetics as they have a tendency to melt under a lot of friction. It's also best to use something else if you don't want to risk losing your boot lace, but it'll have to do when you don't have anything else. Obviously, the amount of string or cordage you have will be the best determinant for the size of your bow. These can work with even a six-inch piece of string, so don't despair.

Cut notches on both ends of your spindle handle about an inch from the ends, and tie either end of the string into these notches, making sure that the tautness of the string creates a bowing effect on the spindle handle (just think of a toy bow and arrow set you had as a kid).

Sit or kneel next to your prepared tepee and tinder nest, lay the base down, and put the shavings and other tinder directly under the "V" notch on the base. With the string taut and in place on the bow, loop it once around the middle of the spindle, positioning the spindle at the middle of the string. Then place the blunt point of the spindle into the base indent, and position the block on the top of the spindle. Now you're ready to begin.

The basic motion you need to employ is like using a saw. Hold the bow with one hand and press down on the block with the other keeping the spindle in place in the base indent, then begin "sawing" the bow back and forth. As you do this, the string will cause the spindle-point to rotate quickly in the notch, creating friction. Once you get a good rhythm going, you will begin to generate significant friction, then heat, then a spark that will light your tinder.

If you prepare all your tools properly, this is one of the easiest ways to start a fire for beginners. It can vary in size and shape, but basically speaking, mechanics and physics do the work for you.

FIRE PISTON

This technique is pretty easy once it is refined. Basically, it is a combustion method based on a piston-style pump. The materials required include one hollow tube such as bamboo, one piston/stick that fits snugly inside the tube, and tinder.

The theory is that by pushing downward on the piston into the tube, high pressure is created which generates heat very quickly and ignites the tinder at the bottom of the tube.

This is sometimes made by fitting one piece of naturally-hollow bamboo tightly into another, or by hollowing out a piece of wood and then finding another stick that fits perfectly into that hollowed out space. You can also use a small piece of string or leather to create a seal and hold the tinder in place. Usually some lubricant such as a fat or oil is used lightly to enhance the seal and increase the performance of the pump itself.

This method makes it easy to get a coal, which is the real hard part of all the other friction methods for fire starting. One still must apply the basic principles of having everything ready to receive that precious coal and actually make the fire, but this technique sure cuts down on all the hard work.

I have seen this in action and find it to be quite amazing and probably the best and simplest way to make fire without modern tools. However, it

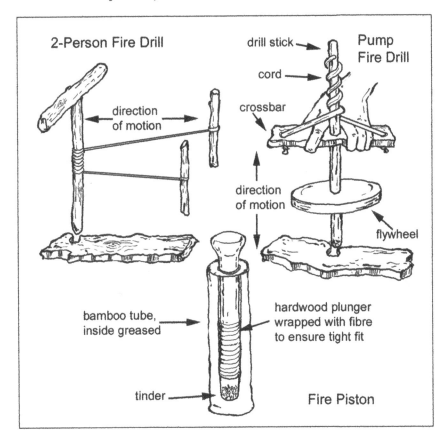

2-Person Fire Drill

direction of motion

drill stick ➔

cord ➔

Pump Fire Drill

crossbar

direction of motion

flywheel

bamboo tube, inside greased ➔

hardwood plunger wrapped with fibre to ensure tight fit

tinder ➔

Fire Piston

may also be the hardest technique for which to make materials, in terms of the details necessary to get the precision seal tight enough to allow movement with lubrication but not so loose as to allow too much air leakage.

Those used by locals are quite small, maybe 6–9 inches. I recommend making one a little longer to compensate for lack of precision and ensure that you generate enough compression to get the heat required to ignite a coal.

Keep this in mind for a situation where you might be isolated for a long time and will have something to keep your mind occupied and the motivation of no longer having to rub sticks is a pretty good incentive. But this is not for the immediate survivor's needs.

BAMBOO FIRE SAW

This is one of my all-time favorite methods, and just another reason why I love bamboo.

Take one segment of bamboo, the driest piece you can get, and cut it in half lengthwise. Take one piece and make a notch in the middle of the outside wall, perpendicular to its length. On the inside of that piece, make a lengthwise notch and load some tinder into it. If you have a knife you can scrape the bamboo and make shavings, which is fantastic tinder.

Now take the other bamboo half and place one end on the ground at an angle, and secure the other end tucked into your stomach or wedged into your lap. Then take the notched bamboo piece and fit the outside notch into the edge of the bottom bamboo—the insides of that bamboo piece and the tinder bundle will be facing you. Gather your tinder around the inside of the notch and start sawing back and forth along the edge of the grounded bamboo. Make sure you keep the tinder in place near the notch that's guiding the sawing motion.

Keep sawing like this until the friction and heat ignite your tinder well enough for you to stop and transport it. Do not stop as soon as there is smoke; keep going until you can see the ember.

ALTERNATIVE FIRE SAW. If there's no bamboo available, you can try this technique with other sticks or small logs.

Find a 3-foot solid "base" log and carve an edge on it as sharp as you can—this will be the piece that you wedge between the ground and your lap or stomach.

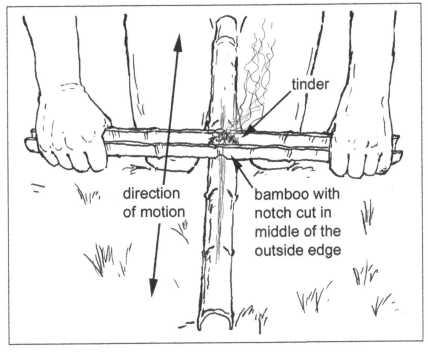

tinder

direction of motion

bamboo with notch cut in middle of the outside edge

Fire saw

Then take another piece of wood that's long enough to hold in either hand while you slide it back and forth across the edge of the base log. Make a small hole in the center of this piece, and pack that space with some tinder, tightly enough to stay in place but loosely enough to allow some air in for ignition. On the other side of the hole, make a notch that will run along the edge of the base log. Then begin sawing just like with the bamboo saw. This will create heat and ignite the tinder.

WHEN IT IS WET
Getting a fire going in wet conditions is particularly challenging for anyone.

It's also one of the times when it's most needed and wanted. It's good to know that it can be done, but there are some tricks to making it so.

Look for dry stuff. Sounds like common sense, but for folks who don't spend much time in the woods, it doesn't seem likely to find dry stuff in such conditions, until you look. Many trees have a slight tilt, or the rain might be coming down at a bit of an angle—look for the dry parts of trees where they're not exposed to the rain. Look for the branches and leaves in these dry areas and scrape some bark off the dry part of the tree as well.

Sometimes you can find dry wood inside the bark: pick up a few branches, peel off the bark, and see if it's dry inside. Sometimes leaves will cover the ground well enough that twigs underneath might still be dry—so look under piles of leaves. There are some tree barks that are very good for finding a dry layer under a wet outer layer, but I don't want to play the name game—just use your common sense and search. Look for dry nooks and crannies and little spaces that might have avoided wetness. If you find dry items, and they are not the right size, shave them down into kindling and tinder.

Of course, it all goes back to initial planning. Prepare your place for your fire and make it as dry as possible. But first bear in mind you'll need enough area around you to stay dry, dry your clothes, and rest safely and comfortably. I've seen almost an entire team come down with hypothermia in early spring from being in the rain too long without heat. At that point, my junior medic and I stopped everything, chose a good location, made a little shelter, got a fire going, and got them all dried out and back into action within a few hours.

It can be done and it can make all the difference in the world, but you have to think your way through the problem. Survival is a lot like chess in that you must always think as many moves ahead as you can.

WHEN IT IS COLD

Another harsh environment is the arctic, or any other snowed-in terrain. I spent three years on a winter warfare team and had my share of snowshoes and igloos. So, I do my best to stay out of the cold. Now most folks will have something to start fire with if they're in this environment. But if you find yourself in such an environment with nothing, this nifty trick—using ice to start a fire—might help when nothing else will.

First of all, it has to be a very bright sunny day. Take a chunk of ice and do your best to form it into a sort of magnifying glass lens. Then, with all the other principles of preparation, supplies, and patience, you can attempt to use the ice as a magnifying glass to light a tinder bundle and make a fire (see magnifying glass technique below).

I admit that this is not easy, nor should it be anyone's first or second attempted technique. But when all else fails, and you're faced with trying something and possibly living or not trying something and certainly dying, you gotta go for it. Note that my mission here is to give you as many tools in your bag of tricks for this one crucial aspect of survival. There are no other areas where I dabble in trying everything that I can because it is this one area that is vitally important for the survivor and can be the trickiest thing for the survivor to actually do.

ALTERNATIVE FIRE STARTERS AND HELPERS

MAGNIFYING GLASS. Let's start with the best option besides the lighter, and that's the magnifying glass. This is a great piece of kit, and I always carry one. It's really an eternal source of fire so long as you have sunlight. The bigger the glass, the easier to start a fire and the better chance you have when the sun isn't as bright. As long as you can capture enough light to harness and focus, you can make fire. This is why I really dislike those survival gadgets that come with the tiniest of magnifying glasses; it can be very tough to get a fire going with those small ones.

The technique is quite simple, and in fact most children have successfully tried to light a fire, or at least get an ember, using a magnifying glass. The first step, as with all of fire-starting techniques, is to gather your tinder nest, kindling, and fuel, and to set up your fire tepee in the brightest location you can find. With your tinder nest next to you, gather an even smaller amount of extremely fine tinder which will be used to create the initial ember.

Next, get into a comfortable position in which you can sit, kneel, or lie very still for a period of time. Hold the magnifying glass about two inches above the lighting tinder, and maneuver it so that the sunlight is going through it and pointing directly into the middle of your tinder. When you begin to see wisps of smoke, begin to gently blow or fan the tinder until a flame or ember appears. Then transfer the ember as described above.

Note that you don't need an actual magnifying glass, though they do work the best. Practical substitutes include flashlight lens, glass bottle, any convex shard of glass, and so on.

Another trick when using a magnifying glass is the cigarette technique. Now I don't smoke, but I always carry a lighter. And when I go to the field I often carry a pack of cigarettes both to trade with local tribes and as a good primitive method for treating parasites (more on that later). The main thing here is that it's much easier to get a fire going with a cigarette than with an ember or coal, and it can be easier to light a cigarette with a magnifying glass than it is to ignite tinder.

HAND CLEANER. Commercially available "hand sanitizers" are very good for starting fires. I once used this in the jungle when the humidity was so bad, that even a magnifying glass in pure sun and clear sky in summer wouldn't ignite the tinder as it was all too moist. A bit of hand cleaner added to the tinder, and it ignited and stayed lit.

VASELINE. Many soldiers carry Vaseline gauze dressings in their first aid kit. These are great for your hands and lips when they get chapped; they're awesome for sealing a sucking chest wound; and they're super for starting a fire as the petroleum jelly-covered gauze catches easily. Campers and outdoorsman for years have used cotton balls soaked in Vaseline as a reliable fire starter.

PERFUME. Depending on your situation, check in your inventory of supplies and see if anyone has any perfume, aftershave, or other astringents. Now, if the first ingredient in the product is water, it likely won't work. But if the main ingredient is ETOH or alcohol, you have a good fire-starting enhancement.

BOOZE. Some of the higher-proof drinking alcohols will also help start a fire. It's a shame to use them that way, but if it's all you have, it's still not wasted.

BATTERIES. If you have batteries with enough juice left in them, and two little wires, it's easy to start a fire. Just connect one wire each to the positive and negative on the battery. Then touch them together on top of your fine tinder to make a spark and get an ember.

STEEL WOOL. Note that some forms of steel wool work better than others, and I have run across steel wool that simply wouldn't burn, even when I threw it in a fire, haha! The principle is that you fluff it up like a nest and it will burn a rather high heat that will be good for setting your tinder alight. The cool thing about steel wool is that you can simply touch it to your batteries to get a spark and start your fire.

CHAR-CLOTH. Now this is the sort of thing only a survivalist would mention as it takes work to prepare it and I don't believe in smoking some cloth to have it ready for fires, when I can just carry a lighter. However, I bring it up here as you might have survived a plane crash. If there was a fire, look for naturally made char-cloth. It might even be smoked clothing off a person who didn't make it. But don't let that cause you to miss a chance to start a potentially life-saving fire for you and fellow survivors. It is created when cloth is essentially cooked without being burned. This material may catch fire when you can't find good tinder—it's desperate, but that's survival.

PINE SAP. This has already been mentioned, but it is such a wonderful thing to find and use in helping to get a flame. Always look for this stuff!

FLINT AND OTHER ROCKS. These take a little practice at finding and identifying, but I always say try anything. If you happen to have rocks lying around, time on your hands, and need for a fire, just start grabbing rocks and striking them against one another to see if you get sparks. If you do, that's all you need to know.

If you have a piece of steel or a knife, this is preferable, but flint and a rock can work, too. Now even with a nice piece of flint and a good strong steel knife blade, it takes a little practice to get the angle strike right for creating sparks. This is the principle for modern lighters—flint and steel make a spark, which ignites the gas, which results in a flame. Flint is found all over, but more so in some places than others. It's grey, brown, or black and if you break it, it will look like a clam shell sort of pattern.

RUBBER. Rubber is a great fire enhancer. Many survivalists cut up small pieces from an old inner tube and throw these into their survival kits. Rubber never rusts or decays, and it can even get wet and still burn. It won't catch a spark, but rubber will help a tiny fire get big in a hurry! So look for any rubber from the wreckage; it will serve you well for fire making especially in inclement weather.

ANY FUEL, OIL, OR LUBRICANT. Take a good creative and thorough approach to making an inventory of your stock in a survival situation. Look for new ways of using all that you have available. Even cooking oil or sun tan oil might come in handy for making a fire, or keeping one going in foul weather.

STUFFING FROM CAR SEATS, ETC. Another potential source for fire starting that is often overlooked. Again, the recurring them here is to look at everything differently. In survival, one needs to start thinking in "extremes." Be willing to rip up a nice car seat to get that stuffing, or break apart some structure to get at some part of it that might be useful. Survival is not pretty; in fact it's downright brutal and sometimes even ugly. But, if the moment of brutal ugliness brings about survival, that is life and that is beautiful!

TERMITE NESTS. These can be used for building fires, and note that they make a lot of smoke. I've heard everything about termite-nest smoke, from curing foot fungus to scaring off jaguars to diminishing mosquitoes. And you can eat termites, too—a 2-for-1 special.

DRY POWDERY PLANTS. Some plants lend themselves well to specific needs of man. The puffball mushroom is a great example. They aren't everywhere, but if they're around, you'll know them as they're an oddly round-shaped mushroom that if you give a little kick, it will turn into pow-der—great for fire starting. So look at all the plants around you and exper-iment with everything you find. You never know; and you might have the rest of your life to find out. Pine cones also make a great way to get your fire going, but they're more for kindling than tinder.

PROCESSED FOODS. Some foods like Cheetos™ and Pringles™ are known to burn well as fire starters, due to their high fat content and being pro-cessed. Most processed foods have a layered structure that permits air to let them burn well.

TAMPONS. If these are available, they're great as tinder—be sure to fluff it up first.

FIRST AID DRESSINGS. These are also great for starting fires as they are perfectly dry and light so they take a spark readily. But only use them if you have no immediately pressing first aid requirements for a bandage. If so, evaluate the benefits of using improvised dressings if they would not start fires as well. But consider infections and antibiotic supplies, too, if a dirty rag might cause an infection, best forego the fire and dress the wound with the sterile bandage.

CONDOMS. These are not for fire starting directly, but condoms are fan-tastic for keeping things dry and/or carrying them with you to stay dry for later usage.

FIRE FROM TRASH. The same principle of the magnifying glass or the flashlight reflector can basically be applied to anything highly shiny and bendable enough to focus the sun's light. I've heard of everything from a dark chocolate candy bar to toothpaste being used to scour and polish the bottom of an aluminum can. Because cans are of a convex shape, they natu-rally capture and focus all the sun's light in one direction. So shine up a coke can or anything you can find and try using it to magnify or focus the sun's rays and ignite your fire.

MAGNESIUM BAR. This is a good piece of kit to have with you whenever travelling. It works in any climate, even wet, and is simple to operate. Like flint, the idea is to strike the magnesium bar to create sparks to light tinder.

CANDLES. Store-bought and improvised candles won't necessarily help you get a fire started, but they're very handy to have as they keep a flame with little effort or oversight—as long as you keep them protected from the elements.

MAKING COOKING UTENSILS

Along with fire making comes another very important, but often overlooked, aspect of fire use in survival—what to cook in. If you have pots and pans, or metal cups or tin cans, you're golden and sorted. But when you're truly surviving with nothing, these otherwise simple things are often the most difficult to problems to solve.

BAMBOO FOR COOKING. Not only can you use bamboo to start a fire, as a food source, as a water source, as material for making shelter and more, you can cook in it too. It's not as crazy as it sounds. The process is simple. Start by cutting out one enclosed segment of bamboo. Then cut a hole into the side of the segment large enough to get your food into, or simply cut one end off the segment to create an enclosed tube.

To cook in this vessel, place it with the food/liquid near the fire, but not actually in or on it, and leave it there until the bamboo blackens and hardens (called "curing"). After it's cured, you can put it closer or even above the fire, but keep an eye on it in case it actually catches fire. I have boiled water for a full 30 minutes using a bamboo vessel, and have used the same cured "pot" for weeks.

COCONUTS. Coconut shells are the best natural thing I've found and used for boiling and cooking in. I've placed them right in the fire and watched them transfer the heat and boil the water and not burn. It's safest to place them on the side of the fire instead of on or above it, but they are fairly resistant to catching fire.

TURTLE SHELL. I have seen turtle shells used by tribal locals for cooking, and so I know they work. I myself have cooked turtles in their own shells, and that works swell!

CONCH SHELLS. I have used these on seashore survival experiences and they can be of limited use for boiling water and such, but their capacity isn't great so they don't hold enough material to be of real value unless there are no other alternatives, in which case, a half dozen of them placed around your fire can sterilize the water quantities needed and cook a little food.

CARVED-OUT WOOD. Given enough free time and lack of other materials, this is a doable venture in terms of making a cooking pot. Get a nice piece of hard wood that when cut, shaved, or otherwise manipulated could become a

bowl is formed by burning then carving with a rock

bamboo pot for heating water

bamboo pot for cooking food

Cooking vessels

pot. Then try to spot-burn it by concentrating fire on its middle while keeping the outsides free from flames. This is best done by using a combination of water, soil, and positioning on the non-burning areas. Once the middle is sufficiently burnt out, use a rock or stick to start hollowing out the area of you want. You may have to do several cycles of burn-carve, burn-carve until you reach your goal.

BIRCH BARK. This bark is great for many survival needs, but it has a fairly flexible and hardy paper-like bark that allows you to form it and place it near a fire without burning, and it will transfer heat and boil water. I have seen bowls and boxes and even rucksacks made from this stuff. I'm not that creative—I tend to make a handful of cone-shaped "things," prop them next to my fire with my food/liquid inside, and get busy with other projects.

TRASH. Tin cans, old barrels, or just about anything else you can find may work better than having to make something from scratch. Just be mindful of potentially harmful pollutants in whatever you find.

GENERAL COOKING CONCEPTS. Make whatever contraption you can to hold or hang your pots over the fire—close enough to cook your food or boil your water, yet far enough so the pot itself doesn't catch flame. There are tons of ways of doing this and no set rules other than the basic principles. You can use one stick as a lever that's held in place by the fork of another stick. You can wedge a stick into the ground on an angle and hang your pot from that. You can prop up a stick using rocks, and hang your vessel from that. You can hang string or a stick with a hook from the fork of a branch and attach your pot to its bottom. Just use the materials around you and your imagination to make something that works.

stick wedged between rocks to
hold pot over fire

Y-stick to hold food
over fire

tongs for holding
hot items

stick can be rotated
so food cooks evenly

General cooking concepts

Food

Obviously we need food to live. But when you find yourself in a survival situation, hunting for food won't be one of your first priorities. Once you have all greater priorities sorted out, then start thinking about gettin' some groceries.

Now when you got it, save it first!

The first thing is the obvious—save what you have, as you just don't know how long you might have to go. But let's qualify that a bit. If you are in a scenario like a sinking ship, you might wanna chuck all food overboard or into your life raft right after anything regarding communication, shelter, first aid, and of course, oodles of H_2O.

But what about when you're on land and gotta move and you just can't store or carry all available food. In such cases, soldiers have a simple saying: "Better to carry it in ya, than on ya!" So, try and eat all you can. If you have to make a long journey and everything is perishable, you might just take a day or more and grub out and gorge for a few days. Just think like a camel—stuff your pie hole and feed your face like there's no tomorrow. It won't be easy to do; won't be easy moving afterwards on a full belly; and it sure won't be easy as the body adjusts from engorgement to starvation—but you might buy yourself a whole week of nourishment for a day or two of feasting.

Now, let's say you got some chow, and you have the wherewithal to keep it for awhile. Whether it was on hand, stored, or simply found around you, you absolutely should consider rationing it.

RATIONING

Rationing is fairly simple math. Take the amount of food you have, divided by how many people there are, divided by how many days you expect to be in survival mode.

Amount ÷ Number of People ÷ Duration

Time is the one thing that you'll have no control over; you could be stranded a mighty long time. So, for this "infinite" potential, you'll need to assign some sort of arbitrary number based on the law of averages.

Most "survival" situations from people involved in airplane crashes or getting lost off-roading tend to be around three days. Survival situations for people lost camping or at sea tend to be around seven days. People lost in the jungles or mountains can face their survival situation for around 30 days. Consider your situation, take into account the laws of averages, and then make that your baseline planning figure.

So, you're either there for three, seven, or 30 days. Heck, any longer than that and you're taking up residence! But for my purposes, I shoot for 30 days as a regular planning figure. This gives me stronger mental preparation in case the rescue or return takes longer. Setting that figure keeps everyone hanging on longer and better than using the shorter day counts. It's one of those "better to under-promise and over-deliver" situations. Do it the other way around and folks can start dropping like flies mentally. It happens a lot more than you might think.

Moving on to the next factor, the number of people is simple if you're alone. But if not, then you have to be realistic in your rationing concepts. There might be kids or elderly folks in your group who might not require as much. You might also consider weight as a factor—to give a 300-pound, 30-year-old athletic male the same rations as you'd give a petite 18-year-old female of 90 pounds, wouldn't quite pass the common sense test.

You might also have some unconscious people present. Do you save their food for three days while they're out of it? What about folks who are seriously injured whose chances of surviving aren't very good in the first place?

So, it's not as clear-cut as just dividing equally per person. You must take into account the other factors because, to ignore them could lead to the demise of the group as a whole. The more concepts you can wrestle with now in your head and heart, the better you'll likely handle them when you must struggle with them in reality. A key aspect of this book—much like training for combat—is that the harder you train and the more you sweat to prepare now, the less blood and loss of life there will likely be later.

CALORIC INTAKE AND OUTPUT

We all need calories for energy and to live. Eat too many and you get fat, eat too little and you lose weight.

Now, the three main elements of food that contribute to caloric intake are *carbohydrates* (starches and sugars as found in fruits, veggies, sweets, cereals, and so on), *proteins* (meats, legumes, dairy), and *fat* (animal fats, oils, nuts). You need all three to have a balanced diet and keep maximum health. If you're going to be survivin' for awhile, after the initial period of stabilization you will really need to do the best you can to cover all three areas. But the goal is always to get out and get home safe as quickly as possible, so this is more of a long-term plan.

CALORIE FACTS FOR AVERAGE HUMANS:

- Men need about 2,500 calories per day.
- Women need about 2,000 calories per day.
- Children and the elderly need a bit less.
- Large people and fit people need a bit more.
- We only burn about 20% of daily calories through activity and exercise.
- 70% of these calories are actually spent on all the organs working all day.
- 10% are burned off while processing the food from which you're getting the calories.

Now, let's say you didn't eat at all for 24 hours. You'd still have to burn calories for your organs to keep functioning. Even if you just laid there and slept, your body would still be burning calories. This is called a "basal metabolism rate," or the base amount of calories your body is burning while you do nothing but sleep and rest.

Though studies vary, most folks will expend about 1,800 calories just sitting there for a day.

A good rule of thumb is the **dirty dozen calorie rule**—12 calories are used up by every one pound of your flesh every day. So a 200-pound man uses up 2,400 calories a day just by existing.

The military assumes that young, fit men need at least 3,000 calories a day. They provide meals that have about 1,200 calories per meal, so that a soldier will usually have more than enough energy to do his job. If the soldiers are static for a while, they will gain weight, or eat fewer meals to avoid it. In extremely vigorous times, a soldier might eat 5 meals a day and still lose weight over a period of time.

Why the heck am I saying all this? Well, whether you're alone or have a group of folks to go on rations, this info will help you better understand how to chop out those food supplies based on some reason, and still mind health needs.

What it means to you in true survival terms is threefold—how much food you need, how much you give each person, and what do you prioritize in the first place.

It is likely that any food you have on hand is pre-packaged and labelled with nutritional values. Use that info to factor into your equation when figuring out how much each person needs.

When you don't have packaged food, it's good to have some rough ideas of what wild foods will do for you.

CALORIES FROM FOOD IN THE WILD:
* One pound of fat is worth about 3,500 calories.
* Wild meats tend to be about 500 calories per pound (rabbit, deer, boar, etc.).
* Fish are around 750 calories per pound on average (the range is wide).
* Shellfish and seafood are around 350 calories per pound.
* Vegetables come in way low at around 100–200 calories per pound

(the range is wide; roots and tubers provide more calories than other veggies).

- Fruits are about double the veggie value at 300–400 calories/pound.
- Milk has about 2,500 calories per gallon (if you can find a wild goat or other source).
- Eggs offer about 100 calories per egg.
- Nuts are great for pure survival energy, with 2,500 calories per pound.
- Beans are an awesome energy food with about 1,250 calories.

Now that you have an idea what humans burn in a day, what the needs are, and what general foods provide in terms of energy-resource value, you should be better equipped to figure out how to ration your chow so it's more equitably shared and applied.

While we're talking general rules, I'll share the following "common knowledge" with you as a guide, and then I want you to chuck it right out the window and prove it wrong.

HUMANS WILL LIKELY DIE IF THEY GO MORE THAN:

- 3 minutes without air
- 3 hours of extreme exposure (heat or cold, desert, arctic, freezing water)
- 3 days without water
- 3 weeks without food

If your will is strong, I say you can prove all these limits wrong. They are, however, good and standard guidelines for planning and assessing any situation.

Now, let's say it all goes horribly wrong. What does *that* look like?

PHASES OF STARVATION

Determined humans can go 8–12 weeks without food, provided they have adequate water and a strong will to live. So, you have at least two months, if you're drinking water, before you're pushing up daisies. So, don't despair if food is scarce. Not saying it'll be easy, but you have time, and that's the important thing to hang onto during lean times.

Obviously, if it's freezing cold or scorching hot and your exposure to these extreme temperatures is high—or your physical demands from your surrounding elements are high—your timeframe of survival without food decreases significantly. Ultimately, know that you can go about 30 days without food in almost any situation. And your chances of rescue or return within a month are very good. Humans can lose around 50% of their total weight and then make a full recovery, so keep the faith. Meanwhile, let's take a look at the signs of starvation.

HUNGRY AND MAD—WEEK 1. The first phase is hunger. Irritability and lethargy or tiredness may result from lack of food and lower blood-sugar levels. There is an initial drop in weight from losing water the first 24 hours, and then the body begins to hold onto that water for the next 24 hours.

After that, it starts to consume the stores of fat.

KEY: This is the anger phase, when people are very grumpy and irritable.

VERY HUNGRY AND SAD—WEEK 2. In the next phase of starvation you have the obvious loss of weight, but now the muscle mass is also diminishing as the body begins to consume itself as a source of energy. During this phase, most people no longer experience normal hunger, and sex drive decreases markedly.

KEY: This is when people begin to suffer serious bouts of depression and self-doubt.

STARVING AND CRAZY—WEEK 3. In the latter phases of starvation, there could be swelling from fluid under the skin, anemia, immune deficiency, chronic diarrhea, and decreased ability of the body to digest food because the digestive-acid production has been reduced.

In this phase, go easy on eating food should you find some. And when you first commence to chow down, start by taking small bites, then wait for several minutes, and repeat. Organs start shrinking and losing some function during this stage.

KEY: This is when people start acting crazy and extreme; in short, they begin getting desperate. Even nice people might find themselves doing things they never imagined.

STARVED AND SUBDUED—WEEK 4 AND FORWARD. In the last stages of starvation, people experience neurologic malfunctions including hallucinations, convulsions, and severe muscle pains, as well as irregular heartbeat and shallow breathing.

KEY: At this point, there is no extra energy for fighting or even crying, so it is mostly a hanging-on phase, trying to sustain and maintain and hope.

In my experience, I have lived hungry and gone through periods of starvation. I know it well and the bingeing that comes afterwards. For the survivor I will share what I have experienced teaching classes where I starve people as part of their training. The first 24–48 hours are easy; after one day, your stomach shrinks a bit and you think about food less. But after that, days 3–5 can be quite severe for most folks. People get mean and they will eat things they never would have before. After about a week, people seem to get more civilized. So, be prepared for these emotional variations.

The best medicine is a slow but constant pace of working towards some practical goal that can keep the mind occupied and not tax the body more than a minimal exertion of energy. Slowly improving your shelter or signals, collecting firewood, working on an escape vessel, or preparing for an escape journey by gathering supplies are all worthwhile jobs, and the key is to keep busy, but not burdened. STICK TOGETHER if in a group or KEEP IT TOGETHER if alone.

ETHICS AND HONOR IN SURVIVAL

Now let's look at something near and dear to my heart—doing the right thing in bad times. I've often heard my SF brethren say that Green Berets are Uncle Sam's extremists. And in spirit, that's true. We hold fast the philosophy, "Who believes longest and strongest will always win," and we DO believe! But I tend to put it another way with less heavy overtones, in short, "SF is where the bad boys get to be the good guys!"

It's that singular statement that makes the difference between SF and everyone else. We work in extreme environments, we live in the grey areas where things happen that people can't even conceive, much less imagine beforehand, in order to make rules for guidance. And we must have that "built-in" moral compass that guides us through. This is one of the things they test for, especially amongst the officers, as they are usually the ones who make the final decisions. They must be able to see things in the here and now, for what they are and aren't, and understand what they mean and will mean. So, let's look at the guiding principle the military teaches its men and women for when things are at the extreme end of human existence and experience: Survival at War.

Now, I don't teach *all* of the S.E.R.E. (Survival, Escape, Resistance & Evasion) training methods of the Green Berets in this book because a lot of it simply isn't applicable to a civilian survivor. For example, while Green Berets seek to use stealth and remain "sterile" in our environment, leaving no trace, I want you to be as loud and large as you can be to get found and rescued.

But there are two tenets at the core of the S.E.R.E. course you should know:

First: plan on walking home. Think about that. You're behind the lines, surrounded by bad guys, in a harsh and alien environment, and you know "friendlies" are around somewhere. But they try to drill it into our heads that our allies might not know where we are, or they might know but simply may not be able to get in because of the enemy's position, or they are over-committed elsewhere fighting. They want us to have a plan and a hope for rescue, but mentally, to have it locked in tight that no one but no one is coming to get you, and that you and you alone are going to get yourself out.

You, too, should lock this thought into your mental programming from the outset of any survival situation. Try for rescue, use your head, but by God, if none comes, you plan on walking all the way back to Fort Living Room if it takes you ten years to do it! Never Quit!

Second: learn to survive, fight to survive, and live to return—with honor. This is probably the most important thing I'll say in this entire book.

The SF trainers know we're going to be tortured if we're caught. We're high-value targets for the bad guys. They also know that everyone has a breaking point, even if it's death. What they teach is to know that, understand it, and accept it. Everyone will break at one point or another. The key is to do your best, bounce back afterwards, and at all times, even during the breaking, try to keep your sense of honor.

And that really applies to a survivor when they are in any kind of starvation situation in a group of people. When you are alone, you can kill, lie, steal, cheat, and do anything out there in nature in order to survive. Those are the rules! You sweet talk that little critter into coming close to you and then you whack that booger on the noggin and eat 'em!

But when you are with others, you are not alone, so those rules don't apply. One day, some way, you will get back home. Or, maybe you won't. If you do make it back, you want to be able to live with yourself and the actions and decisions you did and made while out there in extremis. If you don't make it out, you'll at least face the end knowing that you did right by what you believed and held to be good.

It is this thing that they teach us in Special Forces that I wanted to share with you here. This attitude alone can guide you through much hardship, and this sort of thing is contagious. Set the example; be the standard; and others will follow. Together, your chances of survival will increase.

One last note on attitude and contagion. Fear spreads faster than any virus I've ever seen. If someone is in fear or panic, calm them down ASAP or separate them from the group immediately if you can't contain them. Work with them alone and individually before you return them to the group. And watch them—the seeds of dissention spread quickly, and if the "group think" turns to panic, it could doom the entire effort. Live to return with honor. Remember that.

CANNIBALISM Now, I think it is worthwhile to digress onto a tangent here and discuss the merits and stigmas of cannibalism since we're looking at starvation and potential temporary insanity. Gruesome as it is, it warrants a realistic discussion because it *is* real, it has, does, and will occur, and cannot be ignored just because we find it tasteless, no pun intended.

First, you can immediately throw out the option of auto-cannibalism—for example, chopping off your pinky to nibble on for sustenance. The reasons are simple and pragmatic more than gross and hardcore. The loss of blood, the energy expended from the stress and pain, the potential exposure to infection, all weigh heavily against consuming your own body parts, unless. . . . If you happen to have lost the body part in some traumatic accident already, give it a real think. I know it sounds morbid and horrible, and I personally would be real sad about the prospect. But being a hardcore pragmatist, the idea of burying the dang thing and letting it rot instead of using it for sustenance just doesn't pass the common sense test.

What about how cannibalism might apply in a group situation? I will say this first: we all have a right to do as we please so long as it doesn't harm anyone else. The moment you do so, you're dead wrong! And that holds true here, too. But if someone is dead already, and the group is starving and food is scarce or nonexistent, why let the dead person's flesh go to waste? Their spirit is gone; it's only meat now. If you can't eat them—on principle or due to decay or disease—then use them for bait to capture an animal you *can* eat.

What if someone is not quite dead yet? I say, true friends will let you eat them if they die first. We jest in Special Ops that if a fella dies first, we're dividing up his gear and laying claim to his best kit and beans and bullets. The principle is that you accept the potentiality of death and you give your blessing in life, to the living, so that they know they can go on living and be free of the guilt that might hold them back from doing what may be necessary. So if someone is mortally wounded, or fatally ill, consider discussing it with them while they are conscious and coherent and receive their blessings to dine on their flesh after they pass. Get their messages, and remember them, but eat and live. The only rule is that you must not kill your own kind to live—that is murder and violates all the laws of the universe. Cannibalism after death, for life, is not.

Those are all the philosophical aspects; now let's look at the practical applications. The obvious target areas for consumption are the muscles—the buttocks, legs, arms, and back are the first cuts. Eating the human brain should be avoided. There is a rare viral disease found only amongst people who practice cannibalism called "kuru." It is suspected to be caused by the eating of human brains, so leave the brains be or use them for tanning the skin. The organs in general should be avoided as well due to possible toxins and diseases, but can also be used as bait in traps. If they had an infection, most viruses, parasites, protozoa, and fungi will be killed by cooking well. If the body is in a slight state of recent decay, apply the "drop test." That is, pick up the body part and give it a hard shake. If any muscle mass falls off, then the integrity of the meat is decayed too much to eat. But if it stays on the bone it is still fresh enough to cook and eat. (This principle applies to road kill, as well.) And that's all I got to say about that.

KILLING IS LIFE

MEAT: IT DOES A BODY GOOD! Animals and insects can meet about 90% of all your nutrition needs in a survival situation, and it's an easier and safer bet to catch and kill animals than trying to subsist off of plants alone. Ounce for ounce, pound for pound, you will always get the most calories from meat over any other food source out there, and for the survivor, it's the calories that counts the most. The brain needs glucose to function and the human body can get this from animal fat, as the liver breaks it down to its chemical components, but it does require more water to do this. Also, that glucose is a simple carbohydrate that the body uses for energy, so you can get carbs from meat. The difference is that these are not the complex carbs you get from roots and grains, so they don't give that longer-lasting energy like breads and pastas, but they do give you all you need to survive. So there is no doubt, meat is the stuff that can see you through the hard times!

Another fact is that almost everything out there moving around is edible in one way or another, whereas it's the other way around for plants—most plants are not edible for humans.

And, everywhere you go on the planet, there is animal/insect life. So everywhere on the planet where you might find yourself stranded and surviving, there will be an animal food source that you can find, get, and eat, and know that it is safe and will supply you with almost everything you need.

You simply cannot say the same about plants on any level. They aren't everywhere; they're almost all unsafe to eat; and they hardly give you anything you really need nutrition-wise. Taking these two fundamental principles into account, it is no wonder why the military teaches primarily to rely on hunting food rather than gathering food. Since most soldiers have the killer instinct to begin with, it's simply a matter of place and time.

All that said, in order to survive we must commit ourselves to eating meat.

THAT MEANS GETTING IT, AND THAT MEANS KILLING. There are many, many ways to kill. I assure you right now, for the non-hunters, there is no real *nice* way to kill. Death is death and it is unpleasant to see and ponder, especially when you are the one doing the killing. Be prepared to do so using brutal blunt trauma or some gruesome mangling way via traps and snares.

Life is precious in all its forms. I never hunt for pleasure or sport. I don't like killing anything, not even insects, unless I have to do so. (Well, excluding, skeeters, ticks, leeches, and other parasites, but even they feed something else.)

You never know if you're going to end up killing a baby critter or a mama critter with hungry babies to feed somewhere. It happens. You have to look at it in the bigger picture—that animal is on the food chain for something, so it might as well be you. Heck, if you died out there, it might be the other way around and that critter would be nibbling on your flesh. So, you're only doing what you need to do, and that animal's end is its fate.

All you *can* do is dispatch it as quickly and humanely as you can, and be thankful for the nutrition it is providing you. At the end of the day it is the law of nature, and it is a natural way for an animal to go, being eaten by a larger predator. It just happens to be you as the predator today.

HIT FAST, HIT HARD. The safest and most humane way to kill is to be the meanest and most brutal you can in the offing of the critter. Like with first aid, sometimes you must be cruel to be kind. Don't try to "beat it to death gently." Crush its friggin' skull and end it! It is the only way. Sorry. Once you are over this, understand that you will live another day as a result of this killing. This animal's death means quite literally and directly, your life. And all the little rabbits and squirrels dying and being eaten by you, at the end of it all, have helped you get back home to your loved ones, and that is your mission.

For survival hunting, simple is always best. It is usually a two-part process:

1. **Disable or hurt it enough so that it stops moving, at least for a moment.**
2. **Dispatch or kill it the very second you get the chance to finish it off.**

Try to do the last first whenever possible. And don't try anything nicey-nice for a disabler—just hit it hard and hurt it. Take the mindset that you need to try to seriously injure or mortally wound your prey with the first blow, and then close for the kill to finish it off. If you need to, throw a rock or sharpened stick or weighted club to distract or disable it long enough for you to close the distance and then pummel its brain housing with your war club, battle axe, poking spear, or bleedin' blade. Once committed to the kill, is must be fast, furious, and final.

Now that this is said, let's talk about how to catch a critter.

CATCHING ANIMALS

Before you can kill an animal and eat it, you have to catch it. Too bad it's not as simple as walking into the butcher shop and pointing at what you want to chow on. You have to use all your wits and resources to catch these critters because, after all, they really don't want to be caught, haha! So you'll use tracking, hunting, snares, and various traps in your efforts to find, catch, kill, eat, and live.

TRACKING

Since I'm assuming that you're not going to have this book with you when you get stranded somewhere, there is no real point in showing lots of specific animal tracks and habitat specifics that you wouldn't remember anyway.

Like plant identification, it's its own art and area of study. You just need to understand some general concepts about tracking.

The real deal is that when you are hungry, you start hunting and if the prey is there, you will find tracks or droppings.

Once you find these, make two key determinations:
Are the tracks of something too big for you to bother with?

If they are not too big, are they fresh enough to be worth pursuing?

Tracks usually lead to one of three places: **Home**, **Food**, or **Water**. And the finding of any one of these is a good thing. You might find their food source and be able to eat it, or their water source and drink up, or their home and then you eat them.

Feces is usually found somewhere around tracks, so the two are useful and work together for the beginner survivor. Mainly it's the feces that gets the novice tracker's attention to then notice the tracks around the droppings, then you follow those tracks.

Most of us are familiar with paw tracks as we know them from dogs and cats. The cats have retractable claws, and dogs don't—so look for the claw marks. Generally, paw pads with claw scrapings means some sort of dog or wolf critter, and paw pads without means some kind of feline animal.

Many rodents and small game like weasels, coons, and such have paw pads with or without claws. If there are claws evident, the tracks are likely from the feisty critters; conversely tracks lacking clawed pads are mostly from the class of the easier "prey" animals.

If the tracks are from hooves, then they're likely goats, pigs, or deer-type critters. As long as they don't look like they're too big or heavy, they might be worth hunting. Even if they are too big to hunt, chances are they'll be easier to track and will lead to water or other food sources.

To guesstimate an animal's weight by their tracks, just step beside their tracks and see what kind of impression your foot leaves in relation to the track. The track size will be a fairly straightforward guess as to animal size, especially when compared to your foot beside it.

At all times—regardless of your primary activity—you should be on the scout for any signs of animals. Tracks and stacks of poo are the obvious.

Fresh tracks will have crisp edges; look at the soil and see how dry or crumbled it looks. Take into account what the weather has been lately and you can guesstimate the freshness of the tracks. If they seem to be within a few days, it might be worth further investigation. You might find a lot of tracks or not many, or they may be old, but always consider that there may be more nearby that are fresher. As for droppings, the wetter and more smell they have, they fresher they are. Even if they're dried out, then check around to see if there is a home nearby.

Further develop your tracking skills by looking for signs of feeding and foraging. Things that have been chewed on, scratched at, dug up, turned over, and in any other way disturbed and/or modified from their natural position and condition are all signs that critters are about. Once you see these things, keep looking for more signs until you find tracks that may lead you to your prey, water, etc.

HUNTING

This is the simple act of looking for, finding, and then engaging the animal either by stealth or direct confrontation, usually with a weapon. Hunting is my preferred method for finding chow, but it isn't always the desired technique as it requires time, plus not all the critters in your environment might be best acquired by hunting.

For example, you're in the desert and there simply are not a lot of big creatures to hunt. Since hunting takes some time, the payoff of the animal's size must make it a "value-added" pursuit. Therefore, in an environment with a lot of small game and little larger prey, set the hunting as a secondary kill technique and go for snares and traps, instead. So, the basic rule is: Hunt Big, Snare Small.

Now, while you're out "hunting" for tracks and drops, whether it be for small or big, you're still looking for bird's nests for eggs to raid, as well as anything you can whack on the head along the way such as lizards, snakes, bugs, etc. Everything that moves is a food source for you to hunt. So keep your eyes open at all times, and keep several weapons handy at all times as well.

The Four Basic Hunting Styles, in Order of Effectiveness:

Tracker: You find tracks and hunt down the animal's trail. This provides good chances of success. (Herding animals into a trap or ambush is considered part of this group.)

Waiter: You find a home or watering hole or feeding ground, and wait, hidden. When an animal approaches, wait until it gets near to you and then pounce with your weapon to disable and kill.

Baiter: Set out some bait and hope an animal comes to take the bait. You can set the bait in a trap, or in the open—in which case you would wait and pounce when a critter came for it.

Ranger: Roam around until you encounter and engage. This is not the best technique on its own, but you should always be a "ranger" when on the move or while out doing other tasks like finding water, shelter, etc.

Now let's look at some of the basic considerations of hunting.

TIME OF DAY. Start in the morning, at first light or just before. This is when many critters are most active. The night dwellers will be headed for home and the day dwellers will be looking for breakfast.

Do not hunt at night! And try not to risk hunting at dusk, either, because the predators come out at night, and they can see in the dark while you can't. Also, it is very easy to get disoriented in the dark and you could easily end up spending a miserable night away from your camp. If you must hunt at dusk, keep a fire lit, keep it in sight, and hunt for the things that might come to check out your fire's light. Surprisingly, while big things tend to stay away from fires, smaller, more inquisitive critters often come for a peek.

FINISHING. Everything fights for its life, and as such, everything can hurt you in its own self-defense and struggle to live. *Always* exercise extreme caution with teeth, claws, horns, and anything like stinging tails, spitting, etc. If the animal has it, it will use it on you, even faking you out to draw you in. I've encountered some mighty mean raccoons, possums, and even squirrels—no wild animal is worth overlooking. When you whack little things, step in and finish them off quickly. It's more humane and it keeps you from getting injured, keeps them from getting away or attracting larger predators to their distress sounds, and prevents the animal from sending a distress signal to big mama critter, who might be very unhappy about you eating junior.

APPROACH. With big animals, once you've wounded them, go easier; don't start running after them right away as they could run a lot longer and might get away by outdistancing you. If they're bleeding out, give them a few minutes to drain and lose energy so they can't fight as much when you come upon them. And always approach any sizeable game you've taken down like a downed man in a fight—from the top, rear oblique of the head. In essence, approach from their weakest point, and the angle that gives you the most time to respond if they try to strike at you.

STALKING. Every step you take needs to be purposeful. Watch your foot placement so as to not break twigs and disturb vegetation, or otherwise make sounds and smells that can be detected and give you away. Use your toes to test ahead for potential "crunch factor" before placing your full weight down, and if you detect "crunch," use your toes to clear it, or insert under it. Basically, do like you did as a kid, playing hide and seek—be sneaky.

Look all around you at all times, especially up and behind you. Many things are above you in the jungles and forests, and the view is always different from the rear. Scan near, then mid-range, then out into your distance. This should be a constant process—near, mid, far—every few steps. It takes alertness and vigilance to hunt, and this is why it's so demanding, but rewarding, when you succeed.

The fact is you should be in "Hunter Mode" the entire time you're out there. Carry a weapon with you at all times, regardless of your purpose at the moment. You never know when you're going to bump into a critter or when it will bump into you. When those golden moments present themselves, you must be ready to strike in an instant with a lethal blow. This killer instinct will become natural with a bit of practice, and is highly likely the hungrier you get.

SIZE. Don't tackle anything bigger than you or that is more than you can realistically use.

If something spots you, freeze. Maybe it's curious, maybe it's not sure. Just be still and be patient. When it carries on, so do you. If it runs, determine if you have the energy and any chance of catching it before you make a dash.

If it's after you, try to make a slow, cautious withdrawal. Keep eyes on it at all times. Once it's close, use techniques mentioned for how to handle—pounce and pound.

Always carry a near, far, and too-dang-close weapon. A spear or bow for far; a throwing rock or stick for near; and a club or knife or poking stick for too-dang-close.

Stay mobile and always work to the outside of any game's striking range. All animals strike from their center, be it horns, claws, or jaws, so keep moving to their left or right, whichever is open to you, and keep moving in circles around them to break their concentration on attacking you, whether it's for your self-defense or to counter-attack them.

SCENT. Try to stay downwind, so that your scent doesn't blow to the animals and alert them.

Try to smoke yourself with the fire before you go out to reduce your human smell. Use soil or foliage to cover yourself in as a scent mask. And certainly don't do the morning wash up before goin' huntin'.

SILHOUETTE. Be aware of your visual presence on the landscape to other creatures. Move slowly, cautiously, and steadily, stopping regularly and always with cover (meaning real protection, like rocks or trees). Seek total concealment when possible and wait for a period of time. Be aware that even if you can't see any critters, they may be clocking you, so do all you can to keep from being seen at all times while on the hunt. Animals tend to detect scent and movement over color and shape, so, stay down wind, and move slowly so you don't catch their eye. And always stay away from the ridgeline so you're not silhouetted against the skyline. And stay near the wood-line (edge of the trees before an open field) so they don't see your shape standing out against the trees or bushes behind you.

SNARES AND TRAPS

Outside of hunting, the other way to get food is to capture it in a snare or trap and then kill it. I recommend using these techniques for smaller creatures, as these don't provide much food and so it doesn't justify using a lot of time and energy to hunt them. Also, they can be very difficult to catch, so best to let trickery and technique do the work for you.

The basic principles of traps and snares fall in line with those of hunting, except hunting is all about mobility operations, and "snaps" (snares and traps) are about static operations. That in mind, the old real estate axiom comes to mind—location, location, location! So, you must choose your "real estate" carefully. To do this, you apply the same techniques for hunting—looking for drops and tracks and then finding a home, hole or feed spot—and set up your "snap."

Snaps take a lot of time and work to initially set up. After that, they just require vigilance to check regularly to either get your catch or re-set your trap or improve it, as often the first-time snap setter will find they need to tweak their technique before they get the just right tension on the string, just right looseness of the noose, and just right hold for the trigger. Be patient, expect failures at first, but it will improve.

There are many, many different types of snaps and I have found many simply too hard to make, too difficult, too much work, or too hard to remember how to make in the first place. When these factors come into play, the end result is that the snap doesn't work. If it doesn't work, it results not only in a letdown physically because you go hungry but, because you've invested time that now seems wasted, mentally that can be a surprisingly bigger drain. So, I teach that it's better to know one or two snaps very well, that work very well and easily, than to have a multitude of stuff that sounds cool and looks good but frankly, only works for real pros who do it all the time.

So, I will teach and preach only one of each. What is the difference between a trap and a snare? In the simplest terms: string!

SNARES. If you have wire, twine, string, rope, or cordage of any kind, you can make a simple and effective snare. The cordage provides the mechanism for tension, which is the basis for a snare's spring action. And the trigger is what causes the release of the tension energy, by the animal's movement. So, remember it this way: SNARE the HARE. The hare has springy little legs and hops, and so the spring of the snare will make him hop right off the ground.

Snares are anything that will snatch your prey, ensnaring it by tangling up its limbs or wrapping around its neck. The best snare is the most basic and simplest one, as it is effective and easy to make, so you can make several of them quickly to increase your odds by placing them on numerous low-hanging branches in an area with various animal activity.

The **spring snare** is just what it says on the label. When it is triggered, it will pop like a spring under tension and snare your prey. The best way to make a spring snare is to take a small sapling tree and bend it over to look like an upside down "U"; then tie a small piece of string to its top, and tie the other end of that string to a little hook carved from a piece of wood which is then hooked onto a small stake in the ground with a notch to hold it; then tie another piece of string in a circle with a loosely fitted slip knot, and hold it open using two small twiglets.

Choose a sapling that's just on the side of a game trail, and add bait to lure the critter. It puts its head into the loop to get at the bait, and in doing so, it disturbs and inadvertently tugs on the looped string. This causes the string to pull the little wooden hook out of the notched wooden stake, releasing the tension on the little sapling tree which then springs back up to its original upright position. In the process, it snatches the noose tight around the critter's neck, snatches its body off the ground, and holds it dangling off the ground with the noose choking the life out of it. It dies, you find it and eat it. (If you don't have bait, the concept is such that the snare will be on a pathway that the creature will need to pass, and in doing so, will go through the loop, pulling on the string and the same net result ensues.)

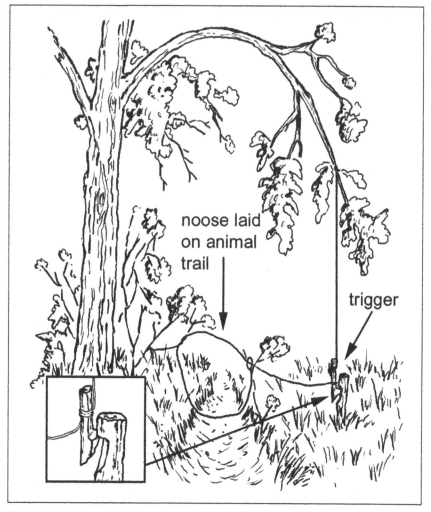

noose laid
on animal
trail

trigger

Snare preparation

Now, there are tons of variations on the simple spring snare, and it all depends on what is available to you—the sapling, the string, the knives for making the notches and stakes and hooks, etc. Most of it can all be made without a knife by improvising, but you do need the string or wire or cordage.

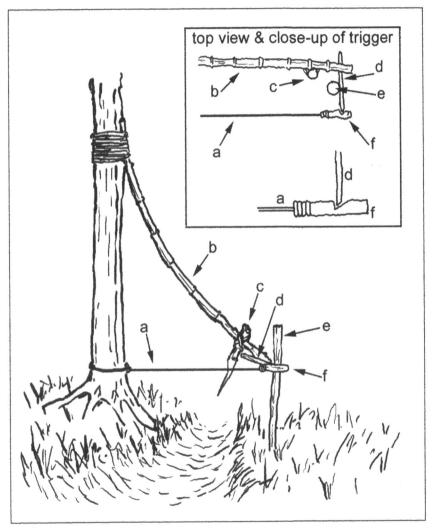

top view & close-up of trigger

Spring snare

The other thing to know is that it doesn't always work out as planned. Often, a limb will get caught or the mid body will get caught and the animal will hang there in pain and suffering until you come along and bludgeon it to death, or another animal comes and steals your meal, or it gnaws its way out, or it gnaws its own limb off to get away. So, check traps at first light and end of the day as a matter of course and habit. Make the rounds to check your snares often, and be prepared to immediately end your prey's life or engage larger game trying to get at your food. Take on the duties of checking your traps in a very mentally alert manner.

BAIT AND PLACE. Now both snares and traps can be used with bait or place techniques. "Bait" involves food or other form of attraction to lure an animal into the snap. "Place" simply means that you situate the snap on a well-used animal trail or lair. Ideally, you'd want to employ both bait and place combined to enhance your chances. Choke points are the key. It's just like setting up an ambush for soldiers—use the terrain to channel them in, then use a ruse as bait to lure them into the channel.

So, choose a good location, right outside of the animal's home, hole, lair, etc. Or choose a spot near the feeding grounds or watering hole that looks well used. The principle to these is that, no matter which route the critter takes, it will always come home, need water, and go to feed. So, these are ideal sites for laying your ambush.

Now, if you don't find such obvious sites, but you're onto a good game trail, as many critters will use a trail like a veritable highway, then use the game trail for your location. But when you do this, be sure to **"channel or funnel"** the critters into your newly made love-nest of hate, by laying logs, rocks, sticks and brush in a way so that it funnels them into your trap *both ways!* This important point is often overlooked by newbie snap layers. Picture an hourglass angle from above, so that a "V" focuses them into your trap from either direction of approach.

IMPORTANT: In all cases of snaps, be sure to reduce the amount of human scent on all of your snap materials. One effective technique is to rub your hands with dirt before making and setting the snap. Then use whatever you have for bait based one whatever you think the critter you're after eats. Often, the guts of other critters will get almost anything to come and smell and nibble, so offal is almost always a good choice for baiting, and usually that scent will overpower the human scent.

front view

top view

animal is
funneled
into the snare
from either
direction

Snare placement

TRAPS. If you don't have cordage, then you have no capacity for tension to make a snare and must use a different principle of physics to create a trap. Basically, traps use leverage or gravity as the mechanism of tension. The trigger is the loss of balance caused by the animal's movement, allowing gravity to apply the energy to execute your trap. Remember it like this: SLAP the TRAP. Just like you'd slap your hand down to catch a mouse trying to escape, your trap will slap down on your prey.

Figure-4 Deadfall. This is the most basic and common trap. You can use a large rock, heavy log, or other similar object to crush the critter. As an alternative method, instead of a large rock or log, you can build and employ a box, cage, or basket to fall onto the critter and trap it there until you come to finish it off.

The Figure-4 is easy to make, and can be constructed even without a knife by using your fingernails or a sharp rock. Picture the numeral 4. There are three lines in the numeral 4—one vertical, one horizontal, and one angled. Each of these lines will be a stick or log in your Figure-4 Deadfall, they will be held together with notches, and they will all stand under the weight of the deadfall.

How to Construct a Figure-4 Deadfall

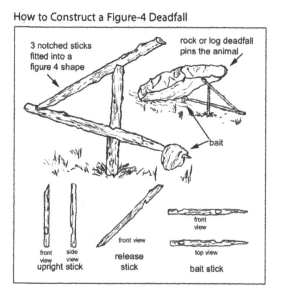

Figure-4 deadfall

The vertical stick needs one notch and one point. Carve the notch facing downward on the stick about 4 inches from where it will rest on the ground. Carve the top of the stick into a point.

The horizontal stick needs two notches. Carve the first notch on the side of the stick about eight inches from the end that goes under the deadfall weight; this notch should fit into the notch on the vertical stick. Carve the second notch facing upward; the angled stick's point will fit into this notch.

The angled stick needs one notch and one point. Carve the notch in the middle of the stick, on its underside so that the point of the vertical stick will fit into it. Carve the end of this stick into a point that will fit into the notch on the horizontal stick.

When the sticks are arranged into a "figure 4," first place some bait onto the end of the horizontal stick closest to where it will intersect with the vertical stick. Then gently place the weight (rock, log, etc.) onto the top of the vertical stick to hold the trap upright.

Now, the critter will smell the bait, walk under the weight to get to the bait, and when it begins nibbling, it disturbs the balance and triggers the mechanism. If no bait is available, then make the end of the horizontal bar long and wispy so that any animal passing through will disturb the balance anyway and set the trap off. Again, set your Figure-4 trap on a trail or in a key location. Make plenty and keep them simple.

With both traps and snares, it takes some time and finessing to make them, and there are no guarantees that the right-sized critter will come along or that the trap will work exactly right. So the real key to success is the "P for Plenty" method, also known as the "Shotgun Hunting" style. In contrast to the "One shot, one kill" motto of the sniper and good hunter, you need to set out lots of snaps all over the place in hopes that you'll get something, much like a hunter with a shotgun who shoots into the bush somewhat blindly, or at a flock of birds hoping something will get hit. So, instead of spray and pray, spread the dread so all the critters live in fear of you.

While the basic snare and the common Figure-4 Deadfall trap are the easiest and best to use for the novice, here are a few other methods of making traps that you may consider trying.

NETS. If you have a net, you can use the snare method but replace the noose with the net. You can also use a net with the basic deadfall method, and instead getting crushed, the animal will get ensnared in the net after it triggers the net to fall upon it. You can also use a net to hunt with, by hiding and then throwing it onto your prey as it comes near unaware. You can also use nets to catch birds and fish.

HOLES. When all else fails and it goes to Hell, start digging holes. It is hard work to dig holes, so this method is not to be undertaken unless you have energy to expend. But know that digging a simple hole is surprisingly effective for catching things. Snakes and small critters just seem to fall into them when placed in the right spot. Dig your holes (size and placement) based on the type of animal you believe is nearby and hope to catch. Regardless of the hole size, try to loosely cover it with light twigs and leaves, making sure that an animal can break through this cover and that the hole is deep enough to contain them once they do. If you have bait, place some in the middle of the cover above the hole.

BOXES. Another technique is making cages or boxes with a small hole for the critter to stick its head in and inverted spikes to hold the animal's head from pulling out, like a Chinese finger trap. The animal will press its head through the opening to nibble at the bait, but they won't be able to get their head out.

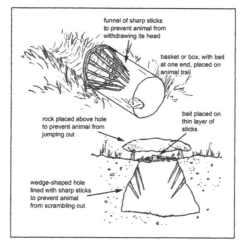

Box trap (top), hole trap (bottom)

HOW TO PREPARE ANIMALS FOR CONSUMPTION

BIRDS can be peeled out of their skins, but you lose all the fat. So pluck them as best you can, save the feathers for other uses such as fire starters, and then burn the rest of the feather stubble off by rolling the birds in the fire before cooking. All birds can be eaten, big or small, predator or scavenger—they are all safe. There are some rare birds with actual poisonous feathers, but they're generally not a concern.

MAMMALS are universally safe to eat. Some have poisonous sacks, teeth, claws, spikes, and many other types of defenses you should be wary of, but once killed and skinned and cooked, they are all safe to eat.

REPTILES are mostly safe to eat. *All* snakes are safe to eat once killed, beheaded, skinned, and cooked. So, too, are turtles/tortoises, lizards, and gators. Frogs get a little dicey, as some have poisonous skins. In general, the amount of meat on frogs is not worth the effort to catch, cook, and clean, but some big giant frogs might be worth the trouble, and all those big ones are safe to munch! Of course, if you can come by small frogs with little effort, grab 'em and eat 'em if they're not of the poisonous persuasion. The general rule for poisonous frogs and toads is that the very brightly colored ones are no good.

The general rule for all reptiles is to skin and gut them and behead them as well. Then cook or boil them. If you are unsure of what kind of critter you've got, try to skin it with sticks instead of using your hands as their skin might be poisonous. But once the skin is off, they're good to hook-n-cook.

TO SKIN OR NOT TO SKIN? Skin all reptiles. Skin most mammals (except pigs, as they cook better in the skin). Don't skin birds; pluck them instead. Scale fish; if no scales, skin 'em.

GUTS are to be put to their *best* use, not necessarily their *full* use. I teach that it's good to eat the key organs—heart, liver, and maybe the kidneys if large enough, but usually they're not. The rest gets a bit iffy and are best used as bait for traps and fishing.

BONES. If you can't use them for tools, or dry them by the fire for chalky anti-diarrheals, then try eating the marrow out of the big bones and boiling the small bones to get the marrow nutrition out of them and into a broth for drinking.

COOKING is best done by boiling, if possible, as it allows you to get good, clean fluids into your body and add some flavor to it. On a practical level, it is easy to drop everything in the pot and let it stew while you do other things rather than have to tend the fire and turn the meat so it doesn't burn. Also, when cooking meat, it helps to throw bugs and plants in for flavor and texture, plus you can avoid eating the bugs directly. If for some reason you can't boil, just cook the meat over your fire, rotating it often to cook it all the way through. You can also cook meat by placing it on a flat board close to the fire, also turning it to cook through (this is called "planking"). Or use sticks and lashings to build a spit on which to place the meat above the fire.

place food on a board close to the fire

place food directly on hot rocks or wrap in leaves or grasses and place in embers

hot rocks placed in liquid will bring it to the boil

Cooking methods

Foods can be smoked for storing and transporting. The key with smoking is to cut the meat into extremely thin pieces of flesh, hang them well spaced out on a rack, and make a small teepee around the rack that is nearly airtight so the strips can get the maximum smoke. Almost never does a survivor have a surplus of sugar, salt or fat, but all of these can be used to store your food for longer periods. Bacteria tends to not be able to grow on food that is completely engulfed in these mediums, so consider that as an additional use for these resources if you have them.

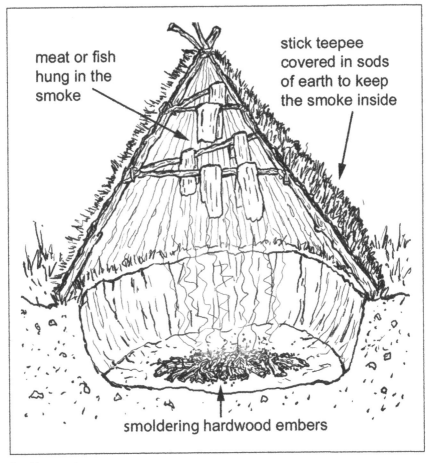

meat or fish hung in the smoke

stick teepee covered in sods of earth to keep the smoke inside

smoldering hardwood embers

Smoking meat

If you have plenty of sun, you can sun dry meat as well. Again, cut it in thin strips, hang a string or rope between two trees and out in the open sun, and fold your strips over the string. The one drawback from this method is that it often requires someone to be on "fly duty" to keep the flies away.

FISHING TECHNIQUES

If you're anywhere near water, going fishing is always a smart option. Tackle is not that difficult to make in the wild, the techniques of catching fish are varied and achievable, and almost all fish are good and safe to eat.

LINES are a bit tricky to come by and create, though very doable. The reality is, you can try to use almost anything light and relatively thin, but that doesn't mean it will work well. One of the most important factors of good workable line is strength. When you get a fish on the end of your line, it is going to thrash about and try to escape; weak line will make that easy to do as it will snap or come apart. Consider all materials that you have to create line. Or use thread or stitching from your clothes, stringy matter from plants or vines, and sometimes, found materials that are laying about. Always scan the shore of a lake or river; you never know what you may find, including actual fishing line. Whatever line you use, always make sure your string and hook can support whatever fish you're after.

HOOKS are very simple to make, actually. Any safety pin, paperclip, or other piece of bendable metal can be used. Make a good anchor point for tying the string and sharpen the working end as best you can, or make a barb or trap so that once they bite down, they can't get their lip back off the hook.

I have made hooks out of thorns, toothpicks, small bones, and many other things. The key is to fashion your material into the classic "J" shape that mark most hooks, sharpen the point on the hook end, and fashion a notch or a barb near that point that will catch on the inside of the fish's mouth once it goes in. If you have no metal or bone available, you can use the small joints in tree branches which provide a natural angle, and then

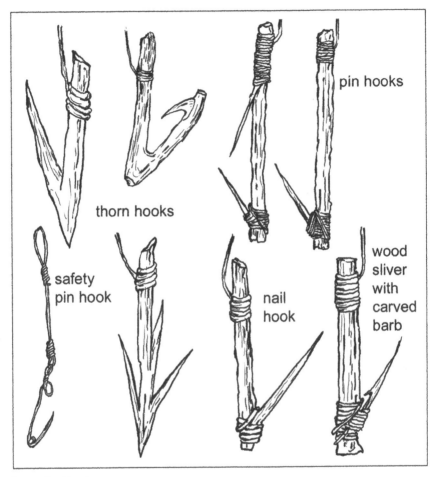

Improvised hooks

sharpen the smaller end's point; then make a notch on the anchor point at which to mount the line.

A good simple technique for any hook you make is to create a "barb." Just imagine a small toothpick with a notch groove around the middle. Tie your string there, put your bait on the whole stick in line with the string. When the fish bites and you pull, the stick turns perpendicular to your sting and in effect makes a barb in its throat that it can't spit out.

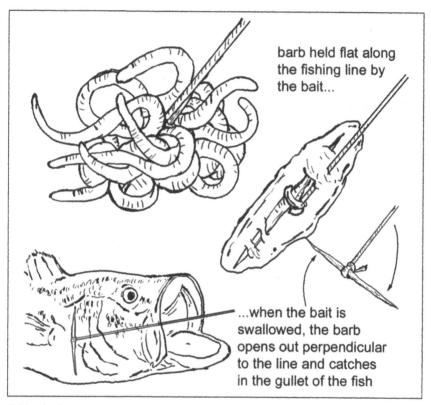

barb held flat along the fishing line by the bait...

...when the bait is swallowed, the barb opens out perpendicular to the line and catches in the gullet of the fish

Fishing barb

POLES are very helpful if you need to get your hook out farther into the water than you can without it. It also helps for taking some of the tension off your hand from pulling in the fish. If you have to put a lot of line on the pole to get it out farther, once you get a fish on the line, place the pole on the ground and your foot on the pole and then work the fish in by the string. I find two sticks or crudely fashioned gloves will help me work the string without hurting my hands.

WEIGHTS are sometimes needed either to cast out or to get your baited hook down to the bottom if that's where you think the fish are. For survival fishing, I find the best way is to tie a rock or other weight to the end of the string and then tie the hook with an additional piece of string onto the line 6–12 inches above the weight. Look for rocks that will be easily secured to your line—for example, a smooth round rock won't work as well as a rock with natural grooves to hold the line better.

BAIT is anything that you think will make the fish bite the hook. Bugs and animal guts are usually the best bait. You might consider "chumming" the water by spreading extra guts on its surface to attract numerous fish into a feeding frenzy, and then whack them with sticks as they feed. You can use insects, worms, berries, or even fish eggs from cleaning other fish. When you use bait in the traditional way, make sure you fasten the bait onto the hook or barb as securely as possible—you don't want to be giving those fish a free meal. If you can hook a live insect onto your hook, all the better.

LURES are a good substitute for when you don't have bait. Anything like feathers or light pieces of cloth can be used to mimic a fly or other insect to get the type of fishies that hop and jump. Anything shiny can be used as a "spoon" to get the underwater biters—tops of coke cans, small pieces of plastic, metal, or anything shiny that you can trim to a small piece and tie off to your string. Tie it just above your hook so it moves around right in front of but won't stop the fish from getting a bite on your hook.

FLOATS are useful in two ways. If you're after mid-depth feeders or just-under-the-surface feeders, then you want to mount to your line a piece of stick or plastic that will float on the water so your eye can see it, but will hold your baited hook suspended underwater and off the bottom, at the depth you set. Once in the water, simply watch the float or "bob" for any motion—when fish bite at the baited hook, the float will bob up and down telling you that it's time to pull in the fish.

The other way to use a float is just to let it get your hook out into the water where you want it. It will still function as a "bobber," but you're also using it to help in your placement by letting it float over to where you want, either with current or wind. In this manner, tie the bob just a couple inches above the hook.

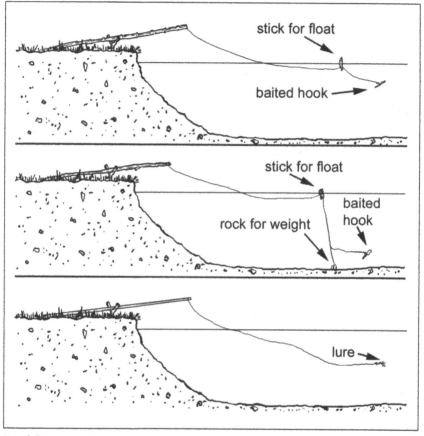

Line-fishing options

POISONS are also an effective means of catching fish, using naturally occurring roots and/or nuts in the water to disable fish and make them easy to whack or simply pick up as they lay atop the water in a daze. Instead of noting here all the specific plants and nuts that can be used, I'll simply give you a couple of specifics and general thoughts to remember. First, acorns are a superb fish poison—simply mash them up as finely as possible and then dump the material into the water. Stand nearby with a stick, spear, club, or net in your hands, and when you see fish begin to float or appear stunned, get 'em. Also, any of the roots or nuts that make water milky when applied are likely to be good. The concept is that these materials make it difficult for the fish to breathe and they float up where you can catch, scoop, or otherwise grab them—and the good thing is, this process doesn't make them inedible. The trick is that you'll need a fairly still area in the water so the current doesn't make your poison dilute and drift away.

FISH TRAPS are another good fishing method, and an alternative when you've got no strings or hooks. You can make traps for use in the sea, rivers, lakes, or ponds. In the sea, find a natural pool that fills up at high tide and becomes visible at low tide, and then build a gated fence with sticks and or stones surrounding it. For the sea, when the tide is high, chum your pool to lure fish in and then block the exit when the tide begins to go or the fish you want are trapped.

fish get trapped
in tidal rock pools
when the tide
goes back out

Tidal trap

The best river trap is made by building a "V"-shaped wall of stones and/ or sticks that will funnel fish downstream into the open end of the "V" and through a small opening at the point that leads to a holding pen also built with sticks/rocks.

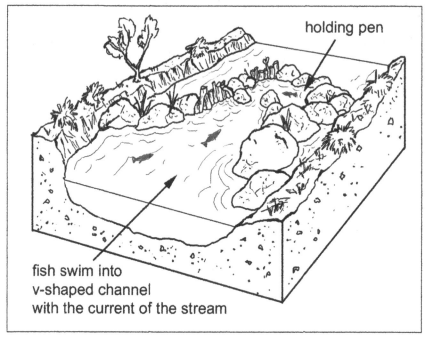

holding pen

fish swim into
v-shaped channel
with the current of the stream

V trap

For ponds, pick an area where you can make a "V"-shaped fish pen, then chum the pen area and try herding or scaring the fish into your pen. Since there is no current to help keep them in place, have a spear or club ready to disable and kill the fish that appear.

SPEARS are good to make and use for fishing, though they take some skill to master. The real trick is that the points have to be very small and very sharp, and to include several points on the end. The best kind are long thin spears with small nails at the end filed very sharp and positioned in a circular pattern, as opposed to horizontal like a dinner fork.

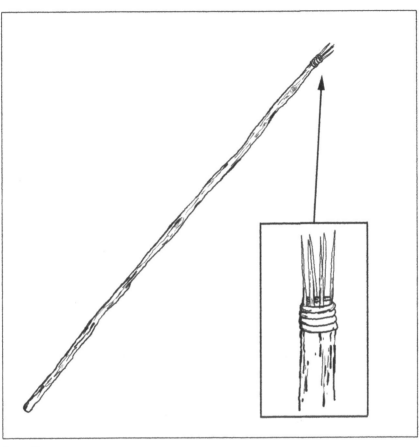

Spear tip

STICKS can be used with some success in shallow waters like ponds, slow streams, and shallow bays. In such settings, it may not be a bad idea to try this method first before spending time on the more time-consuming methods—at least for a few minutes. Stand in the shallow water and position yourself perfectly still, then wait. If you see fish swimming by and close to the surface, swing hard and directly at the fish's head. Often this will only stun a fish, so be ready to finish with several quick and hard whacks, or simply grab them and chuck them onto shore.

NETS are great tools if you have them. String the net across the stream or river in a manner known as a "gill net," placing it close to the inside bank of a river bend and going as far out into the stream as its length allows. In the sea or on a deep lake, if you have a vessel from which to fish, you can fasten weights to the corners of the net to hold it down just below the surface, then pull it up quickly to try to catch anything that may be in it. You can also use a net by standing on the bank of a river or lake and employ it by casting it on top of fish that swim by—just make sure the perimeter of the netting has enough weights tied to it to hold the fish down in the water long enough for you to quickly approach and club. You can also use the simple scooping-type nets to catch fish. If you have a smaller net or finer mesh, use that for the minnows and eat up. Or use the big net to try and head them off or divert them into the net, and then swing them onto shore or your raft.

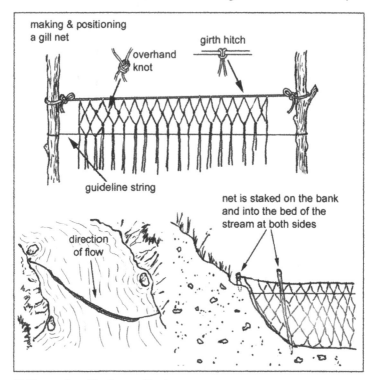

Making and positioning a gill net

LIGHT is actually an effective tool for hunting lots of things—you just need a flashlight or a little pocket laser or even something reflective that you can divert the sunlight with. Laser lights and flashlights that you point and maneuver on the surface can lure freshwater fish as they are attracted to the light and may check it out, allowing you to club or spear the fish. You can also hunt crayfish and frogs and lots of other critters with a flashlight as they are stunned, shocked, scared, or just dumbfounded curious, and they'll stare at that light until the next thing they know, they are seeing stars for the last time as you wallop them upside the noggin.

THE RULES FOR EATING FISH ARE SIMPLE. Eat them soon after you catch them—anything from the water spoils quickly in the air. If they look odd or ill or deformed in any way, don't eat them, but don't throw them away—instead, use them as bait. Anything with bright colors, weird shapes, strange colorings—just keep on fishing. Use all fish guts for bait, don't eat any fish guts. If they seem okay, clean all fish by gutting. Also, skin creatures like eels or catfish, and scale any fish that has them. Use the heads to make soups, and always eat them eyeballs! And some fish, like catfish or eels, can be tricky to skin, so try and stake them to a tree and use a pliers-like took to pull their skin off as if you were taking tight stockings off a fat lady's leg!

WHERE TO DROP YOUR LINE. Fish can usually be caught around the bank where water meets land. They'll often hang where trees and bushes go out into or over the water. They will also work with the sun—in other words, if it's hot they will go to the shaded bank or the deeper water, and if it's cold they'll come to the shallows or sunnier water.

Before you start, look around and scan the water to get an idea what the fish are doing—jumping or chillin'—and act based on that knowledge. If they're chillin', go work your line in front of them; if jumpin', try using flies or top-floating bait.

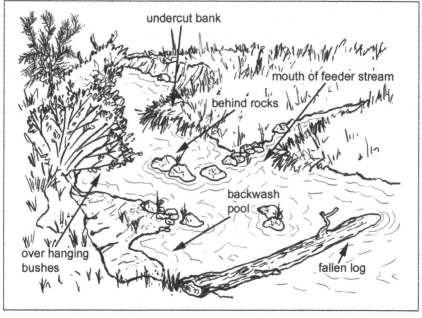

undercut bank

mouth of feeder stream

behind rocks

backwash pool

over hanging bushes

fallen log

Where fish are

EATING PLANTS

If I haven't made it plain and clear before, let me do so now:

Eating unknown plants can be deadly!

It's just plain dangerous to rely on plants as a food source if you do not *know* the plants you're trying to eat.

The other harsh fact is that plants simply don't give you enough bang for the buck. They do have nutrients in terms of vitamins, minerals, fiber, and maybe some starch and carbohydrate action, too. Such nutrition for the survivor is a secondary concern, whereas real energy in the form of calories is critical to the survivor and that comes best in the form of meat, plain and simple. But, if you find a lot of something, and it looks like it might yield a large amount of food, then the taste test comes into play. Of course this might warrant the ultimate risk factor—death.

Use all of your experience and common sense in trying to assess not only the quantity and quality of the potential food-source plant, but also its danger criteria. Use what you know to be good; and only after a taste test.

Does it look like anything you've seen in the store or restaurant before? Does it look like any food source you've heard of or seen pictures of?

Maybe there was something like it in that crazy local market you visited the day before you got stranded out in the bush; maybe you saw the picture on a menu last week in that Asian restaurant. Bring it all to bear in evaluating the next steps, as it might save your life, or end it. Now let's talk about the real dealio with the UET. . . .

THE UNIVERSAL EDIBILITY TEST

Okay, the first thing to understand is that there is NO failsafe universal test to see if something is edible or not. For example, there are plants that are fine when raw but kill if cooked, and vice versa. Likewise, there are exceptions for every rule out there for plants that are safe.

It is important to understand that the Universal Edibility Test (UET) really should be called the "Edibility Test Universally *Applied*." That is its intended purpose and why it was designed by the military. They recognized that wars happen all over the globe and that it was not uncommon for soldiers, sailors, and airmen to get separated during the course of warfare and become isolated in remote regions where they might need to rely on the land for food.

So the military designed a "universal edibility test" as a *guide* for soldiers to use to test unfamiliar local plant life and see if it was safe to eat or not. It's not infallible, nor is it the only way to go about it. Remember, humans have been trying foods forever and a day since the beginning of time, and that's really what it all comes down to—observation, common sense, and a calculated risk. So, let's look at some parameters to help you reduce the risk in the first place and then we'll discuss the UET by the "book" and its alternatives.

Understand that many people die every year from eating poisonous plants. It begins to border on "unintelligent" if you have animals around and the ability to catch and eat them. Almost all land animals are safe to eat, and once skinned and cooked, all of them are!

But let's say there just ain't no animals around, or you ain't caught none lately. When do you start eyeballin' plants to eat? Well, start eyeballing them right away. ALWAYS be on the look out for chow!

First, look for anything familiar. If you know what something is for sure, or you find a plant that looks a whole lot like something you know is edible, then there is a chance it might be of the same family or a local variation of that edible plant. So, that's a good candidate for starters.

Next, make sure there's lots of it. This is really important! No point in taking all that risk, and making all that effort, to get a handful of nibbles. If there aren't a whole lot of little things, or a few really big things, then it might not be worth the risk.

In general: Things that stink, sting, burn, or are barbed are usually not good candidates for the ol' taste test. *Exception:* prickly pears on cacti have mighty mean tiny spines but taste great and are very nutritious. Thistles are tricky ones, too, as are some of the crazier tropical fruits which have heavy "hornage" but juicy innards. Try to pay attention to all the exotic fruits and veggies in your grocers and markets to make a study of what some of these look like. The first time I saw papaya in the wild, I had no idea what it was, though I had eaten it plenty before that time.

The taro leaf, for example, is a food staple for many indigenous folks in the oceanic areas, but it's a poisonous plant because it has *oxalate* crystals which look like barbed spikes under a microscope. However, boiling takes all that out and makes a yummy meal of it. So, there are tons of exceptions. That's why the "universal" part of the edibility test ain't so universal.

Alrighty then, let's look at some of the classic indicators for perilous plants.

PLANTS TO AVOID

MUSHROOMS. These are tasty and they do have some (albeit very little) nutritional value, but the risks of eating any mushroom out in the wild is borderline suicidal! There are experts with years of study who still die from eating the wrong mushroom every year. For the survivor, mushrooms are simply OTL—Off the List!

Now, I know *some* good-to-eat mushrooms well, and when I've found them, I've eaten them because I found a large quantity and I could 100% identify them. But I never teach mushroom class to my students, because it doesn't pass the common sense test. You'll usually simply not find enough, and even if you do, they provide hardly any nutritional value. So, do not risk eating mushrooms.

And here's the kicker for mushrooms; the things can taste fine and you think you're all good and they turn around and kill you 24 hours or even days later when it's way too late to do anything about it. If you're going to try and eat the things anyway, then do try and cook them. But know this: many fungal toxins are resistant even to high heat, and so cooking the shrooms will not always kill the toxins!

SHINY-LEAVED PLANTS are generally taboo, but not shiny like banana leaves, we mean shiny when they look like they have a sheen from a light coat of oil.

YELLOW AND WHITE BERRIES are almost always bad juju, though there are exceptions. But for this book: if it's yellow, white, or even green, stay off it! (While we're on berries, the upside is that 90% of berries that are purple, blue, and black are good to go. Also, raspberries and similar "cluster or aggregate" berries are 99% safe.)

THE RULES FOR RED BERRIES ARE TRICKY. We all know strawberries and cherries are yummy as are cranberries, raspberries, salmonberries, lingonberries, etc. However, many red berries are poisonous, so the guide here is like for mushrooms—if you don't know it, don't eat it. Holly berries are red and juicy but these are toxic, whereas Hawthorne berries are dry but healthy. *Yes, I know the birds eat holly berries!* But that doesn't make them any less toxic to humans. In general, if the critters can eat it, so can you. BUT that is not the rule because some animals have immunities to these toxins.

UMBRELLA-SHAPED FLOWERS are bad.

PLANTS WITH THREE-LEAFED GROWTH PATTERNS are bad. Some of these are also poisonous to the touch, such as poison ivy.

MILKY OR DISCOLORED SAP is usually bad. One of the notable exceptions is coconut milk.

BEANS, SEEDS, AND PODS are generally best avoided unless you *know* them.

GRAINS are just tricky anyway because often it takes too many and too much work to be worthwhile, but if you find any heads with a *pink, purple,* or *black* spur just leave them well enough alone

PLANTS WITH A SOAPY OR BITTER TASTE are best left alone.

FINE HAIRS, SPINES, OR THORNS are signs of plants to avoid.

PLANTS THAT LOOK LIKE DILL, PARSLEY, CARROT, AND PARSNIP are often *very* poisonous, and that's a shame because they sure smell like the real deal. If you're truly desperate and have many of these roots staring at you as a potential food source, then risk the taste test at your own peril as the poison in the plant that resembles the edible persuasion is none other than the deadly hemlock—which can kill you in a hurry. Don't go there.

AN ALMOND SMELL IN PLANTS in general almost always indicates it's poisonous. Some chemical and biological weapons, like cyanide, also smell like almonds. Unless it's an almond, anything almond-smelling should be considered poisonous. Even if the almond smell is on the leaves and/or woody parts—skip it! (The counter to this is the general rule that plants smelling of onions and garlic are usually safe to try.)

MIND THE MANGOES AND CASHEWS if you're highly sensitive to poison ivy and sumacs, as these have similar properties on their surfaces that can cause a bad reaction.

DON'T EAT PLANTS WITH WORMS IN THEM as they are decayed—instead, eat the worms!

BURN, BOIL, WASH, AND PEEL! Try to peel everything first, wash everything you can't peel, and cook everything! Some plants from the water have giardia, and anything from the soil can have bacteria, fungus, and other parasites. So use these simple methods to best prepare your food for safe consumption.

Some plants, like acorns, are highly bitter due to tannin concentrations, but with a few boils and water changes, are excellent to eat. So, it's a bit of work and a learning game when it comes to plant selection and preparation. If you can't get fire, try rinsing in water and drying in the sun.

Now let's dig into the **Universal Edibility Test**. The column on the left includes official U.S. Army Survival Manual procedure, and the column on the right includes my comments and observations based on experience and application. Ultimately, it will be up to you to decide what you do and how you do it.

EDIBILITY TEST

MILITARY EDIBILITY TEST	HAWKE TASTE TEST
Test only one part of the plant at a time.	This is absolutely correct, but also neglects the common sense test. Most folks aren't going to arbitrarily take a plant, and mix it up and try and eat a salad.
Separate all the components—leaves, stalk, roots, flowers, fruit, buds, etc.	This too, tends to overlook the obvious. For most survivors who are starving, they aren't looking for all the parts to eat, they want that one thing they think they know that might be edible food, like a root, fruit, berry, nut, etc.

(Continued on next page)

MILITARY EDIBILITY TEST	HAWKE TASTE TEST
Smell for strong or acid odors; this alone cannot be relied upon.	There are some good foods that are stinky, but mostly, smell will tell you if you're on the right track or not.
Do not eat for eight hours beforehand	If you are starving, you probably haven't eaten for a little more than eight hours. The point is to have an empty stomach for the best "thorough" analysis of the potential food source as viable or not. Most people will surely be here by the time they're ready to risk their life by eating unknown plants.
During this time, test for any contact reactions by placing the part to be tasted against your inner wrist or elbow for about 15 minutes.	Touch it to the outer part of your forearm first, if no reaction there, then try the inner part—if it does flame up, the outer hurts a whole lot less. Nothing wrong with waiting 15 minutes, but really, five will give you a good enough indicator if it's gonna burn or not.
Scratch Test addition: Scratch a piece of your flesh with your nail and see if rubbing the potential food on that causes a reaction or irritation.	Some folks say to actually scratch yourself, and that is an option to be extra safe, but if you've got dirty fingernails and you're in the tropics, I don't recommend tearing holes into your only layer of protection from infection.
During the test, eat nothing except the part being tested, and purified water.	Well, if you've got purified water, you're already doing ok. The other point is common sense, but it is valid: if you've got other food, stay off it while testing so as to not mix or dilute your test results.
Take a portion of the part of the plant you plan to eat and prepare it the way you plan to eat it.	Mostly, if you have fire, cook or boil everything! No reason not to do so and lots of reasons to do so. Yes, cooking or boiling might take away some nutrients, but it will also take away more bacteria and toxins, which will hurt you a lot more. Boil if you can as that makes a broth you can drink to stay hydrated with clean water and still get some of those nutrients from the broth. But if you have nothing and no fire, then this test will be done in the "raw." But do rinse or peel whenever possible.

MILITARY EDIBILITY TEST	HAWKE TASTE TEST
Before tasting the prepared plant part, touch a small portion to your lip and see if it burns or itches.	Yep, this is rock solid, do it!
If after three minutes there is no re-action, place a pinch on your tongue and hold it there 15 minutes.	This is pretty good, though I think you'll know sooner than three minutes. One minute is likely okay for the first touch, but the 15 minutes on the tongue is a bit much. I say five minutes is good. You'll know if it's not right pretty quickly as you'll be so hungry and your juices will be flowing, so reactions will be much more concentrated and quicker.
If there is no reaction, chew it thoroughly for 15 minutes, but do not swallow.	Again, I say five minutes is all you need.
If there is no burning, itching, stinging, inflammation or other reaction, then swallow and wait eight hours.	Yep, if so far so good, swallow and wait. But I'd say, based on your sense of the food, closely resembling a plant you know or think you know, or if it's radically alien to you, wait up to two hours, four hours tops, though 90% of the time you'll know in the first hour or so.
If anything goes wrong, isn't right, or there is any negative reaction at all, induce vomiting and drink lots of water.	Yes, and consider some of the ash, charcoal diarrhea drinks as neutralizers too (see First Aid chapter). For emergency medicine, charcoal is used for poisonings when vomiting isn't possible or warranted.
If nothing happens, then eat ¼ cup's worth of the prepared plant part.	Or thereabouts; eat a decent amount but don't gorge yourself yet. If it's not good, it would be worse to have a belly full of it. So, go easy for starters.
Wait eight hours; if nothing happens, the plant part as prepared is safe to eat.	Again, wait awhile, two-to-four hours and you should know. Take a nap, get up, and move around a bit to see if activity induces nausea. But if all seems good, it's likely ok.
Army says the UET takes 24 hours.	Hawke says it takes eight hours.

UNIVERSAL EDIBLES

FRUITS, NUTS, AND BERRIES are found all over the planet. Even in the arctic it is possible to dig up berries from under the snow. The problem is that they come in so many shapes and sizes and colors. So, all one can do is to be on the lookout for anything that looks like these things, and then apply the rules of the UET:

Amount: Are there lots to eat, or are they big enough to make a real meal from a few?

About: Do they look like something you know or have seen before?

In Doubt: Do any warning signs—smell, touch, taste, look—call it into doubt?

If in doubt, throw it out!

Also keep an eye out for the critters around you. Are they nibbling on something? Could be a nut or berry. Are there lots of insects about? They could be attracted to some fruit. Look on the ground; I've often found fruit and nuts not because I knew what their trees and leaves looked like, but only because I saw some on the ground and looked up—they couldn't have fallen too far from the tree!

AN EASY WAY TO REMEMBER THE BERRY RULES:
* PB&B (like the acronym for Peanut Butter and Jelly, but replace jelly with "Berry") means Purple, Black and Blue Are Good for You (90% good to go!)
* Yellow, Green and White Mean Death by Night (90% deadly to know)
* Red can be good for the head, or . . .
* Red can mean you'll soon be dead (50/50 is the red way)

ROOTS, TUBERS, AND OTHER STUFF TO DIG UP. Anything you dig up should be cooked if at all possible. Not only is there concern about ground bacteria, fungi, and other evil spores, but the real deal is that roots are a concentrate of everything that's in the plant as its storage facility. So, boiling or cooking can neutralize any toxins or otherwise strong concentrations that might cause you some grief.

Secondly, it's real hard to just arbitrarily go around digging stuff up. That takes time and energy. So, try to have an idea what to look or smell for, and only commence to digging if you're pretty sure or, if there are so many of a plant sprouting up that if it does have an edible root or tuber, you'll be in a good stock for a while.

Again, look at the ground for signs of disturbance to see if any animals have been rooting around trying to dig up and eat some yummy grubs. Chances are, if they dug, they got it and ate it, so study the plant stalk they left behind. Look for more of those and try digging one up and see if it's paydirt. It helps to have a digging stick for this sort of task.

GRASS, GREENS, SHOOTS, STEMS AND ALL IN BETWEEN. Many plants that grow in and around water are edible. Also, people can eat grasses—not a lot, and they should only be the brightest green, newly fresh grasses, but they can be eaten—they are not dangerous and have some nutritional value. People do not have the enzymes needed to break down grass and get the nutrients out of it the way animals can, but a little grass in the diet can help a bit.

Many trees have brand new stems that are edible, or, when small little saplings are coming up out of the ground, they are often edible as well. Always apply the UET.

EATING TREES! One thing that really makes me happy is trees. In combat, I go into the trees and have my moment in the quiet before the storm. But the main reason they make me happy is all the good things that they mean. They mean life! They provide shelter, weapons, tools, lookout points, fire, transport in the form of boats or litters, and medicine as well. They also mean food. Not only do animals live and rest in them, providing you a hunting ground and source of meat, but you can actually eat a good many trees!

For example, the spruce tree buds, needles, and stems can all be eaten raw, but they're better cooked. Many fresh baby sproutlings can be nibbled on from a lot of trees like the evergreen (green year round) coniferous (plants with cones) pines.

Birch trees have an inner bark that is edible, as do pine trees, too. See the list of edible plants by region for a better idea, but many hard woods do have some sort of edible inner bark, and many winter trees have nuts, and many spring trees have edible shoots.

It's not ideal and certainly not a complete survival diet to go around nibbling on trees, but if you have an idea of which ones in general offer a food source, apply what you know, all your common sense and the good ol' fashioned taste test and you'll likely be alright and find something you can eat.

REGIONAL FACTORS

Alrighty then, all that said and you're still looking for food to eat other than killing critters. Let's take a general look at some of the most common plant food found in abundance in each of the world's regions.

DESERT

CACTI are all over most deserts and they're mostly edible. If you chop into them and they're green, they're good to go! If they have a white sap, don't rule them out right away—smell, finger-touch, lip-touch, and/or tongue-touch the sap. If no bad smell or burn, go easy at first; but figure it's likely ok. But if it don't look right, forget it.

AGAVE AND YUCCA FLOWER STALKS are good to eat and provide a decent meal. Cut off about three feet of the bud and stalk (which looks like a huge asparagus tip), peel the hard outside, and eat raw, or any way you please. The flowers of both are edible raw, but cooked is better as the yucca flower tastes soapy (in fact it can be used to make soap).

The fruit of both can be eaten as well, and it's best to eat while white inside. You can cut the agave down to its middle section and dig a hole that fills with water. After drinking, cut it off and cook it for a few hours—the agave is like a big potato, and the yucca roots are also just like potatoes.

DATE PALM is a good find. They look like the obvious palm tree but instead of large nuts, you'll see clusters of small round fruit. The best way to get at them is to cut the tree down. If you should happen upon these fruits—which are like coconuts and bananas—in the jungle, you'll know what to do and enjoy.

ACACIA are those little trees with the thorny spines and nice yellow flowers that smell good. These trees are all over the world in good quantities, and the best part is, a tree can feed you a whole meal as the flowers, the buds, and the young leaves are all good to eat.

AMARANTH is found all over the world as well. It is full of vitamins and minerals, and when found, it is usually in abundance. It can be eaten raw or cooked. It is also known in:

- Africa: Vegetable for all, or *yoruba*
- Asia: Different names all over, but the Chinese call it *yin choi*
- Latin America and Caribbean: Here it's called *callalou*
- US: Chinese spinach
- I'm a fan because it is easy to identify, plentiful, and has lots of protein in the seeds. It grows in any areas where it is drier in climate.

SEA

SEAWEEDS, KELP, SAMPHIRE and pretty much anything green from the sea or near the sea can be eaten. The seaweeds and kelps can be eaten raw in a pinch, but only take small amounts unless or until you can cook or boil them. Many of the harder shoreline plants are also edible, but best boiled. In general, most sea greens are fairly safe to munch, just make sure they're healthy and still anchored in somewhere. The only poisonous one you might encounter looks feathery, not leafy. Do not eat any sea plants that are colorful.

Ideally you'll want to boil your sea greens to reduce the salt, kill any bacteria and parasites, and generally make them more palatable. If you don't have fire, try rinsing well in fresh water if available and letting it dry in the sun. They can cause a laxative effect if too much is eaten without anything else in the stomach.

ARCTIC

Green stuff here is generally hard to come by, but it is there. Most of the mosses that you find on trees or the ground, and the lichens you find growing on rock, are all edible. In a pinch, these can be eaten raw, but are best boiled—a few times, in fact—to get out the bitterness and rinse them clean. These have been used in hard times as a food source by Eskimos. They even dry them out after boiling, and then beat them into a powder to make a nice starchy flour for bread.

ARCTIC WILLOW is a plant that you pretty much will only get to chow on its tender little sprouts in spring. If you're there in spring, enjoy!

ALL PINES AND SPRUCE are edible, and the same rules for eating apply to both. The needles are edible and make fine, nutritious tea. The inner bark is edible, as are the baby cones, as well as the pine nut seeds from young cones in spring. Most parts are almost always better boiled just because it's cold and you need the warmth and the liquids. These too have been used by Native American Indians of the Northern Tribes, who found hunting difficult after some longer harsh winters. As did the Eskimos; they would also eat these raw, boiled, or roasted, or dry the bark out to crush and use as a flour to make a nice carbohydrate bread source.

THE FERN is a fine plant for eating. But only eat the freshly sprouted tips that look like their nickname: "fiddle heads." These can be eaten raw, but are also better and safer to eat any quantity after boiling. They often grow in batches, so chances are you'll be able to get a whole meal out of them. They are starchy and high in vitamin C. The roots can be dried, then boiled and mashed to get the more than 50% starchy pulp out so as to be able to separate from the fibers that are also in the root.

FORESTS & MOUNTAINS

Lots of green stuff is out there, in volume, easy to identify, and safe to eat.

OAKS, PINES, AND BEECHWOOD all have edible inner bark, and for all the evergreens (except the yew, which has flat needles instead of round ones) you can eat the raw needles, baby cones, and seeds from the cones. The deal for eating bark is to peel off the brown stuff from the tree, then find a thin layer of slightly slimy but meaty bark, kind of like an inner skin—this is what you peel and eat. Not the dry outer bark, and not the hard wood inside. It will always taste funny, it's a tree! But it is edible and nutritious and filling. It is harsh on the trees, but that is survival.

PLANTS LIKE BURDOCK, PLANTAIN, CATTAIL, ARROWROOT, DANDELION, SORREL, AND SASSAFRAS are all good finds as food sources.

POKEWEED is poisonous if not boiled, but one plant provides a lot of food.

PURSLANE grows everywhere, often in open sunny areas. It is a thick, fleshy-leaf plant with all parts being edible raw or cooked.

CHICORY is one of my faves for making field coffee. To do this, roast the roots until dry and dark brown, then crush and use like coffee. Just look for the sky-blue dandelion-like flower on the base of the stem with milky juice. You're in there! Grows all over the world and all parts are edible, too.

THISTLE is good when you peel and boil the stalk, and eat the roots raw or cooked. It can usually be found in dry woods.

WILD ONION AND GARLIC, WILD ROSE, AND WATER LILY are good for starters. These are found most anywhere in such regions. For the few you might not be so sure about, look them up before you travel as they're very common, and once you know them, you'll always know them.

CAT TAILS are my favorite as they are near almost all swamps and ponds and small stream areas, and they offer so much food in that all of it is edible—raw if you must, but boiled or roasted over the fire, these are great grubs.

DANDELION roots and heads and leaves are good to eat—just discard the stems with their milky white sap (which makes a decent glue). They're good to eat raw or cooked. But try not to eat a lot at one go just because you found a field of them—tummy upset is likely to result if you do.

JUNGLE

PALMS are just wonderful things to find in the jungle. They mean life. Not only in terms of shelters and cordage, but they are a good food source. Cut the tops off and eat the tips, the soft parts, the flowers, the seeds, and the heart of the palm. This is high in fat energy.

ALL NUTS YOU CAN FIND are not only a great source of food, but they are excellent travel food as they'll last for months in their shells. So save these up for any journeys being planned. If you do find a lot of nuts, you can squeeze the oils out of them by wrapping them in a strong cloth and beating them and then using something to "press" the oils out. You can use the oils for your skin, cooking, candles, etc. Also, use the oil cloth as your wick for your oil candle.

COCONUTS are simply the gift of the gods in the jungle. They're easy to identify, but not so easy to get. Chop the tree down if you can't climb it, as that will be less risky than trying to climb and taking a fall. If you must climb the tree, coconut trees usually grow on an angle and you can get up it fairly easily. Use bare feet, and wrap a strong cloth or towel around the back of the tree and hold it on either side to create holding pressure, and walk up the tree by scooting the towel up after each few steps. They're not easy to get into, either, but worth the effort. If you don't have a knife, take a sharp rock and just start jabbing into it. Brace the coconut between some other rocks or logs to keep it in place while cutting. *Do not* use your feet to hold it in place; it's too risky as the cutting rock or knife may miss or slip off the nut and through your foot. Many cultures call the coconut tree the "tree of life" as they have so many uses.

BANANAS are another great source of food. Easy to access and plenty filling, they'll last a week or so depending on their condition, and the banana tree itself is a fantastic source of water as well.

INDIAN GRASS is another plant found readily in many warmer climates. There are many varieties, from the less-than-edible types of North America, sometimes called bison grass, to the more desirable types that are sour and often called lemon grass. The key to ID is simple—if you see a field of grass, it's likely bison, or if you see clumps of fat stalked grasses, these are likely to be lemon grasses. Simply pluck one and taste—if sour, it's lemon; if almondy, it's bison. Both can be eaten and are best added to soups.

PAPAYAS are super to find because they are so huge that one will fill you up. But like any of the soft fruits in the tropics, they will go bad quickly, so consider slicing them very thinly and drying them in the sun for longer use.

BAMBOO is also awesome to find for the absolute all-purpose utility of it. The baby shoots can be eaten raw, although they can be bitter. Boil with a few changes of water to make them a lot nicer tasting.

SUGAR CANE is not a likely find, but it is all over the tropics as a remnant from failed plantations. Peel the outer hard layer and enjoy, as these are very nutritional.

TARO is found all over in the tropics, and again, it has to be boiled to neutralize the oxalates. Once that's done, the leaves and the roots provide super tasty greens and starches, and one plant can make a whole meal.

WATER LILIES are plentiful and actually tasty, but it's real hard to get out there and actually pull up their tuber roots. Once done, boil or roast and enjoy.

SOPS are some crazy-looking fruit to most Americans. They are mainly in the tropics of Asia and there are two kinds—sweet and sour. They are tasty and plentiful.

EATING BUGS

Bugs are everywhere on the planet, and since they are often at the bottom of the food chain, that means there are more of them than anything else. So, they are more plentiful than the animals and a whole lot easier to catch. They are also more plentiful than edible plants and provide a whole lot more energy and nourishment than the plants.

So bugs become, by simple math, one of your best survival food resources, period.

That said, let's look at some basic bug nutrition to help you get your head around the fact that you're gonna need to be eatin' them, and which ones are better to focus on getting if you have a choice.

BUG NUTRITION

That phrase just sounds yummy saying, doesn't it? Okay, I am not one of those folks who likes to eat bugs, or even thinks it's funny to gross people out with as a cool party trick. And I have literally eaten giant cockroaches, huge maggots, big fat grubs, spiky crickets, biting praying mantis, and many other assorted flavors of creepy, crawly critters and slithery slimy worms, etc.

But I've only done it to demonstrate to folks that it can be done, and that I can and will practice what I preach. My first option is always to kill bigger animals to live, but if I were to be wounded or ill, then I might have to eat whatever I can get my hands on within crawling distance, e.g. bugs!

I also teach that while hunting is the best way when able, it would be pure foolishness to ignore the insects as a food source and a good supplement to any diet out in the wild. So if you see 'em, eat 'em! As a matter of fact, many people eat these things daily or as a delicacy in various cultures. So, that said, let's look at the real value of eating some of these, and you might be surprised how they stack up.

Let's use two well-known forms of meat as a standard—pure beef and cod fish.

For 100 grams of lean ground beef, you get about 28 grams of protein and no fat.

For 100 grams of broiled cod fish, you get about 27 grams of protein and no fat.

Now look at comparable protein and fat statistics per 100 grams of the following insects:

BUG NUTRITION

Insect	Protein (g/100g insect)	Fat (g/100g insect)
Grasshoppers	20	6
Beetles	19	8
Termites	14	0
Ants	13	3
Crickets	12	5
Worms	9	5
Caterpillars	6	0

*Compiled from studies from Africa, Mexico, Iowa and Wisconsin.

Making the case for bug eating even stronger is the fact that, while bugs might not have all the protein of the pure meats of the fish and cow, they do have more fat and that makes them actually better for surviving than the pure proteins with *no* fats.

Taking it one step further, and putting to rest the issue of "can you or can't you bring yourself to eat bugs" once and for all, the bugs come with a lot of other minerals, vitamins, and nutrients that the pure meats don't provide. Since an insect is a complete life form, it stands to reason it would have a more complete amount of nutrition provided by its complete consumption.

In short, bugs are probably one of the best survival foods if you can get enough of them. If the quantities are lacking, then the use of them as you catch them to supplement your diet. That said, let's look at the rules for eating them.

BUG DINING RULES

BEETLES, CATERPILLARS, ANTS, CRICKETS, GRASSHOPPERS, COCK-ROACHES, ETC.—all the commonly known insects—are pretty much fair game.

The general rule is if they are brightly colored, smell foul, have spikes or barbs, or bite, then you might want to avoid them, but that doesn't necessarily rule them out. Remember, everything has exceptions!

It's almost always better to boil them or roast them on a hot rock by the fire or on a stick. Remove anything hard like shells, legs, wings, pincher heads and stinger tails.

HAIRY INSECTS should be squashed and the guts thrown into the broth for boiling; or burn the hairs off with the flames.

SPIDERS are edible, but they're really not worth the time or risk as you usually only get one at a time. However if you find a huge tarantula, then chuck him in the stew.

SCORPIONS can also be scarfed. Yup, they're on the menu, just be careful, remove the stinger, and cook well when you can.

BEES are very nutritious and often come in bunches. There are two tricks to eating bees. One, you must kill them before they kill you. And two, you must remove their stingers before eating them. To kill them, use smoke, and try to go after their nest at night. They'll be less inclined to attack then. Smoke them out by putting some good smoky material in their hole and sealing it. Then check the next day, being ready with more smoke. If they're dead, scoop out the score. The honey is delicious and nutritious and you can eat the comb or use it as a wax for other things like candle light or water sealant. If you have a known allergy to bee stings, then stay outta the honey pot!

SLUGS AND SNAILS AND WORMS are all edible, but they require an extra step. Soak them for a day or so in water to get them to purge their guts, then cook them up well. Again, anything brightly colored, especially around the sea, is likely dangerous and is better to leave well enough alone.

That's about it on the bottom of the food chain, and for food in general. The good thing is, there's lots out there to eat! It takes some doing, thinking, and getting used to, but mostly, know that there is food out there and you'll be ok in that regard. Just mind the water and shelter and you've just about got it licked. And Never Quit!

Tools

The first thing you do in a survival situation is make an inventory of what you DO have. Anything in your vehicle (car, plane, train, however you got there!) that can be used as a tool or weapon, take it. Everything else you need to survive—in terms of weapons and tools—you'll have to make do with the materials you find around you in your environment.

Of course, you will likely be in an environment in which you may cross paths with predators that could hurt or kill you. So, as you begin looking for shelter and fire materials, and water, the first thing to do is to pick up a stick or rock to use as a protective weapon.

WEAPONS FIRST

There are absolutely two things that must be with any survivor at all times: a Stick and a Knife.

What you have available will determine which one is the priority. If you have a knife already, reach for a stick as soon as possible from your environment or circumstances.

If you don't have a knife, fine for now—a stick is actually easier to produce and handier immediately in most cases. Let's look at what is so important about these two items and ways to go about making them.

THE STICK

Picture a standard, sturdy walking stick as your intended quarry. But this is much more than just a walking cane. This is you all-purpose survival stick.

THINGS TO CONSIDER IN ATTAINING A GOOD SURVIVAL STICK:

- Find one that is about 6–12 inches taller than you.
- Look for the straightest, strongest one you can find.
- Use a manmade material if it's available, like a pipe or metal rod.
- For your best bet, find a strong sapling tree that you can cut to fit.
- Select a stick just big enough that when you grasp it, your fingers and thumb touch.
- Choose a stick with a natural fork at the top (or make one).
- Carve a point at the bottom.

This will give you the ideal survival stick, which will provide all sorts of uses. Let's look at some of these criteria, and at some of the various uses of this invaluable tool.

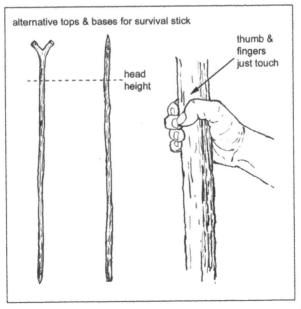

The survival stick

HEIGHT. If the stick is too short, you risk serious injury by having it jam into your eyes or neck if you should fall during night travel or if you're moving under illness or injury. Choosing a stick taller than you will mostly ensure that this will never be a problem.

Also, when it is just a bit higher than you, your stick can serve as a great measuring device. You might determine how deep a river is, and whether you can cross it or not; it may also help you safely find footing while making a river crossing. You can use the stick to determine if you could jump over a chasm—just lay the stick on the ground and see how far you can jump beside it, then use the stick to try and touch the other side of a chasm. If the stick is strong enough, it might even be used as a small bridge. It can help you determine heights—to see if you can jump down from a tree or cliff, etc. It can be used as a pole when rafting, for steerage in the water.

The stick also gives you extra reach for nuts and fruits in trees. This is one area where the fork at the top is very useful as it can be used to wedge between fruit and the tree and then leverage it away from its branch. It becomes a digging tool for you for roots and water. The point makes it a good weapon for deterring any wild animals that might be considering making you their next meal. The fork also becomes a weapon if you need to pin the head of a snake or trap a small rodent until you can finish it off. Finally, the fork might become a bit of an arm rest if you end up using it like a crutch, and this is the only time you should make it shorter than your height.

THE POINT. As soon as you find a good survival stick, spend a few minutes carving and shaving down the end into a point. The point will serve as a weapon, as a poking device to spear fish or birds, and as an extra measure of stability as you use it for walking assistance. Now, the point obviously won't stay a point for long if you're leaning heavily on it while walking. I tend to only use my stick as a pacing aid unless I'm tired or pulling uphill or using it to lean on going down steep slopes. I also use the stick to clear brush out of my path where there might be snakes, or use it to stir critters from bushes into my trap or into a blow by my waiting club.

SAPLINGS. If you don't have a knife, converting a rooted sapling into a survival stick can be a challenge. The thing to do is bend it far enough down to still leave you the desired length, say a foot more than you need near the base, then twist it until it gives way. I generally twist it on itself in its roots. Then take a rock and smash the end off where you want it. Then use the rock and rub it against the bottom to make your point. One of the benefits of using a green sapling is that they have more give so they are less inclined to snap on you when under some weight, plus they won't burn as easily when you're using the stick to hold a pot over the fire. But, if you find a nice, good, dry piece of hard wood that works for you, then use that by all means.

THE FORK. I try to find the natural point where the tree bifurcates or splits off for branching, and trim those down by breaking them off to leave me a nice fork for the top. The fork is optional—use what you can find at first, and after awhile your eye will begin to notice better survival-stick material as you go.

HAND GRIP. If you have time, consider making a hand grip area and attaching a "dummy" cord. This is just a piece of string or rope used as a lanyard that keeps the stick tied to you so you don't drop it or forget it. This is not to say you are a dummy. Any soldier who has done multiple day patrols without sleep will tell you that you become semi-delusional, you start seeing and hearing things, especially at night, and in this state, it is easy to forget something. For example, if you get startled by a creature in the night and run, it would be sad to have lost a good tool; and what's worse, if the creature pursues, without a lanyard you wouldn't have your stick to protect you. So it's a good practice if you have the cordage, to tie all your key stuff to you for just such exigencies.

OTHER USES. I've used my survival stick as a lean-to frame to make a quick shelter. You can also use your stick as sort of calendar/day tracker, by carving a notch for each day you're out there to help you maintain a sense of time. Also, carve your name into the stick in case it gets lost and someone finds it, or to use it as a marker to show that you were there. You may also want to keep track of your kills, or the number of times the stick saved you, in order to give you a sense of accomplishment and pride. In Prisoner Of War training, we call such things, "little victories"—it is exactly these sorts of things that keep you hanging on and strengthen your resolve when it waivers. Yes, the almighty walking stick truly becomes one of the most important and useful tools in survival and is so often overlooked. Acquiring one is one of the first things you need to do in a survival situation—it will quickly become one of your favorite things.

THE KNIFE

If you have one, that's great—you've got a lot of your tasks handled already. If not, look to make one pretty soon into your situation as it is simply the most valuable tool for survival.

If you have any metal, that will be your best resource for making an improvised knife. If you got a blade with no handle, find a piece of wood to wedge it into, or wrap the handle portion in something safe such as clothing or leaves.

You might find a scalpel, a pair of scissors, maybe a butter knife or some other similar household item that can be modified, sharpened and used as an improvised blade. You might find a nice chunk of metal that you can beat with a rock and form into some sort of cutting utensil. Consider anything metal than can be sharpened—like the zipper toggles on your pack, or the metal pieces of your suitcase, or maybe even your belt buckle or purse strap.

Other items that can be fashioned into some sort of cutting or slicing tool include coins, nails, glass, and plastic (if it is thick and strong enough).

SHARPENING YOUR BLADE manually is a bit of a lost art since most modern knives stay sharp a long time due to their excellent machine-made razor edge, plus, many modern folks use an electric or otherwise automatic sharpener at home. Most field people carry a small sharpening stone for this purpose. Many primitive peoples will find a very good flat surfaced stone and it will become the tribe's sharpening stone.

The basic principles of sharpening are fairly easy to grasp and only practice will help to refine your technique. I recommend trying to sharpen some knives at home, as this is the only way to develop the technique.

THE STEPS TO BASIC KNIFE SHARPENING: Use a rough or course surface to grind down the bulk of the blade's edge (this is often called a "dry stone") using a bit more strength in the strokes.

Then use a smoother surface to get a finer edge on the blade. This is best accomplished with a literally "wet stone" (wet it with water) using longer, controlled strokes.

Use soft gentle strokes in a sort of arcing motion to refine the edge.

Start by keeping the sharp edge facing toward you while you stroke the blade against the rock away from yourself.

Change directions when you turn over the blade to the other side; this gives a sort of saw cross-cut on the blade and the end result is a more razor-like edge that slices more efficiently.

It is key to keep the angle of the blade consistent with each stroke—approximately 20 degrees off the sharpening surface.

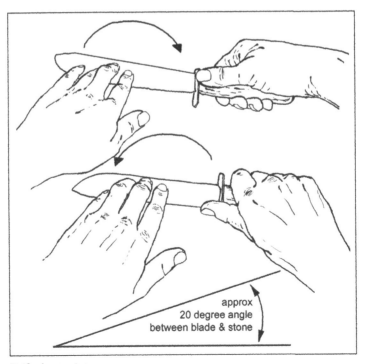

approx
20 degree angle
between blade & stone

Knife sharpening

While sandstone is not good for making a knife, it's the best for sharpening one; if there's no sandstone, any gray-colored clay-like rock, or rock with glitter in it (such as granite), will work pretty well.

The smoother the sharpening rock, the better.

NATURAL MATERIALS FOR MAKING KNIVES

Many things found in the wild can be used to make a knife, as well as other weapons and tools, including wood, stone, bamboo, shells, and bones.

BONES. Animal bones are some of the more handy items that are often overlooked by modern folks in the outdoors. If you find some deer or other antlers, consider yourself lucky, as you'll be able to use them for several purposes. Should you find a carcass—be it recently killed by a predator (make sure they're done and gone; vultures are a good sign of this) or some really old rotted corpse—if the bones are good and strong, pick through them and get the good ones you can still use. The key when working with bones is to first sterilize them by fire to kill any harmful bacteria.

To make a **bone-blade knife**, find yourself a good bone, like a leg bone, and break it in half with a rock. Take the shard that looks most knife-like in size and shape, and sharpen it up with a stone per the method described above. Then wedge it into an improvised stick handle, or wrap it in cloth or natural materials to protect your hands. Try to keep the outside of the bone as the sharpest piece, as it has a harder surface area than the marrow side and will hold an edge longer. This should last awhile; and when it starts to give, make another.

Bone-blade knife with stick handle

Bones can be used for many other purposes as well.

Some cultures use bones to make booze, and some use them as an aphrodisiac. We won't be dealing with those items, but I have successfully used antlers as a good **poking weapon**. The antlers are tough to break, but you *can* break them off. Then sharpen up the point a bit and you will be able to use it in a sort of tearing manner to incise game—it's better than using your fingers by a long shot. You can also lash a rock into the forks in the antlers to make a decent **club**. I have also used dead cattle horns as **drinking cups**; these come off fairly easily after a certain amount of decay has set in.

Femur bones also make great **clubs** (another name for a hammer for the survivalist). While shoulder blades can be made into a **saw**, it takes a lot of work to carve the teeth on the blade, unless you have a knife; best to use it for a club or a modified axe or machete. You can use various bones to make a **rucksack frame**, or **snow shoes**, or other such framing purposes. When you find a nice set of bones, take a moment to study them and then creatively apply them to your problem-solving needs.

Jaw bones of big game can be used as a **make-shift saw**, as well. The skull might become your **bowl**. Look at how much skin is left on the bones; is it worth salvaging to make shoes or a sack?

Bones can be used to make **buttons** by taking a small piece, rounding or smoothing the edges with a rock, and poking or boring a hole in it with a hot piece of steel (like a heated-up safety pin). Or just make a toggle-type button, which looks like a short pencil with a groove in the middle into which you fasten the tie to the cloth.

Bones can be used as **needles** as well. If you can, bore a tiny hole into the top through which to run the line. If that's not possible, make two small cuts in the back end, slightly off set from each other so that you don't cut right through the thing, and then tie your thread material with a small knot so it doesn't slip.

Bones can be used to make **fish hooks**. Fish and bird bones are especially good as they are very small and light and have natural points that are easily sharpened up. So, dig through any dead bird bones you find. But make them safer to work with by sterilizing them in the fire to burn off any residual flesh; or, at least, let them get good and sun-bleached if time is an option.

Bones can be used to make **arrow heads**. When you break the bone to make the knife, sift through all the smaller pieces to find any that have a shape you can work with; sharpen them up and make them into spear heads which can be lashed to sticks (for arrows) and spears.

Bones can be ground up into a sort of **chalk to help slow diarrhea**, but more on that in the First Aid chapter. Hooves can also be melted and used for **glue**, but that's only if you have the materials such as an extra pot to boil them down in.

The point is, use everything, everywhere, all the time.

WOOD. In most environments, wood will be the most readily available thing to use to improvise a knife. It may seem a bit odd at first to think that wood can be used as a sharp-edged tool. In fact, it is more common that we realize and is actually still used by some peoples as a first-choice even today.

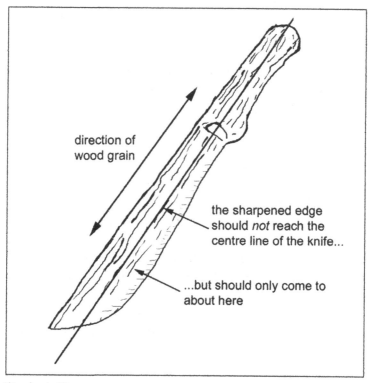

direction of wood grain

the sharpened edge should *not* reach the centre line of the knife...

...but should only come to about here

Wooden knife

KEY FACTORS FOR SELECTING A PIECE OF WOOD
TO MAKE A KNIFE:

- Find a piece about one-foot long.
- The harder the wood, the better (use the thumbnail test).
- Use live wood, not dead dry wood.
- Select a piece where the grain goes the length of your in-tended blade, and not horizontal (the grain is the little lines, of a slightly different color, you see inside the wood; these indicate how the tree grew and as such they show its stronger side).

Once you find a nice piece of blade wood, the next step is to use a piece of stone to shave it down by scraping the rock against the blade area (the top 6 inches or so). You can rub the rock against the stick, or vice versa if the rock is too big. The idea is to make one side of the blade the *sharp edge*, and make the other side flat or blunt.

Rub the intended sharp edge on both sides of the blade so that you have two halves that bevel and taper down to a blade.

The trick here is to make sure that the sharp edge does not go to the center of the piece of wood. It should go 90% of the way there, but not actually to the core or this will make the blade much weaker.

BURNING THE BLADE. Once you have the foot-long hardwood selected and filed down to a basic knife shape, then it's time to temper it with some fire. Place the blade near enough to the fire to get it nice and dried out—this will take some time, maybe an hour or two depending on environment. The drier it is, the harder it becomes. Once it is well dry, then work on the actual edge of the blade. You'll want to hold this right at the edge of the fire so it's almost licking the blade, and get it just barely blackened, but not burned. This area will then be ready to make a finer blade by rubbing a smoother stone against it. The same technique for sharpening steel applies to wood. Go gingerly so as to not break the edge, but once finished, this will actually slice pretty well for a while.

It will need some re-firing and sharpening, and eventually will break or give way, but it will be a very utilitarian item for you for awhile, maybe a week or month depending on how much heavy use you put it through. Nice to know you can make a knife almost anywhere, aye?

SHELLS. On the seashore, wood might not be readily available, but often seashells will be. These make excellent cutting tools. The handle might be trickier to fashion without wood, though you can use cloth or other natural materials. The edges of shells can be sharpened quite nicely against a stone or another shell, and these blades will hold an edge for a while.

BAMBOO. Bamboo makes an excellent blade, and I have used this many a time. The same basic techniques for wood apply to bamboo. Find about a two-foot-long section of bamboo. Break it to get a piece that's about one foot long and about three inches wide—basically make it a width that is comfortable for your hand when you grip the handle area. If the shard is too wide, it's easy to scrap the edges down to a comfortable size. It is better for the bamboo piece to be a bit too wide rather than too narrow, for strength and longevity.

Once you have the raw form of the knife, start to sand down the blade portion. Again, the concept is that one edge should be flat and blunt, and the other edge is to be the sharpened side—do not make the sharpened side bevel above the center point of the blade face. By keeping less on the blade side, this makes the back, blunt side more of a supporting ridge for the knife itself. Remember, at the end of the day, it's only about a centimeter that does the actual cutting work.

In this case, like with the bone blade, as you sand away the bamboo to get the edge, shave down the *inside* of the bamboo as it is softer. This makes it easier for you to smooth but also, keeps the harder, enamel like surface on the bamboo which means it will hold its edge longer and therefore, serve you better as an improvised blade.

Once the bamboo is ready, again apply the fire drying and tempering. Then again, slightly char that edge and smooth it into a nice sharp edge.

COCONUT. I'm not sure why I've never seen it in any books, but I've found that a good hard coconut shell actually makes a good cutting tool.

It's probably not often considered because it is curved and, as such, doesn't fit well on a handle. But a nice triangular shard of coconut shell can be very sharp on one side, and the other two sides will remain plenty dull enough to not injure the hand when working with it. I've encountered many coconuts in the wild and a whole lot less bamboo, so, give that a whirl if stranded on an island with coconuts.

STONE KNIVES

We all know man has been making weapons out of stone since, well, the Stone Age. But for modern man, it may seem unusual if not outright undoable. In fact, it's very doable.

First, not all rocks are created equal. Some are inherently better for making into tools than others. So before you start to smash and break rocks, take a good look around. Try and find rocks that are either exactly what you need or very close to it in their natural state. This little bit of looking could save you lots of time and effort. And in survival, energy saved equals life!

Once you find a rock that looks like a good candidate for a blade, take into consideration its composition. Stones like sandstone or shale will simply shatter or crumble when you start whackin' at them with other rocks. It won't take you long to figure it out, but generally, the dark, harder stones work better for shaping.

By the way, most of the rock knives I've made looked horrible, but they did cut and did the work I needed of them. So don't fret if your handiwork doesn't produce a masterpiece—the goal is simply utility.

Making a knife from stone is one of those tasks best done when you have some time, several hours to a day, to sit down and work on it. It'll take some refining of your technique to figure the right angles for striking the stone to eventually give you the rough shape you're striving for. As the stone begins to take form, pay attention to the pieces you whack off. You might get a most unlikely looking piece that just happens to be a very sharp and thin-edged fragment. If so, consider stopping and using that as your knife blade, or as an arrow or spear head.

THE THREE ROCK TOOLS NEEDED TO MAKE A STONE KNIFE:

BREAKER. This is a large rock, like a sledgehammer, used for breaking a large stone down into manageable knife-sized fragments.

CHIPPER. Think an oval rock, like a small hammer, used for further shaping the stone blade down to its useful dimensions.

FLAKER. This is a flat piece of sharper-edged rock that you use to flake off the last bits of stone in order to give your stone knife its edge.

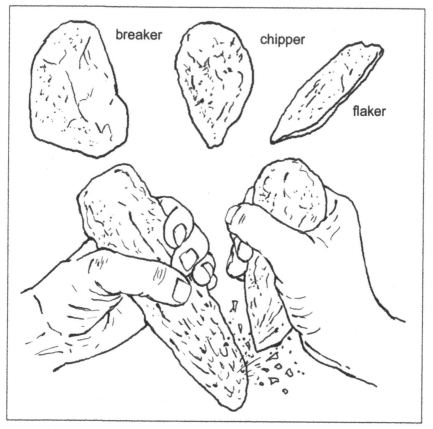

Knife-making tools

Once you break a starter rock with the breaker, look for the best piece to begin forming. Then use the chipper to give it the basic knife shape. Then use the flaker to create an edge with small taps, at a sharp angle, away from you. Then you can try to actually grind this edge against other stone to give it sharpness.

The basic principles of knife-making apply throughout. The ideal length of your finished knife is about one foot—that's six inches for the blade and six inches for the handle. Too long and you run the risk of it breaking while you work on it, which can also cause injury (ask any Amazon native jungle guide and they will tell you all about their "machete bites"). The blade should actually be a few inches longer, maybe eight inches or so, in order to fasten it to your handle. A knife that is too short is also risky, as you may overextend yourself in an effort to counter its shortness, resulting in a cut or gash.

Once you've chipped and flaked your blade, secure it into a handle. You can wedge the blade into a piece of wood, bone, or antler; or wrap cloth around the end and fasten the cloth with cordage; or tie the blade onto a stick or piece of wood with some lashing. The key is to make the strongest, most comfortable handle you can, as a bad handle can lead to blisters, and then infection. If you're going to wedge the blade into a stick, try to find a stick that is slightly split on one end (or split one yourself) and slowly thrust the blade into the slit until it's secure, then fasten it with cordage.

OTHER POTENTIAL WEAPONS

Now that we've covered the basics of the two mainstays in the armament of the survivor—sticks and knives—let's take a look at other potential weapons.

DIRT. Never underestimate the value of good old-fashioned dirt. In a pinch, you can grab a handful of dirt and throw it at a predator, aiming for the eyes to hopefully drive it away. In the absence of anything else, I recommend doing so vigorously and repeatedly!

Also, you can use dirt to try and stun or shock smaller game long enough for you to close the distance and stomp on them. Not ideal, but when there is nothing else, it's worth the effort.

If you don't have any weapons or stones handy—for example, in a desert or beach environment—you can fill a sack or t-shirt with sand or dirt and use it as a rock-like weapon. This can also be fastened to a small stick to make a club; or it can be used as a sort of sling weapon to be spun around and let loose towards your target.

These methods are best used as a last resort. But it's good to keep in mind that everything can be utilized and exploited, however creatively, for your needs.

ROCKS. These were probably the very first weapon humans used. If they are around, keep an eye out for the ones that will make better projectiles for your purposes. Your strength should determine the best weight for you to throw. You want to have the ability to give it a good thrust, and potentially to throw it a decent distance, so it should be manageable. But you also want it to do some damage when it hits, so it shouldn't be too light.

Take some time and practice your aim, as no two rocks throw alike. I find the smoother ones give me a bit better aim because there's less resistance as they roll off the fingertips to change their trajectory. I also find the smoother stones are better as your prey is usually some distance away, and there's less resistance on smooth stones flying through the air. Also, a well-placed round smooth rock tends to impact the prey with a core shock that stuns them or knocks the wind out of them long enough for you to get to them and finish them off. This is particularly true with birds.

I sometimes find that a rock with some nice pointy part or sharper angles and edges work better on rodent-like prey as these rocks have more chance to fracture bones. This means they will either stay in place due to pain or not get as far as fast due to limitations.

You might choose a large rock to drop on prey, or just to have near your hunting site for finishing off what you catch. Basically, it's good to have various types of rocks as readily available projectiles in all circumstances. They are good for all the reasons noted, as well as for flushing game out of bushes, or throwing at predators in an attempt to discourage them from putting you on the menu.

THROW STICKS. Throw sticks are different than your basic walking stick discussed above.

The **rabbit stick** is basically a non-returning boomerang. Find a solid stick with a bend in it the shape of a boomerang. Anything about two feet long should work. The advantage of the rabbit stick is that you get more leverage on your throw due to its angle, and that means it delivers more impact on the target. Seek out a naturally curved piece of the hardest wood you can find. To throw it, point your non-throwing arm at the target, then whip the stick either overhand or side-armed, whichever is more comfortable to you and gives you more power and control.

The **"Hawke-daddy special"** is a modification of the rabbit stick that I've used effectively. I sharpen points onto both ends of the stick so that if they happen to hit, it will pierce or puncture and increase the damage, thereby increase my chances of disabling the critter.

CLUBS. These come in a variety of styles. The simplest is the good ol' fashioned log-type club, usually a tree branch with the heavier side for whacking and the thinner side for handling (sometimes you need to scrape down one side to get a thinner grip). Keep on the lookout for a good animal leg bone, shoulder bone, or jaw bone that could work as a club. Also look for a tree branch with a natural big knot in it—if you can find a fresh one on the ground, great, providing it's still strong and solid. If not, try to cut it from a tree. The hard knot makes an excellent weapon as it's a very heavy, strong, and hard part of the tree and is not likely to break on impact or with heavy usage.

The best sticks for clubs are usually the harder woods so they don't snap on impact. You should try to use a greener stick to keep it from being too brittle and to better hold the rock in place.

The best rocks to use are the darker, harder rocks that have a bit of an oval shape so you get more force of impact over a smaller surface area.

FLOPPY CLUBS. This is basically a stick with a string tied on the end, and a rock tied to the end of the string. The best length for the string after tied to both the stick and stone is about 3–6 inches.

What this does is give a lot more "oomph" power than a regular club in that the extra few inches gives it more leverage as you swing the club, giving the rock more momentum and delivering a more powerful blow.

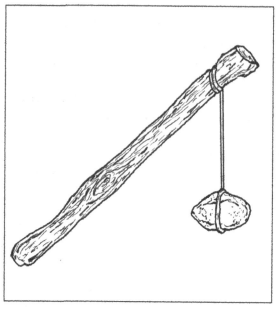

Floppy club

Be sure to make a good notch in your stick so the string doesn't slide off with the weight and force of the whipping stone. Also, the stone should not be too big, maybe 1–3 pounds. Anything heavier is too difficult to wield in the field under survival circumstances, as you are always weaker and tired. Also, make sure the rock is nice and smooth so its edges don't eat through the string after a few whacks. In general, I don't rely on this weapon much as I find the accuracy too challenging to accomplish in a dynamic situation.

HAMMER CLUB. This is great for a number of reasons. Not only does it simply make a great tool—a hammer—but it also makes a great weapon, and is fairly easy to make. Just lash a good stone to the end of your stick and voila, you have a hammer club.

There are three ways to lash the rock to the stick:

FORK TECHNIQUE. The best and most practical way is to use a stick with a natural fork in it that will fit your rock nice and snug naturally, then lash it in with your best cordage.

SPLIT-STICK TECHNIQUE. Split one end of your stick, wedge your rock into it, then lash it in and put extra lashing at the base of the split to keep it from splitting the stick further. This method is okay, but I find the stick often ends up splitting eventually anyway, unless you have a lot of cordage and can really wrap it tightly. But the split method is good for temporary uses and when you have limited cordage as the pressure of the split will do most of the work for holding a well placed, well wedged rock.

BARK-WRAP TECHNIQUE. If you find a stick with flexible bark, you can break it and keep a long strip on the end to fold over the rock at the end of your stick. This is not the best technique, as the force of the rock can sometimes snap the bark. But in a pinch, it's another technique to know.

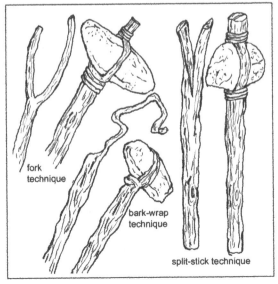

fork technique

bark-wrap technique

split-stick technique

Lashing techniques

HATCHET CLUB. This is similar to the hammer club, but with a rock that has a sharper edge to be used as a hatchet, tomahawk, or axe. Find a rock with a triangular or wedge shape that has more weight at the back and a finer point at the front. Then chip and flake away to give more of a cutting edge, but not too much edge or it will tend to disintegrate on impact against any hard surface. It's good for certain types of chopping, such as when you are trying to make a structure with larger logs, like perhaps a raft.

SPEARS. These have been around for time immemorial. The basic spear is just a long, strong stick with a sharp point at the end. In its simplest form it is best used for lunging and piercing mid-sized game such as a small pig or doe. It takes some skill to effectively throw a spear. Because the standard spear is best for lunging and not for throwing, they should be very strong. When I select a spear for stabbing and jabbing, I use the lion as my guide. That is, I select my spear so that if I came up against a lion, my spear needs to be long and strong enough to thrust into his neck, chest, heart, and lung areas without exposing me to the reach of his deadly claws and without it breaking. Further, the point must be sharp and strong enough to forcefully pierce his flesh. Let this be your guide for spear making.

Making a spear is pretty simple. All you need to do is find a strong, fairly straight, and long stick. Scrape off any knots or other imperfections in the area where you will be holding it, then sharpen the point. That's pretty much it. But if possible, you should always fire-harden your spear(s) by using the method described above regarding fire-hardening wooden knives.

THROW SPEARS. A throw spear is different than a regular spear in that it is a much lighter and therefore frailer stick. It would not hold up well against the lion model. However, with the addition of a good spear head, the throw spear becomes a great hunting weapon for mid-sized game that might be aggressive. Wolverines, boars, coyotes, and bobcats come to mind as smaller critters that will put up a mean fight if cornered.

The best piece of wood to use for a throw spear is a green (i.e. not dead) hard wood, and about thumb-sized in diameter. You can make these into a very long javelin-like spear (about 9 ft.) or very short type of throw-dart spear (about 3 ft.). These can be made even more effective when a sort of sling shot device is added, called a "spear thrower." These have many names in many cultures throughout time, such as "atlatl" or "woomera." With a pouch of leather or paracord, it provides more leverage and delivers more power to the throw of the spear, resulting in a more forceful blow to the target.

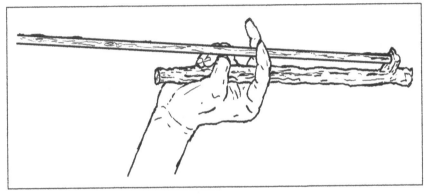

Throw spear

Spear heads come in a variety of options. Anything sharp is good. Usually, the pieces of rock that are too small to be a knife and too big to be an arrow head make a good spear head. Bone can be used—just find a piece about six inches in length and file it down into a long nail-like point. If the bone is wider, you may file it down into two points for a forked spear head or three points for a trident spear head—the more dangerous the working end, the more damage it inflicts, and the greater chance of your dining that day.

Metal, glass, or anything sharp and hard can be made into a spear head. The more weight the better, but too much weight and you'll likely not be able to use it as well.

The lashing is important in order to keep the head attached as it makes its impact upon the game's hide and bones. Any give in the lashing and the whole thing may just be an exercise in futility on your part and lucky for the game.

MAKING AND LASHING A SPEAR HEAD. Choose your material, be it stone/rock, bone, glass, etc. Chip it into a basic long arrowhead shape, then file it to a finer edge and sharp point.

Add a tang (or "tongue") to the base of the spear head that will fit into the stick and help make the lashing that much more secure.

Split the end of the spear *slightly*, and wedge the "tongue" of the spear head into the split.

Use cordage to lash the split stick back together, forging the spear head into the stick as tightly as possible, locking it in.

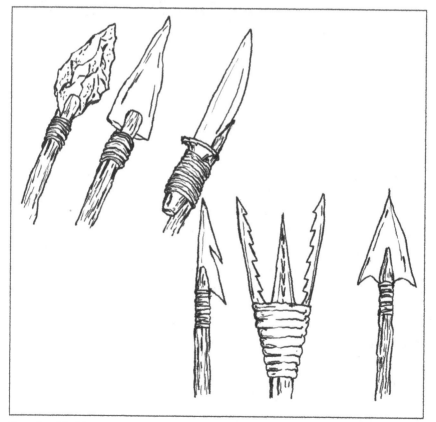

Spear head lashings

One advantage of the throw spear over the regular spear is range. You can project your reach with a throw spear, but to do so accurately takes a lot of practice. The best way to throw a spear is with the hand catapult method. (aka: Spear Thrower)

Basically, spears aren't the best projectile weapons for a survivor as they take some work to make, and a lot more work to master. It is probably best to use your stabbing spear instead, skip the throwing spear for land game, and make a lighter spear with finer spear points for fishing (a much easier proposition than hitting mammals). A spear with three prongs (nails, long thin bones, pieces of wire, or even three long thorns) for pinning and piercing smaller fish works really well—just keep a string tied to it for retrieval and you're good to go!

BOLAS. This is a super easy (to make and use) and fairly effective weapon for hunting. It's just three rocks tied to three strings which are tied together at the other end. The bola is swung overhead and then, after a few whirls, let loose in the general direction of the prey. The concept is that the bolo will either whack the prey with one of the rocks, maybe all three if you're lucky, or, if the rocks miss, the strings have a chance of getting tangled around the critter giving you time to close in and finish it off.

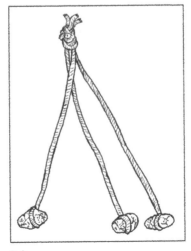

Bola

SLINGSHOTS. Most people know what a slingshot is from childhood. This is basically a forked piece of wood (or any other material that will do the job) with some rubber, tubing, elastic, or other such material tied tautly to both ends and with a pouch in the middle for holding your projectile.

These take a little practice to perfect, and can be quite effective for killing small game. I use it for field mice and birds as it usually delivers enough impact to kill them dead on the spot. Plus a slingshot gives me a good enough range to get close enough to critters without scaring them off. Also, slingshots are fairly accurate and quiet, so even a near miss will often not cause the critter to scurry away, allowing me to adjust fire and whack away.

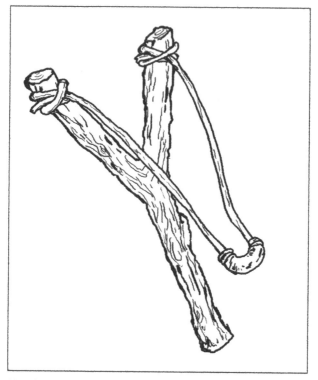

Slingshot

SLINGS. A sling is what David used to slay Goliath. Any cordage of about two feet in length, with a small pouch fastened to the middle, and with a moderate-sized smooth-edged stone, can become a fairly accurate and deadly weapon with some practice. Tie a knot in one end of the string, tie a loop in the other end of the string, and fasten a pouch to the middle of the string (the pouch can be a piece of animal skin or clothing) into which you'll place the projectile.

Here's how to use it:

Place the looped end around your index finger.

Hold the knot end between your thumb and index finger. Place the rock in the pouch, give about three good circular swings overhead, and let it fly at your target by raising your thumb to let loose the knotted end while the looped end stays firmly around your finger.

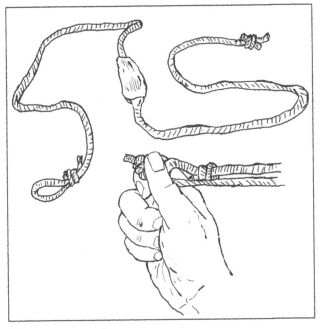

Sling

Before you start hunting, practice for awhile to increase your accuracy and velocity.

BOW AND ARROW. The bow and arrow are the classic weapons of the primitive world. I don't always recommend using these as they are time-intensive to make, but if you find yourself in a long-term survival situation, they can improve your mammal-hunting success. On the other hand, I *have* made and used many bows for short-term fishing as this is an effective method for rivers or ponds where you can see the fish but can't quite get at them. A good bow will thrust an arrow right through the water and into your prey.

For the basic bow, find a nice strong sapling of about 4–5 foot high from top to bottom. Choose a hard wood that is green and fresh. Find the piece that has little or no knots, branches or sprouts. This will give you a good solid stave or bow.

Cut the sapling, trim and slightly smooth down the outer surface. Leaving the middle third of the bow in its whole, solid state for strength and for gripping, you want to shave the top and bottom thirds so that they gradually begin to taper towards the end of the bow—these two thirds should be about a third of the original thickness of the stick. Do this shaving and tapering only on one length side of the bow; the other side should remain completely solid from top to bottom as this will become the backbone of the bow. Then cut perpendicular notches into the top and bottom of the bow, just an inch or two from the ends, for tying your string or cordage.

Start by using the best cordage you have (sinew and paracord woven together is a great combo). Lay the cordage straight out on the ground next to the bow, cut it so that it's just longer than two-thirds the length of the bow, and then tie a strong small loop at both ends. With the shaved length of the bow facing you, bend the bow to about two-thirds of its original length and slide the cordage loops over the ends and into the end notches. The bow is now ready. When not in use, it is best to unstring your bow. This will prolong the life and effectiveness of both the bow and the cordage.

Basic arrows can be made out of any long, thin, strong branches that are as straight and as free of knots or twiglets as possible. Shave them or scrape them down to create as smooth a shaft as you can make. Cut the back end of the arrow to create a flat tip, then cut a slight horizontal notch across that tip into which the string will go. Then cut or file the other end of the branch to a nice point, harden it with fire, and you have the simplest of arrows. About two feet long is ideal.

You might try making simple arrow heads for your arrows as well, to give them a greater efficacy for killing. Take shards of rock, shaved bones, nails, flakes of shells, glass pieces, scraps of metal, or anything you can fashion into an arrowhead shape and wedge in and lash to the point (use the directions for spearhead lashing as a model). Finally, to add finesse and increase control, add two or three feathers to the back end of the arrow to create "flights." These can most simply be fastened with cordage near the back end of the shaft.

Once you've got your bow and arrows made, practice for awhile before you start hunting (shoot your practice shots at something that won't break the arrows). A bow and arrow works well for all kinds of small mammals. Even if the arrow doesn't kill it on impact, a good hit will disable the critter long enough to allow you to move in for the kill.

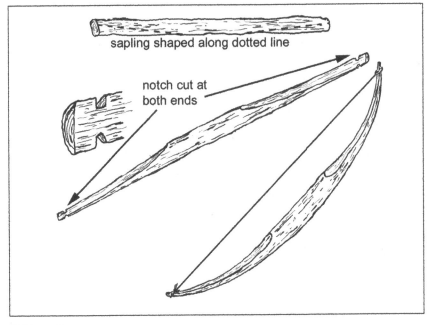

sapling shaped along dotted line

notch cut at both ends

Making a bow

BLOW PIPES. Now this isn't the easiest weapon to make or use, but I don't want to leave anything out of your mental arsenal of possibilities. If you happen to have some tubing, or can find some hollow reeds, or can bore a vertical hole through a length of bamboo, then you might be able to make a usable blow pipe. The basic concept is that you need a long tube (about five feet) that's hollow through the middle and has openings on both sides. If you don't have the materials noted, or the tools to make it, it's best not to try to make a blow pipe—too much time and energy.

But if you do manage to get a decent pipe, you'll need some darts. Small nails, paper clips, or other light, thin objects like sewing needles, thorns, fish and bird bones, thin branches, or even wires can be used. Whatever you use, sharpen the point as best you can. Also, the darts will need a base on the opposite side of the point which will create a good seal once placed in the tube, and which will assist the flight. You can make the base from cork, foam, Styrofoam, feathers, etc.—anything light enough to travel quickly out of the tube and through the air. Think 3–5 inches for the dart length.

To use a blow pipe, place the projectile just inside one end point-side first. Place your mouth around the opening, creating a tight seal with your lips. Aim the blow pipe just slightly above your prey, take a good breath, then release a thrusting puff of air into the pipe to shoot the projectile.

NETS. If you have the time, the patience, and most importantly the cordage, then making a net will provide you with a great multi-purpose tool. Nets can be used for catching fish, snaring birds, trapping small game, as a hammock to sleep in, as a litter for a patient, or as a rucksack to carry your goods on the move. This is why I try to carry the U.S. Army Jungle Hammock at all times, as it does all these things very well. If I don't have it, I use it as my template for making my net. And if I'm lucky and have some 550 para cord, I'll use the guts and the casing to make a net. If not, I make string from sinew or plant matter or whatever I can. Dental floss is a good improvisational material for nets as well.

Start with two 10- to 12-foot lengths of strong string for the top and bottom of your net (the main lines), and as many 12-foot lengths of finer string for the interior of the net (the core lines) as you have. Tie the ends of both main lines to two trees about 10–12 feet apart so that you've got about 8–10 feet of main line across the top and bottom to work with. Tie one at about eye level and the other just below waist level.

Next, take the core lines and fold them in half so that they're about 6-feet long each. Using a prusik knot (see **Knots** below), tie each of these core lines to the top main line—about one inch apart—until you have as many "pairs" of core lines hanging down across the length of the top main line as are available.

Now you're ready to start making the net. Starting with the far left "pair" of core lines, tie these two together about one inch down from the main line, using an overhand knot. Then take the inside line of this pair and tie it to the closest string from the next pair over, also about an inch down from the main line. Next, take the other string from the second pair, and tie it to the closest string from the third pair. Repeat this process until you get to the end, then reverse direction and continue back the other way. Do this back and forth—creating a diagonal pattern of squares—until you get to the last two inches of core lines. Then tie the bottoms of the hanging pairs of core lines to the bottom main line, and you've got yourself a nice 3-foot-wide net.

To catch fish with your net, use sticks to stake it in across a stream, and weight the bottom with rocks if needed. Or, tie small rocks around the edges and use it as a throw net. Or, stake one end down near the riverbank with a vertical stick, tie the other end to another vertical stick, and walk in the water in as wide a circle as you can, coming back and closing in on the original stake—see what you can trap in your net that way.

For birds, you can spread it across an area where they fly through often—such as an opening between trees. For small game, you can throw the net over them and tangle them in it long enough to finish them off. Or spread the net out on the ground and tie the ends to a snare-like spring that can spring up and net your prey that way.

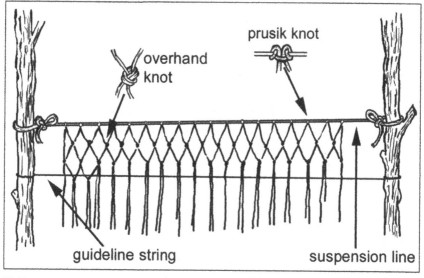

Making a net

NOOSE STICK. These are handy little things. They are really more suited for traps and snares (covered above in the Food chapter), but what I have in mind here are nooses as they can be applied as a weapon.

First, make your noose with a slip knot out of thin wire or strong thin string; even a high-strength fishing line can be used. Then take a strong stick about 3–4 feet long and a diameter that provides a comfortable grip. Tie your noose to one end of the stick so that the loop of the noose is just a couple inches removed from the stick. Now you have an extended-reach garrote that can be very effective if you can get close enough to a small mammal or bird.

Some animals will freeze when they see a human. In remote areas where humans are rarely seen, they might have no fear whatsoever. When you can get close but can't get a clean whack at them with a club—such as with birds perched just a little too high, or critters in a hole or crevice—then the noose stick becomes handy to reach up or in, slip on the knot, quickly and forcefully choke the animal, then haul 'em out and eat 'em up.

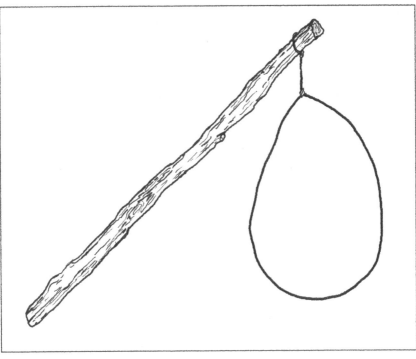

Noose stick

TOOLS

Let's now look at other tools and techniques you can make and employ in the wild using all the materials available to you in nature.

LATRINES

Wherever you are in a survival situation, you'll need to utilize the facilities. Of course, if you're short on water, you'll be drinkin' that first round of urine, or using it in your solar still, or condensing it in a boiling pot, or something! But if your water flow is good, then you'll need to take a moment to reflect on the disposal of your bodily fluids. This becomes particularly important if you're stuck in a contained area or with a larger group of survivors.

URINAL. These are not normally needed for most survival situations. However, you should take note of where you choose to urinate. You might want to do so into a small hole you kicked open with your heel, then cover it up. Or you might want to pee all around your camp site to mark your territory and keep predators out. If you opt for this, do so outside of your own smell range and a fair distance around your perimeter, such as 30 meters.

If you must confine urination to a small area, it helps to build a piss pit, or urinal tube. Make a hole about 1–2 feet deep and 6–12 inches wide, and fill it about two-thirds full with gravel, sand, rocks and bark. Then take some bark or a large-leafed plant, roll it into a cone shape and place it into the hole, fill the rest with dirt so it props up the cone, and then build a mound with the displaced dirt around the cone to support it. This will give you a field-expedient urinal that will contain the urine, disperse it into the ground, and keep the bacteria under control. Keep insects at bay by keeping it covered when not in use with another large leaf or piece of wood or sheet of bark. These are good for larger groups staying put a while. Change them around as needed and keep them about 50 meters from the camp if you can, downwind, down range, and down slope of water and camp.

CAT HOLE. You'll always need to defecate in the field as well, and you *always* have to cover up your feces after you do so. To make a cat hole, dig a hole at least one foot deep and one foot around, and cover it up with sticks, leaves, rocks, whatever is available. But always cover it as it not only attracts insects, which then land on you and your food and spread disease, but it may attract larger animals that find human feces to be a delicacy and will seek it out to eat or just to roll around in. You don't want to invite such critters to start hanging around your survival camp. So, always go further away from your camp to dig your cat hole in which to defecate, like 100 or 200 meters. When the hole is filled halfway up, it's time to dig another one.

If you are in groups, consider having people go out to the cat hole in buddy teams. People are exposed and vulnerable to animal attacks when in the defecation position. Also, when surviving, people will be fatigued and they might pass out with some medical problem. It is a bit odd and uncomfortable but try to use buddy teams whenever separating from the group—the more minds, the more hands, the more solutions and help, the faster and better and easier things are done.

HYGIENE. It is extremely important for survival to maintain good hygiene. Use water, sand, or sun and air if that's all you have. If you don't have soap, it can be improvised by taking some animal fat and mixing it with some slurry ash from your fire pit (slurry is ash mixed with water), then boiling the lot. Let it cool and harden, then slice it into bars you can use. This will clean you to a degree, but is not antiseptic. Try to add some pine sap or pine needles to the brew when boiling to give it some antiseptic properties. Soap-making is an art, so experiment to find a good mix that doesn't dry your skin too much and cause irritation. Use soap for cleaning all your tools, especially after handling game and cooking food. Some plants make a soapy residue when crushed; experiment, and if you happen upon these, use them.

WASTE DISPOSAL. You will always produce by-products and waste if you are living outdoors. Try not to waste anything. For anything you make that results in leftover bits and pieces, find a use for them or save them. Wood shavings from whittling can be used for bedding, insulation, fire re-starting, etc. Save everything—just keep it in a pile or in a makeshift storage area. Take a look at it every day and see if any new ways of using something come to mind.

For leftovers from animals, try to use or save what you can. Clean bones and cook them over the fire to dry and destroy the small bits of meat left, then store—either in a hole covered with dirt, or in a makeshift sack tied up into a tree. For parts like offal or guts, use them for traps or fishing, even if it's just to chum the waters and make fish come to your area for easy feeding—just be sure to chum the water *downstream* from your normal water and hygiene areas. Whatever you absolutely cannot use that is organic and will decay and smell and attract insects and other critters, put in a pile for burning. Just make a bigger fire than normal and slowly put the organic matter in the fire. If fire is not an option, then bury it as well as you can, and do so far from your camp.

WASTE RULES: Organic = BURN, Inorganic = SAVE

UTENSILS

You will always need something to help you eat. This keeps your dirty fingers out of your fire-cleaned food and keeps the food from getting under your nails and growing bacteria which will find its way into your mouth and make you sick.

Spoons are the hardest utensil to make as they require a good deal of carving, which means you need a blade. If you have one, great, make a spoon primarily for eating soup-type meals that consist of water and a bunch of things you chopped or smashed up that are too small for a fork.

To make a spoon, find a solid piece of wood just larger than the size of spoon you want. Scrape off all bark and imperfections, draw or carve an outline of a basic spoon shape, then start whittling. Once you've carved out the shape, start to dig out the bowl. When that's done, sand the entire piece down with your blade or, lacking a blade, a combination of rocks from gritty to fine.

If you need a fork, try to find branch that is already in the shape of a "Y" and use that. Trim and scrape the bark, fire-temper it to dry it, harden it, and take any smell or resin off it. Then use it to jab your chow.

If you're comfortable using chopsticks, they're easy to find or fashion in the wild, even without a blade. If not, try make a "poking" stick by sharpening the end of a strong thin stick in order to stab and jab your food.

Finally, you'll need all types of hanging implements to hold pots, other kit, food over the fire, etc. Try to find joints where branches sprout out from a limb and use those as natural hooks. Bigger ones for bigger jobs and smaller ones for smaller jobs, right down to fish-hook sized jobs. Hard woods with little to no smell are the best choice for these purposes.

Always peel the bark; fire, sun, or air dry the wood; and make sure the wood doesn't ooze any resins when peeled, or bubble and hiss when fire-tempered.

BASKETS AND OTHER CARRYING TOOLS

If you're stuck in the wild for some time, you will eventually start making things, and before you know it, you have a collection of stuff. You might just want to store it, or carry it if you're mobile. Or you might need to gather and transport something, such as a fruit tree you find a mile from your camp. So, some sort of carrying device is always handy.

Whenever possible, keep it simple by using your shirt, poncho, coat, or blanket. If you have nothing, there are almost always plants around that can help out. Look for wide-bladed grass, long thin reeds, willow branches, or large tree leaves such as palms.

Reeds are a particularly useful plant for these purposes. If there are a lot of reed- or willow-type plants around, put them to good use. These are usually 2–4 feet long and are fairly strong by themselves and, when combined with others, can actually form an impressively strong structure. They are not too difficult to break with bare hands, so harvesting them for this use is a reasonably easy endeavor.

BASKET-MAKING TECHNIQUE. Cut 20 reeds (or similar material) about 2–3 feet long and place them about ½-inch apart on the ground. Then lay a number of equally long reeds across them perpendicularly, at about three-inch intervals. Starting with the outside top reed, weave the top reeds above and below each consecutive bottom reed, one after the other, alternating over and under as you go. Once you have a good number of rows woven together, roll the structure sideways into a conical or tepee shape, and tie the narrow end together. Then tie together the two opposite sides that have been pulled together, and trim the excess off the outside rim. Now take one more reed, form it into a circle sized to fit, and fasten it to the open end of the cone as a reinforcing mouth of the basket. Use some good cordage to lash together the rest of the basket. If you can, dip it in water to soak it, then let it air dry in the sun; this will tighten up and harden it a bit, and you'll have a pretty decent all-purpose tool.

If you make such a loose-weave basket as described, there is more space or bigger gaps in the basket. So, if you're filling it up with small things (fruits, nuts, stones, etc.) you can line the basket with your shirt to prevent spillage. However, these loose gaps will allow you to use the basket for fishing as it will allow water to flow through while fish get caught inside. Just tie some string to it for casting and retrieving, add some bait to the inside, add a rock to the inside to weigh it down, and place it in a stream with the opening facing upstream.

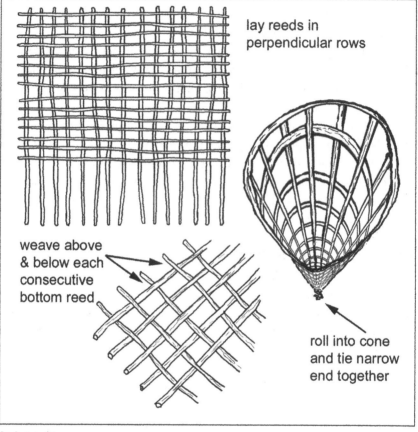

lay reeds in
perpendicular rows

weave above
& below each
consecutive
bottom reed

roll into cone
and tie narrow
end together

Basket making

In addition to fishing, I can use the same basket to trap small game and birds. The best method is to place some bait under the basket, use a stick to hold it tilted up, and tie a string to the basket to be pulled when the prey enters the trap. Just make sure you use good placement, and a long string, out of sight and down wind. A Figure 4 style trap can be fashioned with the basket as well if you don't want to monitor the trap.

LEAVES. You can take large green leaves and make a weave (using the over/ under technique described above) to create a flat area, which in turn can be bent or molded into a circular basket, used as a plate, made into a matt for sleeping on, or used as a blanket, a roof, almost anything. You can use thick branches to make a basic square frame onto which you can mold and lash the woven surface. Or you can take two long thin branches laid across each other into an X shape, lash them together where they meet, bend them upwards and fasten them to another branch that has been formed and lashed into a circle shape. Line this frame with your woven leaves and you have a simple basket without employing all the finer craft skills needed to actually make joints and a proper shape—this will be good enough for your purposes in survival.

BACKPACK FRAMES. A self-made backpack frame will let you carry more weight, more easily. This is important when surviving as you'll be in a weakened state. You can fasten a blanket bundle or basket to the frame to make it easier to transport items with reduction in friction and the resulting blister rubs which cause painful sores and can become infected.

There are three easy ways to make a simple backpack frame:

The **"Wishbone"** frame is a tree branch in a naturally occurring wishbone shape. Find a green wishbone and cut its two separate branches to a length just about the size of your torso. Then cut the joined end down to a 6-inch nub, shaving off any sharp points (this is the top end). Fasten a separate straight branch across the opening between the two long branches to connect them together near their ends (this is the bottom end). To make carrying straps, tie a long piece of cordage into a big loop—around 12–16 feet around—and loop it first around the top nub, then around the ends of the straight branch at bottom. This is your frame. When you're ready to use it, simply wrap the materials you're transporting into a shirt, a leaf basket, or whatever vessel you have, and lash that to the frame with cordage.

The **"A-frame"** is similar to a wishbone frame, but instead of finding a naturally shaped wishbone branch, you fasten together three sticks in the shape of the letter "A." The "A" will be pointing upside-down when mounted, with the apex toward the ground whenever you are carrying heavy loads, uphill, for long periods of time. Otherwise, the A should be pointing right-side-up.

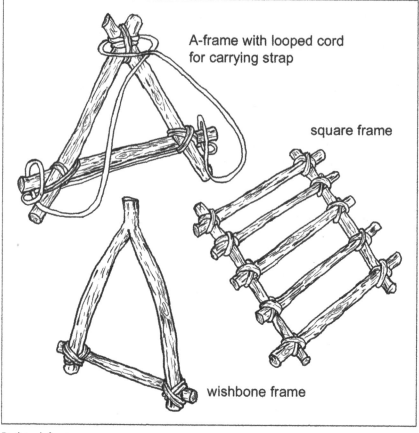

A-frame with looped cord for carrying strap

square frame

wishbone frame

Backpack frames

The **"Square"** frame is simply five sticks lashed together into a square, and then 3–4 sticks fastened horizontally to the frame.

A good tip for the shoulder straps is to wrap the cordage with fleshy leaves for padding around the collar bone area and shoulders. Consider making the frame's bottom horizontal support rest right on the top of your buttocks so you can take advantage of the natural fleshy padding nature gave you there!

BOWLS

Bowls are one of the fundamental implements a human being needs on a regular basis. So they are useful to produce if you are able.

You can make a bowl out of many things. A closed-ended segment of bamboo is easily transformed into a bowl by cutting a hole into its side. You can also take a closed-ended segment of bamboo and cut off one end, creating a cylindrical bowl or cup. You can also make a decent roughly hewn bowl from a block of wood. Just use fire to burn the center and use a knife or rock to dig out the burnt area, then repeat the process until you've got a deep enough vessel for your purposes. Once you've burned and carved it to shape, sand it down to remove ash and any other imperfections.

Some tree barks are just amazing. Cherry tree is one. Birch is another. Neither will burn when placed next to a fire, but water can be boiled through them without the loss of integrity. Perhaps this is why natives use the birch bark for making canoes as it has such a versatile and utilitarian texture. Birch is the white tree that always appears to have peeling bark which looks a lot like paper coils when you get up close to it.

A piece of birch can be peeled off and rolled up into a cone, or actually folded into a box shape. Then take a small twig, form it into a one-inch peg, split it halfway down the middle, and slide it over the edges of the bark like a paper clip and it will hold your utensil in its shape. This will hold water very well, and is just a great li'l field tool to find and use.

If you can't find bark or leaves to shape into a cone and use as a bowl, try playing in the mud! The best kind of mud is the grayish clay you can find almost anywhere, but mainly you can find it on steep river banks higher above the water line.

Take a nice pile of clay and mix it with water, just enough to make it the consistency of modelling clay. Then form it into a bowl shape. (You might try just making a long roll, then coiling the roll, and then smoothing that into the bowl shape if it's a bit too soft to work with otherwise.) Let this dry in the air and sun for a day or two depending on humidity. Then you're ready to fire the bowl—this will make it tougher, harder, and longer-lasting, and will also reduce any mud residues/flavors in your water and food.

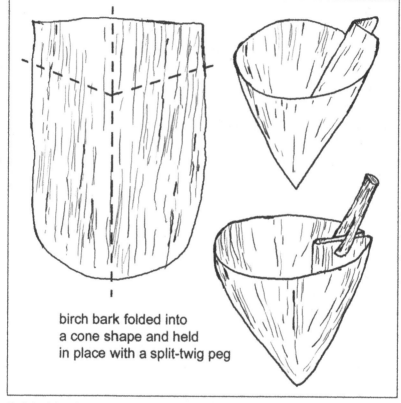

birch bark folded into
a cone shape and held
in place with a split-twig peg

Birch-bark bowl

HOW TO FIRE A MUD BOWL. It's really simple. Make a fairly big fire. Put your bowl by the fire to begin the drying-out process. Once you have some good coals and embers, clear an area in the center of the coals and place your bowl in it. Then push the fire and embers up next to the sides of the bowl. Then slowly place small, light branches over the bowl so as to not damage or dent it with the weight. Build the fire up again around the bowl and let it burn for 1–3 hours. Then remove it, let it cool, and put it to use.

Burn the inside well with fire if you want to use it for cooking, and if you do, place it on rocks next to but not in the fire, and don't pour cold water into it while hot or it'll break.

HAND DRILL

There are many instances in the wild when you want to make a hole in something hard. It might be for a needle, a knife handle or walking stick to add a lanyard, or many other things. Making holes presents a unique challenge. This is where the fire-bow method can double as a regular drilling tool. Simply find and fashion a new spindle stick (*don't use your hard-made fire spindle!*) and a piece of rock, glass, shell, or such material to make a small drill bit. Chip and flake your bit material until it's narrower than the spindle and has a sharp pointy end. Then use it, or something even narrower, to bore a hold into the tip of the spindle in order to hold the bit firmly in place. You may also split the end of the spindle a couple centimeters slide the bit into the split, then lash it in place.

Now you're ready to go. You can use your fire-bow method to create holes in wood, shell, bone, etc. Just create a vice to hold the item in place—using your feet, two rocks, logs, or whatever works—and start spinning the spindle between your hands while pressing down. Once you get the hang of this, you'll find you'll use and actually need it more than you'd expect.

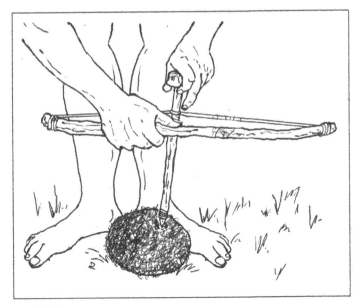

Hand drill

BOATS AND RAFTS

There is a lot of bad advice out there about making boats, canoes, rafts and all that in a survival situation. I'm here to tell you that these things take a whole lot of time and energy, and without good tools, are extraordinarily difficult to make for a single survivor. So, only attempt to make a raft if you have to make a tremendous water journey, and then, make sure you give a lot of time to make it, at least a week or two or more—it's that much work. And don't expect to make a raft like the ones you've seen on TV. People tend to forget that when surviving, the daily food, water, and hygiene needs alone take up most of the day. Add to that low energy and lack of physical strength and you'll see that making a seaworthy raft is a very difficult task.

If you're going to make a raft, find the lightest wood you can. Tap all the trees around you and find the lightest, softest ones. Without an axe or machete, you won't be able to cut fresh trees and will be stuck having to find what you can laying around. If you have the time and can make a stone axe, do it, and cut green logs.

The only method I will describe is the basic log raft. Use as many long logs as you need—2, 3, or 4, if you can get away with it. These should be 8 inches or so in diameter—large enough to hold your weight. You'll also need 4 slightly narrower branches to use as cross beams. In a pinch, the most basic raft of all is just a big ol' log that you put in and hang onto.

Lay the long logs tightly together lengthwise on top of two cross beams, one on each end. Then lay two more cross beams on top of the long logs, directly above the two bottom cross beams, and fasten those beams together like your life depends on it, because it does. Test it with all your might to try and break it, if it gives way when you push and pull against it, keep working on it until you make it strong enough to pass the test. Once you get moving on the water, you won't have much chance to stop and make corrections.

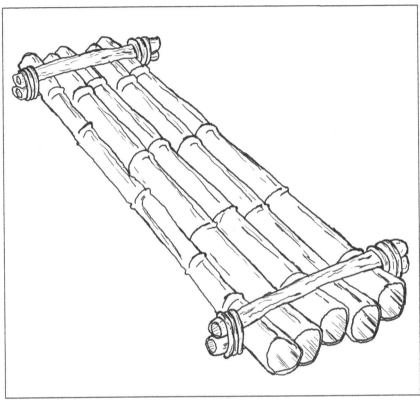

Raft

RAFTING TECHNIQUES 101. There are a few standard rules to follow when taking to water on a homemade vessel. DO NOT raft at night. DO stay to the inside of river bends. DO NOT attempt to navigate rapids; stay away from them if at all possible.

RIVER CROSSING. River crossing can be very dangerous. When attempting to traverse a river, especially one with good flow, you'll need some tools. If you have a walking stick (and you should!), you will be using it to propel your raft by pushing it off the river bottom. If your regular walking stick isn't long enough, find one that is. You also need to find another strong stick, carve a point onto one end, and stab it into the ground where you want to cross. This will be your anchor in an emergency—tied to cordage that will be tied to you on the raft—so stick it in deep and strong. When choosing a location for this anchor stick, find a place where you can wedge the stick into the ground and then prop it against a tree. This way, should you start to be pulled down river, the anchor stick will lock up against the tree and should not come out altogether.

Another key consideration involves the cordage or rope you have made. You put a lot into this rope, so you don't just want to tie off and leave it after the crossing unless you have to do so. You need to rig it so that you will be able to retrieve it once you've crossed. And you need to make sure there's enough rope to reach across the river, including some extra slack just in case.

While your anchor stick should lock against a tree if you get yanked downstream, make sure the same thing won't happen when you pull it from *upstream* once you've crossed. To this end, make the tie-off at the base with a loose loop of about three inches bigger than the girth of the stick. This way, when you're across, you can wiggle your rope up the stick by flicking it a few good times, and then pulling it towards you.

After you've tied the rope to the anchor stick, wrap it over your shoulders and around your armpits—this way, if you slip or get pulled suddenly downstream and the current is so strong you can't recover, you'll be pulling against the string with your head *above water*.

Once you are safely across, walk up stream a bit, flick and wiggle your rope, pull the anchor stick away from the tree, and recover your precious cordage. Then be sure to dry it the first chance you get.

An important note on river crossings in the cold and in general: If you only have one pair of shoes, take them off, wrap them and keep them dry, and then put them on when you get to the other side. Wet footgear will tear your feet up in a hurry! Wear only your socks if you have to, improvise shoes with bark, vines and grass, but don't get your only foot gear soaked if you don't have to do so. Or plan to take some time and dry out your feet afterwards if you must get them wet.

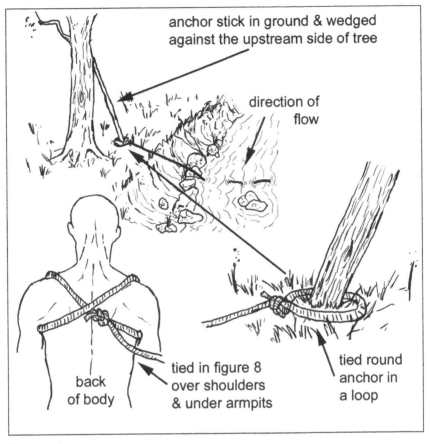

anchor stick in ground & wedged against the upstream side of tree

direction of flow

back of body

tied in figure 8 over shoulders & under armpits

tied round anchor in a loop

River crossing

IN A COLD ENVIRONMENT, DO NOT GET YOUR BOOTS WET AT ALL COSTS, OR YOUR ONLY CLOTHES. Strip and suffer the pain for a moment, but you'll feel warm like you're on fire when you first get out of the icy river and once your dry clothes are back on, you'll feel toasty warm. Getting your only clothes and boots wet in the cold environments is taking a huge gamble that you won't get caught in a blizzard for a long while afterwards. That's a big risk. If you get caught in a cold snap or just stuck overnight in wet clothes in cold regions, you'll likely not make it to see the dawn.

In general, but especially in the cold when you only have one set of clothes or boots, the rules for river crossing ain't easy, but it is simple—get nekkid, get across, get dry again. Staying warm is staying alive, and getting wet is getting dead in the arctic.

ROPE AND CORDAGE

Rope is another important item to have in a survival situation, yet normally in such situations there is no manufactured rope available. In this case, you will have to make your own rope and cordage. Luckily, nature provides plenty of raw materials for this purpose. We'll talk about the materials first, then the process of making rope.

ANIMAL SKIN. If you do bag or find some good-sized game carcass, you'll be able to use the skins to make strands of leather fairly easily. Simply skin the animal the best you can, spread the skin out so there are no folds or creases, scrape as much mucous and membrane off the inside of the skin as you can, dry it out in the air and sun, tamp down an inch or so of dry dirt over it, then remove that dirt and replace it with fresh dry dirt. Adding and removing several coatings of dirt helps get the skin cleaned and dried. Once it's in good shape, cut it into thin strips. When you're ready to use it for rope, tie strands together to get the length you need, then wet it a bit and apply it to whatever tying and lashing you need to do. That's it.

If you need to tan the hide to make cordage that has more utility and lasts longer—such as making string for shoes, or for making foot gear, clothing, shelter, sacks, etc.—then use the brain of the animal. Make a slurry with water and the brain (after scraping all the flesh from the inside if you want the fur, or both sides if you want the leather), and soak it until it feels like pasta. Play with it, stretch it, scrape it some more, and let it set a day or two. Then rinse it and let it get almost dry. While it is still pliable, scrape it some more and work it over a piece of log or stone like you were buffing your shoes with it. Do this until you have the soft suppleness you'd like.

TENDONS AND SINEW. This is messy business but it is how man has done many things for the longest time. The essence is that once you have taken an animal's life, you use every bit of it that you can. In this way, you truly become thankful for the gift of its life for yours. Again, if you get or find a big game carcass, here's what to do.

Once you've gutted, cleaned, skinned, cooked, and smoked what you need, take some time and go through all the animal's bones and limbs and look for tendons. These are the hard, almost plastic-like pieces that you really can't eat. They will come out in long strands and will be tough. Scrape these with a rock and try to get all the extra tissue off of them. Then let them dry. They will be hard and look brittle, but will be quite strong. Use a rock hammer or log mallet and beat on them a bit to break them open into fibrous strands. Pull these apart, and then wet them again to make them pliable. When moist, twist them or braid them together to the desired tensile strength and length. You don't need to tie them together for length as they will dry and harden together and be very secure.

GRASS. Grasses can be used for a wide variety of purposes including bedding, roofing, clothing insulation, and to make tools such as brooms, baskets, and blankets. They can also be used to make lashing and cordage. The key to using grasses as cordage is in the bundling. First gather a lot of grass, then make bundles of same-length grass and tie the bundles about an inch from the top and bottom ends, as well as in the middle—make as many ties around the middle of the bundle as necessary. When grass is bundled in this way, it becomes a sort of flexible log and a very useful tool indeed for manufacturing many types of structures and tools, from dome homes to baskets, frames, seats, etc.

OTHER PLANTS. There are way too many plants for me to list here that can be used for making things. In fact, you don't need to know all their names and uses. What you do need is to have an idea of what *kind* of plant can be used, so I make mention of a few of the more common plants here. With that in mind, look for plants like these as your standard to then use to make cordage. Most of these require some beating and splitting; I often use my teeth to hold one end and then use both hands to split these apart. Once they are separated out, I make cordage as with any other fibrous material, as noted below.

TREE BARK. Many trees have naturally flexible bark that can be peeled off in strands. These strands can then be torn into thinner strips to give the foundation for good cordage. You'll have to practice by peeling some tree bark, but you'll quickly ascertain the good ones in your environment.

ROOTS. Have you ever tried to pull up a plant or small sapling only to find that it had some crazy root system, and the more you pulled, the more came up and you ended up with quite a few feet of thick but flexible cord-like rootage? Well, that's the stuff you're looking for. I don't encourage digging for these, but when you happen across them, put them to use. I don't like to use roots for two reasons. First, they dry out fast and that makes them a bit more prone to becoming brittle and breaking. But also, it is harder on the environment when you go ripping up root systems. However, it is survival, and it's a brutal business.

VINES. What I love about the jungle is that vines are everywhere. You can literally just reach out and grab a vine almost anytime you need some cordage. However, in other areas vines are hard to come by. Or, they are way too fat to be used for cordage. Or so you thought. . . . Often vines will have a bark that is inherently superb for making cordage. So, if you find some little vines, use them, they are nature's twine. If you find big vines, peel them first and then use them.

FACTS ABOUT USING NATURAL FIBERS FOR MAKING CORDAGE:

- Anything green and pliable is possible to use.
- If material is dry, and in the winter, soak the material in water.
- When a fiber is really hard to work with, boil it.
- Test everything with your eyes and hands to see if it's usable before you start working it.
- Test everything after you make it to ensure it's usable.

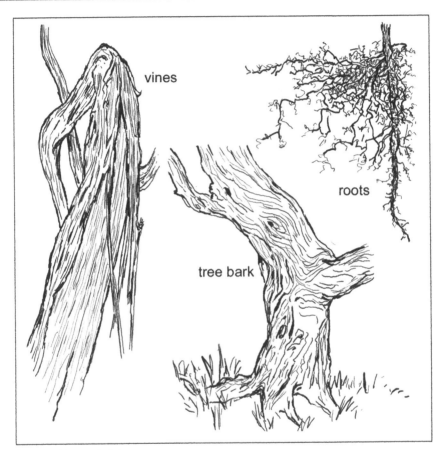

vines

roots

tree bark

Rope-making materials

HOW TO MAKE ROPE AND CORDAGE

Once you have the base material fibers selected and prepared, you're ready to begin.

Take several strands and tie a small knot at one end. Then twist these fibers together to make a strong strand, and knot the other end.

Repeat the last step until you have a good number of strands to work with.

Next, take two of the strong strands you just made, and begin to braid them together by crisscrossing them in an overlapping fashion until you get to the ends. If you have a partner, have them hold the starting ends together. If you're solo, pin down the ends with a rock, between your legs, in your teeth, or whatever works for you to keep the ends stable as you twist.

Make a knot at the other end.

If you need longer cordage, tie two more strands to that end, and start the braiding process again.

That's about all on the basics of making any cordage. You'll use what you have, make what you can, and make it as strong as you need.

KNOTS

I'm going on the record right now, saying that everything you've ever read about the importance of knowing knots is wrong. Every single survival book out there says that you will die if you don't know how to make knots in a multitude of variations and types.

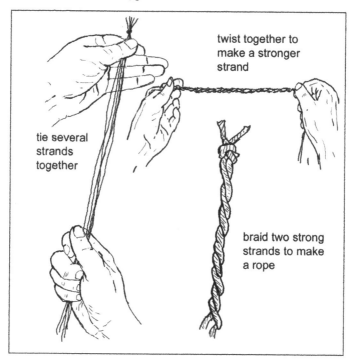

twist together to make a stronger strand

tie several strands together

braid two strong strands to make a rope

Making cordage

That's pure crap! Everything I ever need to know or do regarding knots, I could manage with a granny knot—it's as easy as tying your shoes. To make life even easier, I found a few more knots that have been helpful. But that's it. I'm talking about being in an actual survival situation here, and doing what it takes to get out alive.

OVERHAND KNOT. This is the simplest knot. It's the common knot you make in a single rope to keep the end from fraying, for example. Just make a loop in one end of the string, then pass the other end through the loop and pull tight.

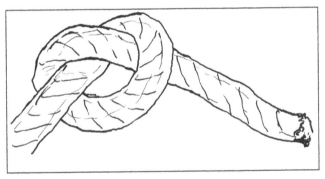

Overhand knot

HALF HITCH KNOT. This one is pretty simple, too. It can be used 90% of the time for almost everything. Simply wrap the string around the object, tuck it in on itself, and pull tight.

Do this twice when you need real security. These are dang hard to get undone.

Half hitch knot

SQUARE KNOT. This is a bit trickier. It's really good for binding two pieces of cordage together.

They say it's not good when joining two ropes of unequal diameter. I say use it even then, just put a half hitch on each end afterwards and it'll hold.

To make a square knot, just remember: **over-under, under-over:**

Hold one piece in one hand, the other piece in the other hand.

Lay one side over the other, it doesn't matter which.

Then take that same piece and turn it under the other.

Turn it back pointing towards its original start point.

Then bring it back under the other string.

Then wrap it back around over the other string.

Pull them together slowly and dress them up a bit as they come together.

They should form a sort of symmetrical square, hence the name: square knot.

When it's in shape, pull it to the desired tightness and you have tied a nice square knot.

Once you learn this, it helps to do it the same way each time. The good thing is, you always know if you did it right or not as soon as you pull it tight. And if it's not tight, simply undo half, re-do it in the opposite way, and you should have it.

You can also remember the square knot sequence as: **right over left, left over right**—or, **left over right, right over left.**

Note: the square knot is really just a double version of a half hitch, with a reverse twist!

Square knot

GRANNY KNOT. The Granny Knot is similar to the square knot, except the sequence is: **right over left, right over left**—or **left over right, left over right.**

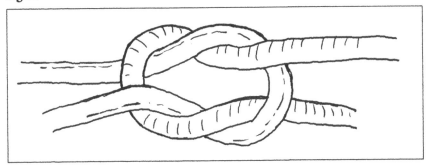

Granny knot

PRUSIK KNOT. This is basically another form of a half hitch. It is ideal for tying into other ropes without cutting up your cordage. It is good for making a slip knot, as well for emergency ascents.

It makes a bight that won't slide under tension, but when loosened it can be slid around and moved easily to a new place on the rope.

To make a prusik knot:

Make a bight or loop or upside-down "U" with your string. Make it a few inches long so you can work with it.

Place it over the rope or object you want to tie into/onto. Then pull the rest of your string through that bight so that it's wrapped around the rope.

Then dress it up so it looks neat like a letter "T" across the rope.

Pull tight to lock in; loosen to move or slide. That's it, all the knots you'll ever need to know.

Now, don't get me wrong, learning and knowing knots is great. The more you know about anything, usually the better off you'll be. However, from years of playing and teaching survival in the bush, I have found quite simply that you really don't need to be a rope master to survive.

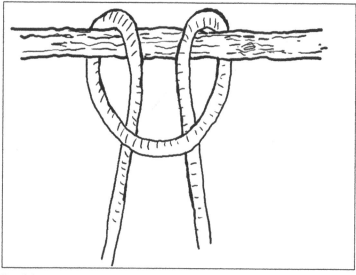

Prusik knot

LADDERS

It seems every survival book includes cool instructions on how to make a neato ladder. There's usually a picture of a rope ladder or the knot ladder with loops of rope tied into one rope. Well, most of the time, you won't need a ladder. If you do, both the rope ladder and loop ladder are hard to make as it requires a lot of cordage and it must be strong and durable. These are great if you have lots of man-made para cord, for example, but otherwise, I say, save your time and stay away from these unless it's completely necessary. If you don't have great cordage, they can break or snap under use anyway.

This is where everything must be put up against the common sense test. If you really need a ladder, I recommend just using tree branches. Use one long tree sapling or a long piece of wood, and cut notches into it for steps or grips when you put it on an incline. Or, use two long strong logs as your two side rails, then use smaller branches for the rungs. Fasten the rungs in place with notches and lashings, and test each rung strenuously before using the ladder. Basically, ladders in survival books are mostly a nice fiction. Use a rope instead.

Navigation

People talk about a walk in the woods like it's an easy thing, and it can be—if you know where you are, and where you're going, and how you're going to get there, and how long it should take you. In a survival situation, you might not know any of these things. And you might be in mountains or desert instead or woods.

SHOULD YOU STAY OR SHOULD YOU GO?

This chapter will tell you what you need to know to find your way out of the woods and back to the comfort of home. But before you learn how to travel in a survival situation, you'll need to decide whether to travel. You might be better off where you are. Should you stay put, signal for help (see Chapter 8) and wait for help to arrive? Or should you set out for civilization on your own? This is perhaps the most important decision you'll make in a true survival situation.

If you stay, you might never be found, or you might not be found in time. Choosing to move raises other questions. Do you know which way to go? How far it is? Do you have the resources, internal and external, to overcome the terrain, the weather, the distance, to get there?

Note: Rescue teams fly or sail or drive to the survivor's last known location, whether it be the entrance to a national park or the source of a "mayday" signal.

Ninety percent of the time, you will be better off making camp and waiting.

If you are with a plane, chances are the pilot called for help and gave coordinates when it was going down, and a search team will be sent. Even if the plane went down suddenly and unexpectedly, planes are fitted with beacon transponders that turn themselves on at impact, recording and reporting your location. That means a distress signal will have been sent when the plane crashed, and that means the authorities have been alerted and a rescue mission is being mounted. They'll be looking for the plane. Staying with the plane improves the chances that rescuers will find you with it.

The same is true for boats, cars, and structures, all of which are easier to spot than an individual person.

If, however, the plane or boat or car or structure poses some sort of danger, move to the nearest safe place. Try to find an area where you can safely camp for a few days, one that will be easily spotted by rescue teams. Assess whether you can safely salvage anything useful from the disabled vehicle or structure. Depending on what it contains—food, a two-way radio, flares, etc.—it could save your life.

While staying put and waiting for help to find you is often your best option, certain circumstances are going to force you to find your own way out.

STAY WHERE YOU ARE IF:

- You are with a plane, boat, or other vehicle.
- You are at a shelter.
- You are with a group.
- (Unless any of the above is in danger of sinking, exploding, burning down, or falling off a cliff.)

PREPARE TO DEPART IF:

- You are completely lost and far from anything man-made.
- You are alone and no one has any clue where you are.
- You are almost certain no one will be looking for you, or they won't begin looking for a long time, or they won't be looking in the right place because you're not where anyone would expect you to be, or you've waited as long as you can at the boat, car, plane, or house.

- You are running out of supplies.
- A member of your party requires emergency medical care.

If you are with a group, you may have to make a decision about whether to strike out on your own, leaving the others behind. If a member of your group is in a bad way medically and can't make the journey, and neither you nor others in your party can transport the sick or injured person, you may have to go it alone. If your party includes elderly persons, infants, and/or children who would not be able to make the journey, you may have to leave them behind.

If you must break up the group, give the travellers their best chance at success by giving them the critical supplies, like canteens, knives, etc. Write down their names and next of kin, with contact information, in case they are lost. Write down or commit to memory their intended route. Estimate a travel time and return date.

If the group is divided over whether to stay or go, try to divide survival assets equally to avoid fighting., but favor the mobile group—their road is harder.

These are only guidelines, and only you can make the decision. Consider your options and think through the consequences. Once you've made up your mind to stay, settle in for the long haul and see the section on **Shelters**. If you decide to move, the following section is for you. By the time we finish, you should have enough information to chart a course and follow it to safety with confidence.

THE BASICS

DEAD RECKONING. The simplest and most effective style of survival navigation. It works in all types of terrain. The method is easy, but it takes some work. Simply look in the direction you want to travel. Pick the farthest "target" or landmark object that you can see and begin walking toward it.

Be sure to estimate the distance before you begin, and be sure to take a pace count as you go (see below). Shortly after you set off toward your objective, turn around and look at your starting point for a moment to consider what it will look like from the perspective of your destination. That way, when you get to your target, you can look back, and see where you came from, confirming that it's on-line and that you're on track. Then pick your next target and repeat.

If you can, try to line up three destinations in your sights.

If all three landmarks are in line, then you are dead on track.

In the thick bush, the distance from landmark to landmark might be only 50 meters, but that's when it's especially important to use dead reckoning to keep you on a straight line, especially if you have no compass. In open terrain, dead reckoning might not be possible, as there may not be a target on the horizon. Look for a bush, rock, change of color in the sand, etc.

ORIENTEERING. For the purposes of survival, we'll define orienteering as navigating with a compass but without a map. You may not have a map for reference, but you can use your compass to maintain your bearings and direct your movements.

For example, say you know there is a mountain range to the east, and north of that is a river. You'll use your compass to keep yourself moving in an easterly direction until you hit the mountain range, then you'll use your compass to point you north.

TERRAIN ASSOCIATION. The art of navigating with a map, but without a compass, is called terrain association. This is a bit trickier, but also has its advantages. With a map, you have a good sense of the overall picture, and a much better sense of where you want to go, but it's not always so easy to know exactly where you are.

Try to match what you see on the ground to the features on the map. It doesn't work the other way around. Read the terrain, then find it on the map. *Don't pick a spot on the map and then try to make it fit the terrain!*

To do this you must constantly be aware of your surroundings. Look for anything distinct and specific. If a river is good, a bend in the river is better! A hilltop is good, but a cliff or plateau is more distinctive, and therefore better.

When you find yourself surrounded by distinctive terrain, don't leave the area until you can place it on your map. It's much easier to stay on track once you have confirmed your location.

MAPS—HOW TO READ, USE, & MAKE THEM

If you have a map, use it. If not, consider making one. Just trying to make your own map can force you to visualize your surroundings from a bird's-eye view. It's a good exercise, if nothing else, and can help you develop a better sense of awareness of your surroundings, which can give you peace of mind.

Making a map from scratch can also help you understand the terrain and its potential impact on you. Even if you are staying put, your home-made map might help you decide on a better place to make camp. And if you're planning a move, it's an excellent help in planning a route.

The simplest form of homemade map is a **sand table**. This is just making a model of the surrounding terrain in sand or dirt, using sticks as small trees and pebbles as rocks, whatever is available as a visual aid.

To make one, simply orient whatever you intend to write on toward the north and then build the map with your camp at the center. Add key terrain features and significant landmarks as you scout the area and discover new elements of your environment.

Note: Mapmaking is especially helpful if you're with a group, so everyone can get a sense of their environment, and everyone can keep active. Fear, anger and depression are extremely contagious and addictive. One person can quickly infect others. These attitudes must be fought off daily and crushed at the first sign. Keeping everyone busy and involved is one of the best ways to fight these emotions, and terrain models are a good way to keep folks productive who might not otherwise be able to contribute. You can use the sand table to show people where the watering hole is, where the latrines are, where the food preparation area is located, etc.

TERMS & CONCEPTS

LONGITUDE AND LATITUDE. You have heard these words many times, even if you don't use these types of maps. In the simplest terms, latitude and longitude are lines used to divide the world into segments. These segments are defined by three measures (degrees, minutes, and seconds) in combination with a cardinal direction (north, south, east, or west).

Here's how the world is divided by latitude and longitude.

A full circle is 360 degrees (just like the compass). 180 is half of 360, meaning halfway around the circle. So when someone says they "did a 180," they mean they turned around and went the opposite direction. Latitude and longitude divide the earth into 360 sections.

Lines of longitude run "longways," north and south, up and down the globe from top to bottom. These lines chop the world into long vertical slices. As you move east or west around the globe, you cross these lines. That's why lines of longitude, despite running on a north-south axis, actually measure location on an east-west axis.

From any given point, we can travel 180 degrees east or 180 degrees west to reach a point exactly opposite our location on the globe

How do we know where east begins and west ends? We define a starting point. This point is a line of longitude called the meridian, or middle line, and it runs through an observatory in Greenwich, England, where this was all originally sorted out. Longitude is measured in degrees east or west of the meridian at Greenwich, also known as the Prime Meridian, or 0 degrees longitude.

Lines of latitude are the lines that run all the way around the globe horizontally.

Latitude lines intersect to longitude lines at 90-degree angles. Think of latitude as a bookshelf with 90 shelves, or degrees, above the waist, and 90 shelves, or degrees, below the waist. What is the "waist"? That would be the equator—the middle, or reference, line for latitude.

It is important to understand that while longitude lines are the same length all around the globe, latitude lines become shorter the farther they are from the equator. The equator is defined as the longest possible circumference around the earth. But latitude circles shrink as they get closer to the poles, as the circumference they travel diminishes.

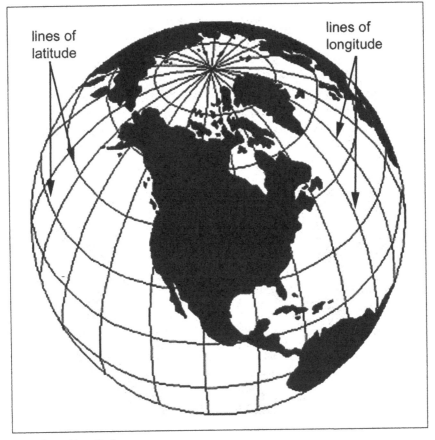

Latitude and longitude

Now that you have the basics of latitude and longitude, let's look at how they're used, and how time zones come into play.

Any particular location is somewhere within 180 degrees to either the west or the east of the Prime Meridian, at 0 degrees longitude. That same location is also within 90 degrees to the north or the south of the equator, which is defined as 0 degrees of latitude. You can think of an area bounded by lines of latitude and longitude as a square.

Near the equator, one square is about 70 square miles. That's quite a big area. To refine with more accuracy, each square is further divided into minutes. There are 60 minutes in each square, just as there are 60 minutes in an hour. To refine still more, each minute is divided into seconds. There are 60 seconds in each minute of latitude and longitude, just as there are 60 seconds in a minute of time. To pinpoint exactly where you are, or want to go, you would say your location in a sequence, as follows:

West ("of the prime meridian" is implied) 94 degrees, 49 minutes, 46 seconds, and north ("of the equator" is implied) 29 degrees, 16 minutes, 22 seconds.

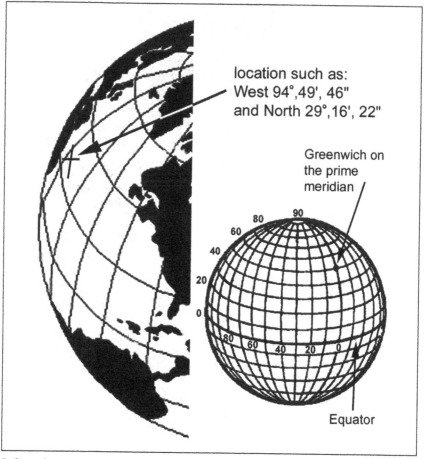

location such as:
West 94°,49', 46"
and North 29°,16', 22"

Greenwich on the prime meridian

Equator

Defining location

Note: Minutes are denoted by the symbol (') and seconds are indicated by the symbol (").

Degrees can be divided into hundredths and even thousandths, so they can pinpoint locations with extreme precision.

Most maps you will find that survive a plane crash or a shipwreck will be marked with lines of latitude and longitude. Now you have some clue how to use them, and this will help you work more easily with maps on a smaller scale, and better understand how to make your own map.

SCALE. A map's scale tells you the size of the area it represents. More specifically, it tells you the size of the area represented by each of the map's squares. The scale can be found in the legend at the bottom or at the side of the map.

Map scales

Many civilian maps are made by the U.S. Geological Survey at a scale of 1:24,000, where 1 inch on the map equals 24,000 inches on land. One square on this map is one square inch, and one inch represents 2,000 feet. These maps cover an area of 7.5 minutes of longitude by 7.5 minutes of latitude.

Most military maps use the metric system, which is more internationally applicable, and are drawn to a scale of 1:50,000. On these maps, the squares are one kilometer to a side. The distance from one corner of this square diagonally to another corner would be 1.5 kilometers, or "clicks."

Note: The larger the scale, the smaller the area covered, and the more detailed the map will be. The smaller the scale, the larger the area covered, but in less detail.

For example, on a pilot's map with a scale of 1:250,000, the area represented by each square contains a lot of ground, but not a lot of detail. Such a map might cover the entire United States. A smaller-scaled map, like 1:1,000, will contain lots of detail, but will cover only a very small area, like maybe a local campground.

GRID COORDINATES. Grids are formed by the vertical and horizontal lines drawn on the map, much as the lines of longitude and latitude divide the globe into square sections.

The big difference between lines of latitude and longitude and grid line is that latitude and longitude incorporate the curvature of the earth. Grid coordinates are designed to divide the earth's surface equally and evenly on a flat surface. The lines of the grid do not run exactly north and south. To account for this variation, see the **declination diagram** below.

Locations on a map are expressed in grid coordinates.

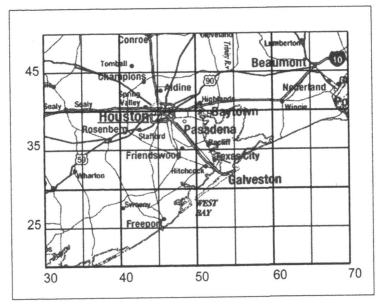

Declination diagram

LEGEND. A map's legend is like a book's table of contents and index all rolled into one. The legend will tell you the map's scale, where and when it was made, and all the visual keys you'll need to understand the map's symbols.

Map legend

SOME THINGS ARE CONSIDERED STANDARD ON A MAP:

Green = Vegetation (white areas contain few or no plants).

Blue = Water (rivers, lakes, intermittent streams, marshes, etc.).

Brown = Contour lines (which indicate elevation).

Red = Roads (or place names or major destinations like air-ports, etc.).

Black = Man-made structures (buildings, cemeteries, roads, etc.).

SYMBOLS. If you have a map at all, look for signs of civilization, like cities or roads. If you cannot find any, look for other man-made structures like oil pipelines, power lines, or railroad tracks. Any of these will eventually lead you to a populated area. If you are lost at sea and have an aerial map, look for the black dotted or dash lines that indicate commercial shipping routes, and try to get yourself near those to increase your likelihood of being spotted.

Black dashes usually mean some sort of trail. Blue dashes mean intermittent stream. It might be dry, but it's a good place to dig for water.

Also look to the legend for the contour interval, which will tell you the distance between contour lines (see below).

Finally, pay attention to the **declination diagram** if you plan to use a compass.

COORDINATES. These are the numbers used to pinpoint a location.

If a map starts at 25 at the bottom left corner and goes to 75 at the bottom right, then one of the 50 squares in between includes your east-west position. If the map's vertical coordinates start in the bottom left-hand corner at 10 and go up to 60, your north-south position would fall somewhere in one of those 50 squares.

To name your position, read right until you find the grid coordinate that corresponds to your east-west position, then read up until you reach the coordinate that corresponds to your north-south position.

When giving or receiving coordinates on a map, remember: Right & Up. This is simply a standardized way of reading or describing a location in a way that someone else can find it. Right gives the east-west coordinate, which comes first. Up gives the north-south coordinate.

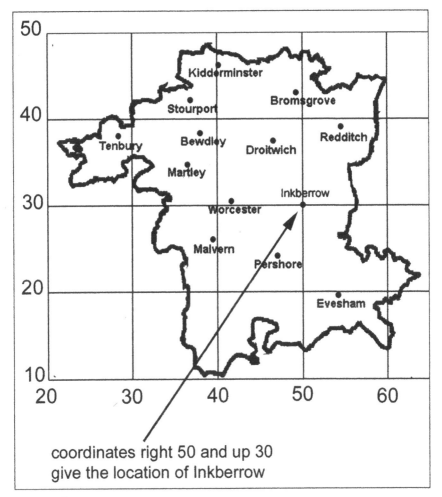

coordinates right 50 and up 30
give the location of Inkberrow

Map coordinates

Say your position is 50 and 30. On a military-style map of 1:50,000 scale, this would place you in the map's middle square. But that square represents one square kilometre. That's a lot of terrain in the middle of the jungle.

To mark the location more precisely, divide the square into 10 equal divisions. Since our square is 1,000 meters by 1,000 meters, dividing it into tenths narrows our square areas to 100 square meters. So the new way to describe the more detailed coordinate would be as follows: Right 50 then, say, 5, then up 30, then, say, 5 again. It would look like this: 505305. This coordinate will bring you within 100 meters of your desired location.

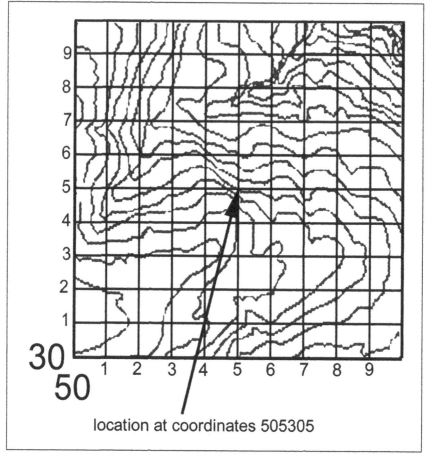

location at coordinates 505305

6-digit grid

At this distance you could make contact by hollering. Mission accomplished. This is called a "6-digit" grid, and it's about the best you can do without a protractor.

Not bad for map-reading 101. With some practice, you can get good at guesstimating an 8-digit coordinate, which will bring you to within 10 meters of your target. At this distance, you should be able to see your objective.

CONTOUR LINES. Each contour line, often a wavy brown line on the map, represents a consistent elevation, which will be indicated on the line. The contour interval is the distance between contour lines, and tells you how steep or how flat the terrain is. This will come into play when you plan your route.

If the lines are close together, the elevation changes a lot in a very short distance, which means the terrain is steep. If the lines are farther apart, that means elevation change in the area is gradual.

Look for areas that have lots of lines in increasingly smaller concentric circles. This indicates a hilltop or mountain peak. The ultimate elevation is usually printed near the mountaintop.

YOU'LL MAINLY USE THE CONTOUR LINES FOR THE FOLLOWING PURPOSES:

- To avoid peaks (or to find them if you need the vantage point for scouting).
- To avoid steep valleys (or to find them if you're looking for water).
- To avoid steep ridges, cliffs, or mountainsides.
- To seek flat ground for ease of travel.

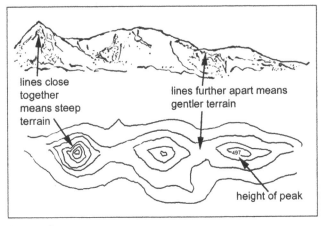

Contour lines

DECLINATION DIAGRAM. First, it's important to understand that there are several definitions of north. This might be a factor, especially if you're close to the poles, and it can be used to your advantage everywhere if you understand the principle.

TRUE NORTH is the actual point on the earth where all the longitudinal lines meet. It is a physical point whose location means very little to the survivor except as an aid in understanding the other forms of north.

MAGNETIC NORTH is the direction the compass points. Magnetic North is not True North. The earth's magnetic wave lines meet slightly off-center of True North, in part because the earth's rotational axis changes ever so slightly, and so the earth's rotation isn't perfectly consistent. What this means is that near the poles, magnetic north can be as much as 300 miles from the actual physical location of true north. Again, 99% of the time this will not affect you, but it can be helpful to understand the differences as you navigate, especially over long distances or from locations near the poles.

GRID NORTH corresponds to the actual lines on any flat map you might be using to navigate. Flat maps are imperfect representations of the spherical earth, and so grid north is not True North.

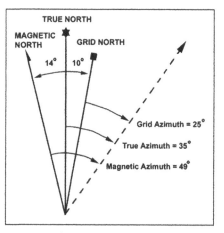

Variations of "north"

For example, imagine an orange. Now, take a black marker and draw a set of perfectly straight lines on it, from top to bottom, evenly spaced all the way around. Then draw a set of rings around the orange, perpendicular to the lines, spacing the rings evenly from a large circle around the orange's middle to increasingly smaller circles as you get closer to the orange's top and bottom. The lines connecting the orange's top and bottom are lines of longitude, running in a north-south direction. The circles around the orange are lines of latitude, running along an east-west axis. The intersections of longitude and latitude describe sections. This is how we measure our globe.

If you wanted to lay this "lined" orange flat on a piece of paper, you would peel and lay it out, but there would be gaps where the peel's curved surface was flattened. But imagine if you could remove the orange peel in one solid piece, then stretch it slightly at the edges so it covers the whole sheet of paper evenly. This is how a map works. It gives us an approximate representation of a portion of the earth's surface, laid out on a grid indicating scale.

What the difference means in actual walking terms is this: A 1-degree variation between grid north and magnetic north will cause you to walk about 250 meters off course over a 10-mile distance. You will walk a mile off course if the variation is 5 degrees, and if the difference between magnetic and grid north is 10 degrees, you will walk almost 2 miles off course over a 10-mile distance.

In a survival situation, you just need to be aware that over long distances, it is normal that you will find yourself off-course. Don't panic or give in to disorientation and confusion.

THE DECLINATION DIAGRAM SHOWS YOU THE DIFFERENCES BETWEEN:

- True north (often indicated by a line with a star).
- Grid north (often indicated by a line with a square).
- Magnetic north (often indicated by a line with an arrow or point).

Declination diagrams are drawn in the form of a "V" displaying the arc and variance between each arm of the "V." True north is not relevant here. What's important is the G-M (grid to magnetic) angle.

When you draw a line on a map from where you are to where you want to be, that line is called the grid azimuth.

Say you're facing north. Your map and compass are aligned pointing north, and your destination is a hilltop at approximately 45-degree angle from north. If you were to turn the bezel ring of your compass to 45 degrees and walk that direction, you would most likely not arrive at your objective because of the disparity between magnetic north and grid north.

We use the G-M angle to convert the map or "Grid" azimuth to the compass or "Magnetic" azimuth.

In some places on earth, the G-M angle can be quite extreme, and in others, it is very slight. The map legend will usually tell you how much the angle is and how much it changes each year, in which case you must look at the legend for the year the map was made, then do the math to get the most accurate updated G-M angle. Then use that for your planning.

The acronym "LARS" is the easiest way to remember how to convert a G-M angle from Grid for plotting to Magnetic for walking:

Left = Add; Right = Subtract

Depending on where you are in the world, the G-M angle could be left, or west, of the grid line, or it could be right, or east, of the grid line.

If the "M," or magnetic line, is left of the "G" or grid line, then you would add the number of the G-M angle.

For example, say you're plotting a 45-degree azimuth on the map. If the "V" in the declination diagram shows the G-M angle to be 5 degrees, and the M line is left of the G line, you'd convert the map/grid (G) azimuth to the compass/magnetic (M) azimuth by adding the 5 degree G-M angle. The result would be that you change your compass heading, or azimuth, from 45 degrees to 50 degrees.

If the G-M angle is still 5 degrees, but the M line is right of the G line, then subtract the 5 degree GM angle from your 45 degree Grid Plot azimuth, resulting in a 40 degree Magnetic azimuth you can then walk.

That's how you take a plot from a map and apply it to a compass. Here's how you go from compass to map, basically reverse it:

If you see a mountain in the distance at 45 degrees on your compass, and you want to plot it on you map, look at the G-M angle. If the G-M angle is 5 degrees, and the M of the G-M angle is left of the G, you would normally "LEFT-ADD" to convert from map to compass. In this case, since we're going from compass to map, the process is reversed, and we subtract 5 degrees. Hence, the 45-degree azimuth becomes a 40-degree azimuth on the map.

MAP TOOLS

Let's move on to briefly cover a few map tools, some fancy, some simple, just in case you find you have access to them.

PROTRACTORS. A protractor is usually a thin, clear piece of plastic with a lot of numbers on it and a few square and triangular holes cut into it for use in measuring distances and plotting routes. Should you find one of these with your map, here's how to use it:

Orient your map toward north as best you can and place the protractor in the general vicinity of your location. Align the square hole with the grid square on your map. With this you can pinpoint location down to a 10-digit grid coordinate using the little tick marks all the way around the outside edges of the square hole.

If you hold a piece of string at the center of the base of the protractor, and then align the protractor with the grid lines on the map, you can run the string out toward your destination and find your grid azimuth—the degree mark where the string crosses the protractor's 360-degree arc.

Convert that grid azimuth to magnetic azimuth on your compass using the G-M angle on the declination diagram and you'll be ready to set off for your destination.

Note: You can also use the protractor's straight edge to measure straight-line distances.

GPS (GLOBAL POSITIONING SYSTEM). GPS is one of the greatest things since sliced bread. It is not within the scope of this book to explain how to use them. Since there are many different types with many different options,

I would expect you to either know your equipment, read the instructions, or simply fiddle with it until you figure it out. Most are fairly simple and straightforward.

Use it like a compass if you have one, but also know that they operate on batteries, and will likely die before you get where you need to go in a survival situation, so be prepared to do without.

COMPASSES

A compass relies on the laws of physics to tell you which direction you're going, and a decent amount of math is required to use one with precision. But in its simplest form, anyone can use a compass effectively, or even create one.

The earth spins. Just as the spinning of a windmill or waterwheel generates energy, the earth's spin generates electromagnetic waves. It is these waves that magnetize the earth, and it is the earth's magnetic pull that makes the compass needle point north. The compass needle is actually a magnet, and the pole's magnetic pull is very faint, so the needle must be as frictionless, or free-floating, as possible to allow for greatest accuracy.

If you have a map and compass, orient them both toward north, then turn your body so you are facing north as well. This will be your point of view and reference for the rest of your route planning. Whatever direction you must travel, keep your compass and map oriented north, and then face your direction of travel and the map will show you what terrain lies ahead.

THE PARTS OF A COMPASS

BEZEL RING. Your compass has a ring around the outside that turns. This is called a bezel ring. The bezel ring is used for precise navigation, especially at night. When you turn the bezel ring, it makes a little click, and each one of those clicks represents 3 degrees. Turning the bezel ring 5 clicks to the left or right means an adjustment of 15 degrees to the east or 15 degrees to the west. This is not intended for a beginner, but if you get really lost in the dark and need to reset your course, the bezel ring can help you do just that.

Disregard for now—just file the information away in the "could be useful" category.

SCALE. Many modern compasses have a plastic, box-like body. These bodies often have scale markings on the edges. You can use these not only as a straight edge to make a line and plot your course, but to measure distances on your map, as long as the map and the compass use the same scale. You can still use it as a straight edge to measure distance even if the map is of a different scale—just mark the straight line distance, then look at the black-and-white checkered long bars on the map's legend to see how many miles or kilometers that distance really is.

SEE-THROUGH BACK. Many modern camping compasses have a see-through plastic back so you can lay the compass on your map and then line up the map with the compass so that the top of the map, which is always north, is pointing the same way as the north arrow on the compass. This is called orienting your map.

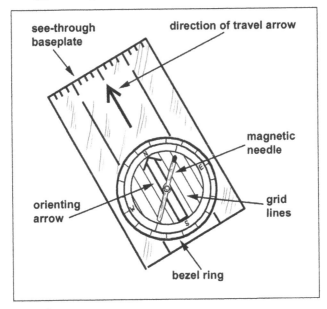

Parts of a compass

HOW TO USE A COMPASS

It's actually very simple. Hold the compass level to the ground so the needle can spin freely. Some compasses have a plumb bubble to help you keep the compass level. Keep the bubble in the center to ensure an accurate reading. Also, be sure to keep the compass away from metal objects, like watches or belt buckles.

Let the arrow spin until it settles in one direction. This is north. Turn your body so that you are facing north. You are now oriented to your environment. The arrow, the lines on the bezel and your nose should all be pointing in the same direction.

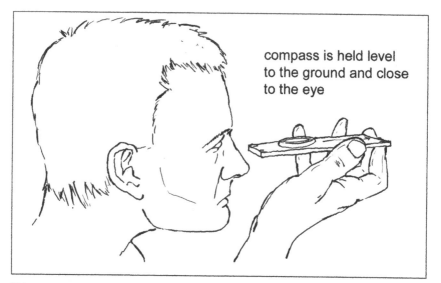

compass is held level to the ground and close to the eye

Using a compass

The compass face is divided with marks into degrees. Some compasses are marked with mils instead of degrees. Mils are for extremely accurate measurements by engineers and such—disregard them. Degrees are usually marked in red, mils in black. There are only 360 degrees, but 6,400 mils.

Stick to degrees.

The **azimuth** is the angle, in degrees, measured clockwise, between north and the direction you want to travel. North is an azimuth of 0 degrees.

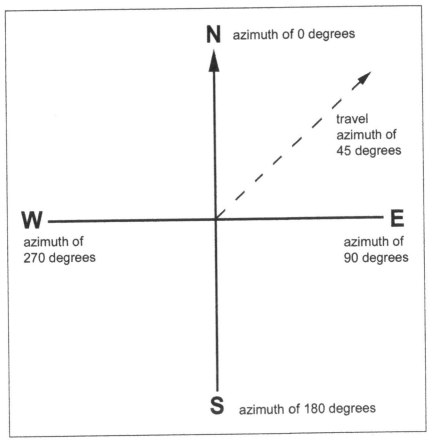

Northeast azimuth is 45 degrees

East is an azimuth of 90 degrees. South is an azimuth of 180 degrees. West is an azimuth of 270 degrees.

When you're facing north, your outstretched right hand points to 90 degrees, or due east. Your back is facing south and your left side faces west. Here's an easy way to remember:

Nose = North
Right = East ("right-ist" or "right-ish")
Sit = South (your butt is south of your head)

Left = West (both words have an "E" so it's easy to remember)

I think of California as the "left" coast, and the East coast as the "right" coast, and I'll let you figure out the political innuendo there—ha!

The easiest way to maintain your sense of direction is to remember where the sun rose. The sun always rises in the east, so point your right shoulder toward where the sun came up and your nose will be facing north, your backside facing south, and your left to the west!

Let's say you are facing north, where your compass arrow is pointing. You know that civilization is to your west, or your left-hand side, about 500 miles or so. This means you want to travel on an azimuth of 270 degrees.

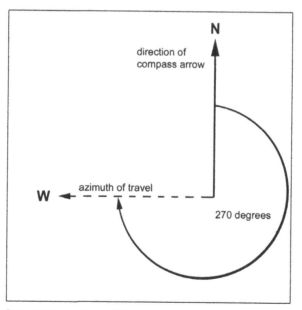

Due-west azimuth is 270 degrees

Finding any other direction is a matter of simple fractions. If you want to travel in a northeasterly direction, your azimuth will be halfway between north, at 0 degrees, and east, at 90 degrees. Your azimuth is 45 degrees.

If you know which direction you want to travel, and want to find that azimuth, simply point your nose and your compass north, then turn clockwise until you're facing the direction you want to go. Look out into the distance and find the farthest object you can see. Keeping your compass level, look down at the dial. Imagine a line from the far object to the center of your compass. Where that line crosses the degree marks on your compass dial marks your azimuth.

Setting the azimuth on your compass is also quite easy. Just turn the compass body toward your target and line up the azimuth with the aiming points of your compass.

Keep the north-pointing arrow lined up between the bezel brackets (these are the two lines on the bezel that bracket the north-pointing arrow when the bezel is set at zero).

Now just face the direction of your pointers and walk your azimuth. By keeping the north arrow between the bezel brackets, you will ensure that your compass is always oriented toward north, and by following the direction of the aiming points on the compass, you will ensure that you are headed in the correct direction, always walking in line with your azimuth.

azimuth is the line between furthest object & the centre of the compass

Determining azimuth

As you walk, check the azimuth every 15 minutes or so to keep yourself on track. After breaks, simply stand up, hold the compass flat, let the north arrow stabilize within the bezel brackets, and resume walking in the direction of your pointers.

BACK AZIMUTH simply defines the opposite direction of your azimuth. Let's say you are walking 90 degrees due east. Your back azimuth is 180 degrees opposite. By adding 180 degrees to your 90 degree azimuth, you get a back azimuth of 270 degrees. If your azimuth is greater than 180 degrees, then subtract 180 to get your back azimuth. An azimuth of 300 degrees would have a back azimuth of 120 degrees.

Back azimuth comes in handy two ways. The first is in helping you find your way back to where you started, especially if you're just trying to get back to base camp after a day foraging. The second is to help you plot a route or find your location on a map.

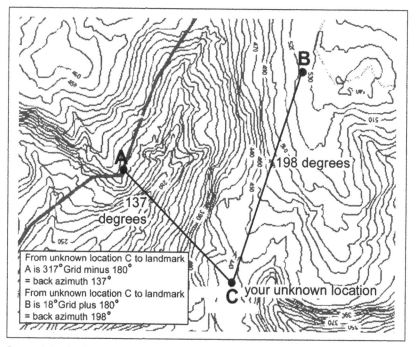

From unknown location C to landmark A is 317° Grid minus 180° = back azimuth 137°
From unknown location B is 18° Grid plus 180° = back azimuth 198°

Determining back azimuth

The terms for this technique are "re-section" or "triangulation." If you have a map and a compass and don't know where you are, but you can see a landmark object in the distance, then you can "shoot" an azimuth at that object. Use that azimuth to determine a back azimuth, and draw that line on your map. Then shoot an azimuth at another distant point, maybe a mountaintop or ridge line. Then convert that to a back azimuth and draw another line on your map. The point where these two lines intersect pinpoints your location on the map. Now you know where you are.

Use three azimuth lines for a more precise location, but with just one distant target's back azimuth and some reading of the terrain, you can get a good idea of your location in many circumstances.

HOW TO IMPROVISE A COMPASS

A compass is a critical piece of equipment if you have to move, especially through low-visibility terrain like jungle, or across featureless landscapes like desert. But what if you don't have a compass? As a last resort you can make one yourself, and if you have to abandon your location and travel, I highly recommend that you try.

You'll need a needle and, ideally, a magnet. A sewing needle is perfect, but many metals can take a charge to become a magnetized pointer. Try a paperclip, safety pin, staple or bit of stiff wire.

Speakers contain magnets, or any mechanical item or electronic device might have a magnet inside. Look around. If no magnet is available, you can use some types of cloth to create a magnetic charge. Silk is best, but use whatever you have. Some synthetic materials work as well. Try everything, even your own skin. The principle is the same as shuffling on a carpet to build up a static electricity charge. Try it.

You'll need to polarize the needle. If you have a magnet, leave the needle lying on the magnet overnight. If you're using cloth, polarize the needle by stroking it against the cloth 50, 100, or even 300 strokes, depending on the material. Stroke in one direction only.

If you have a battery and some wire, wrap a piece of paper or a leaf around the wire to insulate it. Then wrap the wire around the needle and tie one end to the positive terminal and one to the negative terminal. It's best to use a C-cell or D-cell battery, but 9-volt batteries work well, too. Leave it connected for about 30 seconds, or until the wire becomes hot. Repeat this at least 10 times to charge the needle.

Mark one end of the needle as the north-pointing end. The needle will have to float free to point north. You can place the needle in anything that will hold water, like a plastic cup, the cut-off bottom of a plastic bottle, or even a Styrofoam plate, as long as the container is not made of metal.

Place the needle on something that will float. A piece of cork or Styrofoam is ideal. Push the needle through the cork or Styrofoam so it's stable, but will spin freely. If you have nothing that floats, try a leaf. If that doesn't work, try rubbing your finger on your nose and coating the needle with oil from your skin. That may float the needle on the surface of the water, but this method will require occasionally re-oiling the needle.

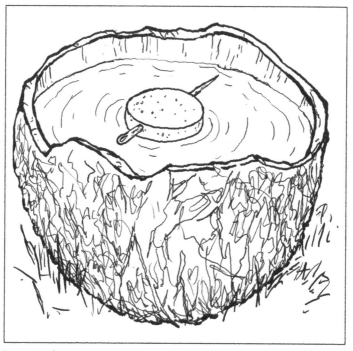

Improvised compass

If no water is available, you can tie a thin piece of string around the middle of the needle and let the needle hang so that it spins freely. But mind the breeze, as wind can make this sort of compass difficult to use. Better than nothing.

Note: Always keep your compass, manufactured or homemade, away from metal.

TAKING DIRECTIONS FROM NATURE

There are lots of myths about moss. Some books say moss grows facing the sun, and that moss will grow on the southern side of trees in the northern latitudes, since that's the side that gets the most sunlight. This is not necessarily true.

THE MOSS RULES:

- In the north, moss grows on the north side
- In the south, moss grows on the south side
- There ain't no rules!

Moss is a special kind of plant that doesn't have the skin to retain moisture like most plants do, yet moss requires a lot of moisture to live. For this reason, moss actually tends to grow on the side of the tree getting the least amount of sunlight, so it doesn't dry up.

Moss is just one of many indicators you can incorporate into your environmental assessment. If you're in the north, and you see a lot of moss growing on the trees, take a moment and look at the big picture. If you see the majority of moss growing on one side of the trees, that side probably faces north.

Then again, it's not uncommon to find moss growing all the way around a tree, especially in moist climates. There's no hard and fast rule about moss. It's just a guide.

COMPASS PLANTS. These are plants that tend to be fairly good indicators of direction. They can be useful, but only if you know what they are and how to interpret them. Since most plants that grow at odd angles are doing so because they are trying to maximize their exposure to the sun, you can sometimes deduce direction from the way they lean. In the southern hemisphere, compass plants will tend to point north toward the sun. In the northern hemisphere, they'll be pointing south. Perennials tend to be thicker and lusher on the side that gets more sun, toward the equator.

If you see a field of plants, take a moment to look at their growth. Are the leaves flat and facing one direction much more predominantly than any other? Do the plants look like they're bent or growing at unlikely angles? If so, chances are they're leaning toward the sun. You can combine that assessment with the knowledge of where you are to roughly figure out the cardinal directions.

TREE RINGS. I've seen a lot of survival books mention tree rings. Yes, they are more distantly spaced on the side closer to the sun, because that side had more growth. But unless you're chopping trees down, or near where trees are being felled, this doesn't help much. If you're near where trees are being chopped down, you're close to rescue already! But all the trees I've seen knocked down by nature were in no state for ring reading.

WIND. Wind can be helpful for gaining a sense of direction in some places, but you'll need to know enough about where you are to know which direction the prevailing winds blow.

Remembering that there are 90 degrees north and 90 degrees south of the equator, you can divide each hemisphere into 3 belts of 30 degrees each. The trade winds are in the belts nearest the equator. Trade winds in the belt north of the equator blow from the northeast toward the equator, and from the southeast toward the equator in the belt south of the equator.

The next belt north of the equator is a band of about 30 degrees containing the westerlies, meaning the wind blows from the southwest toward the northeast. In the corresponding westerlies band below the equator, the wind blows from the northwest toward the southeast.

And finally, if you are so unfortunate as to be lost at the poles, the belts of wind there are called the polar easterlies. At the North Pole they blow

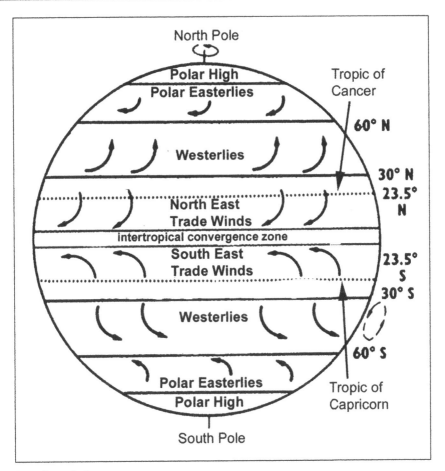

Prevailing winds

from the northeast to the southwest, and at the South Pole from the southeast to the northwest.

In places where the winds are particularly strong, they, like the sun, can make plants lean a certain direction. Look for signs like bird nests and insects—these will tend to concentrate on the side protected from the winds.

Such observations of local life, combined with a basic sense of the prevailing wind direction for your region of the world, could assist you in navigating to safety.

HOW TO READ THE SUN, MOON, AND STARS

Maybe you don't have a compass or the equipment to make one. You still need to get some idea of where you want to go and how to get there from where you are.

Will you have to circumnavigate a mountain range, for example, before you can get to a river, which you can follow to a village? If so, you might need to walk three days due south, then two days due east, to reach your intended destination.

How do you manage this without a compass or a map? You do it the way shepherds and travellers have done since the beginning of time: You read the map of the heavens.

Remember, the sun rises in the east and sets in the west. Once you have that locked in, you can always find north by orienting your right shoulder toward the east, which points your nose north. Simple.

WHAT TIME IS IT?

The 24-hour solar cycle is divided into day and night. These are roughly 12 hours each. We all know that days are longer in summer and shorter in winter, and that daytime light and nighttime dark each last for months at the poles. Still, even with all these variations, there is always at least a slight darkening at night and lightening by day. And even when it is cloudy and overcast for days or even weeks, you can often see little edges of light on the horizon at the break of day and at dusk before complete dark. These are your east and west markers for those climatic extremes.

You have to mentally calibrate according to your location and the season, but you can make a good guess at the time of day by where the sun is in the sky. When the sun is highest in the sky, it's noon. When it first rises, it's approximately 6 a.m. And when it sets, that is approximately 6 p.m.

Now, divide the sky into sections. The eastern horizon is 6 a.m., the western horizon is 6 p.m., and the middle of the sky, directly overhead, is high noon. To see what time it is, just look to see where the sun is and guesstimate. If the sun looks like it's halfway between 6 a.m. and noon, it's about 9 in the morning. If it's halfway between noon and 6 p.m., it's close to 3 p.m. It's pretty simple. I test this all the time and I'm usually within 15 minutes of the actual time.

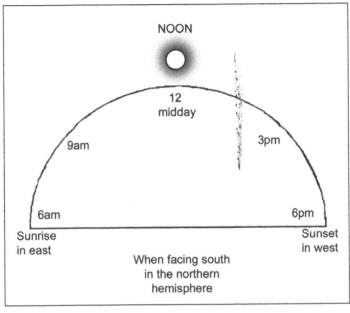

Telling time

You can use the skies to tell the time at night as well (provided you have a clear sky), but I find using the stars to tell time overly complicated and not practical. I recommend sleeping at night anyway, in which case knowing the time isn't critical. But if for whatever reason you need the information, here it is.

This is for the northern hemisphere folks only. Find the Big Dipper. Its position in the sky changes every quarter of the year. Just remember that at midnight on March 7 it is at the "high noon" position. Three months later, on June 7, it will be at the 9 o'clock position.

Note: The constellations move counter-clockwise in the sky.

The point is, if you can find the Big Dipper, and you know what time of year it is, you can tell when it's midnight. From there, divide the night sky into a 12-hour clock face and you can work out the approximate time based on the Big Dipper's relationship to its midnight position.

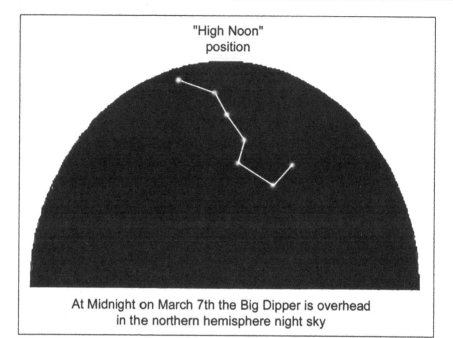

"High Noon"
position

At Midnight on March 7th the Big Dipper is overhead
in the northern hemisphere night sky

Telling time at night

But maybe you just want a general idea of what time of night it is, without all that math. Maybe you want to know how long you've been resting, or how much longer before the sun rises. Use the moon.

A full moon can be used just like the sun—it rises in the east and sets in the west. On the nights of new or "no" moon, you'll have to use the Big Dipper.

Telling time by the moon is a two-part process. First, look at how much of the moon is lit up. If half of the moon is lit, then the moon will be up half the night, or 6 hours. If one quarter is lit, it will be up only 3 of the night's 12 hours. If the moon is three-quarters lit, the moon will be up for 9 hours.

For the second part of the equation you have to know when the moon came up and where it is in the sky. You can guesstimate from there.

For example, if the moon is half full, you know it will be up for 6 of the night's 12 hours. If it came up at dusk, and is half way to the "high noon" position, then it's 9 p.m. If the moon didn't show up until midnight (you'll know this because it first appears in the high noon position) and the moon is only half lit, and it's halfway toward the horizon, or 6 a.m. position, then you know it's 3 a.m.

Knowing the time can help you plan your movements based on available light, and it also applies to navigation.

TRAVELLING AT NIGHT

Generally speaking, you shouldn't be travelling at night. But if you're stranded in the middle of the desert in the middle of summer, when movement by day will surely kill you, here are some tips for how to move at night without a compass.

NAVIGATING BY THE MOON The moon orbits our planet every 29.5 days. This means we get about 2 weeks of a moon with one side lit up and about 2 weeks with the other side lit up. We really get only one night per month of proper "full" moon, but for survival purposes, there are roughly 3 days before and 3 days after the true full moon that we get a full moon's worth of nighttime lighting. The same holds for the new or "no" moon phase—there is really only one night of pitch blackness, but the little sliver of moon that is lit a few days before and after that mean we get about a week of effective darkness.

This is significant to the survivor planning to move at night. If you know you're facing nearly a week of fumbling in the dark, you must weigh very carefully the decision to move or not. Likewise, the full moon has a strong effect on tides and if your movement involves crossing water, this factor must be considered as well.

Now let's look at how the moon can be used for navigating. If you look up at the sky in the early evening, you will notice one of two things. Either the sun will go down and there will be no moon until about midnight, or the sun will be setting and you will see the moon is already up. Here's what either case means to you:

If the moon doesn't come up until around midnight, then the side that is lit is pointing east. Since the sun is already down, you have only one celestial body to point the way. The phrase "one at least, to show the east" may help you remember.

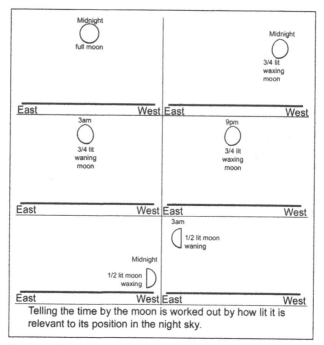

Telling the time by the moon is worked out by how lit it is relevant to its position in the night sky.

Moon positioning

Moon phases

If the moon is up at the same time as the sun, then the bright side of the moon is pointing to the west. Remember the phrase "two is best to show the west."

ORIENTING TO A FULL MOON. When the moon is full, provided the sky is clear, you can use the **shadow tip method** (see below), just like with the sun, to orient yourself. Since the moon also rises in the east and sets in the west, all the same techniques apply.

ORIENTING TO A CRESCENT MOON. Regardless of which side of a crescent moon is lit, either will show you south. Just imagine a line from tip to tip of the crescent, and then continue that line down to the horizon, and that will point you generally due south every time.

NAVIGATING BY THE STARS

THE BIG DIPPER. The Big Dipper is a true "gift of the gods" for navigators, in that it stays in the position of true north throughout the year. Depending on where you are and the time of year, it might be near the horizon or even obscured by mountains in the distance, but it will always show north, and it can always be found in relation to other supporting constellations.

The Big Dipper is known by other names, like The Plough in Europe, or seen as part of a larger constellation called Ursa Major. But in the U.S. it's called a "dipper" because it looks like a soup ladle, and it's called "big" to distinguish it from a smaller dipper in the same section of sky. It's one of the easiest-to-recognize constellations.

In case you're uncertain, there's another easy-to-find constellation called Cassiopeia, which looks like a sideways "W," with the open parts of the top of the "W" facing the Big Dipper.

THE POLE STAR. The Pole Star is the North Star. Here's how to find it.

First, find the Big Dipper, and trace from the handle down to the ladle and around the bottom of the ladle and up the front of the ladle to its upper lip. If you extend an imaginary line along the front of the ladle and out beyond its upper lip, that line will point the direction to the North, or Pole, star.

The North Star is actually the last star at the end of the handle of the Little Dipper.

Just to be sure, look for the "W" of Cassiopeia. The middle point of the "W" points right at the Pole Star.

Don't confuse the North Star with the planets Venus or Mars, which are very bright in the night sky and can be mistaken for stars by novice stargazers. One sure way to differentiate between them is that Mars is red and Venus is blue, and while both will be bright, neither will twinkle.

Once you have the North Star located, you will know for sure where north is, and you can determine the other directions from there. If you're headed east, keep the North Star off your left shoulder, and you'll be facing and walking due east.

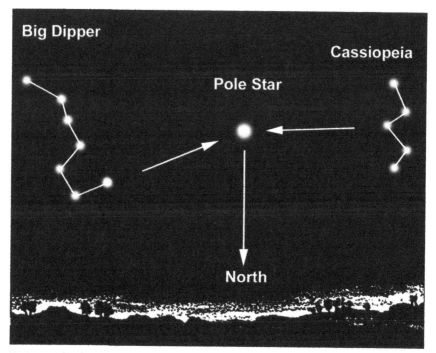

Navigating by the stars

STAR GUN. (Also discussed on page 280.) A star gun is a bit fancy, but can be used for those nights when no moon is visible and you must move at night with some sense of your general direction. This method can also be used when clouds obscure the sky and visibility is limited.

To make the star gun, choose one bright star in the sky, then place two sticks in the ground, one taller than the other, several feet apart, and align their tips as you would align the sights on the barrel of a rifle.

Sight in on your star and keep track of it. Don't stare, just take a look every minute or so for about 15 minutes until you've got a sense of the star's movement. Once you know which direction it is moving, you can find your cardinal directions.

If the star is moving to the right, you are facing south.

If the star is moving to the left, you are facing north.

If the star is dropping down your stick, you're facing west.

If the star is rising up above your sticks, you're facing east. Here's the memory key for the star gun: "East-star rising, the south is right"

If you know a rising star means east, then the opposite is west. And if you know the south is right, then left is north. Easy!

Star gun

GETTING YOUR BEARINGS IN THE NORTHERN HEMISPHERE

This applies to most of us, as most of the earth's landmass is north of the equator. But because they are less populous, the lands south of the equator are often the most remote.

Either way, try to always pay attention to where the sun came up and mark that location with a feature of the terrain. Since most survival movements are based on a general direction of travel, like north or south, instead of any precise angle of azimuth, all you really need to do is locate your cardinal directions. Follow those and you'll be fine.

For example: You see the sun rise over a mountain in the distance. That mountain is to your east. You know that a large city is somewhere to the south of you. So, you point your left shoulder toward that mountain and you're now facing south. As you walk, keep checking over your shoulder to make sure that the mountain is in the same relative position, to your left, and you'll know that you are still headed in a generally southerly direction. Make sure to use a fixed, identifiable feature of the terrain, the farther away the better. Do not use the sun as your reference feature, since it moves, and you'll end up going in a big U-turn.

During the daylight hours, there are a few fairly easy ways to figure out your direction without a compass. These are the most common and easy to use.

SHADOW TIP METHOD. As the sun rises in the east, it will cast a shadow pointing west. As the sun passes the high-noon position, toward the western horizon, the shadow will move to the opposite side, or toward the east.

So as the sun rises from east to west, it casts a shadow that moves west to east.

Find an open area, place about a 1-foot stick in the ground, and look to see where the shadow falls. Mark the tip of the shadow with a rock, a small stick, or a line in the dirt. Wait about 5 minutes while the tip of the shadow moves. Now, mark the new position of the shadow. Mark a line connecting the two positions. This is an accurate east-west line. Extend the line in the dirt about a foot to each side so it's long enough to stand on.

Put your left foot on the end nearest the first mark and your right foot on the end nearest the second mark. You are now facing north. Your left shoulder is pointing west, your right shoulder is pointing east, and south is behind you.

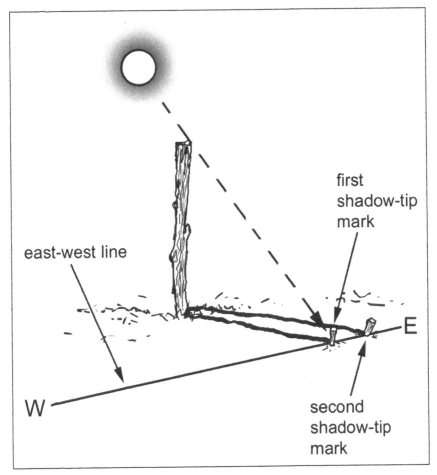

first shadow-tip mark

east-west line

E

W

second shadow-tip mark

Shadow tip method

The following two methods are variations of the shadow tip method.

ANALOG WATCH METHOD. If you have an old-fashioned analog watch with hands, hold the watch parallel to the ground and point the hour hand in the direction of the sun. Mark an imaginary line between the hour hand and the 12. This will give a north-south line with the south line going away from you as you face, meaning the north side of the north-south line is usually at the bottom of your wristwatch as you face it or pointing towards you. (Which means you'll need to turn around to actually be facing north.)

But always spot check yourself with the basic knowledge that the sun rises in the east. So, if it's 9 a.m., and you bend your left arm to look at your watch as normal, then turn your body so that you point the 9 at the sun (the 9 makes a line towards your elbow, and from the center to the 3 makes a line pointing towards your left hand as it sits in your dial on your wrist), then make your line between the 9 and 12 noon—that line will give a north/ south that means you should have to turn around to face north at 9 in the morning. One variation on this method is to place the watch on the ground and use the shadow of a stick to give you your imaginary line for north and south. Or you can keep the watch on your wrist and use a twig or pine needle to make a shadow and see that as your imaginary line.

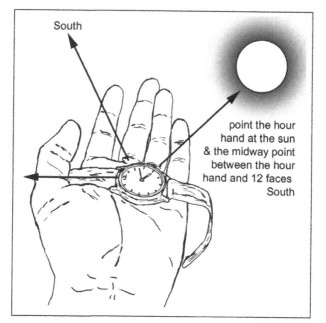

Analog watch method

Note: If you're on daylight savings time, use the 1 p.m. instead of the 12 noon.

DIGITAL WATCH METHOD. All you really need is the time. Whether you get it from a digital watch or a radio announcement, just draw an analog watch face on the ground that has the current hour pointing at the sun, and draw a line between that hour mark and noon on your circle in the dirt. This will give you the same north-south line.

I have found that if I have a watch, I already know what time it is. If I can see the sun, I know where east and west are, and so I really don't need these methods at all!

The only exception is at high noon, when the sun is due south. So, again, you don't need this method, and it's hard to use at 6 a.m. and 6 p.m., too. But then, if you can see the sun, and you know if it's getting lighter or darker, then, you know east for sunrise at dawn and west for sunset at dusk, so, again, you have your cardinal directions and as such, really don't need the watch method to find directions at all.

Example: At sunrise, you get up, and need to move due north. You put your right shoulder to the sunrise in the east and your nose is now facing north. You walk all day until noon. Now, the sun is at due south and should be directly behind you. After high noon, the sun will be moving towards the west, so, you now keep your left shoulder to the west until the sun sets. In this way, you will walk on your path in the correct direction all day.

The watch method can be helpful when you lose your bearings—say a small boar jumps out and you must hunt it or evade it. And then get back on track. Or you are following a compass azimuth and then lose or break your compass. In these cases, the watch method can be of use.

GETTING YOUR BEARINGS IN THE SOUTHERN HEMISPHERE

DURING THE DAY. The sun always rises in the east and sets in the west, so many aspects of navigating in the northern hemisphere are applicable in the southern, just in reverse.

Telling time by the sun is a simple process. The method's accuracy will vary throughout the seasons, but it will always give you a rough approximation you can work with.

Divide the daylight into 12 hours, with 6 a.m. being sunrise and 6 p.m. being sunset. High noon is when the sun is directly overhead. Now chop the sky into sections. If the sun is halfway between 6 a.m. (the eastern horizon) and noon, the time is around 9 a.m.

When the sun is at high noon, it is due north.

THE SOUTHERN CROSS. The Southern Cross is the major navigational constellation of the southern hemisphere. It looks like a tilted cross composed of 4 stars. Whatever its position and whatever time of year, you can follow the long axis from top to bottom in a straight line for about 4½ times the length of the cross to a point in space corresponding to the southern celestial pole. Draw an imaginary line from this "point" straight down to the horizon and you'll have located due south.

The cross rotates around the southern celestial pole throughout the year, but it is always visible. To find it, look for two bright pointer stars that, when you draw a line from left to right through them, will point straight at the stars that form the short arm of the true Southern Cross.

Be aware that there are two false crosses in the same general area. To make sure you've found the true Southern Cross, look for an irregularly shaped black hole in the constellation.

SOUTHERN SHADOW TIP METHOD. Place a stick in the ground so it sticks up about a foot high in an open area. Look at the shadow it casts, and place a pebble at the tip of that shadow. Wait 5 to 10 minutes for the shadow to move, then place another pebble at the new shadow tip. Mark a line connecting these pebbles, then extend the line about a foot longer on each end.

This is your east-west line.

Place your left foot on the first mark and your right foot on the second. You are now facing due south

Note: The shadow will still move from west to east in the southern hemisphere, but the movement will be counter-clockwise.

ANALOG WATCH METHOD. Take an analog watch face and point the 12 in the direction of the sun. Make an imaginary line between the 12 and the hour hand. For example: If it's 5:25 p.m., use the 5 o'clock position for the hour hand. The imaginary line between the 12 and hour position will describe a north-south line.

DIGITAL WATCH METHOD. Apply the same principle, but use your digital watch to determine the time. Then draw an analog watch face on the ground or on a piece of paper, with the 12 oriented toward the sun. Mark the time from your digital watch on the paper or the ground. Mark a line between 12 and the hour hand. This is your north-south line.

AT NIGHT. The sky in the southern hemisphere looks quite different from the sky in the northern hemisphere, since it faces out into the other half of the galaxy. You will see a different set of constellations. But the moon will still rise in the east and set in the west, as does the sun.

HOW TO TELL TIME BY THE MOON. The moon has roughly 4 phases, loosely described as full moon; new or "no" moon; one half lit; other half lit. Each phase lasts about a week.

Nighttime is roughly 6 p.m. to 6 a.m. With the night divided into 12 hours, you can approximate time by the moon's position in the sky, much as you can with the sun. When the moon is directly overhead, it's close to midnight. When it's near the horizon, it's either dusk or dawn. The amount of the moon's surface that is lit will determine how long the moon will be visible. A quarter moon will be visible for about 3 hours. A full moon will be visible all night. A half moon will be up for half the night.

HOW TO DETERMINE DIRECTION BY THE MOON. When the moon rises after the sun has set, usually around midnight, the lit side indicates east.

When the sun and moon are up at the same time, the lit side faces west. Remember: "One at least to show the east, two is best to tell the west."

When the moon is in any type of crescent shape, you can draw an imaginary line from one tip of the crescent to the other and continue that line down to the horizon and the point at which that line intersects the horizon will give you a rough indication of north.

When the moon is full, you can use the shadow tip method just like during the daytime with the sun. Mark the first shadow tip, then 10 minutes later mark the second shadow tip. Draw a line connecting these marks to define an east-west axis. Place your left foot on the first mark and your right on the second. You are now facing south.

STAR GUN. (Also discussed on page 273.) A star gun is a technique using two sticks like gun sights to aim at a star in order to determine its direction of movement. This movement will give you an indication of the cardinal direction you are facing. The star gun is useful when inclement weather prevents you from observing the whole sky.

Pick a bright star, place a stick in the ground as a sighting point, and then place another stick in the ground 2 to 3 feet away and reaching higher, so that the line of sight from the top of one stick to the other aligns on the targeted star.

Observe the target star every few minutes for about 15 minutes to determine its direction of travel. Then use the following key to determine the cardinal direction you're facing.

If the star is moving to the left, you are facing south.

If the star is moving to the right, you are facing north.

If the star is moving down, you are facing east.

If the star is moving up, you are facing west.

WEATHER

Weather doesn't do much for us in terms of determining direction, but it does mean a great deal in terms of travel, movement, and shelter. You are at the mercy of Mother Nature, and you must respect her temperament and her terms.

It helps to have a basic understanding of how weather works. In the simplest terms, the earth rotates, and this makes night and day. The earth also circles the sun, accounting for the four seasons. During each season, general patterns prevail, such as heat in summer and cold in winter. The sun heats the earth by day, and its absence cools the earth by night. Wind patterns are caused by changes in temperature, and the sun evaporates water from the oceans into the atmosphere, where it rains down onto the land below. All these processes work together to give us what we experience as weather.

Where on the planet you are, and what time of year it is, will determine what types of weather you can expect to be exposed to. If the skies look like rain, you'll want to make sure to pitch camp on high ground. If the wind is whipping, you'll want to avoid exposed ridges. These are factors to be considered as you decide whether to hole up or set out to find help.

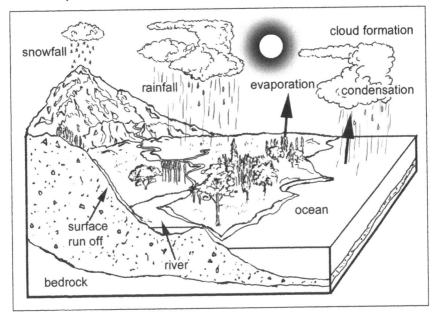

Weather cycle

My purpose in this section is to give some general weather-prediction tips so you can do a decent job of reading basic weather patterns. Plan your moves accordingly.

There are a few pithy sayings that go a long way toward reading the weather:

Red sky at night, sailor's delight. (This means the sky is dry and it's not likely to rain for a while.)

Red sky in morn, best to warn. (If the light of the sunrise is more red than yellow, expect stormy weather.)

Grey-breaking day, all is ok. (This is the normal morning sky before the sun comes up, and means a normal day.)

Grey at night, wet all right. (This means the clouds are so thick they cover up the setting sun's light. Expect rain.)

WHAT TO LOOK FOR

Sometimes you can smell moisture in the air, or things sound different, as if you can hear farther. This is the quiet, dead space between the atmospheric pressure waves before a storm comes. Or you can see the smoke from your fire dancing about instead of just trickling upwards. Or you can feel the drop in atmospheric pressure, or change in temperature, or just feel the wind either stop suddenly or pick up rapidly. Other signs of weather to look for include:

PEOPLE. Some folks get aches and pains in anticipation of wet weather, or their hair curls up with moisture, indicating that rain could be approaching.

ANIMALS. Excessive activity in the middle of the day may be an early warning of bad weather. When animals go all quiet, a storm is imminent.

SKIES. A rainbow usually means the storm is past.

If there's enough moisture in the air, you can sometimes see a ring around the sun or moon. If the ring is large or loose, then the moisture is thin and the weather will be ok. If the circle around the sun or moon is tight and small, it means denser moisture in the air, and an increased chance of precipitation. So . . .

The bigger the ring, the better the weather.

Small ring in the sky, you won't be dry.

CLOUDS. Aside from hard and increasing winds, one of the best ways to predict oncoming weather is to look at the clouds. There are many different types, and many varied combinations, and they all have funny names that I can't be bothered to memorize. What I care about is what they mean to me when I'm stuck outdoors. The main things to know are that when they're dark, they're full of water. When they're close to the ground, they're ready to dump on you. That said, here's your class on clouds:

The Good: Bright, white, puffy, cotton ball-looking clouds. Rippled, sand dune-type clouds.

High-flying, light, wispy, thin-looking clouds.

Also, ground fog in the morning usually means a sunny day is ahead.

The Bad: Clouds that look like someone stretched out a big cotton ball over the sky, leaving small pockets and slight gaps where the cloud is thinner.

Clouds that look like a solid grey blanket has been unrolled across the sky.

These usually mean precipitation is coming. The time of year will determine whether it's rain or snow, and the speed and strength of the wind will determine how long before it gets to you.

The Ugly: These are those very serious tropical storm-type clouds that move in rapidly, and the sky goes black before it pitches down on you.

Also, when you see any of the above cloud formations with one large, tall, fat, pillar-looking cloud, usually with a flat head at the top, it's pushing a bad rain.

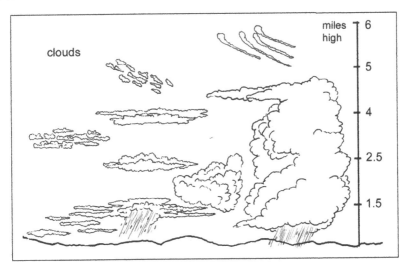

Cloud heights

When you see driving rains moving like a shower wall, these are from a mean storm. Look to see if it's headed for you or not.

If you're in the mountains, a storm can slip up on you in minutes over a ridgeline that blocked your view. In the desert, you might want to make tracks *toward* ominous-looking rain clouds in hopes of finding life-giving rainwater. Use your common sense—you'll be fine.

LIGHTNING. If you can see it in the distance, prepare to seek shelter before it gets to you. If you can hear it, best to take shelter right away. Shelter is way back in a cave or at the base of a tree in a large cluster of trees at the lowest point you can find. Stay away from high ground and single trees. In open terrain, lay down flat on the ground or in any small gulley or ravine.

To calculate lightning's distance from you, start counting seconds from the moment you see the flash until you hear the thunder. Then divide that number of seconds by 5. So, if you count 10 seconds between the flash and the boom, divide 10 by 5 to get your distance: 2 miles.

GETTING THERE

Now it's time to put theory to practice in the real world.

Mind how you go. Route selection is everything.

When choosing your route, choose the path of least resistance. You will probably be weak and tired and hungry, or maybe even ill or injured.

Try to stay on the high ground. Don't drop down unless you have to, since climbing down and back up will wear you out fast.

Walk the ridgelines as much as possible. That way you can see both sides of the mountain, and double your chances of spotting water or civilization.

If you have to drop down to lower elevations, try to read the ridges and stay on a path that keeps you as high as possible on the land as you and it descend. Beware of "dead ends" that force you to backtrack and waste energy.

Don't walk in valley bottoms unless you are shielding yourself from the wind or looking for water. In low-lying areas you are more likely to encounter thick brush that can make movement difficult. In these cases, drop low to the ground and try to find a game trail to follow out. Then stay out.

Try to give yourself "handrails" by using terrain features such as rivers and ridgelines to keep you on track in case you get disoriented in thick cover or dark.

Try to avoid traversing swamps and mountain ranges. Better to take more time and go around them, unless you're running out of time and forced to take the risk of not making it at all.

Be aware that on sloping terrain you will inevitably drift downward. Try to offset your elevation loss by walking back up a few meters every click or so.

If you find yourself fighting too hard, consider altering your route to an easier path.

Don't dogmatically push to reach a planned destination. Your schedule is arbitrary. It's not worth wearing yourself out.

Incorporate food and water stops and rest and sleep areas into your route.

ESTIMATING DISTANCES

Try to estimate the distance to your destination before you set out. After a day of travelling, you should try to estimate how far you've come, and compare that to how far you expected to get. The difference can help you adjust your planning to better match your actual performance.

If you have a map, use a straight edge to estimate the distance to where you want to go before you set out. The straight edge can be the compass, a protractor, a ruler, a piece of paper, a piece of string, or any flat object that can be held against the scale in the map's legend and transferred to your azimuth.

A piece of paper is handy for estimating distance on a route with many legs or curves. Simply place one corner of the paper at the start point, then move the paper, keeping the edge on your line of travel at all times and making little pencil marks at each change of direction for a new leg or at each bend of a twisting route.

In this manner, you can "walk" your paper edge along the entire route, making marks along the way, so that when you are done you can look at the distance along the straight line of the paper's edge. Place this against the map's scale legend to see how far your journey will be on the ground.

Remember that elevation can be deceptive. For example, a 45 degree incline will add about 50 meters for every 1,000 meters, or "click," travelled. A 10-click journey on a steep gradient could add an extra kilometer to your overall distance. This can add up over the course of many miles in mountainous terrain.

A good rule of thumb is to allow 1 extra hour travel time for every 1,000 feet of elevation gain. An 8-mile journey that might take only 2 hours on flat ground will take 3 hours if the path climbs a 1,000-foot hill.

ESTIMATING DISTANCE WITHOUT A MAP. The easiest way is the way you know. Use whatever point of reference you're familiar with. Most folks know that a football field is 100 yards, and a basketball court is about 25 meters long. Use these known quantities to estimate unknown distance.

Your arm is about 10 times as long as the distance between your eyes. This is a fairly constant biological fact. You can use your knowledge of basic anatomy to your advantage.

You may know the length of something nearby, say your crashed plane. To make the math easy, let's say it's 100 feet long. You're on a hilltop overlooking your base camp near the crash site. You want to estimate the distance to camp to make your homemade map as accurate as possible. Here's how. . . .

Hold your arm out in front of you, elbow straight and thumb pointing up. Close one eye and line up one edge of your thumb with one edge of the plane. Then close that eye and open the other one, being sure not to move your head or arm. Your thumb will seem to move due to the change of perspective.

But how much distance did your thumb jump over when you changed eyes?

Let's say it moved over about 3 times the length of the plane, or in other words, 300 feet, since the plane is known to be 100 feet long. Based on the known size of the plane and the fact that your arm is 10 times longer than the distance between your eyes, you can take that "jump" distance and multiply it by the easy-to-remember constant of 10.

This is applied basic trigonometry (or geometry for purists)—but this is the triangle formed from one eye down your arm to the point, then the short base line distance over from the eye change, then the distance back to you forms a triangle, so, this is how to apply it. Multiply that known size, by the amount of itself that it moved over by the eye/arm ratio of 10.

The boat of 100 foot length, jumps over 3 times its own length when you switch eyes, means a 300 foot distance, multiplied by 10 means a 3,000 foot distance between you and the boat. Now use this measurement and apply it to the terrain around you to get a sense of your estimated distances.

ESTIMATING DISTANCE WITHOUT A POINT OF REFERENCE. This is basic algebra—you have an equation, 10 x JD x ??

The JD is jump distance. The ?? is the unknown measurement. All you need to do is find a known measurement and use that factor for your formula. Here's how . . . .

You know your own height. You're likely between 4 and 6 feet tall. So, use that known measurement and find something in your environment that you can measure against that height, like a tree. Say there's a tree near you that you can estimate as being about 10 times taller than you. If you're 5 feet tall, the tree is approximately 50 feet tall.

Now you have a known factor to plug into your equation

Now, select a hilltop off in the distance, extend your thumb, close one eye, line up one edge of your thumb with one edge of the hilltop. Then switch eyes and estimate how far your thumb jumped over, keeping in mind that you measure the jump distance using the same edge of your thumb.

Now, consider that jump distance in terms of your 50-foot tree. You'll have to approximate, so there's some room for error here, but it's a better guide than nothing. Let's say your thumb jumped about 8 times the size of that tree. That's about 400 feet of thumb jump, multiplied by 10 for eye-to-eye distance, giving you 4,000 feet. That's about how far that hilltop is from you.

This theory is called parallax. In the desert, use boulders. If you have a person-sized object out at a distance and your thumb just about covers them when you hold it out in front of you, they are about 500 meters away from you.

If you're out to sea, you will have a hard time measuring distance without an object on the horizon. If you see an object on the horizon, you should be heading for it. If you're not moving that direction, you probably don't have a motor or sail or even a rudder to help propel you, so it won't help much, other than to give you a sense of distance. In these cases, and if you have some rope or cord, tie it to something that will float and let out an arm's length of rope.

Use this piece of rope to estimate the distance and then use the parallax formula method to guesstimate your surroundings. In general, it won't help much at sea or the desert or arctic where there is literally nothing on your horizon as far as you can see. But, it might be helpful for determining if you can swim to shore or out to recover an overboard object.

These techniques for estimating distance without a map should be incorporated into your planning for how far you can or want or need to go, and how much time you'll need to get there. They can also be used in conjunction with your pace count to calibrate your distance estimations to your specific environment. It's all about learning and applying and continuously incorporating old data with new information to develop the best analysis of your situation.

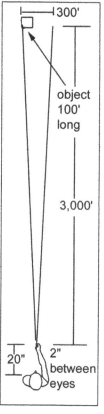

Estimating "jump" distance

KEEPING TRACK

PACE COUNT. This is a technique used by the military for millennia to determine distance travelled. It is absolutely vital information for helping you know with any degree of accuracy exactly where you are at all times. It is also critical knowledge in planning how far you can expect to go in any given terrain and amount of time. Experience helps to modify it for variables such as terrain, load weight, weather, and other factors including food, fatigue, and morale.

In Special Forces, we use the pace count with GPS-like precision. We navigate many kilometers, in the dark, under a heavy rucksack, against the clock, repeatedly, through thick terrain. We are able to do all this successfully because we fine-tune our skills and rely on our pace count for accuracy and backup.

In its simplest form, pace count is just a matter of counting your steps. For this to have meaning, you need to know how far your step carries you. So we measure.

On a flat surface, like a road, I walk 100 meters at a comfortable speed in 63 paces. If the terrain is uneven, but still fairly flat, like out in the woods, I take 68 paces to make 100 meters. This is an average pace count.

The more difficult the terrain, like thick jungle, or the steeper, the more steps I take, so my pace count increases. If I'm carrying a full rucksack, or moving at night, or sick and tired and hungry, I will take smaller steps, and so again my pace count will increase.

To determine your pace count, measure 100 meters on the most level ground you can find. Use a piece of string measured against your own height, or any other known entity, and tie it at both ends to a stick or stake. Place the start-point stake in the ground and stretch the string to its length. Repeat the process until you've measured out 100 meters. This is your scale.

Starting with both feet together, take two steps. Where your trailing footsteps pass the first-step foot and land on the ground again, that is one pace.

Count each time your trailing foot strikes the ground. Walk the 100-meter distance at a normal stride. Do this 4 times. Remember the number. Write it down if you need to. Your mind will tend to wander, so count out loud to stay focused. Walk back to the beginning counting all the way. Remember that number. It should be the same or very close to the first one. Go up and back once more for a total of 4 counts.

Take the average of these to find your approximate pace count.

For most men, this is about 55–65 paces. For women it is usually 60–70 paces.

Bear in mind that many factors will affect your pace count and only practice and experience helps refine it so you can adjust or "calibrate" on the fly.

BASIC MEASUREMENTS TO KNOW:

1 meter is approximately 3 feet.

100 meters is the distance you'll be measuring with your pace count (approximately 65 paces).

1,000 meters is a kilometer (KM), or one "click". This is 100 meters times 10, or 650 paces.

1.6 KM is 1 mile. (This is good to know if your map scale is in miles.)

So, you start walking with your right foot forward, and you're counting every time your left foot strikes the ground. You're taking your time, minding your steps, always looking ahead and keeping track of your pace count number in your head as you go. What do you do when you get to the end of the pace count?

You start again. But how do you keep track of how many 100-meter segments you've walked? Here are some options.

PACE CORD. A pace cord is the most common and easiest-to-use strategy. It only requires a few minutes to make. Take a piece of cord or string. Double it up a few times if it's very thin. Make it about 1 foot long. Tie a knot at the top and a knot at the bottom, and one more about 2/3 of the way up. Then take 9 smaller pieces of string and tie them into knots around the longer segment the cord. Now tie 4 smaller pieces in knots around the shorter segment. Make the knots tight enough to stay put, but loose enough to slide up and down the cord. Now you have a pace cord.

Tie it to your shirt or belt loop. Slide all the knots to the top on each segment. Begin walking and counting your pace. When you get to your 100-meter pace count, slide the bottom knot on the 9-knot segment down to mark 1 100-meter segment walked.

After your second 100-meter pace count, slide down another knot. Keep repeating this. Let's say you get to your destination, a watering hole down the hill from your base camp, and there are 6 knots at the bottom of your pace cord. That means you have travelled 600 meters.

After 9 knots, you'll mark your tenth 100-meter walk by sliding down the bottom knot of the 4-knot segment. Each of these four knots indicates

1,000 meters, or 1 KM, or 1 click. Rest your 9 knots to the top of the cord's longer segment and begin again.

With this technique, all you need to do is count your 100-meter pace mark of 65 steps or so, and let the cord keep track of the rest.

Some alternatives to the pace cord are to pick up a pebble or break off a piece of twig and put it in your pocket every 100 meters. Once you have 10 of them, just move them from one pocket to another until you've travelled a click. Move them back to the first pocket for the next click, and so on.

After a while you will get into a groove so that the counting becomes a comfort, your song, and your way of keeping worry at bay.

If you want more accuracy over shorter distances, you can chop your pace count in half to the 50 meter mark, or in quarters to the 25 meter mark. After a while, you will find many uses for your pace count, including using it to move around your camp safely in the dark.

TRACKING DISTANCE WITH TIME. Sometimes, you may have too much on your mind, or other matters to deal with, to effectively do a pace count. If you have a watch, another—though much less accurate—way to measure distance is to let time do the counting for you.

It takes a person in decent shape and average health, on average, about 15 minutes to walk 1 mile at a normal pace on a flat road. This means the average person walks about 4 mph. Folks who are older, ill, or not in shape may walk at only 3 mph, meaning they cover a mile in 20 minutes.

> If 1.6 KM = 1,600 meters = 1 mile = 20 minutes, then:
> 400 meters = 5 min, and:
> 100 meters = 1 minute, 15 seconds

Generally speaking, and depending on your rate of speed and specific circumstance, you'll travel about 100 meters every minute or so.

Now, take this info and factor in your terrain and circumstances. Are you carrying a litter? Is someone on crutches? That might mean only 1 mile per hour. If you are in extremely thick terrain like a swamp or a jungle, you might only move 1 mile in an entire day.

Keep in mind that if you're 100 miles from anywhere, that could mean 3 months of walking every day!

This is how to use time to estimate distance. If you have no watch, you can use the sun and moon to tell time. Just remember to factor in a wider margin of error with these less accurate methods.

GIVE YOUR JOURNEY LEGS. You will rarely walk in straight lines, like we see on a map or measure with a compass. We have to take the actual terrain to be walked and break into manageable portions. Give your journey some legs.

For example, say we need to walk 10 KMs. There's one mountain and two rivers between our start and end points. So we look at how far it is to the first of these obstacles, and call that the first leg of our journey. It might be 2 clicks to the first river. Then we have to walk another 4 clicks to the mountain. Call that the second leg. From the mountain, it's 3 clicks to the second river, and then 1 more click to the destination—each of these segments becomes a leg.

Take a look at the terrain contained within each leg. For example, you might be going due south and gradually downhill on the first leg toward the river. After you cross the river, you might travel southeast on a steep uphill slope toward the mountain. From the mountain, you might turn due east and follow a gentle downhill slope toward the second river.

In this way, we chop up a long journey into smaller sections called legs. Within each leg we look at the distance, the direction and the terrain we must traverse, and approximate the time it will take us to get there. By doing this, we accomplish many things.

By envisioning the terrain in our mind's eye, we familiarize ourselves with what to expect, and when and where.

If we lose our way, get hurt, or otherwise become distracted, we will find it much easier to get back on track having already mentally rehearsed the route.

For example: You're walking through some thick woods at night. You're worried about an infection on your hand and you've forgotten your pace count . . . but, you know that you're on the third leg, so you should be going downhill. You sense that the ground is indeed sloping downward. You know you are headed for a river, so you keep walking. When you find the river, you are at a known point again, and you can pick up your pace count. You know you are supposed to turn due east, and a full moon is out early in the evening, so the moon, rising like the sun in the east, let's you know which direction to go. With this fore-planned knowledge you can confidently continue even when confusion sets in, knowing you're just a leg away from regaining your orientation.

Even if you have no map or compass, you can use whatever landmarks you find to divide your journey into legs. Use terrain features as stopping points. Write down your pace count so far and start over. Check your direction and make adjustments based on what you've seen. Then begin anew.

Note: If you truly have no clue where you are, and you're determined that you must go, then make your best guess at which direction is likely to take you toward help and do not change your direction unless you have a very good reason to do so.

Such a very good reason might be a power line, pipeline, stream or something else with real promise to steer you out of the wilderness. Otherwise, stay the course, or else doubt will creep in, you will begin to wander, and before you know it you'll be walking in circles or inefficient zig-zag patterns, crisscrossing the same terrain, wasting energy, and getting no closer to anything but death.

TRAVEL TIPS

THE HIGH ROAD. When moving uphill toward high ground, go slow, try not to get your pulse and respirations so high that you get sloppy and slip and fall or, worse, push yourself so hard that you pass out and then roll down. Try resting with one leg up-slope and one leg down, and resting your elbow on your knee to catch your breath. Also try locking your knees as you take steps up a steep incline so the muscles get a rest. Remember that your pace count will be much higher—maybe even double—when going up steep hills.

THE LOW ROAD. Moving downward toward lower ground can be deceptively difficult. Not only can it cause injury through the pounding of your heels as you go down, but there's also a tendency to want to move quickly, which could lead to a sprained ankle, an open fracture, or a fatal tumble. Best to go slow, making sure to place each foot solidly each time, as if your life depended on your sure footing. It does.

OPEN GROUND. This type of terrain can also be deceptive. Try not to go too fast. Speed can lead to injuries and cause you to miss a lot of subtle signs that might help you out of your jam, like tracks and trails.

THICK COVER. Presents certain challenges in that you often can't see very far ahead of you, and so can get disoriented. Try to look as far ahead as you can and pick a target to walk toward, like a dead tree or a hill, etc. Watch your step as you go, looking for holes, and be careful stepping over fallen trees—bees will often make a home under fallen trees, or a snake might be nesting under the back side of that log. Try to look over logs before you step over them.

WET GROUND. Wet ground can be extremely challenging. Try to stay as dry as you can. Look for dry mounds or little islands of dryness as you go, but try to plot them on a line so that you keep to your general direction of travel. Swamps can be some of the most difficult terrain to travel because it's just plain hard to lift your feet out of deep, sucking mud, over and over again, and also because the tendency to "island-hop" can take the traveler well off his path. If you have no choice, just get in the water and walk as straight as you can and take breaks to dry out along the way. It comes down to which is the greater risk: parasites and predators, or jungle rot and being lost.

BOOT CHECK. For the survivor, the most important element of transport is the LPC, or Leather Personnel Carrier—your feet and your footgear. This cannot be stressed enough. Many men have died because they neglected their feet. Many wars have been lost because soldiers pushed their feet too hard and could not stand and deliver when they needed to.

A good rule of thumb when travelling in standing water or rain is to stop for 15 minutes every hour and take your shoes/boots and socks off. Let your feet air-dry at least enough to keep the skin from disintegrating for the next 45 minutes. Put your feet in the sun if you can to dry them out. Wring out your socks and swing them around while you're waiting to help them dry as well.

You might even consider not wearing socks at all if you're travelling in swamp or very wet jungle. Surprisingly, most decent shoes or boots won't tear up your feet without socks. In fact, when they get wet they stretch a bit, and actually become more form-fitting as a result.

When I served in the jungle, we took off our socks, t-shirts, and underwear to keep that wet clothing from keeping our skin so moist that friction with the fabric would cause sores. This also had an added benefit in that every time we took a step, the extra space in the boot would suck air into the boot, helping keep the foot dry. We left our clothes hanging from our frames to dry as we walked. Then we wore the dry clothes at night to keep warm and sleep a little better. Try it.

TRACKS. Always be alert to your environment. Even though you are tired and fatigued, do not walk with your head down, or staring out at the distant horizon. Study everything around you as you go. Be like a sponge soaking up data; and be like a computer, always analyzing information; and be like a survivor, always looking for ways to exploit the situation to your benefit.

Always be on the lookout for tracks. We've covered tracks and tracking in the **Food** chapter, but for our purposes here, tracks have a different significance. Animal tracks could lead you to their lair, which could mean food. They could lead you to where they are eating, which could mean food. Or they could lead to water, which you may need, and which could lead you to rescue! So pay attention and always looks for tracks!

GOING 'ROUND IN CIRCLES. It's easy to find yourself travelling in circles if you aren't careful. Anyone who has been lost in the woods and tried to find their way without a compass back to their car or campsite can tell you, it really does happen.

The reason is quite simple. Most people favor a dominant hand and, although most of us aren't aware of it, a dominant leg.

When a ball is thrown at you unexpectedly, you'll automatically try to catch it with your dominant hand. As you walk, you tend to step longer and stronger with your dominant leg. Over long periods of time, this will tend to steer you around in a giant circle in the direction opposite of your dominant leg.

Countering this is easy. Ask yourself with which foot you kick best. That is your dominant foot. For most people, it's the right leg. Now that you have determined your dominant stepping leg, you know that you'll tend to walk in a circle toward the left. To correct this imbalance, step to the right whenever you come to a tree or any other obstruction that causes you to deviate from your straight-line path. This will keep you much closer to on course.

(If you find yourself stepping around obstacles frequently, you should alternate stepping to the left and to the right. You'll need to develop a sense of flow and balance based on your terrain and movement. Just being aware of the "circle phenomenon" and knowing how to counter it is 90% of the solution.)

Another phenomenon to be aware of is the "fear factor." When you're lost and uncomfortable in unfamiliar surroundings, there is a psychological tendency to move toward your dominant or "preferred" side. This tendency is exacerbated at night, and that's when folks make tracks in a circle.

CLIFFS, RIDGELINES, AND RIVERS. You will most likely come upon natural obstacles during your travels. Most can be surmounted or skirted. Here are a few ground rules:

Never jump off a cliff into unknown water! There is almost always a better way down, and it might even be better to try climbing and fall half way than to jump and risk death from not clearing the cliff or landing on rocks in the water below.

Never try to climb up anything if you can help it. Try to walk out, always looking for the easiest path out first. Climbing is a last resort, and you should never need it unless you're trapped, since civilization and water and rescue are almost always in valleys.

Stay out of freezing cold rivers. You will become hypothermic within

45 minutes and could very well die. Best to either build a raft or just keep walking beside the river.

If you must cross a river, your pants can act as a flotation device. Simply pull them off, tie off the legs in a knot or with string if you have some (string will allow more of the leg to act as a balloon). Once you're in the water, hold the pants by the waist behind your head and throw them over your head like you're trying to scoop air into the pant legs. Because they are wet, the pants will actually trap air and act like a float. Put your head between the legs and hold the waist together and this will hold your head above water. Depending

Rappeling method

on the material, you may have to re-inflate, but that's just a quick overhead throw and you're back in business. Now get across the river and get out of it.

Any number of scenarios might force you to descend a cliff. First, try to find some way to walk or scramble down, but if you must descend a steep face, use a rope. If the rope is strong enough, like 550 parachute cord, it can be used for an improvised rappel, but this is not recommended. It hurts and can cause burns, loss of grip, and a fall.

In an emergency, there are two methods of doing an improvised rappel: Faced with a steep slope, you can run the cord under your trail arm, around your back and then under your lead arm and lean into it and walk down the steep slope. To stop, just turn and face back uphill and bring your lead arm in as a brake arm and this will lock you into position.

For when you're on an actual cliff, run the paracord between your leg, being sure to run it under one of your butt cheeks, say the right one, then across your chest and over your left shoulder and then held by your right hand so that your left hand is the trail/guide hand while your right hand is the feed and brake hand. If you need to stop, just pull your right hand in to your waist. This is called the *Dulfersitz*, and I don't recommend it.

In either case, anchor your rope well and tell it goodbye, as you most likely won't be recovering it.

But let me say again: Stay away from cliffs! Walk around!

There's a multitude of scenarios one might encounter in the process of navigating your way toward safety. Hopefully we've covered techniques and strategies to allow you to adapt or improvise your own unique techniques.

Whatever it takes, remember: Never quit!

Signals

Get seen, get heard, get found, get home!

Signals are some of the most important tools in survival. Rescue often starts when the survivor sends a signal, be it audio or visual, that catches someone's attention. Everything else is the hard but happy road home.

The principles of signalling are pretty straightforward: Make yourself seen or heard. So let's look at some ways to make a scene and make some noise, because it's the squeaky wheel that survives.

The first thing you want to do in any survival situation is let someone know where you are so they can come help you, just like calling 9-1-1 in an emergency back home. The thing is, if you have a working radio or a phone, you're probably not truly surviving so much as just tolerating temporary discomfort until help arrives. When you have no means of direct communication and you're stranded, *that's* a survival situation, and it's in these situations that signalling is so important. Now what can you signal with?

First off, take an inventory of any resources you have at hand. Some, like a whistle, are good for signalling over short distances, and some, like strobe lights, are better for longer distances. Some signalling tools are one-time use only, like rocket flares, or limited-use, like a beacon with just a few days' worth of battery power left. Simple, low-tech signals like clothes can be laid on the ground to spell "help" or "SOS" without too much effort, or you may be able to arrange rocks and branches in similar fashion (if they'll contrast with the background enough to be seen). But only go to the effort if you have the time and energy to gather a bunch of rocks and branches, and if you're sure you plan on staying put for a while. There's no point marking a camp you won't be at.

Now let's hope you got lucky and got stranded with some sort of communications equipment. . . .

RADIOS

If you have an actual rescue two-way radio, and you can see an aircraft or vessel, be sure to keep the antenna perpendicular or "broadside" to the target instead of pointing it at the vessel you're trying to signal. The strongest signal radiates out from the length of the antenna, not at the tip. This applies to any sort of antenna you might rig up.

It's also good to know that most radios and beacons have only about 72 hours' worth of power, so use them wisely. But also know that all aircraft and sea vessels monitor the distress channels, and if you don't think you'll survive for 72 hours, it might behoove you to just turn it on and leave it on and hope for a speedy rescue.

Search through your supplies for any type of standard communications items before attempting anything more complicated. Most signalling tools will come with instructions, and even if they don't, they can usually be figured out without much trouble. But even though you can often figure out how to use a signal, you may not know when and where to best use it, and for how long.

Here are some good general rules to follow when implementing any communication plan, especially when the power supply, whether batteries or engine fuel, is a finite resource:

WHERE. Always broadcast from the highest, most open, and most likely to be spotted vantage point, where visual signals can be seen from the greatest distance, and broadcast transmissions travel farthest.

WHEN. Try to concentrate your power-based communications in the first 24 hours, as this is when most search parties will be initiated. Broadcast your signal continuously during this window if you're able.

Consider delaying your 24-hour broadcast period for a day or two if you have reason to believe it will take folks that long to begin looking for you.

After the initial broadcast period, you'll need to go into power-conservation mode. This means spacing out the broadcasts and standardizing their length.

Transmit at Dawn, Dusk, Noon, and Midnight. Dawn and dusk are when atmospheric changes can help broadcasts travel enormous distances. At midnight the sky is "stable," as it is at noon. These will be your standard broadcasting times. Should someone stumble across your SOS pattern or beacon, they'll have a better chance of finding it again the next day at a standard time that's easy to remember. For example, if a radio operator thinks he hears an SOS around noon on a particular channel, but he can't tell for sure, he might try the same channel at the same time the next day to confirm.

Transmit from 5 minutes before until 5 minutes after the hour and the half hour. Most radio broadcasts begin at the "top" or "bottom" of the hour, so that's when most people start tuning in their frequency. These will be the most likely times for someone to accidentally happen across your Morse code SOS signal.

If you do have a radio, tune to one of the big channels, like 5.000, 10.000, 20.000, etc., as these are used to broadcast WWV universal coordinated time, and people all over the world use this to set their watches. SOS tapped out in code has a good chance of being heard by someone on these frequencies.

And remember, it's illegal to broadcast without a license, but if you're trying to get rescued, just dare the authorities to come arrest you!

BUILD YOUR OWN RADIO

Speaking of radios, I'm going to share with you how to make the most basic radio in the world. All you need is some wire and a battery, like from a car, aircraft, or watercraft engine. If you have access to a large battery, like from a car, and you're 100% certain you cannot use it in any other way for rescue, consider converting it into a survival radio.

You'll need wires to make an antenna, but if you have a large battery, chances are there's wiring nearby. Scrounge around. I have used barbed wire fences, metal rucksack frames, even a bed's box springs in a pinch.

Antenna theory is complex, but in its simplest form it works like this: the longer the antenna, the farther it will transmit, and the higher off the ground it is, the better it will transmit. Radio waves radiate from the antenna in lobes that are biggest, and therefore strongest, off the sides of the antenna, not off the tip end. Radio waves travel farther when the sun is down, so try to do your transmitting at night. Place your battery up off the ground on a piece of wood, with one terminal—let's say the negative one—wrapped tightly with wire and tied off to a metal rod stuck in the soil to act as a ground. Then wrap the positive terminal tightly with wire and run out 30 to 50 feet to a tie-off with one end of a plastic spoon. From the other end of the plastic spoon, without letting the tied-off wires touch, run more wire up and around a high tree branch. Try not to let the wire sag, but be careful not to break it under too much tension.

You are now ready to begin transmitting your SOS.

You can do this by using a piece of metal with an insulated handle to connect the positive and negative battery terminals, creating a spark. A metal hammer with a hardened ceramic handle and a rubberized grip or a screwdriver with a plastic handle will keep you from shocking your hand. Slowly tap out SOS by arcing the terminals for three short intervals, followed by three long intervals, and then three short intervals again, with longer gaps separating the three patterns.

(To see how this works, take a 9-volt battery and a coin and any AM radio. Tune the radio to a frequency with nothing but static, then put the battery very close to the antenna and touch the coin across both terminals briefly and quickly. This will cause a break in the static, a "crackle" that can be detected by the human ear. This audible signal, metered out in Morse code, can say anything you want, including "Get me outta here!")

Granted, this is a pretty desperate measure, and there's no real way to test how well this method will transmit, since there are so many variables at play. But if you have a battery and some wire, you might as well try it. Someone might hear you.

If your homemade radio transmission does make contact, it's probably because some amateur ham radio operator is scanning the lower spectrum AM and shortwave frequencies for a remote Morse coder with whom he can communicate. Hams like to practice communicating with others at great distances at low power based on efficient antenna construction and good application of radio wave propagation theory. Thousands of people are into this hobby and practice it every day in very remote regions indeed. Contact with one of them could save your life.

The key is to establish a regular pattern of transmission and repeat it every night around the same time, a clear indication that you're a real person calling for help, not an atmospheric fluke.

Such a pattern also allows you to preserve your power, and gives you something to look forward to at night when there is nothing else to do and the temptation to succumb to depression creeps in.

Don't give up. Some ham out there just might detect your crude signal and report it to the authorities. Or a military radar system could detect your pattern in the static and use triangulation to pinpoint your location and send help.

Either possibility is very much a shot in the dark, but every once in a while we get lucky, and it's possibility that gives us hope.

LIGHTS
Radio contact isn't the only way to call for help.

Any light, even a pocket penlight, can save you in a survival situation. Although its range may be limited, even a small light in an otherwise blacked-out area can attract life-saving attention. And just as a combat soldier should have his weapon on him at all times, you should keep your method of signalling handy at all times. That brief and unexpected moment when a plane flies overhead or you glimpse a ship on the horizon or maybe even another flashlight on a mountain across the valley might be your only chance to catch a rescuer's attention, so always keep your light signal at the ready.

FLARES. Flares should be fired overhead and at a slight angle away from you, but never directly at a ship or aircraft. Only use flares when you can see the craft you're trying to signal, or, if visibility is poor, when you can hear it. These are one-shot dealios, so use them wisely.

LASER FLARES. Laser flares are bright and fan out to cover wide areas for long distances, but there's one catch: They often look like disco or rave party lights, and so might not be taken seriously as a distress signal. Still, if you're in a remote area and folks are looking for you, the chances are great you'll attract help.

FLASH LIGHT. The standard handheld flashlight can typically be seen at a range of approximately 5 miles, depending on weather and terrain.

STROBE LIGHT. The individual-sized strobes found in many survival kits can be seen for about 10 miles on a clear night, and perhaps as many as 20.

VEHICLE/AIRCRAFT/WATERCRAFT LIGHTS. These can be seen for 5 to 15 miles over open terrain under various weather conditions. Note: Even if the weather is foul, if SAR crews know you are out there, they will continue to look, provided the weather is not so bad as to put their vessels and lives at risk. Don't give up hope just because the weather is bad—rescuers might still be looking, and they may still be able to find you. If the weather is extremely dangerous, best to save your lights and settle in to ride out the storm.

LASER POINTERS. These are often overlooked as a means of signalling, but they have very good range (at 1 kilometer, these beams fan out to cover about a 20-inch area that can't be seen from the point of origin without binoculars), and can be used to signal to aircraft and ships at sea. Laser pointers are also very visible to pilots who might be flying with night-vision goggles.

They say there's a danger of damage to the human eye, so don't aim it at anyone's face at close range. Also, civilian laser pointers are many times weaker than the lasers used for military purposes, so the risk of injury is minimal. If you can find a laser pointer in the wreckage, include it in your signalling arsenal.

CHEMLIGHTS. Also known as glow-sticks (or CYALUME lights), these have a range of about 5 miles, and are very effective when tied to the end of a string and swung around in circles. In the early days of night-vision goggles, this was an extremely effective and simple mid-range signalling method. Just remember that once you break your chemlights to illuminate them, you'll only get about 12 hours of light out of them—basically one night's worth. If your supply is limited, try to wait until you're sure you see something worth signalling to before breaking one open.

HOMEMADE LANTERNS. Find some cups, tin cans, or chunks of sandstone, clay, chalk or other soft stone that can be hollowed out to contain animal fat or engine oil or any other liquid fuel. Use a piece of twine or cloth cord, or even pith from a fibrous plant, as a wick, soaking it in the oil until it's fully saturated. Position the wick so it hangs partway out of the container while staying in contact with the liquid fuel. Light the wick and you've got a lantern. When protected from the wind and arranged in a triangle, three lanterns can make a very effective SOS signal.

FIRE. This is the most likely resource for the survivor in most situations. If fuel is scarce, fire's use for cooking and warmth must be weighed against its potential use as an emergency signal. Likewise, if your resources for starting a fire are limited, you'll have to make a decision whether to use them now or later. But if your resources for starting and feeding fires are plentiful, you'll definitely want to make signal fires. As a general rule, high points and open areas are the best places to build them.

It's a good idea to build some sort of platform under your fire, especially if the ground is wet, as in snowy terrain, swamps, jungle floors, etc. Platforms also help if you're hemmed in by a lot of dense vegetation. The higher the fire is off the ground, the more likely it is to be seen.

Try to make multiple fires if you can. Make three fires approximately 10 to 25 feet apart when possible. This arrangement will be clearly distinguishable as a distress signal at great distances.

If multiple fires are too difficult to build or maintain in your situation, stick to just one. Also consider preparing a bonfire that you can set ablaze quickly when the moment comes to send a signal.

Trees can be used as natural fire beacons. If you happen to find

set fire to a dead
tree or a living
pine tree that
stands on its own

build signal fire on
a platform to
elevate it

Fire signals

a nice, big, dead tree that's still standing, build up a pile of kindling around its base to make an ignition station for easy and quick lighting. Be sure to protect your ignition station from wind and weather, and keep everything you'll need to light it nearby so you can start your fire—and send your signal—quickly when the moment comes. Opportunity often arrives without warning. Don't miss your chance at rescue due to lack of preparation.

If no dead, dry trees are handy, look for a large, living pine tree. These have a resin that burns very well, making them good candidates for signal trees.

Seek out lone trees to prevent the fire from catching and spreading.

In an extreme emergency, you might have to consider starting a forest fire to draw attention to your area. Just know that fire can spread quickly and could very well be deadly. If you find yourself trapped by a forest fire, try to get to water. If you're surrounded, try digging in and waiting for it to pass, but don't expect to survive. This is an extremely high-risk option, and will likely put innocent people, including your potential rescuers, in harm's way. If you do survive, you'll probably be arrested after your recovery, but at least you'll be alive.

A NOTE ON FLOATING FIRES. In some places, like deep jungle, a river might be the only clear space for miles. The survivor is not likely to be able to make a clearing in thick jungle, and so the river might be the only place where a fire can be seen from the air. Most survival books recommend building 3 small rafts, tying them together in the shape of a triangle, building a fire on each raft, and shoving them all out in the river as a floating signal.

I have to throw out the bull-crap flag on that. A fire is very difficult to build in the jungle, as is a raft, as is crossing a river to tie off to the other side to hold 3 burning rafts in place. Add to that the constant work of pulling them in to maintain the fires and floating them back out into position and *this does not pass the common-sense test.*

However, if you hear a plane in the area and can tell that it's searching, it might be worth floating a single fire out on the river. The fact is, no one does this for any normal reason, so if the SAR bird sees even one fire on a float, they will know it's a signal for help.

Better yet, just tie a flag or something shiny on a pole and mount that on the raft and let that be your signal on an open river, since any SAR plane will fly all the area rivers in a search.

Even better: If you're able to build a raft, float yourself down the river. You will find people and they will find you.

SMOKE & MIRRORS AND OTHER SIGNALS

Many other visual signals are available to you, some obvious, some not so obvious, and all should be used at every opportunity and in whatever ways time and resources permit. There is virtually no limit to what you can use to signal for help.

SMOKE. Light is only one aspect of a fire that can be seen at great distances. Don't neglect smoke as part of your signalling plan.

Try always to make smoke with your fire, and try to make smoke that contrasts with your environment. For example, use **white smoke** to mark your location in the jungle, and use **black smoke** in snow-covered terrain.

Green leaves and green plants are excellent for generating white smoke. Just try not to burn any poisonous plants, as the poison can enter your lungs if you inhale the smoke.

Burning rubber creates a thick, black smoke. Again, be careful to stay upwind, as inhalation can cause sickness.

Petroleum products can be used to not only get a fire started in a pinch, but to create dark smoke. The trick to using any petroleum product is to start with a small amount, wait a few minutes for it to soak into whatever fuel you're pouring it on, and keep the container a good distance away from the flame. Petroleum can be extremely flammable, so use caution and experiment before the actual moment of need. It would be a shame to send a signal and attract a rescuer only to have them find a French fry instead of a survivor.

MIRRORS. This is a classic. The military estimates the effective signalling range of a mirror at 50 to 100 miles. That is stronger than any other visual signalling device, and stronger than most emergency radios. Metal shards from wreckage or any other type of metal can be polished to a mirrorlike surface, if they're not sufficiently reflective already. On a sunny day, metal can reflect sunlight as far as 10 miles.

The technique for aiming flashes of reflected sunlight with metal or mirrors is simple:

First, if you have an actual "signal mirror" made for this purpose, just follow the directions. This store-bought item has a hole in the middle of the mirror through which you can look and see exactly where the reflected light beam is hitting in the distance. Simply hold up the signal mirror, note where the beam is going, then direct that beam at your target.

If you are simply using a piece of metal or solid mirror, you will have to aim it manually, but this is not difficult to do. Face the sun, hold the mirror or piece of metal as close to your eye as you can, and aim the reflective surface at something nearby, such as a tree, rock, etc. This will show you the angle at which to hold your device, which can then be turned at an aircraft, ship, or target area in the distance.

Once you've got the beam locked on or near your target, move the reflector just a bit up and down between the sun and the target. This will cause a twinkle that is very bright and will catch the human eye at great distances.

To see what I mean, next time you're on a commercial plane at midday, look for vehicles and buildings on the ground below. As you fly overhead you will see glints and glimmers as the sun reflects off metal and glass beneath you. This is a much higher altitude than any search and rescue

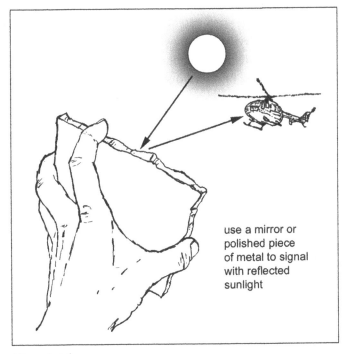

use a mirror or
polished piece
of metal to signal
with reflected
sunlight

Mirror signal

aircraft would be flying. If the aircraft was closer to the ground, with crews looking for you, and they saw a flash like that in the middle of nowhere, it would certainly get their attention.

PANEL MARKERS. These are swaths of brightly colored cloth made primarily for the military with the express purpose of signalling. If you have these, use them. Keep them displayed at all times and deploy them where they're most likely to be seen. You can cut them into strips and tie them to treetops surrounding your position. The breeze will make them move, helping SAR aircraft to locate you. Panel markers are usually bright orange or yellow or pink and made of tough, weather-resistant material. You can also use them to help construct a shelter.

SPACE BLANKETS. These are thin, lightweight, shiny silver blankets designed for retaining body heat in emergency situations. They make excellent temporary shelters or water catchments, and their reflective side makes an excellent signalling device. The drawback is that they are not very durable and will fall apart after a little use. But even when they do, they can be torn or cut into strips and tied or staked out to blow in the wind.

CLOTHES. Even the shirt off your back can be used as a signal. Clothing that's bright, white, or shiny is best, and can be spread out on the ground to spell HELP or SOS. This should only be done when you have enough clothing to spare for warmth and protection from the elements, of course.

FLAGS AND POLES. These are simple and effective means of sending signals. Any time you can find or improvise a pole in a clearing that can hold up some strip of plastic or scrap metal or cloth to form a flag, you should do so. You might even consider climbing any hilltops near your position and raising a pole on each one with arrows pointing toward your camp. If you've got nothing to make flags with, a grouping of three poles will stand out and draw attention if anyone should come near them. Skin the bark off of saplings so they look white and better contrast with the surroundings.

"The rule of threes" pole signal

MOUNDS AND SHADOWS. This is another low-tech way to get a signal out, especially when the terrain is bare, as in a desert. You might try stacking three rock mounds. By themselves, they may not really stand out in the ter-

rain, but in the afternoon they will cast shadows, and a pattern of three dark shadows in a geometric shape just might be what saves you. There are specialists who do nothing but study shadows on satellite photos looking for anomalies, and this is the sort of thing they would spot easily.

Rock signal

UPTURNED DIRT. Another way to send a signal when you have no other options. If you're in a tundra-like area, and have something to dig with, overturn shovelfuls of dirt so the moister, darker side is facing the sky. The combo of the small ditch you've dug and the dark dirt will stand out against the surrounding grassland. Dig in the pattern of a geometric shape or a word and you'll have a signal.

STICKS AND STONES. If you're really beat up and don't have the strength to try these other methods, simply stack small piles of rocks, or arrange them in lines. You can do the same thing with sticks. Try to make a pattern, or a grouping of three.

BEACH SAND. Try writing your message in the sand in large letters carved with a stick or large shell. Use wet seaweed or sticks to line the letters. These darker materials will help your message stand out.

SEA MARKERS. The open ocean can be an especially difficult place to improvise signals unless you have a light or mirror. Sea markers (there are many dyes and powders available specifically for this use, which when placed in the sea create a fluorescent cast upon the surface) are only good for about 3 hours in calm seas, but they can be seen from several miles off. If you have a packet of sea marker available, use it only in clear weather and when you suspect that someone may see it within the timeframe.

MORSE CODE

Morse code is an old-school but effective way to communicate that you can use with almost any means of communication: light, mirrors, whistles, even fires.

Morse code is also the only signal that will transmit through a nuclear-charged environment when the airwaves are full of static and charged particles, Morse code can still be heard because it is simply a pattern in the otherwise steady static background. See Chapter 10 for more.

When I first started in Rangers and Special Forces I was a communicator, and we learned Morse code at ridiculously fast speeds. However, the fact is that *you do not need to learn Morse code at all.* If you did learn it and didn't practice it, you'd just lose it, so don't waste your time. All you really need to know is SOS!

• • •——— • • • (dit dit dit, da da da, dit dit dit), and that's all there is to it. Just think of that song by The Police—the doo doo doo, the dah dah dah—and that will help you remember. Three fast taps, three slow taps, and three fast taps again. Memorize it right now—tap it out on your wrist with your eyes closed, and don't leave this paragraph until you have it lodged in your head!

But even though you don't need to memorize and practice Morse code, you should keep a copy of the full code somewhere. Either keep this book with you, or tear out the page and stuff it in your travel bag. Here's why:

Let's say you do manage to make contact via Morse code and—holy smokes!—someone actually replies. It would be good if you could make out what they are saying, and say something back that might assist in your rescue. So keep a copy of the code where you can find it.

A flashlight's beam can be seen from shore or from the air for a surprisingly long distance, especially when it's flashing, and this is one good way to send Morse code.

Remember the Native American's smoke signals in old stories and films? You really can use a blanket over a fire to control bursts of smoke that can send a clear message for a long distance.

Even a broken radio or phone can transmit sparks of static that can be controlled to send Morse code.

If you have a radio with no handset, you can use a wire, nail, ballpoint pen or any piece of metal to short out the pins where the handset would normally be plugged in, and this will create an arc spark that will transmit a break in the static that can be read as code. Experiment with briefly touching 1 pin at a time, then holding the piece of metal against that pin. Try all the pins until you find the "hot" pin that would normally key the mike or handset. This takes some practice, but you can keep arcing out the handset pin against the sidewall to make the sparks in longer and shorter bursts that will form the basis of your Morse code.

Now you can start learning to communicate basic messages.

Just think of a dot or dit as a 1-second sound, long enough to say "one" or "dot." Think of the dashes as a two-count, "one and two" or "da-ash." Whatever it is, work out a dots-and-dashes rhythm in your head and practice it.

THE MORSE CODE

A •—	J •———	S •••	1 •————
B—•••	K—•—	T—	2 ••———
C—•—•	L •—••	U ••—	3 •••——
D—••	M——	V •••—	4 ••••—
E •	N—•	W •——	5 •••••
F ••—•	O———	X—••—	6 —••••
G——•	P •——•	Y—•——	7 ——•••
H ••••	Q——•—	Z——••	8 ———••
I ••	R •—•	0 —————	9 ————•

The numbers are easy, and I suggest practicing those first. For the alphabet, start with the easier and shorter letters, like E (•) and T (—), and work your way through the alphabet. At the very least, learn and practice SOS.

KEEP IN MIND

THE RULE OF THREES. There are 3 dots and 3 dashes in the 3-letter Morse code for SOS. That's no accident. The universal distress signal is anything in threes: 3 fires, 3 whistle blasts, 3 rifle shots, 3 stacks of rocks, 3 crosses made of sticks, etc. Let this principle guide you in all your communications. Anything presented in a pattern of 3 will tell observers that it's not mere coincidence or chance, but rather a man-made attempt to send a signal, to make a message, to ask for assistance.

ARROWS. I find that forming arrows on the ground make good markers as they are easy to construct from sticks and stones and they are easily spotted as a pattern that doesn't occur naturally. Always make the arrow's head a triangle, since geometric shapes stand out in nature, and so attract the human eye more effectively.

Three arrows pointing in your direction of travel or toward your base-camp is a good survival signal plan. But you should also make a path, or a sign, or a disturbance everywhere you go, at least as much as your energy, time, and resources permit. Every day you should hold on to hope of rescue. Every time you take an action designed to signal or communicate, it's a tangible reinforcement of your commitment to the fight for survival. That's life-affirming, and it nourishes the will to live.

Arrow signals

WHERE TO MAKE YOUR MARK. When it comes to the placement of your signs, seek the highest point you can get to. In the case of multiple clearings, try to place signs in the areas most likely to be seen first, and if resources permit, mark them all. If there is no high ground nearby, or you can't reach it, use the largest clearing or open space you can find.

HOW TO TELL IF YOU'RE WASTING YOUR EFFORT. Any form of communication requires energy. Conservation of energy is a critical component of survival, and your energy reserves should be rationed out only as needed. It won't always be practical to expend the effort necessary to create a signal. Be prepared to prioritize your physical resources over signalling if the situation calls for it.

WHAT YOU NEED TO KNOW (AND WHAT YOU DON'T NEED TO KNOW) ABOUT SIGNAL CODES. Most survival books contain all the different codes for panel markers and body movements and aircraft responses, etc. For 99% of civilians, that is extraneous crap.

The reason the military has all these codes is so that folks who are prisoners or trying to evade capture can communicate with aircraft when they don't have radios and can't be picked up due to dangerous terrain, bad weather, or enemy fire.

The truth is, you just don't need to know several dozen different panel configurations or body gestures. For civilian survival, just getting the attention of an aircraft or ship is all you need to do. Rescuers will then send in the right type of craft and personnel to get you as soon as possible, or perhaps drop supplies and messages to keep you alive until they can.

A simple waving of the arms, or a nice big "X" to mark the spot, or "H" for helicopter pad is all you really need to know about using panel markers.

If you have lots of time and energy, clear an open area in the shape of a circle about 100 feet across to prepare for a helicopter rescue. Clear away all the loose rocks and debris you can. Try to avoid gradients of more than 5 to 10 degrees, and cut any ground growth down to less than 2 feet high.

This is really just a "make-work" to keep you busy, since rescue helicopters have hoists that can get you out, or lower rescuers to you, without having to land. If a helicopter does drop a hoist to you, *let the ground wire touch the earth first* or you'll be quite impressed with the shock you'll get.

But even if the helicopter doesn't actually need it, a big, fat, circle-shaped clearing with a nice H or X inside will send a message loud and clear to any passing aircraft that someone is down there hoping for a ride out.

CHANGES IN THE AIR

The best way to make a good decision is based on accurate information. To that end, here's an overview of how search and rescue teams work, from the rescuers' point of view, to help you maximize your chance of survival.

I have been on combat search and rescue teams in the jungles of Latin America and West Africa, and have conducted nationwide disaster recovery missions in the West Indies after hurricanes, so this information comes from first-hand experience.

During World War II, the U.S. Air Force was the lead agency for rescue. During the Cold War, as joint operations became standard, the Defense Department became the main entity overseeing rescue operations. We used to practice clandestine recovery missions, since almost everything was behind enemy lines, and few overt rescue attempts could be launched.

After the Cold War, rescue and recovery saw tremendous change and positive growth. The reason I'm giving you this history lesson is that it might be applicable to you because things are changing, and the old system of an emergency broadcast channel monitored 24/7 by the authorities is giving way to a new high-tech method of reporting and tracking emergencies: the satellite.

The military utilized two primary frequencies as distress channels in the old days. These were 121.5 MHz and 243.0 MHz. These became incorporated into the civil aviation and nautical fields and then served as the official international standard for global distress broadcast for many years. This is important because some of you may find these old radios along the way, and it's important to know that these are legacy systems that won't necessarily assure rescue.

There is a newer entity called the JPRA (Joint Personnel Recovery Agency), which has been the lead proponent for all search and rescue for the Department of Defense since 1999, and their standards were being adopted universally as this book was first written in 2008–09.

The new system takes advantage of some half-dozen satellites specifically dedicated to search and rescue that circle the globe every 100 minutes or so, like the National Oceanic and Atmospheric Agency's SARSAT. Some military and government satellites can read a license plate from space, so imagine how useful they can be in finding you.

Note: In 2007 The U.S. Coast Guard made use of the old EPIRB (Emergency Position Indicating Radio Beacons) illegal, since they use the old 121.5 and 243 frequencies. The Coast Guard had found EPIRB was only effective in 1 out of 50 incidents. Satellites are much more effective.

The new frequency is 406 MHz, and any devices transmitting on this new frequency must be registered. The old frequencies are still used, but are only monitored by local ground-based units without satellite access. By February of 2009, all satellites will stop processing distress signals from 121.5 & 243.

What this means to you is that if your absence is known—if your aircraft or ship called in a distress message before going off the airwaves—there are assets available to help find you. In some cases, official or even commercial satellites can be re-routed to aid in a search attempt.

If you look into the sky and see a star that seems to be moving very fast, chances are it's a satellite. And if satellites can read a license plate from space, they can definitely see your giant flaming SOS.

But satellites have limitations as well. Most cover only about 60% of the earth's surface, so there are "dead" spots. They depend on a clear signal, which means they might read a distorted position in heavy jungle. They use a "doppler" effect to approximate a location within 1 mile of the signal, so make your signals strong enough to be spotted from a mile away in case rescuers begin their search in the wrong area.

When one of these satellites detects a signal, it will relay that signal back to any and every receiving station on earth for the next 48 hours. If the first stations don't detect or respond, other stations will, so even if your batteries die, know that any satellite that picked up your signal will still be working for you for two more days. Don't lose hope.

Once a receiving station detects the signal, they relay it to a mission control center, which contacts a local rescue center. Note that weather, distance, and terrain will be factors in how quickly the response reaches you. Keep the faith.

Try to keep your triad of fires burning or your SOS sign burning at night, and if you notice a satellite overhead, or notice the same satellite night after night, try to time your signals to coincide with its journey across your little piece of sky.

Always try, always do, always communicate, always signal, always transmit, always send a message for help, always keep the fires of hope burning, and never quit!

First Aid

Before we get started on medicine, you should understand that everyone gets ill and injured as a part of life. Keep this in mind when you get hurt or sick so that you do not despair or spiral downward. You will probably get ill or injured, maybe multiple times, before you get out or rescued. Do everything you can to prevent it. But should it happen, learn from it so you don't repeat your mistakes.

In this chapter, I will share my years of training, education, experience and practice to give you every chance at survival. And I'll tell you right now, it can get real ugly. Use this knowledge wisely because it's your own life you'll save.

Just so you have a better feel for the source of this information, here is a bit more on my background in the medical field. I have an undergraduate degree in Pre-Med Biology from the University of New York. I was also a U.S. Army Medical Services Officer. But the real medical training is from becoming a Special Forces Medic (18D) and National Registry Paramedic. I have worked the streets and seen what is done for American citizens when they experience a traumatic accident or sudden illness. As a Special Forces Medic, I was trained to be a sort of Jungle Doctor, often receiving better training than physicians from developing and underdeveloped nations. On military bases, Special Forces Medics are authorized to operate as a fourth-year medical resident, still under an MD's supervision but with broad leeway to practice based solely on training.

18D training includes much of the training of a paramedic, nurse and physician's assistant. We must create, run and train all the staff in our jungle hospitals.

We are also trained in surgery, anesthesia, lab work, obstetrics/gynecology, pediatrics and other specialties. What makes the Special Forces Medic truly stand out is the fact that we are also trained in dentistry, veterinary care and certified for trauma to the same level as an emergency room physician—one trained to practice without the benefit of technology and with a special emphasis on tropical, primitive and improvised medicine.

All these factors combine to make a Special Forces medic uniquely qualified to supply a high level of medical care, for extended periods of time, behind enemy lines, and without any outside support. Sound like survival? It sure does to me.

GROUND RULES

While much of this is actually proper medicine, recognized as such by authorities as acceptable practices, some of what you'll learn is just plain extreme medicine that no one could recommend or do unless faced with dying or watching someone else die.

There's a connection between medicine and law that doesn't always fit a survival situation. Medicine has been around since the beginning of time. No one knows it all, and no one owns it. You have a fundamental right to learn as much as you can to be able to do as much as you can when your life or the life of someone you love is at stake. As such, no law restricts what you can do to save yourself. The laws governing medicine were created to protect patients and regulate practitioners. When survival is on the line, the law cannot hold someone responsible for what he does to save himself.

There's another thing you should know about the law and medicine: the laws protect you under the "Good Samaritan Act." If you try to help someone using reasonable measures, you are protected from legal action. The protection varies from state to state, but the spirit of it allows you to help without fear of being prosecuted later if something goes wrong. In fact, some places require you to help. Whatever you decide, once you intervene, do not abandon your patient unless you have no choice or are turning him over to someone trained to continue rendering care.

Finally, the first rule of medicine is known as the Hippocratic Oath: "First, do no harm." And as a guideline, that is true. But also, let me tell you here and now, sometimes you have to be downright brutal to save a life and ultimately do the patient more good.

For example: If a man has a dislocated arm, you are going to yank that thing back into place to help him.

If a woman fractures her femur, you are going to have to pull the bone hard to splint it.

If a kid slices open his arm and it won't stop bleeding, you will reach into the wound and pinch that artery closed.

When your friend deeply scrapes his back from sliding down a mountain, you will scrub the dirt out—ouch!

Get it into your head now that the practice of medicine is a labor of "tough love."

Okay, that said, let's start from the beginning, so you know what things mean. If you understand the principles, you can adjust and modify sensibly in tough circumstances.

ANATOMY & PHYSIOLOGY

The human body can be seen much like a car, with a series of systems that cooperate to make the machine work. A fault in one system may show up as an improper response in another system, but usually, an electrical issue shows up as an electrical issue and an engine issue as an engine issue. So let's learn the systems of concern for survival and how they might get fouled up.

BASIC SYSTEMS AND SYMPTOMS

Integumentary (skin): Watch for rashes and infections.
Musculoskeletal (muscle & bone): They don't work, you don't work.
Respiratory (breathing): If this stops, it's game over.
Circulatory (blood): Got a leak? Plug it fast!
Digestive (food): Sometimes things get blocked up, or won't stop flowing.
Genitourinary (water & sex): Dehydration is the main problem.

Nervous (brain & pain): Headaches and injuries.

EENT (eye, ear, nose & throat): Something going awry with the senses.

Endocrine (hormones): Outside the scope of survival medicine.

FEVER. This is the human body's number one "engine" light, if you will. When something is wrong, the human body tries to fix it. And, whether ill or injured, white blood cells get mass produced and go to work. As they do, their increase in the blood stream increases body temperature. This is a simple explanation so don't get hung up on it. The key thing is this: **fever is a symptom**, not a cause. Still, it needs to be controlled because it reduces the body's overall function. So, cool down your patient, give him aspirin or try some of the other techniques we'll discuss. Do not let a fever rage out of control. A fever above 106 degrees can damage brain cells or cause death. Be on the alert for black urine, which is a sure sign that the brain is cooking and your patient needs to be cooled down!

VITAL SIGNS. In general, most folks have the same vital signs. Below are the normal ranges. More fit people tend to have them just a bit lower, and less fit folks a bit higher.

T—TEMPERATURE: 98.6 degrees Fahrenheit (37 degrees Celsius) is typical, but normal temperature may vary one degree F in either direction.

Without a thermometer, body temperature is very hard to estimate so all you can do is try. Begin by factoring in the ambient temperature and feeling your own head as a baseline then, if the patient is conscious, ask him if he feels fevered. If you are sick, try to record what you observe when are you with it enough to write.

THE BASIC RANGES OF TEMPERATURE ARE BROKEN DOWN INTO GROUPS OF THREE DEGREES:

98–100 degrees F (37–38 degrees C) is a low-grade fever. Usually, the body will handle it fine.

101–103 degrees F (38–39 degrees C) is a mid-grade fever. Control the temperature with aspirin and consider employing antibiotics if they are available.

104–106 degrees F (40–41 degrees C) is a high-grade fever. Keep cool at all costs. Try submerging in cold water or placing cold, wet cloths under armpits, on neck, on groin and behind knees. Strip naked.

In a worst-case scenario, do what you can and hope to pull through, eating food and drinking water if possible. Keep patients from becoming delirious and hurting themselves. Many people have recovered from days of fever, and supportive care is all you can do if nothing else is handy.

P—PULSE: The pressure we feel on arteries close to the surface of the skin tells us how fast the heart is beating. This is important to measure and anyone can measure it by feeling the neck, the wrist, the ankle or anywhere arteries are close to the surface. The average pulse is 60–100 beats per minute (BPM). Fit people might have a pulse up to 10 BPM lower than typical and unfit folks could have one as much as 20 BPM higher. Pulse may also be affected by running, working or worrying.

Take a pulse by placing two fingers on an artery and using your watch to time the beat. **Do not use your thumb; it has an artery and you'll only measure your own pulse!** You only need to count the beats or "pulses" you feel for 15 seconds. Multiply what you count by four to get one-minute pulse. For example, if you count 20 pulses in 15 seconds, the person has a pulse of 80 – Normal!

Note: In trauma or illness, there is usually an increase in pulse and breathing during the early stages. In the late stages, both of these can slow down below normal.

R—RESPIRATION: The amount of times a person takes a breath in one minute is his respiration rate. On average, this is 16–20 breaths per minute, which translates into 4–5 breaths in a 15-second period. Trauma and pain or working and running will cause an increased breathing rate.

B/P—BLOOD PRESSURE: Another important vital sign is blood pressure. It is difficult to measure without the right tools however it is an important assessment tool, especially when there is traumatic blood loss.

B/P is measured in two ranges. The top range (*systolic*) is the higher pressure caused when the heart contracts and pushes blood through the system. The bottom range (*diastolic*) is the pressure that stays in the system, even when the heart is relaxed or dilated. Systolic blood pressure ranges from 100 to 140, averaging about 120. Diastolic blood pressure ranges from 60 to 100, averaging about 80.

The main reason these ranges are important is they allow you to understand what's typical versus what I'm about to describe now: how to assess a patient's blood pressure in the field, when there is significant blood loss. Gauging this will tell you a lot about how bad off a patient is and what survival measures you need to consider.

Say that your helicopter crashes and you find a fellow survivor in the wreckage and he's lost an arm. He managed to get a tourniquet on himself using his belt but then passed out unconscious. Check to make sure the scene is safe, determining if you need to move or not, and then assess the patient.

The patient's blood pressure can be estimated by looking, in order, for a pulse at the following locations:
Behind the ankle bone = B/P about 90 systolic; still low but far enough from the heart to be good news
Femoral pulse (groin area) = B/P about 80 systolic
Wrist = B/P about 70 systolic
Neck (side of windpipe) = B/P at least 60 systolic; worst-case scenario

If the first pulse you can find is on a patient's neck, you know he's alive and has a chance if you prevent any further blood loss and get fluids into him. If you don't have an IV, H_2O enemas will be the best bet for a while since the patient will be unconscious and unable to drink water.

That may seem like a rough scenario, but I warned you survival medicine would be full of them. The good news in this situation is that the patient has a chance at survival and you have a way to approximate B/P in the field without tools.

TRIAGE

Now that you have some basic tools, let's talk about a harsh fact of life–Death! In a major accident, chances are some people with you will have died and some more will die soon.

No matter who you are, where you are, or who is with you, not everyone can be saved all the time. Accept that, because you'll need to if we're going to tackle triage.

When a mass trauma event occurs, you will be faced with enough casualties to overwhelm the system. If you are the only first responder, **you are the system**, and you must decide who gets what care, and in which order.

Basically, there are four categories for triage, which you can remember with the acronym D-E-A-D (although the technical terms are in parentheses):

DEAD OR DYING (EXPECTANT)—These patients will die no matter what. Also, patients in this category could be people who would require so much effort to save that others who could recover might otherwise die. Do not attempt to save the hopeless, like someone who is chopped in half but still alive. **Leave them be and attend to others.**

"E"MMEDIATE (IMMEDIATE)—These are patients who will absolutely die without help but absolutely can be helped. For example, a quick tourniquet can save the life of someone with a leg amputated at the thigh. Without it, he'll be dead in one minute. **Deal with immediate cases on discovery.**

ASAP (URGENT)—These patients have serious wounds and require treatment soon but could survive for up to 60 minutes without treatment. A typical instance of this triage level includes a gut wound with some guts hanging out but no massive bleeding. Another example would be someone with some fingers chopped off. It's bad news but no one is going to bleed to death from that. **Get to it as soon as you can.**

DELAYED (MINIMAL)—These injuries range from a broken forearm to an eye hanging out or a good cut. The patients can make it up to six hours without attention and still be okay. Address these cases at your first chance but **understand that they can wait**.

After doing the best you can on the people with a chance, go and look at who you assessed as expectant. If they're still kicking, do what you can. (If not, still do what you can—but more on that in the Food chapter.)

Once you've made it through the first round of triage, begin reassessing your patients and the treatments you rendered. Some may still be bleeding; others will have loosened their dressings. On the bright side, you'll have a bit more time the second time through. Unfortunately, your patients' vital signs will have become more complicated as the true effects of their trauma take hold and their shock wears off or worsens. Here are a few additional assessment tools to use while remembering that triage is a continual process.

LEVELS OF PAIN

There's a fifth vital sign you'll need to gauge in addition to temperature, pulse, respiration and blood pressure if you want to understand your patient's condition: pain. It's classified as follows:

ALERT—If you can hear a person yelling and screaming, he's okay for the moment. The noise means he's conscious, breathing, awake and talking. In short, it's a good sign that his body is stable enough that all systems are still functioning.

VERBAL—When someone clearly traumatized stops yelling but still responds when spoken to, even if it's only a groan, things have actually gotten a bit worse. Still, a reply shows he's still hearing and processing what's going on. Not so bad, yet . . .

PAIN—When a patient is no longer chattin' atcha, you will have to resort to more extreme measures to get his attention and figure out how much pain he's suffering. One way to do this is a sternal rub, rubbing your knuckles hard on the sternum (the hard flat bone in the middle of your chest) to elicit a response. (It hurts like heck. Try it on yourself.) The patient should shudder or groan in response, even if he's unconscious. If the sternal rub doesn't work, try plucking him in the eye with your finger to see if he twitches or blinks. Any response means your patient is still functioning at some level. If there is no response at all, that ain't so good.

UNCONSCIOUS—The lowest category of being in touch with reality, unconsciousness means your patient shows some kind of vital signs of life but isn't responsive at all. For these cases, check the following:

Eyes: Remember **PERRLA**, which will tell you to look at your patient's eyes to see if the **P**upils are **E**qual, **R**ound, **R**eactive to **L**ight, and **A**ccommodating (meaning they focus when they should). If so, chances are that brain function is still okay. If they don't dilate or constrict at all, that's not a good thing.

Ears: If blood is coming from the ears, that isn't good either but it is better than clear liquid leaking out. This clear stuff is cerebrospinal fluid (CSF). If you see this (and, if you do, it will be mixed with blood), it indicates that your patient has suffered a head wound that caused a leak from the brain cavity to the outside of the skull. Subsequent blackening around the eyes, also called "raccoon" eyes, will confirm this diagnosis. There isn't anything you can do about it except understand your patient has a serious injury combined with everything else and factor that into how you triage him.

You must understand that pain is a very subjective thing. It's relative to a person's perspective and experience. I have seen grown men crying from small wounds, and women and children hacked with machetes merely whimpering as they patiently awaited treatment. The best way to get an idea of how bad someone hurts is to ask him, on a scale of one to ten—10 being the worst pain of your life—how do you rate this pain?

Next—and remember this—the operator feels no pain. Pain is the patient's problem because pain is not a cause; it is only a symptom.

As you began to see with the sternal rub, trauma assessment sometimes demands measures that will cause the patient to feel some pain on the way to healing. Pain is a healthy sign that the body is working and only indicates that something isn't working right. You are there to fix it.

TYPES OF PAIN

The sensation of pain as experienced by your patients will help you understand which systems are damaged. There are a number of ways to categorize pain and a few different theories used in the field of medicine. What's important for you in the field is that pain can tell you about what you can't see or measure any other way if you classify it this way:

THROBBING PAIN usually indicates that something is restricting blood flow, maybe swelling from a bite or a fracture. Move the fracture just a little to allow the blood to flow better and stop the throbbing. Try to reduce the swelling by elevating the limb, loosening a dressing that might be too tightly applied or applying cold or hot compresses on the affected area.

ELECTRIC IMPULSES AND TINGLING usually indicates an issue with a nerve. A slipped disk in the spine or a pinched nerve in a fracture is the usual suspect. Do what you can, but treatment is very limited without pain control medications. This type of pain sometimes feels like fire and is sensitive to hot and cold.

DULL, CONSTANT PAIN is usually found with musculoskeletal injuries like sprains, fractures and strains of bones, tendons, ligaments and joints.

SHARP PAIN usually indicates actual damage to something and is the type of pain felt in most traumatic events where *lacerations* (cuts) occur.

COLICKY OR SPASMODIC PAIN is usually felt when something is wrong with an organ or large muscle mass. The cause could be a lack of oxygen due to decreased blood flow, which in turn could be caused by either swelling from a hard impact or loss of blood from hemorrhaging. Not much can be done in the field for organ damage other than to make the patient comfortable by treating signs and symptoms while offering rest, food, water and time to recover . . . or not.

TRAUMA MEDICINE

Now that you have a good handle on the basics of what is normal in terms of vital signs and traumatic events, actions to take and outcomes to expect, let's get into the real matter of medical issues and actions for survival: how you approach patients or treat yourself in order of assessment and treatment priorities.

FIRST AND FOREMOST

SCENE SAFETY

If you get hurt entering the situation, there will then be two patients that need treatment. And if you two are the **only** two, you both might very well bite the dust. So check the scene for safety, and if it's not safe for the other person, your first problem-solving challenge is how to either make them safe or make the scene safe. So if your patient gets bitten by a snake, and you can't scare the snake away, can you drag him away from the snake?

C-SPINE

The cervical spine has to be on your mind before everything else. Controlling the c-spine is taught religiously in modern street para-medicine, with one thing beat into every paramedic and trauma nurse's head: **control the c-spine**. Fortunately, there's a way for you to remember anyway.

Since A for airway is first in the sequence of methodical checking, and the airway opens to the mouth and nose, then you can take control of the c-spine while checking the airway. To do so, place your hand on the patient's forehead and, from that point onward, make sure not to move his neck. Free your hand up by stabilizing the neck as soon as possible with either a brace or by placing something near the sides of the head to keep the head from turning like the patient's shoes or some logs or rocks. Movement risks damage to the c-spine and can cause paralysis or even death.

Nearly all the time, the c-spine is not important. If there are no impact injuries from a car or plane crash or a fall, there is likely no damage to the neck and, as such, c-spine is not an issue.

ABCs OF METHODOLOGICAL CHECKING

A IS FOR AIRWAY.

Traditionally, clearing the airway is considered the starting point for medical care. **Airway is not the starting point for care in survival medicine. If there is trauma, circulation is the number-one priority. Stop the bleeding first and foremost** because massive bleeding can kill a patient in one minute. If someone is not breathing, he can last a couple of minutes without oxygen—and you can supply air to your patient but not blood.

When you come upon a survivor and have assessed the scene as you approached, begin calling to him to assess his level of consciousness. A response means he's conscious to some degree and that his airway is open because he can speak through it and, so, A is OK!

If the patient doesn't respond to hailing, check these things:

If he's unconscious, make sure he's breathing and turn his head to the side to keep him from choking on his own tongue.

If he's unconscious and not breathing, check his pulse because he might be dead already. If there's no pulse, he's dead. Consider CPR if no one else needs help.

If there is a pulse but no breathing, your patient might need CPR. Before beginning CPR, open his mouth and make sure nothing is blocking the airway. If the airway is blocked, stick your finger in and try and sweep it out. Be careful not to get bit by his gag reflex or push any obstruction deeper.

If there is a pulse but no breathing and no obstructions, give two quick breaths. Do this by pinching the nose, making a good seal around the mouth with yours and giving a good deep breath. You should see your patient's chest rise. Then, let go of your patient's nose and break the seal with your mouth to let the air come out. If your patient was just winded and needed a kick start, this should do it.

That procedure will cover checking the airway and responding the vast majority of the time. **Very rarely, though, the airway will be obstructed because of trauma.**

If your patient's face is torn off, don't panic. They can still recover, and plastic surgery can do a lot of great things. For now, treat the damage as a wound and stop the bleeding, making sure any blood, flesh or cartilage is cleared out of the throat area. If the tongue is in the way, tie it down to your patient's shirt or stick a safety pin in it and tack it to a strong piece of flesh on the face so it stays out of the way. The key is to not freak out, so they don't freak out. And keep the airway open so they can breathe and live.

If your patient's entire face is destroyed and there is nothing but a bloody mess and he can't seem to breathe through it all, consider making a hole in his neck. The lungs are like two balloons that inflate and deflate through one tube: the throat. If the tissues of the face are obstructing airflow through the normal passageways of the nose and mouth, they can be bypassed, which is what a *cricothyroidotomy* (detailed later) describes how to do.

B IS FOR BREATHING.

Checking the airway means just making sure the passage way is open; breathing is making sure the patient is actually sucking air in and out. We got into how to breathe for someone who's not pushing air in and out above. But what if the patient is breathing, but with difficulty? Here's what to look for and what to do about it.

Look very quickly at what other injuries he has. Is it just panic causing rapid breathing or is some trauma causing it? Checking for a sucking chest wound will tell you. For the survivor's purposes, any hole in the chest sucks. There are two kinds, though, with two different actions required.

PNEUMOTHORAX (COLLAPSED LUNG). When you have a hole in your chest, it's easier for the air to come in through the hole than through the pipes of the throat. So, every time the chest rises mechanically when you try to breathe, air rushes into the chest cavity through the hole rather than through the windpipe. That air then gets trapped inside the chest instead of blowing back out because the tissue around the wound seals in expiring air and keeps the air inside the chest.

As this happens, the lungs, being a lot like a wet sponge in their actual texture, start to get smaller, like a sponge getting wrung out by squeezing it. The more air in the chest, the smaller the lungs get until they can't hold enough air to oxygenate the blood. If you see the neck veins protruding like they're under a lot of pressure or see the trachea or throat moving opposite to the hole, your patient is in a bad state. You must get the air out of his chest.

The treatment is fairly easy. Cover the wound with your hand—or with your patient's hand if he's conscious. Find something waterproof like plastic and cover the wound with that. Put a dressing on it and secure it. Turn the person on his **uninjured** side with the hole pointed to the sky if possible. (Think about an air bubble in a water balloon where the air rises to the highest point. Wherever the hole is, lay your patient so the air gets nearer the hole.)

It might be necessary to "burp" this wound every once in a while, maybe every five to 60 minutes depending on its severity. If the patient is conscious, he can do it when he feels pressure building up by sticking a finger into the hole, letting the air out to relieve the pressure and then covering the wound back up. The ribs have a lot of nerves, and burping will hurt, but it will save your patient. Ultimately, surgical intervention will be necessary.

If there is only a small puncture into the chest but the same symptoms are present, you won't be able to burp it with your finger. If you have a medical needle with a hole in the center, stick it into the wound to drain the air. You can also try forcing your finger in or, in the worst-case scenario, cut with a small knife to make the hole big enough to drain air. Only incise enough to widen the hole and drain the air. There will be small amounts of blood but failure to drain the air will result in death.

HEMOTHORAX. If there is an injury to the chest and no is air is sucking in and out but breathing is getting increasingly difficult, then chances are your patient is suffering from a hemothorax or blood in the chest. The effects are the same as a pneumothorax, as blood fills the cavity around the lungs. Do not drain this blood. The blood will only fill up so much space and will then cause enough pressure to *tamponade* or stop itself from bleeding. In this case, you cover the wound and do not "burp" it. You lay the person on their injured side so that some pressure on the bleeding can help to stop it.

If your patient does not lose too much blood into the chest, he will be okay, but this too, will require surgery.

JUST REMEMBER THESE:
Pneumothorax (air-lung) = injury up, air rises.
Hemothorax (blood-lung) = injury down, blood sinks

Tell the difference if you're not sure by *auscultating*. Do this by tapping on the chest to hear what sounds it makes. Practice on yourself, and you'll hear the difference. Take your two main fingers from one hand and place them flat on the patient's chest, then take the two main fingers from the other hand and tap on your fingers. You will hear a thud.

Tap your right side on the top half of your chest and then your right side on the bottom half. This is the side without the heart, so it is all lung and will sound hollow. Then tap on the left side of your chest, first the bottom, then the top half where your heart is. You will hear a distinct difference between the hollow areas of lung tissue and the solid area filled by the heart. This is the difference you'll hear when you auscultate a patient with a chest injury.

If their chest is filling with air it will sound "hyper-hollow" and if it is filling with blood, it will sound "hyper-dull." If you get the diagnosis wrong, no worries; if you burp and air comes out, great, and if you burp and blood comes out, now you know, so don't burp it anymore.

C IS FOR CIRCULATION.
This is a doozy, but for the survivor, it's really easy. Circulation means blood, so basically it means stop the bleeding.

DIFFERENT TYPES OF BLEEDING:
Desanguination is loss of major amount of blood, like if two legs get ripped off.
Arterial blood is the bright-red spurting kind that squirts out with every heartbeat like if a forearm were severed off completely.
Venous blood is the dark, oozing kind; while it might be copious, it's rarely fatal.

Minor bleeding is what you might see from a small cut or laceration. The type of bleeding must be taken into account with the location of the bleeding to have a better picture of the situation and what kind of treatment is warranted.

EXAMPLES OF BLEEDING: Minor bleeding inside the brain can cause major neurological signs and symptoms very quickly whereas a minor bleeder on the arm will clot and heal even without treatment in most cases.

Major arterial bleeding from an amputated leg can be controlled with a tourniquet in seconds, but major bleeding from a ruptured spleen or torn aorta will cause enough internal bleeding in a minute to cause death without one drop of blood being shed.

Most venous bleeding from say, a seriously *excoriated*, or scraped-up, chest from a slide down some steep cliff will hurt but will clot fairly soon on its own. A venous bleed on the scalp could cause a person to lose enough blood that they go into shock and die because the scalp is so vascular that it just keeps bleeding.

Rarely will a minor bleed be an issue unless it involves an internal organ or two and the person is slowly bleeding out and becoming anemic and weak over a period of time. In a survival situation, this could cause death in just a matter of days.

So, the **type** of bleeding and the **location** are the two major factors for considering what the final outcome might be, but the treatment is always the same: **Stop the bleeding!**

It's easy to do. **Just slap your hand directly on the wound and push down.** If your patient is conscious and coherent, make him do it while you find or improvise a dressing. **In case of an amputation, go straight to the tourniquet. If blood is spurting, reach in and pinch it off. If there are two or three spurters, place your knee on one!**

Get aggressive, go after the source of that bleeder and stop it ASAP. If you have to stick your finger into an open gut wound and pinch a piece of intestine to stop it bleeding, do so! It's that easy.

This is not time to be thinking about gloves and AIDS, and it's no time to be worried about infecting the wound. You are already dirty so the wound is already infected. If you lose too much blood, you won't get any infections because you'll be dead!

THE SEQUENCE FOR HEMORRHAGE CONTROL:

DIRECT PRESSURE. The first thing to do is put your hands on the wound or a dressing covering the wound.

MORE PRESSURE. Add a dressing if there is none or add a second dressing and pack it into the wound more by tying the dressing down with the knot on top of the wound to create more pressure in an attempt to stop the bleeding.

ELEVATION. Raise the wound above the level of the heart to decrease the blood flow by reducing the amount of pressure on the hole in the circulatory system. This is particularly useful for a bleeding arm or leg if the person is sitting. If you can't get the limb above the heart, get the heart below the limb by laying the person down then raising his arm or leg.

PRESSURE POINTS. On some locations on the human body, blood vessels are closer to the surface and, as such, pressing down at these points will reduce the blood flow through the vessels to the wound. For instance, if pressure and elevation weren't stopping the blood flow in a hand wound, you could squeeze the area on the wrist where you would normally take a pulse and that will reduce the blood flow to the hand. Pressure points coincide with the places where you can take pulses and this method is particularly useful to a survivor if you are treating yourself or need to hold off the bleeding until someone can produce a suitable dressing.

TOURNIQUETS are considered a **last resort** in modern medicine, however combat medicine has changed this to the point that a good tourniquet, quickly and correctly applied, is often the first choice for any significant bleeding. This tourniquet will staunch the blood loss and provide the caregiver more time to get the right dressings ready to apply. After the dressing is

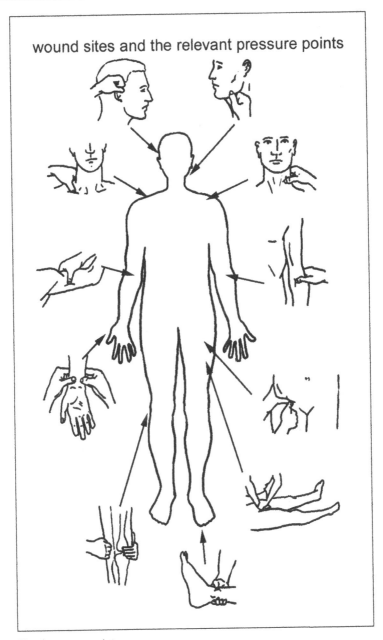

wound sites and the relevant pressure points

Blood pressure points

applied, the tourniquet can be eased up gently, striking a balance during the transition. Also, you can re-tighten a tourniquet while adjusting a dressing. Finally, once the dressing is in place and the bleeding is under control, the tourniquet can be removed completely.

RULES FOR TOURNIQUET USAGE:

- Tourniquets should be two inches wide or wider but not narrower unless nothing wider is available.
- Tourniquets should be placed two inches above the wound or amputation. Placing lower could damage the wound.
- Placing higher could mean that, if the tissue below the tourniquet dies from lack of blood, the patient will lose more tissue than necessary.
- Tourniquets should be tightened only enough to stop the major bleeding; some oozing is okay.
- Tourniquets should not be loosened until you have a proper dressing in place and ready.
- Tourniquets should be kept ready to be tightened or re-applied if the bleeding begins again.
- Tourniquets should be placed **below joints** when possible. If the patient loses his limb later due to amputation, the joint is important to having a better prosthetic.

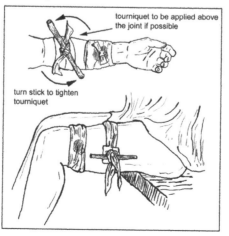

tourniquet to be applied above the joint if possible

turn stick to tighten tourniquet

Tourniquet application

DEALING WITH DISCONNECTED BODY PARTS

Amputations are obviously treated initially by the application of a tourniquet, but what do you do with the body part? Most likely, you will simply bury it later if the survival situation gets extended. But for the short term, in case rescue happens quickly, try to salvage the limb, provided circumstances allow taking these extra measures. **No body parts should be re-attached in the field unless done so by a trained person.** Re-attaching is an invite to infection, gangrene and septicemia, and possibly death. When it's gone, it's likely gonna stay gone.

However, you should wrap the part in some clean plastic or other water-proof material and put it on ice or snow if you happen to have some. If not, perhaps cold lake or river water is near and can be used to keep the body part cold. Do not let the water get to the body part, however, as the part will absorb the water, rupture the cells and destroy the appendage. Also, do not let the part freeze as this too will rupture the cells and destroy the tissue. Depending on how well the temperature is regulated, the part might last up to three days.

Eyeballs pop out. It happens. If they do, try to place them back inside. Most medicine will say this is a **no go** but the fact is, it will only get worse and without the chance of immediate first aid from an emergency room, most of the time, it's best to put the eyeball back in. If the orb is destroyed, the eye is lost. It cannot be repaired or replaced. In this case, do not place it back in but treat it like any wound and cover it with a clean dressing. If the orb is intact, some muscles that move the eye are probably torn but the vision should still be okay since the optic nerve is like a tough piece of stretchy plastic. Try to place the eyeball back in gently after cleaning it the best you can. Finally, cover the eye and dress it like a wound.

If the eyeball can't be placed back in the socket but the orb is intact, put it in something like a Styrofoam cup or plastic bag, keep it moist, cover it gently and secure the whole contraption to the patient's head. Cover both eyes in most cases because wherever one eye looks, the other will turn. This twitching will cause more pain and discomfort to the patient.

DEFS OF TRACKING PATIENT PROGRESS

D IS FOR DISABILITY. This is mostly addressed when you determine the patient's level of consciousness (Alert, Verbal, Pain, Unconsciousness) but becomes particularly important when you notice a significant change, one way or the other.

If your patient is starting to come around after your treatments, this is great. But if you notice that he is deteriorating, you need to reassess what you are doing and what you have done. That leads to E.

E IS FOR EXPOSE. In a survival situation exposure is not usually warranted or desired. However, if there was a major crash, or a person tumbles down a cliff, or you found someone unconscious and there are no obvious causes, you might need to remove their clothing to see everything, in order to find problems and treat them. In the cold, this might not be ideal, but it will help you look beyond the obvious. For instance, someone might have fallen and broken a leg, which gets your attention and his right away. Meanwhile, no one notices that he's also suffered a puncture wound to the chest cavity. Exposure and inspection will find this.

F IS FOR FULL (SET OF VITAL SIGNS). In a survival situation, you are very limited without tools. But you can get a basic amount of info by measuring vital signs, knowing what they mean in general, and then reassessing to see if they're getting closer to what they should be normally—or getting worse. Remember, breathing and pulse increase initially in response to trauma and shock, and then slowly decrease. Keep this in mind when you first begin treatment so that you're not lured into a false sense of security because the vitals look good early on. Reassess regularly, and when you're not sure what to do next, reassess again with systems checks, body part checks by function and reexamination of all your dressings and treatments.

SAMPLE: A DIFFERENT DIAGNOSTIC TOOL

SAMPLE is another medical acronym used to help get a handle on what might be going on. While not so relevant in trauma scenarios, it is good for later as people have problems and you try to help.

"SAMPLE" STANDS FOR:

Signs & Symptoms: What you see is a sign, a bruise for example. What they say is a symptom, such as "no feeling in the hand."

Allergies: Always ask people if they have allergies.

Medicine: Ask a patient if he is taking any medication. That might be the cure for him!

Past Medical History: Ask patients if they've had something similar in the past and what was done to make it better. This single most important question could give you everything you need to know to help them.

Last Meal: This is especially important in case of a rapid onset sickness when surviving because people might be trying to eat new things around you.

Events: Ask what's happened recently and why and how you might be able to make it better. With injuries, ask about the *mechanism of injury*, or how they got hurt. Have him demonstrate or explain so you can visualize how something might have been bent or broken and what else might have been injured but is being over shadowed by the pain of the main injury.

Armed with this basic assessment methodology, you are ready to do the best you can to help yourself and those around you. You can even ask yourself these questions so that you can best understand how to help yourself when something unknown is making you sick or causing you pain.

CARRY TECHNIQUES

Sometimes you will need to move patients from the scene of an injury, either right away to get them out of harm's way or later after you stabilized them. Here are a few tips that I find especially useful and practical.

MOVING AN UNCONSCIOUS ADULT:

- Always get your patient's help if he can assist in anyway.
- Always use as many people as you can to move someone. Bodies are heavy!
- Always try to squat while lifting, letting your legs do the work.

IF YOU HAVE TO CARRY THE PATIENT ALONE:

Stand behind your patient and hold him under his arms, your fingers interlocked across his chest. Drag—don't lift—using your legs instead of your back to walk backwards.

If your patient is a child, carry him in your arms.

If your patient is big and heavy and the distance is great, an over-the-shoulder carry is best. Begin by putting a knee on the ground and pulling your patient's arms over your head. Slide your shoulder lower while wrestling your patient onto your shoulder. Slowly stand up while holding onto something. Then get comfy and get moving.

If you can, use a rope or something similar to make a loop under your patient's arms. Then tie the loop across your shoulders and you can carry your patient like a backpack.

Finally, if time permits, make a pole stretcher. Place your patient in it and drag the poles like it's a cart with no wheels. This works well, but the sticks will wear down and need to be replaced so make them long.

IF TWO PEOPLE ARE CARRYING YOUR PATIENT:

The stronger carrier holds the patient under the arms with fingers interlocked as above. The weaker one holds under the thighs while standing between the patient's knees and lets the ankles lock under their armpits; the carrier locks his fingers together. This works much better than trying to hold a tight grip over any period of time or distance.

The two carriers lock arms like a cradle and let the patient sit in your arms like he was in a chair.

Again, time permitting, make a pole stretcher or litter to drag.

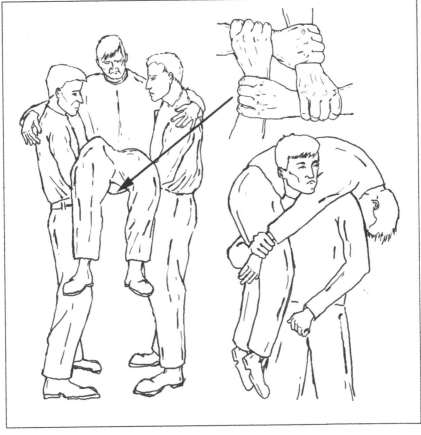

Transporting a patient

LEAVING AN UNCONSCIOUS PATIENT

Sometimes, a person is not conscious, but you can't move him and need to leave. If at all possible, once the person is treated and stabilized, turn him on his side, the uninjured side if possible. Raise his top leg so the knee is bent and place his top arm with the elbow bent so his hand supports his head. This should keep him from choking on his tongue or vomit. Try to leave a message in case the patient comes to and make sure you note where you left him.

The real hard part here is abandoning someone with no idea where you're going, if you'll make it and whether you'll ever be able to find your patient again. Chances are that your patient will perish if he is ill or injured and you cannot take him with you for whatever reasons. But he might perish on the journey. Also, trying to carry him might actually kill you or the other survivors. It is not an easy decision, but it is one that might need to be made. There are no easy answers here.

PREVENTION

Prevention is the most important thing anyone can do for first aid and health. This is especially true for the survivor since there is limited or no access to health care and medicines in survival situations. So, everything you do in a survival situation must **err on the side of caution**.

Survival situations are no time to take chances and unnecessary risks. If you need to climb a tree, descend a cliff, cross a river or even just use a knife, **go slow**. Take some time and think about what you want to do, why you need to do it and how you can do it in the easiest and safest way possible. Simply slicing your finger from being too hasty can change everything.

Prevention is all pretty much common sense. If you're thirsty, drink. If you're cold, get warm and stay dry. But mainly, if you're tired, get rest and sleep. This is the number one key to a good prevention plan. Rested people think better and better decision making decreases the chances of unnecessary injuries and illness.

The first question for prevention should be: How can this go wrong?

From there, you can plan around potential problems. If you have no choice, then take whatever chances as cautiously as you can.

HYGIENE

Try to maintain your personal hygiene and general cleanliness as a top preventive strategy. This will also help with your sense of general well-being and positive mental outlook. But it also decreases diseases by reducing the bacteria that grow naturally on the human skin and multiply quickly in dirty conditions. These become opportunistic infections waiting to happen if you get a cut or scrape while your skin has this excess build-up of bacteria. So, keep clean.

You can do this under almost any circumstances.

HYGIENE TIPS:

THE SUN kills bacteria. If you have no water, try to take off your clothes and expose your skin to the sun for a while, being mindful not to get sunburned.

THE AIR itself can still help kill some bacteria if there is no sun. Just airing out your body for a little while each day, or a few times a day if needed and plausible, can reduce the amount of bacteria on your body.

SAND can be used when there is no water, especially in the armpits and groin. Be careful to get it all out of the butt cheeks to prevent chafing and a rash.

SHOWER in the rain if you get the chance or use some snow if practical.

TEETH are vitally important in life and become even more so in a survival situation as dental problems can cause misery and grief unlike any other. So, keep your teeth as clean as possible. You only need a stick or some cloth to do so. Many folks use a twig of sassafras or pine to scrape all their teeth; to me, this actually works better than a toothbrush. You can also take a piece of cloth, like from your T-shirt, and wrap it around your finger and then rub your finger over your teeth, very firmly. The key is to take your time, and go over every area of every tooth. Do this at least twice a day or more if you're sitting around bored. Stay busy; conduct dental hygiene.

FEET are the most important thing for any soldier, and this rule applies to the survivor as well. Take care of them! Massage them every single day before you start your day and every single night before you end it. Keep them dry at all cost. If you can't keep them dry, stop a lot and air them out so they dry. No matter how cold it is, air them out. No matter how wet it is, take them out of your boots, even in a downpour of rain, and air them out. Try to rotate socks and keep them clean.

That takes care of your body. Clothes are the next most important thing to keep clean. They will keep you warmer in the cold and will last longer in the heat if they're clean.

CLOTHING TIPS:

SUN will kill germs on clothes just like on a person. Lay or hang your clothes in the sun whenever you can.

AIR will also work on clothes to reduce bacteria loads. Air out your clothes when you can. If you're wet, get nekkid and let the clothes air dry. Heck, you hope someone sees you. That means you're rescued!

BOIL your clothes if you have the luxury of fire and a pot as this will kill all the bacteria. Or just rinse your clothes in any water or sand you can come by.

POST-DEFECATION CONTAMINATION is the number one way that many campers and survivors get sick. Do your best not to contaminate your hands during defecation. Use some nice, safe-looking broad leaves for tissue. I prefer to use the dry leaves on the top of the leaves on the ground because it reduces the risk of sap causing irritation if the leaves are already dead and dried. After some trips to Russia and the Middle East, I think the dry leaves are actually softer!

Most important is to always wash your hands, all the time, after everything, before everything. Keep those dirty paws clean!

NUTRITION

This is another key element of the prevention strategy. Most likely, as a survivor, your food intake will be very limited. However, if you understand nutritional basics, then you have a chance of balancing your diet. In long-term survival situations, this alone could mean the difference between life and death—not primarily because nutritional deficiencies cause death but because weakness that results from these deficiencies leads to higher degrees of incapacitation from which death could result. If left to scavenge in a survival situation, see if non-survivors had any vitamins or supplements in their personal effects.

FOOD BASICS: FOUR FOOD GROUPS VERSUS NUTRITION SOURCES

There are essentially four food groups, even though nutritionists will get technical and divide these into further sub-categories. For a survivor, it's very simple.

MEAT. This includes nuts, beans, eggs and fish.

MILK. You won't find butter or cheese, but you might just get some goat milk.

FRUITS & VEGGIES. These are obvious and we don't care if a tomato is not a vegetable.

BREADS & CEREALS. You're not going to find any bread out there, and cereals actually take a lot of work to make, but you can find some good substitutes like roots and plant stalks that provide starches and carbohydrates.

But the bottom line is that you will not eat a balanced diet. You will eat what you can get. And that's why for the survivor, it's more important to understand what you need and what can give it to you out in the wild.

When you are surviving, basically, you need to think "caveman diet," 'cause that's pretty much what you're gonna be on. This is mainly meat and some fruits and veggies if you're lucky.

PROTEIN is the number-one thing that is going to give you strength and you are going to need it. The best source of protein is meat. That means animals and that means killing.

All this means hunting, traps, snares, fishing, etc. now come into play. If you're lucky, you'll find some nut-bearing trees or some occasional eggs or legumes. But mostly, you'll need meat.

FATS are one of the best sources for energy there is. They aren't great for you when you work in an office, but when you're out in the bush, using all your muscles in ways you never have, fat tastes delicious and keeps you going. You're not likely to be putting on weight when surviving and if you do, good on ya! But the bottom line is to never waste fat and throw it away. Eat as much as you can. Use it for storing other foods, or making soap or candles if you have to, but try to eat it all first!

CARBOHYDRATES that we normally get from breads and pastas aren't naturally occurring entities. But many roots will provide carbohydrates, as will many plants like cat tails. (See the Food section for this.) Carbs are important for energy so eat them when you can.

VITAMINS & MINERALS kind of fall into the same category for the survivor. You're not likely to get all you need, and surprisingly to most health nuts, you don't really need that many, but the lack of them will cause you major problems over a long period of time, which we'll look at next. For now, it's important to know that you need them and they are harder to get so this is why you need to try to find some fruits and veggies around you, as these contain the trace minerals and occasional vitamins humans need. Mentally prepare yourself to try some as you do need them to survive. The following chart explains why.

VITAMIN-DEFICIENCY DISEASES TO LOOK OUT FOR

Vitamin	Sources	Deficiency	Symptoms
A "Retinol"	Liver, eggs, carrots, many fruits and veggies	Night blindness	Self-explanatory
B1 Thiamine	Liver, eggs, pork, peas, oranges, potatoes	Beriberi	Weight loss, emotional disturbances, weakness, pain in limbs, and edema or swelling
B2 Riboflavin	Meat, eggs, fish, milk, bananas, okra, few veggies	Ariboflavinosis	Swelling and redness of mouth and throat, cracking at corners of mouth, pseudosyphilis or scaling on genitals

Vitamin	Sources	Deficiency	Symptoms
B3 Niacin	Meats, eggs, fish, nuts, seeds, beans, lots of veggies, liver, heart, kidney	Pellagra	Aggression, insomnia, sensitivity to sunlight, weakness, mental confusion, skin lesions, dermatitis and hair loss, swollen oral cavity, diarrhea, dementia, limb paralysis, death
B5 Pantothenic Acid	Meats, some veggies	Paresthesia	Pins and needles feeling on the skin without being caused by sleeping on a limb
B6 Pyridoxine	Meats, nuts, some vegetables	Anemia	Often overlooked, feeling tired, weak, generally aching, irregular breathing and heartbeat, pale skin and nail bed, cracks at corner of mouth, and pica, the craving of unusual things to eat
B7 Biotin	Milk, liver, eggs	Dermatitis	Any condition of inflamed skin such as a rash, eczema
B9 Folic Acid	Greens, beans, seeds	Birth defects	Not a major issue for most survivors
B12 Cyanocobalamin	Meat, shellfish, eggs, milk, termites	Anemia	Same as B6 above
C Ascorbic Acid	Fruits, roses, pine needles, tomatoes	Scurvy	Dark purple spots on skin, bleeding from nose and gums, tooth loss, sunken eyes, opening of old scars and broken bones
D Ergo or Chole-Calciferols	Dairy, sunlight, fatty-type fish	Rickets, osteomalacia	Weak muscles, painful cramps, easy bone fracturing
E Tocopherols	Nuts, seeds and darker greens	Rare	Hemolytic anemia in newborns
K Mena or Phyllo-quinines	Darker greens, meats, eggs	Bleeding diathesis	Blood fails to clot

Note: The technical chemical name is given in case you can find some substances with these compounds in the label's ingredients for treating severe deficiencies.

MINERALS are in the same category for the survivor as vitamins. You'll get what you get from whatever you eat and you'll eat whatever you can get. The above chart is to give you an idea of what you need, where it comes from, what deficiencies cause and what to look for. When you see these unusual symptoms, they should ring a bell. Look for the causative shortage and try to find similar substitute items from the source list.

There are no real significant diseases caused by mineral shortages that will not be taken care of if the basic vitamin sources are found and eaten. The key thing to note here is that **almost everything you need nutritionally to survive is found in and provided by meat!**

The only two not really provided by meat are Vitamin E, which has no real known deficiency disease and Vitamin C, which is one of the most widely occurring and easy to find vitamin sources almost everywhere in the world! Seaweed at sea, cacti in the desert, lichen in the arctic, and many plants in the jungle, mountain and forests can provide Vitamin C. With meat and one plant from each of the world's environments, you can survive with a healthy diet!

Note to vegetarians and vegans: This is not a natural or healthy diet for human beings! The human body developed natural enzymes to pull vitamins and minerals from the meat of animals, but **we cannot pull the essential vitamins and minerals from the plants.** We need animals to do this for us because animals have their own special enzymes that break down grasses and grains and absorb the nutrients we need, which they store in their meat and organs, and which we can only get by consuming the animals, not the grasses directly.

Therefore, the natural order of things is not to be vegan or vegetarian, but to be a meat eater, as we are omnivorous by nature and that's all there is to it. **The bottom line is that a vegan will die in most long term survival situations if he does not eat meat.** Unless a vegan is fortunate enough to have enough nuts and legumes and other supplements around, his body will simply shut down and die since such a diet relies on manmade nutritional supplements to survive in good health.

So, note to the vegans and vegetarians out there surviving: Either take a hiatus from the diet or figure out who gets to eat you when you go! If you're out there surviving and food is scarce, but water is plentiful, consider the vegan among you to be on the future menu!!

FIBER, simply put, is purely a nicety. Yup, it keeps you regular, and that is important. Without it, you can become constipated and that can cause debilitating pain. But constipation is easily treated by drinking a lot of water and consuming some oil or a lot of fat cooked to be nice and greasy. Either will lubricate the fecalith, or feces "stone," causing the blockage and the resulting pain. Get fiber if you can, but plan to live without it. Enough fruits, veggies, fats and water will usually suffice for the survivor.

Okay, that's all I gotta say about nutrition as preventive medicine for surviving.

IMMUNIZATION

Now let's look at some things you should have in general, especially before any trips, and what it might mean if you don't have your shots aka vaccinations.

Immunizations are very, very important. You might not realize it because they have become commonplace in our lives, but these measures alone have single-handedly saved millions, maybe billions, of lives through prevention. It is imperative that you get your vaccinations and keep your shots up to date. It is especially important, before you travel, to look at your local website—the Centers for Disease Control and Prevention for Americans and the National Health Service for the British—so that you will know which diseases are prevalent in the region to which you are traveling. Get the necessary precautionary injections before you go and do so as soon as you know you're traveling as some vaccines require a series which may take weeks or even months.

The way these things work is simple. You get a low dose of a weakened disease that has been studied and tested plenty before you are getting it to make sure you can handle it. Our bodies then adapt and adopt the sickness so that we now have a resistance and are protected. These are not 100% sure but, mostly, they work. Get the details when you get the shot if you're interested, but do not skip it, as it sure would be hateful to die from some disease you could have prevented with a little poke before you left home.

There are many immunizations that children require during the course of growing up, and these vary from country to country and periods of time based on current medical practices. It is not within the scope of this book to address shots for kids since this is for adults who might end up in a survival situation as a result of work or recreational pursuits.

BASIC IMMUNIZATIONS MOST PEOPLE SHOULD GET

NAME	FREQUENCY	PREVENTS	NOTES
Meningococcal	Maybe a booster every 5 years or when travelling to endemic area	Brain disease	Can kill you quickly!
Hepatitis A	There are lifetime immunity vaccines that usually require multiple doses over a period of time	Hep A, mostly from dirty water in poor countries	Hep A hurts a lot like a bad flu, but most survive
Hepatitis B	Series with boosters	Mostly for healthcare workers who deal with blood	This does kill
Pneumococcal	Maybe a booster every 5 years or if traveling where endemic	Lung diseases	Can kill too
Influenza	Annually	Flu	Not really needed for healthy adults, mostly for elderly and young
Varicella	Usually once	Chickenpox	A herpes virus

NAME	FREQUENCY	PREVENTS	NOTES
HiB (Haemophilus Influenzae)	Maybe 5 years or when travelling to a risky area	Bacterial infections of brain, heart, lungs	Can be lethal
MMR (Measles, Mumps, Rubella)	Might need for travel	Stops what it says on the label	Helps fight other virals
HPV (Human papillomavirus)	3-part series over 6 months, once in life	Prevents disease that could cause harm and is difficult to detect	For sexually active women under 26
TDP (Tetanus, Diphtheria, Pertussis)	Booster every 10 years	Primarily prevents Tetanus, which can kill a survivor quickly	Usually caused by infected puncture wounds

Note: The purpose of this chart is not to teach you what the diseases are or what the vaccination schedules are. These diseases are complex and have many signs, symptoms and ways of spreading. The main reason for this chart is to remind you that there are preventable things out there which can harm or kill you, but it requires you to take the steps to prevent them. **Check your shot records. Get them up to date!**

DISEASE

Simply put, diseases are naturally occurring organisms that cause a reaction that has a negative impact on the health of the human organism when encountered by the human body. They come from many sources, cause many symptoms, and not all have cures. Some go away on their own, some are easily treated, and some are fatal if untreated.

Most diseases can be either treated or cured. Treatment means the disease can be controlled and managed to make it less harmful but not stopped or killed completely. Curing means the disease can be completely removed as a problem.

Since most things can be cured, or at least treated, the key will be lasting long enough to get treatment or a cure. To this end, it is helpful to know what diseases are out there and what causes them so you can try to **prevent** them when possible while recognizing signs and symptoms if you do get something. This way, you can understand what is going on if you get sick, try to keep any sickness from getting worse, have some idea what to expect so you don't despair, and have a concept of the timeline you are up against to help make better decisions to effect a rescue or escape to civilization. I will include treatments just in case you happen to have medical supplies. How to use them will depend on more variables than I can cover here. Read the label; then use your common sense and best SWAG (scientific wild-ass guess!).

DISEASES TO LOOK OUT FOR

DISEASE	VECTOR/CAUSE	SIGNS/SYMPTOMS	TREATMENT
Malaria Protozoan Parasites	Mosquito (dawn/dusk biter) Tropics	Fever in cycles, chills, jaundice, sweats	Chloroquine and other options
Leishmaniasis Protozoan	Sandfly Africa, Asia, Mediterranean	Cutaneous: Skin ulcers, fever Visceral: Liver and spleen enlarge	Fatal if not treated. Antimony, Amphotericin, Miltefosine
Leptospirosis (spirochete bacteria)	Rat urine but many animals can carry and cause it	High fever, bad aches, chills, headaches then stops, then brain, liver and kidney damage leading to death, brown urine is a bad sign	Doxycycline, Penicillin, Ampicillin, Amoxicillin
Histoplasmosis (fungal infection of the lungs)	Bat & bird feces, usually from being in caves or near cliffs with birds	Harsh coughing for no apparent reason two weeks after being around bat or bird droppings	Amphotericin-B or other Systemic antifungals. Consider Diflucan. Unexplained dark lesion around nose mouth is indicator

DISEASE	VECTOR/CAUSE	SIGNS/SYMPTOMS	TREATMENT
Scabies	Mites from poor hygiene in environment, primarily bedding for survivors	Itchiness and red skin and rash as mite burrows into flesh and lays eggs	Permethrin, Lindane Ivermectin
West Nile virus	Mosquito bite with robins and crows making virus worse	Fever with chills, sweats and swollen lymph nodes	No treatment. Consider antivirals
Rickettsia causes Typhus, Pox and Rocky Mountain spotted fever	Ticks, Fleas, Lice usually off of rats, causes some types of encephalitis, too	Fevers, chills, aches, nausea, vomiting, there are vaccines	Bacteria is gram negative and responds well to antibiotics, looks a lot like dengue
Filariasis or Elephantiasis Nematode Worm	Mosquito bite carries thread-like worm, gets into lymph system	Skin thickens like an elephant's, mostly lower legs, can affect anywhere	Diethylcarbamazine Albendazole Doxycycline
Onchocerciasis or River blindness Nematode Worm related to above	Parasite in black fly bite near flowing rivers	Gets in body and lives 15 years, causes severe itching, then thick lizard skin, then leopard patches, they migrate to eye, causes opaqueness and blindness	Ivermectin Doxycycline
Dengue	Mosquito (day biter) Asia, Africa, Caribbean, Latin America, Australia	Rash on lower legs and chest, high fever, abdominal pain, constant headaches, loss of appetite	Goes away on its own, but if there is hemorrhage do not give aspirin, which will reduce clotting and mean more bleeding
Sleeping Sickness (Trypanosomiasis)	Tsetse Fly, Africa Attracted to dark clothes and fast moving objects	Fever, headaches, joint pain, swollen lymph nodes, daytime sleepiness, fatal if untreated	Eflornithine, Pentamidine

(Continued on next page)

DISEASE	VECTOR/CAUSE	SIGNS/SYMPTOMS	TREATMENT
Chagas Disease or American Version of Trypanomiasis	Assassin or kissing bug bites Latin America	Causes a nodule at bite site, then disease spreads for up to 20 years	Drugs from Azole family- Benznidazole, etc. but only early on, hard to treat later
Yellow Fever	City or rainforest mosquito Central & South America	Fever, chills, and bleeding into skin Hits in two to three days with jaundice, coffee-ground-looking vomit, goes away after jaundice, then comes back and often kills	Vaccine is 99% effective. No treatment, only for symptoms
Bilharzia or **Schistosomiasis** (Trematodes)	Parasite from snail in fresh water called flukes	Rash and itchy skin one to two days after wading in water, then fever and aches	Praziquantel, Antimony

Note: The type of parasite is listed not to be fancy, but to help you as a survivor and improviser extraordinaire. In case you come across a medication for one type you might use it for another of the same type. For example, you might find the anti-helminthic, Praziquantel, which is used to treat Trematodes also called Flukes. But you might actually have a flatworm, also called tape worm, from the Cestode family. The Praziquantel can be used for both even though the second is an "off-label" use, meaning the parasite is not the medication's intended target. Still, it can still kill that other parasite because they are similar. Use what you have and think outside the box.

ANTIBIOTIC THERAPIES FOR THE SURVIVOR

RULES. There are a lot of rules, regulations and laws out there regarding antibiotics and their use. These are mostly good things because, if antibiotics were readily available to everyone, many folks would take them for many reasons and many of them would be wrong.

REASONS. What's the harm? Humans change and develop immunities to things the more we're exposed to them. Many diseases that can kill people are easily cured by antibiotics but these antibiotics took time to discover and develop. If people take a lot of antibiotics, and the bugs in their bodies develop immunity to these antibiotics, then the chances are, we will no longer have effective treatments for many diseases and might not find new cures in time. So, in the big picture, doctors are trying to save lives by controlling and restricting the misuse of antibiotics. That's why they're regulated.

EXCEPTIONS TO THE RULES. The survivor has but one mission, to stay alive. Illness can cause this mission to fail. So, antibiotics are to be considered fully acceptable for use in a survival situation. That said, you need to know some basics about bugs and drugs.

TWO TYPES. There are primarily two types of bacteria that have significance to the survivor, the kind that need oxygen and the kind that don't (called *aerobic* and *anaerobic* bacteria, respectively). They have different shapes and such, but that is only important in a lab with a microscope. This is only intended as kindergarten-level class.

THREE TERMS. There is some terminology that will help you though: *gram negative* and *gram positive*. In a lab, a stain on the bacteria differentiates between the two and this information tells what type of antibiotic will work better against it. The other key term to know is *broad spectrum antibiotic*, meaning the drug works against both kinds. These are what you need.

TWO WAYS. Antibiotics usually work in one of two ways. *Bactericidals* either get inside the cell and destroy the nucleus or attack the outside of the cell and destroy its membrane; either way, the bacteria dies. *Bacteriostatics* prevents the bacteria from dividing, stopping its proliferation throughout the body.

DIAGNOSING. The types of bacterial infections you might get on a cut on the outside of your arm are usually aerobic and gram positive and less severe. The types you might get inside you, where there is no air, are usually anaerobic and gram negative and are usually more severe.

When you attempt to diagnose a bacterial infection in the field without the benefit of proper tools and lab techniques, this is called *empirical diagnosis*, or based purely on experience and observation. Use the info you gather to try and decide what kind of infection is being presented. That will drive the determination of which drug might be needed. In short, it is a best guess.

A good rule of thumb is that green is bacterial, yellow is viral. This is useful for determining if you actually need that antibiotic or not when there is a cough, runny nose or phlegm.

It is important to grasp that not all antibiotics work for all bacterial infections. So if you are taking an antibiotic for something that it is not designed and intended for, it might not be doing you any good at all and you've squandered a valuable resource that could have been of benefit later if used for the bugs it was intended to work against.

What it all means to you is this: incorporate what you now know about the basics of antibiotics and bacteria and make the best guess for what will work based on what you have available to you. In most cases, a broad spectrum antibiotic will work. If in doubt, take the antibiotics.

TREATMENT. When it comes right down to it, it is best to have some broad spectrum antibiotics. Try to get them, try to keep them in any first aid/survival kit and if you have them, chances are, they will help. Here is a list of a few; these will change over time so do some research for the most current medicines. I include here one common broad-spectrum antibiotic from each of the major categories so that if you encounter one of these, you will know it can be of good use.

Clindamycin
Ciprofloxacin, Levofloxacin
Doxycycline

Trimethoprim-Sulfamethoxazole
Ceftriaxone
Amoxicillin
Erythromycin, Azithromycin
Kanamycin

Note: Most medications will last much longer than their shelf life. Very rarely is an out-of-date medicine actually more harmful as a result of being expired. Consider the temperature and conditions of storage and time expired, but if the container looks good and the medication looks normal, give it a try.

OFF-LABEL (ALTERNATE) USES OF DRUGS

Most medicines have three names: a generic name, a brand name and a chemical name. For example, *aspirin* is a generic name, *Bayer* is a brand name and *acetylsalicylic acid* is a chemical name. Aspirin was first marketed in the late 1800s but it has been around for thousands of years. My point here is that medicines all have a starting point and usage grows based on the discovery of its benefits. I want you to shake off any preconceived notions you have about predefined uses of drugs; this is survival. Here are a couple of examples of how to think about using a drug for other than its marketed purpose.

There is a well-known antifungal used to treat oral thrush and candidiasis or vaginal yeast infection called Diflucan or Trican. (I use both these trade names as that is most likely how people will know and recognize them.) This drug began its life as a simple solution to the long regimen of tablets that was needed to be taken in order to treat common vaginal yeast infections. With this new drug, treatment went from seven to ten days of tablets a few times a day to a simple one-tablet dose to cure the candidiasis. Now, some physicians took note of these "anti-fungal" properties and began to experiment with *off-label* uses by, say, using Diflucan or Trican to treat fungal infections of the toe, which were very difficult to get rid of. They found these tablets worked! They are now used this way by doctors, although the drug is not marketed for this use at this point. So look at the big picture and apply common sense but try to improvise solutions based on what you have to heal yourself.

There is another well-known anti-viral agent called Acyclovir used for treating Herpes Simplex I, usually found around the mouth, and Herpes Simplex II, usually found around the genitals. Now, this is a very limited scope of marketed use indeed. If your patient is suffering from a viral disease, and you are pretty sure it is viral because antibiotics have not touched it and the patient is getting worse, then maybe you should try this antiviral for herpes you found in the wreckage as a last ditch effort to save them? Food for thought. I cannot encourage or condone this practice. I can only present a concept for thinking outside the constraints of society when you are clearly outside the ability of society to help you.

DIARRHEA

This perennial plague on the survivor has many nicknames but will be experienced by almost all survivors. There are simple general concepts and rules for dealing with diarrhea: **Let diarrhea go for the first 24 hours** to clear out any causative organisms unless you are moving or already ill.

If you are moving or already dehydrated, try to stop it up. If diarrhea lasts more than a day, chances are it is a bug, not just bad food.

Viral diarrhea will be very aggressive, hit hard and fast, and pass in one to three days.

Bacterial diarrhea takes a while to build up and is slower to go away.

When fever, vomiting, blood or pus are present, consider antibiotics.

Antibiotics will not help with viral causes of diarrhea. In all cases, drink fluids, stay hydrated, treat symptoms and reduce fever.

Here is a chart of some of the causes of diarrhea and how to help you determine what type you might have so you can best determine how to deal with it. It is important to know that the majority of diarrhea is from a bacterial cause.

CAUSES OF AND TREATMENTS FOR DIARRHEA

TYPE OR CAUSE	MAJOR SIGN OR SYMPTOMS	PRIMARY TREATMENT
E.coli (many types)	In survival situations, usually shows up without fever, often from dirty food, poor hygiene	Usually gram negative so use narrow spectrum antibiotics if available or Amoxicillin
Dysentery: oral-fecal Amoebic: E.Histolitica Bacterial : See below- Shigella, Salmonella, Campylobacter	Can vary but usually are considered to be of the worst types with longest persistence. Fever, blood, pus maybe, but frequent diarrhea after anything is ingested	Primary mission is to keep hydrated with fluids, enemas, IVs. Oral rehydration solutions made with some salt and sugar, etc. Flagyl will treat E.Histolitica and Cipro will treat the three bacteria.
Shigella (gram negative) oral-fecal route means dirty hands after latrine or flies landing on feces then food, causes about 1/3 of cases of diarrhea	Usually with fever, blood, pus in stool, often with cramps, nausea, vomiting and straining to defecate, starts in two days, lasts four days or longer	Ampicillin, Ciprofloxacin
Salmonella (gram negative) found on turtles/reptiles, usually food-borne from food cooked but not eaten right away	Mostly from eggs and poultry, fever with headache and rose spots and diarrhea with blood and mucous	Usually hits a few hours after ingestion, lasts a few days and goes away on its own.
Cholera (gram negative), causes an enterotoxin which makes it meaner than most	Painless, watery diarrhea, rapid onset usually two days, rarely with vomiting or fever	Fluids, symptomatic, sometimes antibiotics, no vaccine
Giardia Lamblia is a protozoa, no antibiotic will work, usually from drinking bad water, these cysts survive many filters (boil drinking water)	Diarrhea rarely has pus or blood, but often foul-smelling flatulence and eructations or burps, rarely fever	Metronidazole or Flagyl but this is a long course. Tinidazole is a single dose, can go away on its own in a few weeks

(Continued on next page)

TYPE OR CAUSE	MAJOR SIGN OR SYMPTOMS	PRIMARY TREATMENT
Campylobacter, oral-fecal, sexual, contaminated food, water, raw meat	Fever, diarrhea usually without blood, cramps	Mostly goes away on its own
Vibrio P (gram negative)	Usually from brackish water and seafood, watery diarrhea within 24 hours	Mostly goes away on its own
Rotavirus causes a lot of diarrheas from contaminated hands	Usually within two days, can last four to eight days, profuse diarrhea, sometimes vomit low grade fever	Hydration is imperative, this will go away, but loss of fluids is worse with this since antibiotics will not help
Typhoid Fever is a strain of salmonella	It causes diarrhea without blood, but a high-grade fever of 104 degrees, rose spots on chest, nose bleeds	Usually not fatal, antibiotics help like Chloramphenicol or Cipro

Note: There are many other causes of diarrhea but these are the most common ones. The key is to try to let it pass for one to two days, keep hydrated, treat the symptoms, and when all else fails, try some antibiotics and use the anti-diarrheal medicines if you have some and, if not, try some of the alternative remedies listed in this section. Also worth mentioning here is that many of these are internal, and therefore, without oxygen—as such, they are of the gram negative variety.

REAL FIRST AID

Alrighty, now we've covered a lot of ground for all the basics of trauma and disease. So let's look at the other types of medical and health problems a survivor might encounter. But first, let's clear the air about a commonly misunderstood practice: CPR.

CPR—THE REAL DEAL

The fact is that everyone is going to die. Sometimes, in very rare circumstances, this can be reversed by CPR. In some states, the out-of-hospital survival rate for CPR patients is as low as 3%. Think about that.

If most folks who survive as a result of CPR were already in a hospital, with folks looking after them and **all the follow-up care** that goes with the cause for needing CPR in the first place. The rest of people who actually survive after CPR being administered survived because they were **witnessed** at the time they dropped.

This means two very important things to a survivor. First, if you didn't witness someone go down, and you come upon them, assess them, and find no breathing or pulse, chances are, they will not recover. Second, if you do recover them, consider what might be the cause of the problem in the first place. Most likely, you won't have heart monitors, drugs, IVs and oxygen to sustain them if you do recover them. This could be a painful process to recover a life, only to then actually watch it slip away again. Consider this.

Now, I'm not saying not to try CPR. If you're fit and strong, there are no other patients, you're not in danger from the environment and you think you can recover and sustain them, then give it a go.

The main reason for CPR in a survival situation is twofold. The first reason is trying to do something for yourself. If you don't want to accept your patient's death, then get down there and try if the situation permits. The second reason is to help the surviving loved ones. If there is a husband present who just witnessed his wife die, you might try and administer CPR, for him! He'll see that you are trying, and knowing that you did try, he can more easily accept the hard facts. Later, this will help with group cohesion in the survivor dynamics because there is no anger at you for not trying and maybe even a closer bond for having tried.

So, what I am saying is that CPR in a survival situation is mostly for you and the other survivors, not for the dead and dying. It is hard work and will drain you and this must be considered, especially early on in any traumatic crash type scenario.

EXCEPTIONS—LIGHTNING & DROWNING

Now, for every rule, there are almost always exceptions and this is true for Survivor CPR, too. If you see a fellow survivor get struck by lightning, or have a bad fall, or drown and you rescue them, in these cases, CPR is very effective and can very much stand a chance of bringing someone back to life!

Therefore, we'll cover some CPR basics since this is not a certifying class. Still, you'll have the concept in case you need to apply it.

The first thing is always to assess. If you try to do CPR on a conscious person they're either going to hit you or hug you! If they are unconscious but breathing, they might puke on you and now you've created a choking situation. If they have a pulse and you start pushing on their chest, you might actually throw the heart out of sync and kill them, so assess first. **No breathing, but pulse, give two breaths. No pulse or breaths, then do CPR.**

PRECORDIAL THUMP

CPR has already been covered in the early assessment phase. But before you do CPR there is a great little trick to know about called a *precordial thump*.

This is old school, and some CPR classes no longer teach it since it is optional and it might lead to lawsuits from people breaking ribs, but for the survivor, it is the closest thing to a defibrillator you're gonna get in the field.

The heart is amazing and works by *automaticity*, meaning that it generates its own electrical impulses. It has built in backups as well. Nodes at the top fire quickly and regulate most things; when they fail, nodes in the middle pick up the slack, but at a slower rate; when they fail, the emergency nodes at the bottom kick in, usually too slow to be healthy, but enough for life. When someone has a fall, gets struck by lightning or has drowned and the heart has shut down so it no longer creates a pulse you can detect, often, the little electrical nodes are still firing away but either very weakly or out-of-synch so that the heart is not pumping but just quivering. In a short period of time, without blood flow pushing oxygen, major organs start shutting down and dying from the lack of oxygen. Your job is to get the oxygen there by returning the blood flow. The way to do this is to get the heart pumping again.

Because the heart is like a little electrical battery, sometimes a jumpstart is all you need to get it back to work. And that is what the precordial thump does. Execute it with one good blow, striking with the bottom (palm aspect) of your fist, right on top of the center of the heart. Use a firm blow but pull back so as to not break ribs.

Very often, if you witness a case of cardiac arrest, a precordial thump will kickstart the heart back into operation. It can save a life and save you a lot of work. It shouldn't really be done more than once, or two to three times tops. If it doesn't work then, it ain't gonna work, so get to doing CPR. Good luck with that!

GOLDEN 60, 60, 6

This is a guideline to help you understand the bigger picture and what things might mean to you in terms of realistically planning and managing expectations for yourself and other survivors.

GOLDEN MINUTE. The first 60 seconds will often dictate a lot about the chances for a patient's survival. If they have a leg chopped off and are bleeding out, chances are, if you don't intervene within that first minute, they will bleed out and die. For you, that means, if your leg gets chopped off, there is no time for screaming or asking why or looking for help. You better rip off your belt and slap a tourniquet on yourself, hard and fast, or by the time you finish yelling your head off, you'll be dead. Keeping focused on applying the tourniquet will also keep you from going into shock before you can get the tourniquet on.

If someone has their face smashed and can't breathe for over a minute, chances are they will suffocate and die. If you see this, or it happens to you, stick your fingers right into their neck and hold a hole open for them to breathe out of. The chances of someone surviving without the two critical requirements of blood and air, after more than a minute, are very slim indeed. If there are other pressing matters, you might opt to not attempt rescue. This point is usually where first aid rendered by first responders makes all the difference.

GOLDEN HOUR. The upside to the human response to trauma is a shock response that makes a patient hyperventilate to get more air while his blood vessels constrict to save loss of blood. This passes quickly, however, and then the blood flows and the breathing shallows. During this time is when your treatments will most impact a patient's chance of survival. If you can get good dressings on the wounds to stop bleeding, and make sure the airway and chest injuries are treated so your patient can breathe effectively, chances are good that he can survive—**if** he can get further medical treatment. This is the level where, back home, a good paramedic saves lives a lot.

GOLDEN SIX HOURS. After first responder aid and stabilization care is given, your patient will need medical or surgical intervention, depending on the damage done. For the survivor, these first six hours will likely come and go without rescue or aid. Most trauma victims with significant organ and tissue damage will begin to expire without surgical intervention.

You must understand this concept. If you are the caregiver in a mass casualty situation in some remote area, chances are that a lot of your work and effort to save some folks might come to naught if no real medical care can be rendered so you must weigh heavily some considerations.

To whom do you give limited time, energy and medical supplies?

Who do you move or not?

Do you let the person know they are likely not going to make it?

Do you tell their loved ones what the realistic expectations are?

The golden six hours isn't necessarily when your patient will die. It just means that, by then, major damage will have taken its toll and death is likely not stoppable in the field. Without lots of antibiotics, infection sets in so gangrene and septicemia begin. Major organs start to fail as a result of diminished function and systems begin collapsing. Understanding the long-term importance of the first six hours should help you mentally prepare so that you can better manage the remainder of your survival strategy.

Note: I have found that 95% of the time, people prefer the truth, so be honest in your assessments to both the dying and the living. Only in a few cases have I seen that people actually know they're going to die but can't or don't want to face it . . . you'll know these if you see them. In these cases, I suggest you play along, and they will go just a little bit happier. It is not easy. That's all I got to say about that.

SELF-TREATMENT

Most of this is for you, but if you're with others, it applies equally. For self-aid, everything must be considered from the perspective of you being the person injured or ill. Having to do this for yourself is not easy!!!

SELF DE-CHOKING is tricky business. When someone else is choking, always try a few hard pats on the back first; that usually does it. If not, get behind him and give a bear hug, squeezing right under the rib cage real hard with your thumb knuckle driving into their guts. Your patient will heave-ho in a most impressive manner. Heck, you can put out an eye with the force of their vomitus projectile. For self-choking, neither of these really work. I have choked a few times and leaning on something never really did it for me. All I could do was shove my fingers in and pull out the object lodged while givin' up some of my chow along with it. Food for thought, hehe!

DEHYDRATION is a real problem for most people in a survival situation. As addressed in the Water chapter, you can survive for a very long time on small amounts of water if you're not losing too much to the environment or exertion. Survivors, however, will often get diarrhea or other illnesses that cause vomiting. Both of these can significantly contribute to dehydration. While we covered the signs and treatments for this already in the water chapter, what is important for the survivor here is an occurrence that actually happens a lot and is overlooked: kidney stones.

KIDNEY STONES or *renal calculi* occur a lot in the field for people who are dehydrated over long periods of time. They result from low fluid levels that allow naturally occurring crystals like calcium to build up into deposits that become like small rocks or pebbles in the *ureters*, or tubes the drain the waste fluid from the kidney to the bladder.

When these occur, there is sudden and very severe pain in the flanks often accompanied by fever. Usually, they will pass. Have the person rest, often on the opposite side, to allow gravity to help move the stone along the ureter into the bladder. Give pain meds and water if available.

Sometimes, kidney stones actually build up and cause an obstruction in the urethra right near the bladder. This is a medical emergency as the person cannot urinate, and urinary retention has the bladder full and hyper-extended to the point of extreme pain from loin to groin. In these cases, you have three things to try.

Try having your patient lie upside down, with their back against a tree and their feet up in the air, and massage the bladder area so gravity can help dislodge the stone.

When you have the tubing, consider catheterizing the person, or putting a tube into his urethra and up into the bladder to drain it that way.

Worst case scenario, if you think the person is going to die, then consider making a hole straight into the bladder. Be as clean as you can and use a big fat catheter or needle with a hole in the center so there is something the urine can pass through. This is an invasive procedure and there is a risk of infection and complications, but it is important to know that it can be done. The location for the puncture should be in the center of the body, just above the pubic bone. This is called a suprapubic cystostomy and is practiced in emergency medicine.

GOUT is a buildup of uric acid and pseudo-gout is a buildup of calcium pyro-phosphate but both can affect a dehydrated survivor by manifesting as extreme pain in the joints, especially around the lower extremities. The best treatment in the field is some aspirin and topical hemorrhoid medicine applied locally. If there is gout, there is a chance that kidney stones will surface.

JAUNDICE is yellowing of the eyes first and then the skin. It is nothing more than a byproduct of bilirubin backing up into the blood stream and turning the external tissues yellowish. It only backs up when the liver is inflamed, a condition called hepatitis. But this too is only a symptom because something must cause the liver to swell up. It might be a virus or parasite or physical obstruction. Remember, if you see jaundice, look to treat the cause.

DIABETES affects a lot of people and as such, you might see it manifest in a survival situation. There are two main types: the kind where the patient needs insulin and the kind where they need sugar.

If your patient needs insulin, he'll have some, or he'll have told you he's out or running out. The bad news is, without more insulin, your patient will not make it. The good news is that only about 10% of diabetics are this type (or Type 1) of diabetic. The problem for this type of diabetic is that he has too much sugar in the blood. Often, stressful situations like survival will worsen the condition, which takes time to set in, anywhere from hours to days.

If your patient's breath smells fruity and he is both thirsty and urinating a lot, his skin is hot and dry, and he is breathing deeply and rapidly, he is going down. Another sign is if your patient gets very tired and then irritable. The problem is exacerbated by starvation as this causes the liver to start generating more ketones and glycerol which worsens the condition. Make your patient comfortable; chances are that he realizes his prospects. In a crash situation, search for insulin among the wreckage since finding some is your patient's only hope.

If your patient needs sugar, the problem has a much easier fix—a shot of sugar—but, without it, your patient could be in real trouble, too. If he is suddenly hungry, confused, angry, cold and clammy skinned, chances are he is going into *insulin shock*, meaning too much insulin sucked up all his glucose or blood sugar. Check to see if your patient is wearing any diabetes tags. Be sure to get him to drink a sugary drink or eat something sweet while he is conscious or you'll be in a jam. If you're having trouble telling which way your diabetic patient is going, the good news is that giving a candy bar to the other type of diabetic won't hurt him. If in doubt, whip it out.

POISON. There are really only two courses of action available to the survivor for first-aid responses to poisons.

If poison is ingested:
- Vomit it out. If you can't do that, or it's been too long . . .
- Try to neutralize the poison internally by consuming char-coal-based fluids.

If the poison comes from contact:

- Suck out poisons from bites with something other than your mouth and clean the wound.
- Clean off the area and treat the symptoms.

SHOCK

Most people have been exposed to and understand allergies in principle. The concept is that something in the environment comes into contact with the patient and their body has a negative response to that stimulation. Sometimes, the reaction is mild like a runny nose and watery eyes; sometimes, it's worse like a rash or difficulty breathing; sometimes it's so extreme that without intervention, the body kills itself by over-responding.

This is true of **anaphylactic shock**. When someone is stung by a bee, for example, the body might have a strong response that ends up killing the person because a constricted airway prevents breathing and swelling constricts circulation. This can happen to anyone at anytime. You can be stung 100 times by a bee and on the 101st time, the body decides it's had enough, doesn't like it anymore and reacts violently with anaphylaxis. This is a life-threatening emergency if untreated. The good news is that only a few hundred people die a year from it, but many of those who lived had two things handy that you likely won't have. Epinephrine or adrenaline injections and diphenhydramine or Benadryl are the two drugs used universally to treat anaphylactic shock. These can be purchased from most pharmacies and should live in everyone's first aid kits at home, work, etc.

The chances of surviving true anaphylaxis are slim without these. If you have them, get them into the person right away or he could die within minutes. If you do not have them, be prepared to put something down your patient's throat to keep that airway open. In time, chances are that the swelling will go down, but you must keep them alive long enough for the body to do that. In a worst case scenario, consider the *cricothyroidotomy* taught in this chapter. Also, any antihistamine type drug is better than none, so if anyone has motion sickness tablets or sleeping tablets, try them while your patient can still swallow.

The other types of shock are nice to know but not really relevant to the survivor.

NEUROGENIC: When the brain is damaged and the nerves are not passing their signals correctly, major organ functions are impaired. In the survival situation, this is mostly fatal.

HYPOVOLEMIC: Losing too much blood can cause shock. Without stopping the bleeding quickly and replacing the volume of fluids lost with IV fluids, chances are someone in this type of shock will die, and quickly. Stop the bleeding right away, at all costs. For hypovolemic shock you can try elevating the patient's legs, even wrapping his limbs tightly to reduce—but not prevent—blood flow to the limbs. That way, the blood can stay concentrated in the chest and keep the vital organs functioning.

CARDIOGENIC: This accompanies a heart attack. See the CPR section but remember the chances of surviving in a survival situation are extremely low. If someone is having a heart attack, here are some field things that might help.

Put the patient's face in a bowl of ice water. I know, I know. Where are you to get that in a survival situation? But you might be in the snow . . . Doing this invokes a mammalian dive reflex which slows the heart rate down and can stop a potential "V-fib" heart problem, when the ventricles fibrillate and can't pump.

Rub the patient's neck where the jugular veins are located. This can also cause a slowing down of the heart rate and preclude a heart attack. This is called a carotid (type of blood vessel) baroreceptor (type of nerve) response and can be used to calm people down when stressed as well.

SEPTICEMIC: When your patient has a systemic infection, he'll be burning up with fever. Without antibiotics, he will not make it.

PSYCHOGENIC: This is my favorite kind of shock. Sometimes, people just see things or hear things that cause them to faint. When this happens, momentarily, the brain lets go and the blood vessels all expand or *vasodilate* at the same time, which causes blood pressure to drop and the brain to temporarily lose oxygen. This will pass quickly and completely. Just make sure the patient doesn't hurt his head when he passes out, lay him down and wait a minute and he'll come back 'round and be fine. The same goes for when someone hyperventilates . . . let him. He will over oxygenate, pass out and stop breathing for a minute or two but as soon as the carbon dioxide builds back up in his lungs, it will trigger restarted breathing, whether the patient likes it or not, and he'll come to.

The best thing for any type of shock is to try and treat the cause. Keep the patient comfortable, care for the symptoms and hope.

ELEMENTS & EXPOSURE

Braving the weather is mostly common sense. If it's hot; stay cool. If it's cold; stay warm. If it's wet, get dry. If it's dry, find some wet. But what about when you can't and you start to suffer? Here's what to look for and what you can try to do about it. In severe cases, you might not be able to do anything except take it and drive on, with the hopes of making it out or getting rescued: your only real chance of surviving.

SUNBURN is something most of us have experienced to one degree or another, no pun intended. But basically, sunburn is like any other burn in that there are three degrees. Chances are that you'll never live long enough to see the third. The treatments are the same as well.

First-degree burns are the top layer of skin turning red.

These hurt but aren't serious.

Second-degree burns go deeper and cause blisters. Later infection is the real danger.

Third-degree burns go past the skin and do not hurt but are the most dangerous.

The treatment is the same for all burns, as follows:

Keep cool and dry.

Use pain medication when needed and available.

If the burn is deep, consider using topical antibiotics. Burn victims need a lot of fluid, as they will ooze white blood cells and dehydrate.

Do not lance blisters. If you must, lance at the base, not at the top.

If the burn is third-degree, the skin will be grey and painless; the nerves are burnt. These people will need antibiotics because the skin is open and the body exposed to infection.

If a large surface area is burned, like an entire limb, consider *escharotomy*. This is done by slicing through the burned flesh with a scalpel or knife, not too deeply. If the entire limb is burnt, there will be swelling inside, but the skin will not give so make a slice along the entire outside and inside burned part of the limb. This will allow circulation and promote healing and prevent *necrosis*, or the dying of the tissue, which causes *gangrene* to set in. Gangrene of an extremity, without amputation, will lead to septicemia and death.

LIGHTNING STRIKES can cause burns and are to be treated in the same way depending upon the severity. Unfortunately, serious internal damage might be done as well. Dark urine indicates that the prognosis for survival is poor. The good news is that while thousands get struck every year, less than 10% of strikes are fatal.

HEAT EXHAUSTION is merely getting overdone in the sun. The key to avoiding it is to rest regularly, drink lots, stay cool and don't work too hard in the heat. If your skin is cold and clammy, you're still okay, just take it easy as heat exhaustion can quickly lead to heat stroke.

HEAT STROKE is a flat-out killer. It strikes when the body gets so hot and so dehydrated, that the cooling mechanism of sweating stops. If a person passes out and presents hot and dry skin, he is in a bad way. If you're working, and don't feel well and notice that you've stopped sweating, **stop immediately**. This is a life threatening emergency. **Cool down** by any means. Get into shade, jump in cold water, strip naked and fan yourself, put a wet cloth on your forehead and face, underarms, groin, side of the neck, behind the knees and in the arm joint. The same places you can take a pulse or use for pressure points can be used to cool the blood and reduce the core temperature. Dark urine is a bad sign; the brain is already cooking. Without fluids and reduced temperature, someone in this state will expire.

SUN STROKE is some people's way of saying sun burned and dehydrated. This mostly happens when people party on the beach, getting drunk and burnt at the same time. It is not to be confused with heat stroke, which is a life-threatening emergency.

PRICKLY HEAT is an interesting phenomenon. In hot environments, when sweating a lot, especially on the oily parts of skin, the pores will become blocked. This stimulates the tiny nerves on the hair follicles and will be interpreted by the brain as a burning or electrifying sensation. Usually this presents on the back when wearing a heavy pack. The solution is simply to wash the area with soap and water to clean it.

JUNGLE ROT OR IMMERSION FOOT is just another name for when the tissues of the feet start to disintegrate as a result of being wet too long and then being torn off from too much friction, usually from the boot during walking. The treatment is easy: dry your feet. Take breaks and air them out. Failure to do so will invite infection and become debilitating. This can be fatal if it immobilizes you in a bad place or infection is systemic.

INGROWN TOENAILS happen a lot for soldiers and there are many techniques for dealing with them. As a long-term survivor, chances are that you will encounter this if you have to make a long movement as most people do not own or wear shoes designed for long distance movements. (For me personally, if I can't "fight or move" in my clothes, I don't own them.) There are two main schools of thought on this problem, as follows:

Trimming: Shave the top of the nail so it is paper-thin then trim a deep "V" into the middle, and the toenail will come away from the side, easing the pain and pressure.

Removal: I go for this. It's painful, but if it doesn't solve the problem permanently, it certainly solves the problem for a long time and right away. The trick is to simply slice the very edge of the toenail out. Take a small blade, with the cutting edge facing up, slide the point under the nail and try cutting the nail only, with as little damage to the quick below as you can. The secret is to cut right down past the cuticle to the root. Once the blade slides easily without resistance, you're past the nail and can stop. Slide it out. Drain the pus, stop the bleeding, clean the wound and put a good dressing on it. Contrary to popular opinion, a person who undergoes this can walk that day. Still, it's best to wait at least one day. Rest with the foot elevated, and the pain will subside in a day or two.

FROSTBITE happens when the skin is damaged by cold, rupturing cells and causing blisters. You'll know when you have frost bite because it burns or stings at first. And like third-degree burns, once the body part stops hurting, you're in trouble as it's then frozen. Treat the symptoms just like a burn but remember some important differences about recovering from frostbite.

Do not thaw things out unless you can keep them thawed. Re-freezing of digits or limbs will worsen their condition and outcome.

Use the body to get frostbitten parts warm again: feet against stomachs, hands in armpits. Do not use water or fire for re-warming; this must be a gentle process or tissue damage will result.

SNOW BLINDNESS happens very easily when your eyes experience direct, prolonged exposure to the strong UV rays from bright sunlight reflecting off snow or ice. Protect the eyes when you can with glasses or goggles. Two sticks worn like glasses so you see through the slits or a strip of cloth with a small slit you can see through will also work. In a worst-case scenario, put something dark like shoe polish or mud under your eyes to deflect some of the ultraviolet light.

COMMONPLACE HEALTH PROBLEMS

Okay, now that we've covered some serious stuff, let's look at some of the more commonplace, and less life-threatening, health problems a survivor might face.

BOILS—an accumulation of pus and dead tissue—occur as hygiene and health deteriorate. They can become quite painful and unnecessarily infected but treatment is rather easy. Use a warm compress to try and raise the infection closer to the surface then lance the boil with a hot pin and drain the boil from the head. If the boil is very large, use a clean piece of cloth as a drain by stuffing it into the wound and leaving a piece hanging out so the remaining pus can ooze out as the wound closes and heals. Keep clean afterwards.

FUNGUS. Athlete's foot, crotch rot and ring worm are all fungi that can form anywhere on the body and that are common complaints of survivors. The best treatment in a survival situation is sun, but this will only keep the fungus at bay and will not cure it. Only anti-fungal drugs will remove these once they take hold of human tissue. They are unpleasant and uncomfortable but will go away once treated so don't dismay.

HEMORRHOIDS cause a lot of people grief and this can be especially true for the survivor suffering from ailments that cause excess strain on bowel movements. Avoid hemorrhoids with the following tips:

- Maintain a balanced diet
- Stay well-hydrated
- Don't push too hard during defecating
- Lubricate bowel movements

If these don't keep you from getting hemorrhoids, try sitting in a river or some water to let it reduce the swelling a bit.

Deal with persistent hemorrhoids using a rubber band or piece of string. Tie off the offending protrusion and cut off all circulation, which will kill that piece of tissue and stop the pain. Eventually, it will drop right off. Sounds rough, but it will work. It's called *ligation*.

TICKS are a common problem in the woods. Whatever you do, **do not burn** them off. This is just like squeezing them. You make them vomit all their bad stuff right inside of you and defeat the whole purpose of taking them off, which is to stop disease. Use tweezers or string tied around them or even a small toothpick-sized twig to slowly dislodge a tick. Don't squeeze to get them off or just rip them off. If you leave the head, this will get infected fast.

LEECHES are the ticks of the jungle and swamp world. Don't rip them off; that'll just cause open sores and infection. The best way is the same was as with the tick: slowly take them off by separating the sucker head (small end) from the flesh. If leeches get up into your nose or somewhere you can't use the gentle removal technique, **do burn** these boogers with a match or cigarette cherry, or **use salt, ash, or tobacco spit**. Better to deal with a little fluke puke than to have those guys settin' up shop in your nose hairs.

BUGS IN EARS. The best way to get rid of bugs when they're diggin' into your ear canal is oil. Digging can lead to rupturing the *tympanic membrane*, or ear drum, which not only hurts (although it does heal with relatively little scarring or hearing loss) but could open you up to a bad infection since there will be a dead bug carcass rotting inside there. Try some oil, any type, as this will drown the critter quickly and then you can drain him out.

SPRAINS & STRAINS

Sprains and strains are typical injuries for survivors, required as they are to do many physical activities in an unstructured environment. The two types of injuries are often confused.

MUSCLES EXPERIENCE STRAINS when you lift too much and the muscle tears or tendons stretch from hyperextension. You'll know it when it happens as there is a lot of pain in the muscle group.

LIGAMENT STRAINS. Ligaments connect bones to bones, holding the skeleton together. Sprains often happen to ankles when people are running and step on something that cause the weight of the body to force the ankle into an over-extended position.

There are three types of sprain. Here's what they mean to you as a survivor:

- If you twist an ankle, but don't fall, it is a Type 1 sprain with a one-week recovery.

- If you twist and the pain makes you fall, it's a Type 2 sprain with a one-month recovery.
- If you twist and hear a pop, it's a Type 3 sprain with a one-year recovery.

All three sprains hurt and all three swell; the difference is the healing time required. You can move on a sprained ankle the same day as the injury if you need to, but rest time is required in order to prevent it from happening again and becoming a permanently weak point in your structure. Many athletes hurt their ankle and are too impatient to let it mend properly.

The good news for a survivor is that treatment of strains and sprains is the same regardless of severity. The bad news is that you won't likely have the main component: ice. When treating strains and sprains, remember RICE during the first 48 hours.

Rest, get off the injury and give it a break if you can. If not, favor it, a lot.

Ice reduces swelling during the initial 24 to 48 hours following a sprain or strain.

Compress the injured area using an ACE wrap elastic bandage for support.

Elevate the injury to take your weight off it and reduce the inflammation.

After the first 48 hours, the equation changes and you should apply heat to the damaged area, which increases circulation to the area and speeds circulation. So you keep the RCE and swap the "I for ice" with "H for heat" and get CHER. Remember: when you sprain you ankle, eat your RICE for 24 hours before meeting CHER.

DISLOCATION

Dislocation is a possible medical issue in the wild that is extremely painful but easily managed. It's also relatively easy to diagnose: when a shoulder is popped out of socket, for instance, usually from a bad fall, it looks grossly deformed and the person either cries to high heaven or passes out.

If someone else experiences this injury, follow these steps to relocate the limb:

- Take a seat on the ground beside your patient.
- Wrap something like a towel around his wrist so you can grip it; it will likely be sweaty.
- Place your foot into your patient's armpit.
- Slowly pull backward until the arm is stretched out towards you.
- Let the arm slide back into place; the muscle will guide it there for you.
- The arm will ache and not be right again for a long time but the immediate pain relief will be extreme and your patient will love you for it.

If you experience the injury, relocation is more challenging:

- Wrap something like a rope around your wrist, padding it if you can.
- Tie the other end of the rope to a tree.
- Place your feet against the base of the tree.
- Push yourself away at an angle so the rope extends your arm.
- Allow your arm to pop back in.
- Try not to pass out.

The same principles apply when a leg is dislocated to the front or back. Instead of placing the foot into the armpit, you'll use the groin, so mind your manners and pull like heck. Common sense will help you get the leg back into the groove; you'll know it when you've done it.

FRACTURES

Fracture is a fancy name for a broken bone. There are many different kinds but it comes down to two major ones for the survivor.

CLOSED FRACTURES break the bone but keep everything still inside the person.

OPEN FRACTURES are the kind where the bone is not only broken, but it's decided to go and stick out of the person's body. These present the additional problem of deciding whether to try and put the bone back in or not. The fracture checklist will move you through the few key considerations for treatment:

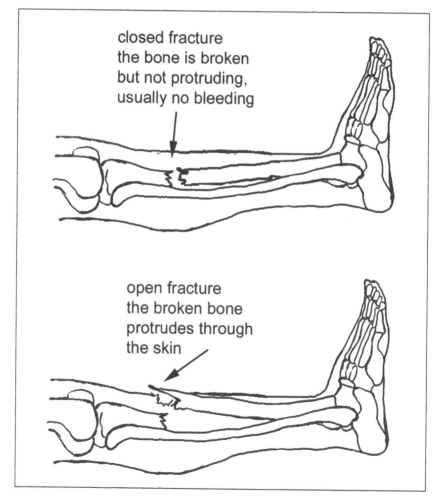

closed fracture
the bone is broken
but not protruding,
usually no bleeding

open fracture
the broken bone
protrudes through
the skin

ASSESS BONE

These indicate the presence of a fracture.

Check for an obvious deformity like a right angle where it shouldn't be.

Check for *crepitus*, a crunchy sound of moving broken bones around.

Be gentle and don't cause additional damage even though you must feel and manipulate a bit.

If there is pain upon any manipulation or movement of the joints, consider the bone broken.

ASSESS FLESH

If the answer to any of these is "no," you've got repairs to do before splinting:

Pulsing: Is there a pulse below the fracture?

Temperature: Is the part of the fractured limb below the break as warm as the part above it?

Feeling: Does the patient have feeling in the part below the break?

Movement: Can they move anything below the break?

PREPARING TO SPLINT A CLOSED FRACTURE

If there is no major deformity, you can splint the break mostly as it is. If there is some major bend in the road, you have to move it.

Normally, you'd only move it enough to get a general sense of normalcy and to keep the pulse flowing so the limb doesn't lose circulation and die, *but*, for the survivor, the chances are that you will be there awhile so you must consider moving a highly deformed broken bone so that it can heal properly. **That means moving the deformity all the way back to a normal position.** Follow these guidelines when doing so:

- Assess the patient's pulse before and after the manipulation. The pulse must be kept open.
- If the limb is cold, there isn't enough blood flow and you'll need to move it some more.
- Stroke the patient's skin with your fingernail to assess whether he has feeling. If so, great. If not, that's not great but it's okay.
- The same goes for whether your patient has function or not. If he can wiggle his fingers or toes, super. If not, it can wait.
- If your patient can wiggle an extremity, see how much strength he has by having him push a little against your hand in all the normal directions.

- The key is to keep the same amount of function after splinting as your patient had before you applied the splint.

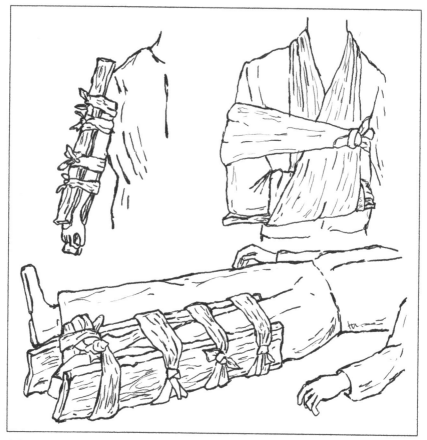

Splint preparation

Assessment is important because it allows you to make sure you are setting their splint the best you can without the benefit of x-rays.

PREPARING TO SPLINT AN OPEN FRACTURE

You will encounter additional challenges from an open fracture. All modern medical practice says not to put the bone back inside. This is mostly correct except if you are in some jungle and think you're going to be there a while since an open bone is a lot like a highway for bacteria with a big neon sign sayin' "Come on in!"

If you have nice clean dressing to place on the bone, and can pad it so it doesn't get bumped or moved around, then this is the recommended course of action. Dress it and keep the dressing dry, not wet, so it doesn't invite more bacteria in. Pad and protect the break, splinting the limb the best you can, and keep the patient immobilized.

If you are sure help is nowhere near and dressings and antibiotics are in short supply or nonexistent, consider placing the bone back inside and letting the body be the dressing and the immune system be the antibiotics. Clean the bone the best you can before you place it back in the body. This is how it was in the days of old; they didn't leave the bone hanging out since there was no choice. The break might not have healed right, but it healed and the patient lived and so can you or your patient.

If you make it back, your patient can always have surgery to repair and correct the break but if they don't make it back, what's the point? This is a harsh reality a survivor must take into consideration. Reapply the principles of assessment to determine if your job is done.

SPLINTING A FRACTURE

The principles of splinting are simple:

- Splint broken bones in a functional position or as close to it as you can get.
- You can use boards or sticks or anything inflexible as a splint.
- Tie the splinting board in two places above the fracture and two places below it.
- Immobilize one joint above the fracture and one joint below it.
- Pad all the bony parts to avoid causing ulcers or sores.
- Reassess the pulse after you place each tie to avoid cutting off circulation.
- Use ice and heat to promote healing as with sprains and strains.
- If you have them, use anti-inflammatory drugs like aspirin or Motrin

for fractures, strains and sprains. If the wound was open, use antibiotics if you have them.

* If you have nothing, use an anatomical splint. Tie the broken limb to the body to immobilize it. Tie a broken leg to the other leg, tie a broken arm to the chest, etc. Broken fingers and toes are easily taped to the neighboring good digit.

MORE EXTREME MEASURES

TREPHINING

Skull fractures present a unique challenge to survival medicine. All you can really do is cover the fracture, dress it and hope. And, here's another big one, if the person has a head injury and it looks like they are going down hard and you have no other choice, consider making a hole in their head. This was called *trephining* in old times.

The following indicators that a patient has blood building up in his brain or that the brain is swelling from trauma might make trephination a good idea:

* Headaches, nausea and irregular respiration without signs or symptoms indicating trauma anywhere else
* A confirmed cause for head trauma
* Unconsciousness
* Dilated pupils
* High blood pressure in the neck veins
* Slow heart rate
* Rapid breathing that stops altogether then starts again (the tell-tale sign)

This treatment is controversial even in modern emergency medicine and you might not even have the tools, but if you do, consider decompression craniectomy. It sounds crazy but humans have been making holes in the skull for thousands of years, long before surgery, anesthesia and antibiotics as we know them came along. I will not teach the techniques of surgery here other than to say, be as clean as possible, use the best tools you have (even a hand drill might be helpful if skillfully applied) and realize that the chance of infection once you expose the brain will be very high. However, if your loved one is about to die from a nasty bump on the head that caused potentially fatal bleeding in the skull, and if a burr hole might save them, it is worth considering, yes?

CRICOTHYROIDOTOMY

When there is simply no other way to get an airway open on someone because of trauma or anaphylaxis, consider making a hole in the neck. It's not as bad as it sounds.

Find the Adam's apple, which is the highest bump on someone's neck near the "voice box."

Just below that, you'll feel a dip and, below that, another less protruding bone. That dip is where you want to make a hole.

In a neat environment, you'd lift the skin there and make a one-inch incision across the throat so it leaves a less noticeable scar later.

In an emergency, stick your knife in sideways and poke through the skin and the cartilage.

Turn your knife so the blade opens the cartilage more and props it open so air can get in and out of the hole.

Stick something in there to hold it open—your finger if you have to—but do not let the hole close back up. (There will be only a little blood but enough to make it slippery.)

The hole can be closed up when the swelling goes down in your patient's mouth or when you clear the traumatized tissue out of the airway.

If you can't get the *cric* open for any reason, consider going lower down to the trachea area. This is right above the V in the base of the neck. If you make a hole here, your patient will have to use a speaking aid the rest of his life, but, he'll live. There are even recent cases of people performing a cricothyroidotomy on themselves successfully and living as a result. Speaking of doing it to yourself. . . .

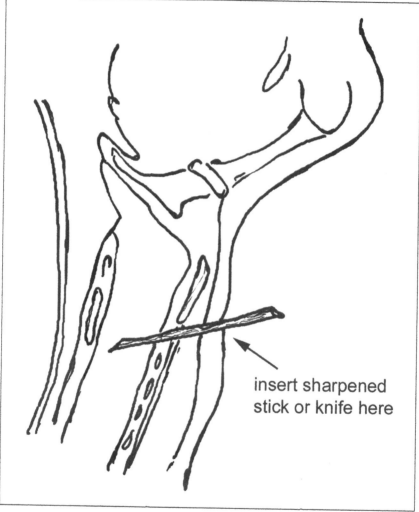

insert sharpened stick or knife here

Cricothyroidotomy

AMPUTATION

Cutting off your own limb is not high on anyone's list of fun things to do when alone in the bush, but it might come right down to it. If your limb is trapped, crushed or becoming gangrenous, amputation might be necessary.

Some principles guiding amputation:

- Cut as low as you can and save as much as you can, especially the joint. I hate to say it, but for most people, cutting through the bone is too difficult, especially without anesthesia so cutting through the joint is exactly what you'll end up doing.
- Wrap the limb tightly to squeeze as much blood out of that part as possible before you lop it off.
- Apply a tourniquet about two inches above where you intend to slice.
- Start slicing. Good luck!
- Once the limb is severed, treat it like any wound. Stop the bleeding and apply a stump dressing by tying the dressing very tightly to the best anatomical anchor point you can find.

If the bleeding won't stop, consider these options:

TIE OFF BLEEDERS with string, fishing line, small wires, anything you can find. Arteries are easy to spot in an amputation; they are deep vessels that carry oxygenated blood from the heart to the rest of the body and run closer to the bones. So any big fat straw-looking thing that is squirting bright red stuff atcha is an artery and needs to be stopped up. Tie these off just like tying off a trash bag, but tighter. Then apply the dressing.

CAUTERIZING should be considered if all other attempts to stop the bleeding fail or you are alone and can't tie off the bleeders yourself. Of course, you'll need a fire, so be sure to have this built before the chopping part starts. Use metal, like your knife blade. Get it red hot and touch it to the flesh and it will sear it and seal it shut. Will sting too, but heck, you just chopped of a body part, why not a little more?

If you had to use a stone to do the cutting, consider putting the whole stump into the fire to sear and seal all the bleeders before you dress it. The upside is that the fire will kill most bacteria on the spot. With a clean dressing and good wound management, you just might be alright. This is an ancient practice from the battlefields, so you are not alone.

DEBRIDEMENT is one option to try prior to axing the ol' pitching arm. It just means cutting out the dead tissue to save the live tissue from contamination.

MAGGOT THERAPY is an all-natural alternative to manual debridement, say with a knife or stone. The practice has been around a long while and is still practiced by some primitive peoples. It was discovered when soldiers with maggots had better results in recovery from battlefield wounds. In fact, it has been shown that maggots do a better job of debridement than doctors since sometimes docs take too much or not enough and have to go back in. Maggots eat until all the dead tissue is gone and, when you feel the pain, that's when they hit the live tissue and you clean them out.

Maggots are the perfect field debridement which saves on antibiotics, stops gangrene and reduces chances of potentially fatal septicemia. Maggots save lives and they are actually regulated by the U.S. Food and Drug Administration as a treatment. And they actually secrete juices with anti-microbial properties so they, in fact, promote healing. So let some flies on that wound, cover it up when the maggots show and let them eat until you say uncle.

OPEN-WOUND MANAGEMENT

Whether to sew a wound closed is an important consideration unique to the survival situation. Most people want to see closure. This is especially true of wounds; they're not natural and we don't like to see them open. But in a survival situation, most of the time, that's exactly what you need to do: leave them open and let them heal from the inside out. It will leave a bigger scar but the chances of infection are greatly reduced.

If you close a big laceration or cut out in the bush, there is a great chance that you sewed it shut with some bacteria in there that is going to grow out of control, unable to be checked and cleaned until it bursts open at the seams with pus or infects the patient systemically and kills him.

CLOSING A WOUND

If there is bleeding and the only way to stop it is by suturing, then do so, but leave a nice clean strip of cloth in there as a drainage device and be sure to take good care and pay close attention for the first signs of infection: redness, heat to touch, swelling, obvious pus and foul smell. You might need to open it back up and clean it out. Best to skip this if you can.

SUTURES

Now, I'm not going to give a class on sutures. It is mostly common-sense basic sewing. You can use any thin thread or fishing line in a pinch if you have a needle.

Start in the middle of the wound, moving out toward the edge or corner.

Stitch in the middle of these two stitches, called approximating the wound.

Sew the wound up so there is not a big buckle of excess skin somewhere along the suture line.

Don't make the sutures so tight that there is a big lip sticking up and don't make it so loose that there are big gaps in the suture line either. Make it look good.

SUPERGLUE, ETC.

Consider superglue if you're going to make a closure, especially if the wound is not too deep but might leave an unacceptable scar if left open, like a face wound. Also, if you don't have suture material, you can use superglue. Staples have also been used. It's a bit more brutal than poking holes in someone repeatedly as when stitching them up, but it can work. And many sources have reported tribes using bull ant heads as stitches. This requires catching them, using tweezers to hold them, and then cutting off their heads once they bite. I've not done it but I've heard from buddies they've seen it done. I recommend just using some tape and making butterfly stitches instead.

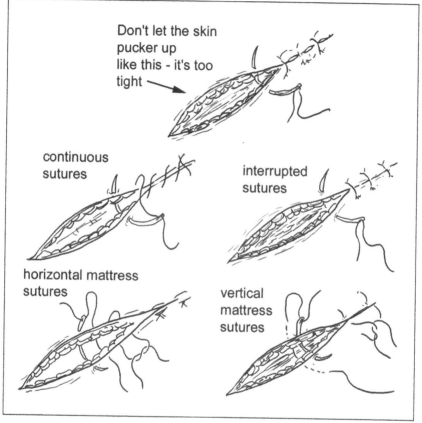

Don't let the skin pucker up like this - it's too tight

continuous sutures

interrupted sutures

horizontal mattress sutures

vertical mattress sutures

Sutures

APPENDECTOMY

The last bit of real craziness I'll throw at you is the appendectomy. These symptoms indicate you should consider cutting out the appendix:

- Someone is going down hard and fast with pain in the lower right side of the abdomen
- High fever
- Extreme abdominal pain and tenderness

In a remote situation with no access to medical care, if an appendix ruptures, the patient will get peritonitis and die. This is a true life-threatening emergency and field appendectomies have been done successfully many times by lay people in urgent need and away from medical care.

An appendectomy can be done with a simple knife and some suture. The suture must be sterile or it will cause infection, and give the patient antibiotics if they're available. Do not do this lightly but, if it's a choice of death *for sure* or death *maybe*, it's not a hard cut to make.

CRITTER ISSUES

Animals are there as a food source for the survivor. But they can be a health threat as well. After all, we're in their environment and must respect the rules of that situation. While our brains make us superior in our ability to create tools we can use to dominate the rest of the animals, without many of these tools, we fall very nicely under some of them in the food-chain pecking order.

Some critters like tigers, sharks, gators and the like see humans as a soft target for chow. The secret to not becoming a meal is making yourself a hard target. But you can only do this by understanding your environment.

ALWAYS MAKE NOISE is the first rule for survivors. This contradicts everything I learned in Special Forces but you do not want to be stealthy if you are surviving, for two reasons. The first is that you hope someone hears you and comes to your rescue. The second and more important reason is that you want to give all the critters out there every chance you can to get out of your area. Most animals will leave humans alone. Snakes, big game and everything in general prefer to get away from some noisy humans. The exception to being noisy is if you are hunting.

So, what do you do when you encounter critters that can hurt you? Let's take a look.

AQUA-CRITTERS

We'll just cover a few things about sea creatures in this chapter. See the chapters on Nature for surviving in the water and Food for the usefulness of sea creatures to you. For now, be concerned with the dangers and treatments for these.

POISONOUS SEA CRITTERS to keep an eye out for include surgeon fish, zebra fish, stone fish, cone shell, auger shell, blue-ringed octopus, weaver fish, toad fish, and sea snakes. If it's brightly colored, avoid it. If it bites, stings or pokes, consider the bite, sting or poke poisonous.

POISONOUS CRITTERS TO AVOID EATING include trigger fish, porcupine fish, and puffer fish. If you're unsure, and it doesn't look like something you'd see in the market, chuck it.

POKING-PUNCTURING-STINGING SEA CRITTERS should be handled carefully. These include sting rays, which have the extra kicker of being a poisonous poke; sea urchins, with nasty puncture infections and venom too; box & pom jelly fish, which can kill; and even catfish and the like can poke you hard when you try to handle them. Be very careful when fishing and removing any fish from your line or net. A bite or puncture can change your life.

JUST PLAIN DANGEROUS

PIRANHA can be dangerous if you're trapped in there, but mostly, you can get away. Just brush them away as you exit if they start on you upon entering the water.

CROCODILES AND ALLIGATORS of any kind should be respected and steered clear of, but mostly they'll steer clear of you, or at least grant you passage. If in the water above the waist with them, be wary as you are technically on the menu. The ones near salt water tend to be particularly ornery, and they can move very fast over short distances so give them a wide berth. You can fight back when they're not too big and stand a chance, but in the water, once they get a good grip, your chances are slim. Avoid water at night and movement near water at night when they're most active hunting.

SHARKS is sharks. If they're bigger than you, and you're in the water, well, you're on their terms. You might get lucky and be left alone, or get some good whacks or pokes in their nose and eye, and deter them. Try and skip this step. Otherwise, try not to urinate in the water or make irregular pan-icked swimming motions. Be prepared to fight hard if attacked. People have fended off sharks successfully before but this is not meant to give false hope. Fight is all you can do, or sit there and be eaten. Mostly, sharks don't seem to care for the taste of people, so, you might get a chomp or two and be left alone to tend your bites. The good news is that more people are bitten by other people than are bitten by sharks each year!

BARRACUDAS are rarely a concern for a survivor, but if caught on a line they can be fierce. Be careful when capturing, but they are mighty tasty.

MORAY EELS are not a real concern in general for the survivor as they hunt at night, are generally shy and will avoid people. If free diving for lobsters you might get bitten, but try to never stick your hand where you can't see. If that lobster went in there, he's gone, find another. Moray eel bites aren't poisonous, but they can get infected.

All bites are treated the same. Stop the bleeding, clean the wound and apply a dressing. Do the best you can to avoid these and if it happens, treat it the best you can in a survival situation. With stinging and poisonous crea-tures, there are a couple other things to think about.

Box jellyfish, Portuguese man-of-war, fire coral and many other stinging sea creatures use similar mechanisms, called a *nematocyst*, to cause a sting. These cause a painful burning sensation. Factors like how much skin was contacted, where on the body the stings were situated, and the condition of the victim (whether elderly, ill, etc.) will determine your patient's systemic response. Sometimes people get sick, nauseous, vomit, have anaphylaxis or even paralysis and death. Usually, they just get a bad sting that passes in an hour or two and then leaves blisters within 24 hours.

The first treatment is obviously removal of the cause. Get the stingers off the person. Don't use bare hands. Even dead creatures can have some sting left in them. Use vinegar, ammonia or alcohol to stop the nematocysts from firing. If you have nothing else, use sea water, but **not fresh water** because this will trigger the stinging. Urine can help; it won't hurt but hasn't been shown to make a difference. Mostly, just use sea water. Baking soda or shaving cream is helpful for removing the nematocysts. Treat the sting site like any burn, relieving the pain and dressing the wound.

There is really danged little that you as a survivor can do for poisons from bites, stings or ingestion. A little knowledge, a lot of caution and common sense will serve you well for prevention. But accidents happen, and when they do, symptomatic treatment is really all you can do.

GROUND CRITTERS

Knowing habitats is one of the best methods of preventing conflict with critters, many of which like to live in and under things. Try to avoid these places or approach them cautiously. I have grabbed snakes I thought were vines and nearly stepped on snakes sunning themselves in the open early in the morning on a cold day. Carelessness and complacency will get you more times than not, so stay hyper-vigilant. Every time you lift up a stick for fire wood or to build a shelter, look first. Stir the foliage with your stick and give anything that might be in there a chance to either leave or make its presence known to you so you can avoid it . . . or eat it!

I don't recommend anyone try and take on any big game when surviving. The chances are that you will lose, or even if you win the battle, you might lose the war by incurring injuries or losing or damaging supplies. If confrontation is unavoidable, some species-specific recommendations to help you deal with it the best you can follow. That said, if you can't prevent an animal injury or bite, and if the animal hasn't eaten or killed you, treat the wounds, bites, scratches and fractures like any other.

BEARS. Big and bad bears should be avoided at all costs. They're great hunters, can smell a good distance, run fast and far, and climb, too! So, it's not like you can really escape them unless a small cave is near but, then, what's in the cave? So, the best plan with bears is to try not to move too fast and see if they'll pass you by. If it looks like they're headed your way, consider your options at that moment and see if gently walking away will get you out of there. Never turn your back and run; this will make a bear see you as prey. If you have food, toss it to them! If you think the bear wants to eat you, look for a river or a tree. Be prepared to engage. Try the passive technique of balling up, letting it whack you a few times and then it might leave you alone. If it looks like a bear is going to try and munch on you, give it all you've got and fight. See the Tools chapter for making weapons like spears and how to use them. For all of these creatures, a sharp poke or stab in the eyes and face with a heavy, strong stick or spear just might discourage them from dining in your restaurant tonight. Black bears and grizzlies are different—color doesn't always tell which is which, but a big hump in the back means it's a grizz. The rule is to "fight back if they're black," and, "if they're Grizzly brown, hit the ground" and play dead. Me, I'm gonna fight.

CATS. If you encounter a big cat in the wild, try and make your physical presentation bigger so you look less like something small for them to prey on. Raise your arms and raise your voice. Wave your weapon above you but not at them, **yet**. You want to discourage, not challenge. If the big cat tries to circle you, it is determined and you will have to fight. If it starts looking off to the sides, give it room to pass you by.

General principles of fighting and self-defense apply here. Wait for the cat to swing and draw inward with your spear during its swing, and as soon as the swipe with the paw passes by you, make your strike straight inward for the eyes. This will prevent the animal from trapping your spear within its grasp since your pole will be on the outside of its arm, allowing you to thrust into its face and neck with all your might and reducing the chances for it to spin around towards you. The cat will have to peel away from your spear and, psychologically, this breaks part of the animal's momentum as it must now square back up on you to refocus its attack.

Tangling with a big cat is not some place you or I want to be. But I have been in enough fights to know that this principle works very well as it is based on simple anatomy. We can grab and hold something into our chest easily if it gets in our grasp, but if it stays on the outside of our embrace, no matter what we do, we cannot hold it and this is where you need to stay when defending yourself against any large creature.

DOGS. Direct is the best way. Wolves and any wild dog-like creature which has decided to directly confront you must be directly confronted. You can't hide from their amazing sense of smell and you can't outrun them as they can gallop for days. Wolves have a pecking order and much of it is in the gaze. If confronted by a wolf or pack of wolves, keep eye contact. If you must look around, do so slowly and purposely so as to not convey a hint of fear, panic or intention of flight.

The upside to fighting wolves—unlike big cats that can fillet you with four paws and big jaws—is that wolves only have a mouth full of teeth to contend with. They are, however, team hunters and one or two will attack you while the others flank you. So get your back up against a tree if you can, channel the attackers to your front and then commence to eye-poking, neck-gouging and throat-jabbin' with your life stick.

BULLS, RHINOS, HIPPOS AND ELEPHANTS. These guys are just too dang big for you to do anything against. You sure ain't gonna stop them with a stick so your best bet is to outmaneuver them. Find a strong tree and run circles around it like you did as a kid when playing tag. If they can't touch you, they can't hurt you. And if they can't pummel that tree over, chances are, you can turn circles around that tree over a shorter distance and faster than they can. With enough frustration, hopefully they will give up. If you don't see a tree or boulder, just try waiting until they get close and then step or jump quickly to the side bullfighter-style. Do not get off your feet, or you might not get on them again. In an emergency, try to remember, **"Run-around the rhino."**

TOXIC CRITTERS

Many creatures in nature have the ability to defend themselves with some sort of bite or sting. They often inject venom with this bite or sting. Poisons come from contact or ingestion; anything else toxic is delivered by *envenomation*. There are many different types of venoms but they can be broken down into three main categories.

HEMOTOXINS get into your blood stream and cause the rupturing of cells, preventing clotting or destroying organs by *lysis*, or breaking the cells. With these kinds of bites, the bleeding usually doesn't stop and there is a lot of pain and swelling and fever. These symptoms usually present with blood or blood-filled blisters at the bite site and a lot of pain.

NEUROTOXINS paralyze the victim by attacking the nervous system and cause death through respiratory failure. The key indicators here are very little pain and bleeding at the site but rapid onset of heart palpitations and abdominal cramps.

CYTOTOXINS actually destroy cells. This type is not so much of concern for the survivor except for the Brown Recluse spider.

SNAKE BITES
Many snakes only bite humans out of fear from a surprise encounter, which means most snake bites are non-envenomating. Even then, there is still the chance for a nasty infection so the wound must be cleaned; also, the person should be treated as if there was envenomation until time and lack of symptoms prove otherwise. Snake toxins are usually quick-acting so if you don't see signs and symptoms within a few hours, chances are, you are okay.

The treatment for snake bites is very simple. Keep calm. The venom will act faster if you panic so move slowly, relax your breathing, lie down (away from the snake hopefully) and raise the bite above the heart if possible. Remove rings, watches or any articles of clothing near the bite that might cause constriction once the person swells up. With hemotoxins, swelling can be quite severe.

DO NOT:
Cut. This will only cause wounds while letting the venom contact more blood.
Suck with your mouth. The venom will get absorbed into your blood stream too!
Use ice. Not like you'll have any, but it won't help, though it won't really hurt either.
Use a tourniquet. The venom will get in anyway and this hurts the limb if there is no venom.

DO:

Use suction devices if they are available and you happen to be "Johnny-on-the-spot" at the time of the bite. These have been shown to reduce the amount of venom by some 30% if applied within the first 3 minutes. After that, what is done is done and there isn't any point, but hey, I'd try anyway.

Use a constricting band two fingers or two inches **above** the bite—**between** the bite and the heart. This reduces the amount of venous blood flow, or blood flow through surface vessels carrying blood back to the heart. Test the difference between a constricting band and a tourniquet with two fingers, which you should be able to get under a constricting band but not a tourniquet.

Treat the symptoms. If you suspect a hemotoxin, try not to give aspirin as that is a blood thinner and will only speed up hemorrhaging.

Clean and dress the bite. Always apply the principles of wound management.

The truth is that bees kill more people every year than snakes do. Most snakes won't attack people and will flee the first chance they get but, if cornered, most snakes will fight back. This is when they are ready with venom waiting.

OTHER BITERS

SCORPIONS, SPIDERS, ANTS AND WASPS bite too. They hurt but most either do not inject venom at all or rarely inject enough to be dangerous for healthy, full-grown adults. Children, elderly people and, unfortunately, weak and famished survivors can succumb to these venoms. So, it is good to know that some scorpions are venomous and others aren't and the same is true of tarantulas and other spiders. But treat them all like they have venom, try to avoid them; if bitten, treat it seriously and hope. As a survivor, there isn't a lot more you can do.

For most bites of this nature, wilderness first aid treatment calls for *cryotherapy* or ice. Chances are, you won't have it so clean the wound, dress, it, keep your patient calm and look for signs of hemo- or neurotoxin. Remove stingers gently, by scraping away from the point of entry so as to not push more venom into the injection site. Gently brush off furry little, brightly colored critters like caterpillars as these things can sting and some have barbs. The rule of thumb is to go gentle with the little creatures.

SPIDERS come in many shapes and sizes and a bite is a bite, but if you get bit and see the spider the basic rules of which ones have venom are these: **yellow, red or white spots** and **dark black or brown bodies**. Most spiders do not kill humans except for the Australian Funnel spider.

THE BROWN RECLUSE is an interesting case. It is a little brown spider with a big bite but not how you would think. Often people don't know they've been bitten until they find a little swollen area with blister and a bulls-eye look. It might have a little pain that, after a few hours, turns itchy. The reason is that this spider injects a cytotoxin that kills cells. What's happening is that ALL the tissue is being killed: the nerves, the blood, the muscle, everything is being destroyed and necrosing. Usually, the toxin wears itself out as it spreads and stops killing cells. The skin usually stays on the top, looking dead and grey until the whole thing sloughs off and leaves a small crater.

Normally, the cytotoxin wears itself out after only one to two inches but wounds have been known to be up to 10 inches. This becomes significant when a person can't afford to lose six or seven inches of flesh at the bite location. As they're not aggressive, most Brown Recluse bites are on the butt or back from sleeping on these spiders. But if someone got bit on the neck or face, you might not want to let the necrosis spread. A medical person would excise or cut it out to stop the necrosis. For most survivors, this is not a medically viable option, but should be considered depending on confirmation of the necrotic bite in an area where a serious threat to health might result. A little digging into the bulls-eye will show that it is all dead tissue under the wound.

It's up to you. Treat what's left like all wounds.

BEES deserve special mention. Not because they kill, and they do, but because the key here is avoidance. Bees normally make a hive 10 to 30 feet off the ground and it's a big roundish looking brown thing. Avoid these. Yes, you can get honey, and yes, I've used smoke among thousands of bees to run them out of my area without a sting, but this is too risky for any survivor to consider. Give way and move away. If you happen to stir them up and they come for you, try squatting and holding still. If they spot you, the gig is up. Run! Run through thick brush to keep them off you and head for water if you can. They'll give up pretty quickly, but do not hang around, keep moving.

WORMS

Now, for everybody's favorite—**worms** aka *helminths* or internal parasites. Most people have them and live with them just fine. As a survivor, there is a good chance you'll get them as you'll be subjected to uncontrolled food and water sources. Mostly, you'll be fine, and they'll have little impact immediately. But in some circumstances, they might immediately cause poor health. Over a period of time, they could become very medically significant to you. For these reasons, I address them in the chart below so you can help diagnose and treat these conditions if possible.

The bottom line is to expect to contract worms, but know that you'll mostly be alright. Seek testing and treatment once you're rescued or recovered if any long term abnormalities present after the experience. (Note: wear footgear at all times to prevent many worms!)

WORMS AND TREATMENTS

Type or Name	Cause/ Transmission	Signs/Symptoms	Treatment
Hook worm (Nematode)	Get into skin, usually when barefoot	Itching early, one week, maybe, but then not much until late when they might cause abdominal or respiratory problems	Albendazole, can use ice during first week to kill them while still migrating into deeper tissues
Roundworm or Strongyloidiasis (Nematode)	Penetrate skin from soil, migrate to lungs and intestines	Abdominal and respiratory problems	Thiabendazole

Tape or Flat worm (Cestode)	Undercooked or raw meat, burrow into muscle	Major stomach pain, flatulence, vomiting	Praziquantel
Pinworm, also called threadworm (Nematode)	Lives in the upper colon, sometimes gets into vagina, not found in tropics	Doesn't harm much but causes itching at night around the anus	Piperazine
Round Worm, Ascaris	Gets in through contaminated food	Usually no symptoms until late, when worms are found in stool, fever, abdominal pain	Mebendazole
Whip worm, Trichuriasis	Usually from soil ingested on food	Often no signs but can cause bloody diarrhea	Mebendazole
Cutaneous Larva Migrans CLM, also called sandworm (Nematode)	Gets into skin and lives just under the surface, usually on beaches, sand	Itches and leaves burrow trails, dies on its own in weeks to months	Albendazole, cryotherapy also called freezing with ice, using some cold aerosol spray might help
Dracunculiasis or Guinea Worm from Cyclops water flea	Drinking water with flea, worm gets into gut, migrates to lower legs, grows	Will take a while, maybe six to 12 months, then forms a blister that itches a lot	Simple cloth filter on water will keep out water fleas, cut boil and slowly pull out worm

RABIES

The last bit I have to say on animals and bites and stings is about rabies.

Hard fact of life: rabies cannot be cured!

Now that I have your attention, listen up. Rabies is pretty rare and even rarer for people to get. To contract it, you have to find the critter with it during the few days it can spread rabies, and then go and get yourself bit.

Rabies is a virus that affects mammals. Dogs, cats, possum, bats, all kinds of critters can get it. It is a virus that gets into the nervous system and causes great pain to all the senses and makes it difficult to swallow or speak, causing excessive salivation and tearing of the eyes. It is extremely painful and death is always the result.

There are preventive vaccines that will help increase the chances of the post-exposure vaccines working. The post-exposure vaccines will work most of the time if given early enough. The incubation period is about two weeks to two months but can be as long as two years. Once rabies kicks in and the first signs appear, there is no hope of surviving, no matter what level of medical care is available. So, here's what it means to a survivor:

Treat all aggressive animals as if they have rabies. Avoid being bitten.

If attacked by an animal under circumstances that seem out of character, assume rabies exposure.

Make all attempts to get to medical care ASAP.

If you or another survivor starts to manifest rabies symptoms, consider quarantine measures for the protection of everyone else.

PRIMITIVE PLANT MEDICINE

The last portion of this chapter covers when you have next to nothing or absolutely nothing. It is not meant to cover everything but to give you enough examples of common alternatives that might be useful to you. As ever, take every opportunity to learn all you can. You never know what might come in handy!

HOW AND WHEN TO INGEST MEDICINAL PLANTS

There are simply way too many plants to know them all. Try to know a few from each category and/or each region of interest. Once you know a few, there are a good many ways to render them but it comes down to these main three for a survivor.

- **Teas:** mix something with hot or cold water and drink the fluid
- **Concoctions:** something chunky like a slurry soup
- **Paste:** anything mashed up and mixed with little water, mostly for topical application

Always have positive identification before using any plant. I try to include only the most common ones that Westerners would be familiar with as well as highly available regional plants that are extremely valuable.

ANTIBIOTICS: (COUNTER-INFECTIVES, REALLY)

- **Honey:** Use it like a paste as a topical antibiotic on wounds. Drink it with teas, especially for sore throats.
- **Salt water:** Gargle as a mouthwash to control cavities. Also, use it as a wash for wounds.
- **Onion:** A natural low dose antibiotic, you can eat it or crush it and put it on wounds.
- **Garlic:** Same story. Make a paste and cover wounds with it.
- **Broadleaf leaves:** Good as wound dressings for their antibiotic properties. Consider cabbage leaves, mullein leaves (don't eat seeds) and plantain leaves in particular.
- **Tobacco:** Use as a paste for wound care to take advantage of its antibiotic properties.
- **Mullein tea:** is a good anti-infective for throat and mouth.
- **Oatmeal:** Apply topically to use antibiotic properties.
- **Vinegar:** Works well for cleaning wounds.
- **Clover:** Use as an eye wash for conjunctivitis or as a vaginal douche.
- **Dandelion root:** Boil into a concoction for use on acne and eczema.
- **Oak bark:** Boil into tannin that's good for unbroken skin rashes. Don't drink.
- **Fruit pomace:** Citrus and other rinds have antibacterial properties.
- **Booze:** Outside of iodine and rubbing alcohol, alcohol is good for wound cleaning and it tastes good too and might come in handy around amputation time.

EYES, EARS, NOSE AND THROAT TREATMENTS

- **Sore throat:** Treat by ingesting tea made with plants containing vitamin C such as pine needles, rose hips or any citrus plant.
- **Hemorrhoids:** Use oak bark, willow bark, witch hazel bark and leaves as well as any tea or tobacco.

- **Congestion:** Topically apply toothpaste under the nose. Also, pepper can help clear the sinuses.
- **Earaches:** Onion juices can ease these; just squeeze, add some water and rinse.
- **Throat aches:** If you can find it, cinnamon is very good for the throat.

DENTAL

- **Cavity pain** can be eased by oil of clove, salt water or draining pus.
- **Fillings** lost can be replaced with wax or twigs as a stopgap measure.
- **Broken teeth** can be repaired with super glue.
- **Knocked-out teeth,** if still whole, can simply be put back in!!!
- **Extraction** can be done in a worst-case scenario. It's difficult but better than excruciating pain and uncontrolled infection.

ANTI-DIARRHEAL

- **Mint teas:** Soothes mild tummy aches.
- **Sassafras:** Calms abdominal cramps.
- **Hazel leaves:** Relieves stomach upset.
- **Rose hips:** Reduces discomfort.
- **Apple pomace**
- **Citrus rinds**
- **Oak bark:** The tannic acids in this and many other hardwood trees' barks are helpful for mild diarrhea. To make tea, boil the bark for two hours; it will make a vile smelling and tasting concoction that will help. Repeat every two hours until stoppage is achieved.
- For worst-case scenarios, **grind chalk, dried bones, and/or charcoal** from the ashes of your fire and make a slurry, suck it down and repeat every two hours until stoppage is achieved.

ANTACIDS

- **Ash, charcoal, chalk and bones** in a lighter brew than the anti-diarrheal slurry above will calm an acid tummy.
- **Dandelion, mint and sassafras** leaf teas also help.

ANTI-CONSTIPATION
- **Soap** will lube and stimulate a bowel movement.
- **Oil** of any type that is ingestible will lube the guts.
- **Dandelion root concoction** is good too.

URINARY PROBLEMS
- **Yams** help decrease urinary tract infections.
- **Dandelion tea** eases discomfort.
- **Rose hips tea** eases discomfort.

ANTISEPTIC
- **Peat moss** is an ancient treatment for wounds as it absorbs well and has a highly anaerobic acid which inhibits bacteria from growing.
- **Urine** is sterile and if it's all you got, whip it out.
- **Oak bark** and many hardwood barks boil down for tannin juices.
- **Burdock root**
- **Dock leaves**

ANTI-PARASITIC
A **worm-removal stick** can be used for Guinea worms. Cut the blister, pull a small piece of the worm out, wrap it around the stick and then slowly pull and spin, wrapping the worm like spaghetti on a fork.

- **Kerosene,** taken once in a two-tablespoon dose, will clear out gut worms. Don't repeat for 48 hours.
- **Salt.** Mix four tablespoons with one quart of water to do the same.
- **Cigarettes.** Eating one-and-one-half cigarettes will shock gut worms enough to make them let go and pass.
- **Tannic acid.** The inner bark of hardwood trees can have this effect.
- **Hot Sauce and/or peppers** as part of a regular diet can reduce parasite loads.
- **Fern stems.** Crush the subterranean root into a powder that is known to fight parasites.
- **Jesuit or Mexican tea.** Make a strong concoction that goes by this

name from the seeds of a common weed in the South-Central desert region that smells like licorice, fennel or anise.

INSECT REPELLENTS
- **Garlic or onion** rubbed all over the exposed skin can also be consumed afterwards and sweated out pores.
- **Oak bark** boiled into tannin is good as insect repellent. Don't drink it in this treatment.
- **Smoke** from a fire or cigarette will help keep bugs away.
- **Sassafras leaves for bedding.** The scent keeps 'em away.
- **Mud** covering exposed skin makes it harder for insects to get a blood meal.
- **Make a face screen** with cut-up strips of cloth.
- **Tobacco** can be used as a skin rub and for smoking.
- **Pepper** rubbed all over keeps bugs at bay.

ANALGESICS (PAIN RELIEVERS)
- **Strangling fig root:** Smoke the dried root.
- **Garlic juice:** Paste for skin and joints.
- **Onion juice:** Paste for stings.
- **Yams:** Reduce muscle spasms and fever.
- **Clover:** Good for bites and stings, also good as an eye wash for infected eyes.
- **Coca leaves:** When chewed, these have a good analgesic effect!
- **Willow bark:** Boil to make a tea or just chew the bark.
- **Toothpaste:** Apply topically for heart burn.
- **Pepper:** Reduces joint paint and muscle spasms.
- **Oatmeal:** Has pain-relieving properties, also has antidepressants.
- **Coconut meat, ash, mud, dandelion paste:** Relief from stings of bees, scorpions, spiders, centipedes.
- **Bleach:** Remove poison ivy, oak and sumac. (Also, use ash or drying agent to absorb resin from these plants.) Bleach can also be used to treat chiggers (any smothering agent like sap will also work).

ANTI-INFLAMMATORY
- **Willow bark:** Tea for systemic inflammation, paste for topical application.
- **Aspen bark:** Soak the bark and lay on the affected area.

ANTI-HEMORRHAGE
- **Puff ball mushroom:** Helps the blood clot.
- **Plantain leaves:** Can stop bleeding as a vasoconstrictor.

ANTI-FUNGAL
- **Onions:** Rub on infected area.
- **Toothpaste:** Has fungicidal properties, apply topically.

ANTI-PYRETIC (COUNTERS FEVER)
- **Willow bark tea**
- **Aspen bark tea**
- **Oak bark tea**
- **Yams**

There are literally millions of plants on the planet. I believe everything out there has a purpose and function, even if we Westerners and our modern scientists have yet to discover them all. Many so-called "primitive" people have been living this principle for thousands of years. It could be a lifelong pursuit to study everything out there.

I learned many of these treatments in the U.S. military as doctrine in their courses. I have also seen some applied, or been taught them by locals, indigenous soldiers and some of my peers over the years. I have even seen some used by shaman and other "witch" doctors. On the whole, I'd say half the stuff out there really doesn't work or works only half as well as modern, highly concentrated medicines. But if it's all you got, then you gotta go hot and give it a shot!

No one human can know it all, and I don't purport to that here. I only hope to give an introduction to some of the better known alternatives so that a novice survivor has a starting point out in the wild. I highly encourage everyone to study on your own and learn for yourself.

BEING WELL IN THE WILD

There are no limits to the trials and tribulations that the survivor might encounter. This chapter gave you a decent foundation in the basics of the body, health, medicine, trauma and general first-aid care as it applies to someone with limited means of surgical treatment, physician counsel and pharmaceutical support. There is no way to teach years of medicine, training, knowledge, experience and science in the short space of this book or any one book.

Instead, my purpose is to give hope to people in extreme situations by telling them what to realistically expect and supply emergency measures to consider during extreme circumstances, measures that can't be learned legally anywhere else for many reasons. Be aware of these facts and procedures. They will be power in the hands of the powerless survivor and can mean the difference between dying alone in some remote corner of the planet or returning home for a fine family reunion. Given the choice to withhold or share this information, I choose life.

The next choice is yours.

REFERENCES

The U.S. Army Special Forces Medical Handbook
The U.S. Special Operations Forces Medical Handbook The U.S. Joint Personal Recovery Agency Survivor's First Aid Course
The Emergency War Surgery Book
The Merck Manual
The Wilderness First Aid Manual

Nature

The First Rule of Nature is to know the "R.O.E."—or Rules Of Engagement.

Nature is a wonderful and beautiful thing to be admired and enjoyed. It is also something that is delicate and we should strive to keep balanced. But for the survivor, know that it can also be deadly mean and change in a heartbeat.

Therefore the survivor must have a firm grasp on the handle of the rules for engaging when out in nature and subject to the whims and fancies outside of our control. To best engage in the challenge, it behooves the survivor to know the rules.

HAWKE'S DIRTY HALF-DOZEN R.O.E.

RULE # 1—KNOW THYSELF Know what your strengths and weaknesses are, know who you are, and know where you are when in a *survival* situation. And before you find yourself in such a place, study and practice the essence of survivalin' at home and in the field. Learn about your home surroundings, your neighborhood and outlying area, your routes to and from work, and also study any areas you may be travelling *before* you travel.

It's only in the practice and application of yourself in test/practice/training scenarios, that you can really come to know yourself in the absence of the hardest and harshest test of reality. So, practice survival to understand your skills, abilities, and weaknesses *before* you have to put them to use.

RULE # 2—"BE PREPARED" It's the old boy scout cliché, but it's been around and stays around because it's true and it works. The better prepared you are now, the better you'll fare later. Can't say it any simpler, and no point in saying it any further.

RULE # 3—FORGET WHAT YOU WANT This is the big thing that crushes most people physically and spiritually. You might want to be home or anywhere other than where you are, but that clearly is not what happened. Forget about it for now. "What you want" won't help or change a thing. The only thing that matters is where you are, what you have, what you know, and what you can do.

RULE # 4—DO WHAT YOU MUST This is really another way of saying "necessity is the mother of invention." Regardless of your feelings, opinions, biases, prejudices, perceptions, and religious or philosophical beliefs, anything that is not practical, pragmatic and that doesn't pass the common sense test, simply holds no sway in the survival situation. Do what you need to do to survive—eat strange foods, get naked to cool a fever, tear apart your clothes to make twine or bandages, spend hours looking for food and water, kill to eat, sleep with an enemy in the cold to stay warm, take the hand of an antagonist to be rescued—whatever it takes.

RULE # 5—NEVER QUIT! This should be said on every single page of this book, and in any book about survival. It is the essence of the entire field of study. Never quit!

RULE # 6—FORGET THE RULES The one rule that applies to all rules is to know when to bend them and when to break them. But when it comes to survival, there are no rules, really. There are only guiding principles, founded on tried, tested and sometimes-true tenets. But the main thing is to not let the rules set any kind of limits or parameters on you that make you give in or succumb to some statistics spouted off by someone, somewhere, but not there with you. If the rules say you can't climb, but you need to, then by God climb!

Alrighty, those R.O.E. stated, let's take one last look at all the regions of the world and the additional considerations for them that didn't fall neatly into any other category already discussed. Since nature is far too vast and diverse to put in any one chapter or topic, these are my parting thoughts on situations based on my experiences and observations that I feel might be of some benefit to you.

THE COLD—ARCTIC AND MOUNTAINS

The main thing in cold environments, perhaps obviously, is to try to stay warm. A big part of this is staying dry. Never jump in cold water, it's suicidal—unless you have a fire or dry clothes to get into, you can be dead in no time. I've seen Special Forces teams shivering to the point of not being operational, just because of too much water exposure in the swamps of the Deep South in the autumn, so getting wet in hard-cold winter is plain foolishness.

Now, staying dry is fairly easy to do, just by staying out of the water and trying not to move so fast or work so hard that your get yourself wet with your own sweat.

But what about staying warm? Obviously if you have a fire you can get warm, but what about when you don't? First, work on the practical and simple principles of physics and terrain analysis. If you keep moving to an adequate degree, your body will generate heat and, provided your flesh is not completely exposed, this can provide a basic level of warmth.

But what about when that's not enough? The simplest things are often the ones that work the best. Think about it. If you're high in the mountains, just go down. Be smart, be safe, but move down! If you're in mountainous terrain, head for the base of the mountain and get/stay out of the wind, such as in the trees. If you're in wide-open terrain, get under the snow or behind a tree or rock or small hill. If there's nothing to shelter yourself with, get into the snow or the ground. Any of these will be warmer than open exposure.

And now, let's discuss the metaphysical aspects of getting warm in the cold. I personally hate the cold. I've lived in it and it is no fun. Yet I have been very surprised by the effectiveness of one simple technique that has helped me every time—breathing. That's right, **breathing**. When I have been in the cold—miserable, shaking, wet, freezing and feeling like I just couldn't move from cold penetrating so deep and only made worse by lack of food and sleep—I found that I could change these outer realities *from within*.

The first thing I do is change my point of view by recalibrating my perspective on my situation. I realize that yes, it's cold, and yes, I could die, but at this particular moment, I have done all I can and there is nothing else I can do to change the external environment—so I do what I can to change the one thing I can control, my internal environment. By simply letting go, breathing in deeply, and relaxing—accepting that I am cold, indeed, but I am still alive and I am ok—I can function and continue to function.

I mentally reprogram my mind to lower the thermostat. I will surely be colder, and slower, but I will function and manage. I breathe in deeply and imagine the cold no longer beating on me, beating me down, pushing me around, but rather, I let it in, all the way, and let it pass through, no resistance, almost joining it and accepting that I am in its space and place, so I must become more like it instead of trying to make it more like me.

I know it sounds crazy, but every time I've done this, I've instantly stopped shivering and actually been fine and happy—well, almost anyway (did I mention, I hate the cold?). It's an amazing technique, and the only thing I can compare it to is vomiting. Crazy, I know! I'm one of those folks who doesn't like to vomit when I'm sick, so I fight it and fight it and remain miserable, until I finally realize that it needs to happen, and then, once it does, it's all better and why did I wait so long! Sorry, that's the closest I can get to explaining it. Those who live in the cold, know. Those who don't, should try it. I'm not saying it will keep you from freezing to death, but I am saying it might help you to get through a tough time and find a way to do what you need to do to actually stop your freezing to death.

THE HOT—DESERTS AND DRIED-UP ENVIRONMENTS

The desert is no joke. It's hot, it's dry, and people die there, it's that simple. Trying to stay out of these areas is the "duh-no kiddin'!" answer. But when you find yourself stuck in such a place, it is important to realize that people do live in the desert and always have. In fact, some live rather comfortably there. So, know that you can manage—that's the way you must approach the desert-survival scenario.

The thing that puts the "zap" on most people's brains, literally, is the huge expanse that is visible to their eye because of the lack of foliage and vegetation. This visual reality makes it seem like a truly daunting endeavor to make it out alive. And it is, to be sure.

But again, keep in mind that people do live there, and someone most likely is somewhere near you. And the very thing that scares you by day, is the thing that works for you by night. You see, in the darkness of the desert night, you can scan the horizon for any signs of life by looking for light. You can listen for sounds as they'll carry a long way in the desert night air. If you see no lights, then look for the glow. Off in the distance, the lights of even a small village will glow like a dull ember off the horizon sky. It's faint, it's subtle, but if they are there, it is there. Mark it and make for it. As the twilight comes and takes away your guiding light, make marks on the ground pointing in the direction of the light or glow, and use your daytime navigation skills to keep you on your course.

Also use the other techniques taught for movement and desert survival, never failing to be on the scout for water hints and animal signs. Use your smarts about resting in the heat of the day, etc. But chances are someone is out there, so keep faith and a sharp eye and wit. This will more often than not get you out of a hot spot. That's all I gotta' say about that!

THE THICK—JUNGLES, SWAMPS, AND NASTY PLACES

Now jungles can be the worst place in the world, as it seems everything in there wants to eat and kill you. But the upside is that heck, really, you can dang near eat and kill everything there, too, and there's plenty of resources available to make rope, shelters, etc. Yes, there are big predators—gators, mean snakes, wildcats, and more—but you can fight back and win, too, so long as you use your wits and don't lose your head.

The big difference of the jungle over every other kind of terrain is that you can't see very far in front of your face, and it's that sense of not knowing where you are at any time that becomes very disconcerting—like scuba diving in the pitch black with no lights when you can't see your bubbles, it can throw you off balance. And that's the thing you have to accept, like getting your sea legs on a boat in the ocean—you must accept the "flow" of the jungle and get into its groove.

To best do this, you must throw out any sense of your timelines and accept the dictates of the jungle or swamp you're in. Remember that it does have a beginning and an end. It has waterways and ravines and hills. It has thicker areas and thinner ones. The secret to managing yourself in the jungles and swamps it to settle in for a long, slow journey. Focus on the day-to-day needs as you gently go with its flow in your movement. Don't fight, don't resist, don't get angry and don't get frustrated. The jungle will beat you down so hard and fast if you do, you'll never, ever win. You can't. It's just too great and strong. *But*, with a gentle approach, you can actually manage to guide and slide through and out. This is the way ahead for the jungle.

Move slow, mind every step, slowly reach for branches to move or hold yourself. Always look through and up and around and down for the signs of freedom of passage. Look up for those breaks in the trees that might indicate a thinner vegetated area or even a waterway. Actively and constantly look for those gaps of vegetation that will give you another 50 meters of movement with less work, even if it's off direction a bit—take the open way. Look down for any sign of a rise or fall of terrain that could lead you to a draw and into a stream and a way out, or up to a ridge that could give you view to find the way to escape. Always take food, water and rest as you need, airing out the flesh as required, and, taking the pace set for you, you'll get out.

Obviously, lots of people live in the jungle and enjoy long and happy lives. It's okay. It has its dangers, but it is just a place at the end of the day, like an overgrown garden park. Things live there and it is unkempt, but it has boundaries, it has an end, and you can find the edges and places where people are. Slow and gentle is the way.

THE OPEN—SEAS, SHORES, AND DESERTED PLACES

The seas are one of those places where humans venture, but it is not our natural space and place. When we are there, more than anywhere else, we are at the mercy of nature. If you have some things and resources, then you have some blessing; and if you are without, then you are without any real options or control other than hope. If you have a raft, as long as it floats, there is a chance of survival. If you have nothing, you can float for a long time without hardly any energy—don't bother swimming and tread as little as possible to look around. Mostly, you must wait and wait. And that is all.

The thing about the sea that gets to people is the vast openness giving the feeling that they are so small, that they can never be found. This is not true. Anything that put you out there would have been on some route that someone somewhere uses sometimes. You just never know. So, don't despair not being found. It's only a matter of time. How long it might take, no one can know. All you can know is that the longer you stay afloat, the greater the chances are that someone will find you.

The other thing that overwhelms folks at sea is the fear of the unknown and unseen. There's an entire planets' worth of strange sea life under them, with some that can kill and eat them, and they can't see any of it. It is very easy to start to feel like any second, a giant shark is going to come up and eat you. But it's closer to the truth to realize that most likely, nothing below is even paying you any mind, unless you're bleeding into the water. In which case, see the section on shark fightin'! So, the key is not to panic and to be patient.

There is nothing else you can do but wait and float. For you, the single-minded purpose of being is staying afloat like a human bobber until you are picked up or drift close enough to anything you can swim to. Not a great place to be. But that's all anyone can say about that.

THE DARK—WAR ZONES AND UNRULY ENVIRONMENTS

WARS AND COUPS. These things happen—always have and always will. Very often, they're unexpected. Usually, a lot of factors build up and lead to these outbreaks of violence, but often enough, it's some small and seemingly insignificant occurrence that triggers someone or something and then it explodes like a powder keg. There is only one factor that really matters to you when these things occur—are you involved and a target in any way by either side, or not?

Most likely, you won't be involved or targeted. Famine, religion, politics can all lead to abrupt violence. The general way to best manage these scenarios is to play it low key. If it's crazy all around you, wait until it settles, then make your way for safety. Maybe it's the embassy or a border, but the best survival strategy is to move about in a low-key manner. Blend in, act like you belong and that you know what you're doing. Have a sense of purpose and urgency but do not have fear or rush. Fast movement gets attention quicker, especially in war fighting. Fear is palpable from a mile away and will attract danger. So, stay calm and move surely.

Try not to move at night unless you know your way. Everyone is afraid and more alert at night, and there is this fear that makes people shoot wildly and not hold themselves accountable to the same rules at night as they might by day. If you encounter anyone, do not act ashamed, embarrassed, or afraid. Be polite, be sincere, be humble, and be friendly. Maybe a bribe will open the way, maybe a promise of something; but be cautious and judicious with those efforts, as undelivered promises can provoke worse hostility.

Depending on the culture, sometimes an authoritative stance will work. Use your best judgment. But if you really think they are going to take you out, then act. More times than not, attacking an aggressor will change the dynamic and give you an edge. More times than not, trying to run will only result in you being shot in the back. It's no joke and it's not TV. When things get like this, people can go "kill crazy" and no rules matter.

If you are for any reason a potential target for the violence, then only two options are open to you. Use pure stealth in sitting tight, or in moving absolutely undetected. For you, cover of night might be the only way. And if confronted, action is the only answer. If they are looking to kill you, they will do whatever it takes to do so. You didn't make these rules or create this scenario. You don't have a choice if they draw down on you, and so it is truly a situation of "kill or be killed." Be ready for this and be ready to live with your actions.

For both cases, target or bystander, all conflicts have a battle rhythm. Listen for the sound of fighting and run away from it at first. Most fighters will be running to the action and assuming all the innocent and scared civilians, women, children, and elderly are simply escaping. In the periphery, you'll look like one of them. Dress like a local for this escape, if possible. Once clear of the fighting, move well around it. The good thing is, while there is fighting, the killers are busy and so this is your best time to make time and distance.

GANGS AND RIOTS. These things occur all over the world and at any time. Mostly, they are easily avoided and in fact never seen. But sometimes, you just might happen to be in an establishment on disputed territory or engaging in business with someone's enemy and as such, you suddenly become an indirect or direct target of bad guys. This is a 50/50 dealio.

If your understanding of the history and track record of these guys says they'll let you go, then try to just get down and out of the way and do not interfere, no matter how much you like your business counterpart. But if you know these folks are notorious for treating all people brutally, you might consider extreme measures to escape. It is not encouraged to attack, as they will likely be vindictive and on a vendetta, and as such, they will make it a mission to hunt and track you down. But if attacking one who is blocking your only chance of exit, and escape is necessary, then consider taking that risk.

With gangs, the best route of escape is usually to the busiest public place or place of authority you can get to, or to the bush as most gang members are city-dwelling urbanites and would rather not go after you into the bush. If you find yourself stranded or passing through gang territory, the survival strategy to adopt is simple but requires focus, determination, and a bit of acting. You must move and act like you belong there, have a sense of purpose or reason for being there, and have a deliberate movement. You must not stare at anyone as that is a challenge, and you must not look nervous or act afraid as that is an invite for predation. Make glances as you would anywhere, do not quickly avert eye contact as that says fear and something to hide, which begs further investigation by the gang members. Yet, holding the gaze too long is an affront and challenge for confrontation. So, balance it—look, see, move away, be a non-entity, be not a player and be not prey.

I've often done this when I went to some foreign, new, big cities, by asking the taxi driver to take me to the worst place and drop me off, just to walk through, see and learn. It works, I've been through some bad places and not had any problems, surprisingly. I've had more fights just going to regular tourist places where predators made the mistake of targeting me as a soft target, only to get a trip to the hospital as their consolation prize!

For riots, the best policy is often to stay put, or if you're in the middle of it, head away from it. Go up, go down, go deep, but go where ever it is quiet. Try to travel at an oblique to the chaos as many will be rushing to the madness or directly away from it. Seek to go at angles so as to not encounter interference either from enthusiastic would-be rioters, or not to be caught up in an angry and aggressive quick reaction force response from the authorities which can harm anyone in its path until they re-establish peace and stability.

Take a moment to review the CIA & DHS (or Home Office for UK) websites to review dangerous gangs and groups wherever you might be travelling. These sites will educate you on what their tactics are beforehand, and this will guide your decision to be passive or take action.

TERRORISM AND NBC (NUCLEAR, BIOLOGICAL, AND CHEMICAL).

These are the extreme ends of the survival spectrum. I don't purport to teach the surviving of them here, but want to convey a sense of what to do, inasmuch as any of these things can lead to a survival scenario for you.

Terrorism is a deep, divisive, and diverse topic. For me, in its simplest form, the difference between a guerrilla and a terrorist is simple and is inherently defined by the words themselves. A guerrilla is an irregular war fighter who only targets militarily significant targets. A terrorist is someone who targets anyone, with the purpose of striking terror into the general public mind. By this definition, anyone, anywhere, and at any time could encounter and be subjected to a terrorist or act of terrorism.

This means at anytime, you could be forced to flee an act or an individual or group of individuals and in doing so, might find yourself in the wild, having escaped the problem or people only to face a harsh environment which might ultimately claim your life.

When these acts occur, you must make a quick assessment. If it is something quick, like a bomb, that you have survived and as such, there isn't much chance of any further damage being done, so you can stick around and render assistance, look for signs of bad guys to give info to the authorities later, and/or seek assistance yourself if wounded.

If something deeper is going down—like a group or an individual appear to be actively seeking to catch and harm people—you must assess the situation quickly. Do you think they mean harm to you, or do you think you can get off eventually unharmed? You must make this decision in a split second because that will dictate your next course of action. The facts are simple: your best chance of escape is during the moment of capture and it is also the most likely time that they will kill you. Make an assessment and make a choice.

If you decide to bust free, give it your all, go all-out extreme on them. You're either dead or free as a result. If they get you before you realize what's happening, the same rules apply for the next step—movement. This is your second best chance to escape, and they are still just as likely to kill you in this phase as well. Once you get to where they are taking you, you are in the worst place, as they now have what they planned for—100% complete control. Escape from here is the most difficult, dangerous, and least likely for you. Be prepared.

Assess your situation, your condition, and the conditions of those around you if there are others. If you bust a move and get away, then again, you might be out in the wild, trying to survive, avoiding them, and moving back toward safety or rescue.

NBC stands for Nuclear, Biological, and Chemical environments. Following the war and terror models, any one of these could, theoretically, occur at any time, anywhere. If you're at ground zero, then chances are there are no more bills for you to worry about paying as you won't survive. But if you do survive, what are the realistic chances and expectations of survival?

NUCLEAR blasts come in all shapes and sizes. But basically there are three types of concern: Ground, Air, and Subsurface bursts. This will determine how far the waves spread and the amount of fallout kicked up. This is complicated by the size or yield of the explosive, and then terrain and weather play a big role in how bad the final result is in terms of wind spreading fires and raining down of radioactive fallout particles. Common sense rules apply as ever, but here's a bit more info to give you a guide.

There are three main types of nukes based on yield. Those that are 1–20 MT (megaton) and up are only wielded by the big superpowers. So chances are you won't encounter these and, if you do, we're all in trouble and we probably will never know what hit. The next are the 20–80 KT (kiloton) types that might be utilized by a renegade country. The third type and most likely prospect are the 1 KT yield in the form of a backpack nuke used by a terrorist.

The good news is that the worst damage, about 50%, will be from the blast itself. So, the farther away you are, the better your chances of survival. The thermal or heat wave will cause about 35% of the damages, and the radiation only causes about 15% of the total damages or destructive impact. Now that you have an idea of the realistic damage radius, so as to not be panicked, let's look at estimated destruction ranges.

ESTIMATED DESTRUCTION RANGE—NUCLEAR BLAST

YIELD	BLAST DAMAGE Total Destruction	BURN DAMAGE 1st–3rd Degree	RADIATION DAMAGE Lethal Doses
1 Megaton	2.5 Miles	10–20 Miles	2–3 Miles
20 Kilotons	¾ Mile	2.5–4 Miles	1–2 Miles
1 Kiloton	¼ Mile	½–1 Mile	¾–1¼ Miles

As you can see, the actual damage ranges are not as wide as one would imagine. The radiation is less of a risk initially than the burn damages that will result from the heat wave and the secondary fires that will occur. But speaking of radiation, what about it?

The radiation emanated is measured in two ways. In the simplest terms, the REM is the damage to our body and the RAD is the radiation absorbed into non-living materials. Organic matter can absorb and keep this energy, which can cause an accumulation of REM, and that is what causes damage to humans. Let's look at what it takes in terms of REM to cause biological damage and what that means to us.

REM EFFECTS ON HUMANS FROM A NUCLEAR BLAST

REM DOSE	SURVIVABILITY	DURATION	CAUSE	EFFECT
800 REM	Instant Death	On Site	n/a	n/a
600 REM	90% Death	1–7 Days	Usually from massive organ failure	No cure, only symptomatic treatment
400 REM	50% Death	1–30 Days	Usually from organ failure	50% will recover but with issues
200 REM	10% Death	1–6 months	Sickness takes time to develop	Many other side effects for the survivors
100 REM	1% Death	Years later	Mostly cancer	n/a
50 REM	0% Death	None known	Mostly okay	n/a

For all matters of nukes, there is a lot of math and way too many variables. I went to Army training as a Medical Officer to handle these mass casualty events, and the formulas they teach are mind-boggling. So, I've reduced these to very simple, general figures.

There are three main ways you can get these REMs. The first, already addressed, is direct **exposure**. The other two ways are **inhalation** and **ingestion**. These are fairly self-explanatory, but we'll look at these more in a moment.

There are also three main types of radiation rays. I'll lay them out in bone-simple terms. **Alpha rays** are like the radiated dust particles. They are not really a threat or concern unless you breathe them in, have open wounds, or ingest them after they've gotten onto food or have fallen into some open source of water and you eat or drink them. So keep covered up, wipe everything off, and keep a wet cloth over your mouth and nose to breathe through.

Beta rays are the ones that can burn the skin and eyes, but they're mainly a concern at the time of detonation. In short, you see a flash, turn away and hit the dirt or head for cover, and hopefully, you'll be ok there.

The last kind of REMs are the worst. These are the **Gamma rays** which can penetrate a lot of things. Lead, thick concrete, lots of dirt, stone, mountains, even large quantities of water can absorb these and deflect them from penetrating you. There are, again, so many formulas, based on materials, how far away you are, and how big the bomb is, etc., that all come into play for measuring what is "safe" for shielding. The bottom line is to get behind, under, or inside the thickest, strongest thing you can—and hope.

That said, let's wrap up on the biggie—explosions leading to exposure.

Now, not that all the math matters nor will it stand up to an actual situation when/if it all came to pass, but let's consider how you can implement your survival strategy. If you're really close and you survive, look at the chart to approximate your survivability and then apply it. If you make it out and get to family, and you know you're ill and not likely to pull through, perhaps you want to give up your food for the other members to have a better chance?

Maybe you know you're toast already, so you can do a few extreme things to help or rescue others before you bite the bullet. It's all your choice, but it helps you make better decisions in extreme times if you have some idea what your reality is.

Speaking of food, what will the effects of the radiation be on foods, waters, etc.?

In general, whatever happened to people and buildings, also happened to animals and crops. The closer to the incident's ground zero, the greater the potential for food being "radiated."

So, try not to live off the land too close to the epicenter of the destruction. And if you must, the further out you go away from it, the more you decrease your chances of consuming REMs and building up your RADs.

Provided that the food was not destroyed, if it was covered, concealed, and otherwise sealed, chances are that it is ok. Again, distance, shield, and exposure factors should be considered and applied. Without a meter to measure, the human senses cannot detect radiation, so you'll have to guess and assess on your own. The general guidance is that sealed and covered items are okay to consume, if far enough away from the source of contamination. Just be sure to wipe off everything as weather patterns can disperse fallout and cause it to spread for thousands of miles. Speaking of fallout. . . .

Fallout loses about 90% of its danger after 8 hours, 99% after 48 hours, and 99.9% after two weeks. But that remaining 0.1% can still kill you. So mind the dust, and stay tight for two days minimum. Shoot for two weeks and if you really must move, try to sit out the 8-hour wait period. If it's critical you move, at least wait two hours, but you'll be risking high exposure that could kill you in one week to one month, in a most unpleasant and uncomfortable manner. Sit it out, and live a while longer.

EMP is the Electro-Magnetic Pulse that occurs as a result of a nuclear blast disrupting the airwaves. It causes most electronics to stop working as it essentially fries their circuits. So, they won't recover without repair or replacement. The good news is that small radios with little antennas are likely to be okay, and the better news is that these EMPs don't seem to affect humans at all and pass in a heartbeat. The bad news is that one high-yield weapon, detonated high above the surface, could cause EMP damage from hundreds to possibly thousands of miles. That means all the stuff we know, use and rely on could be knocked out of commission, very easily, for a long while, and for a wide ranging distance. In this way, this topic is essential to the survival preparation and strategies of this book.

EMS—the local Emergency Medical Services—will be affected not only by the loss of communication but they will also be overwhelmed with the obvious need for fire control, life saving, and other issues. Also, the police need to control panic-induced riots.

The federal government will be engaged protecting national interests in terms of financial, transportation, communication, and petroleum industries as vital for any future survival. In that respect, they have authority and plans to secure whatever communications and systems that are still working to support this mission. Along those lines, all government buildings from schools to hospitals, highways and bridges, all become crucial entities for the government to control and assist in the recovery response. What all that means to you, is that even if you are not affected in the least by the actual nuclear event, you might be affected tremendously indirectly, as a result of being cut off from any access to information or support—all forms of supplies to stores and hospitals could be shut down. In this way, a major nuclear catastrophe could create a survival situation for a great many people.

Note: Morse Code is the only thing that can still transmit through a nuclear particle charged atmosphere!

There might not be food, water, electricity, utilities or communications for days to weeks, depending on your proximity to the explosion. So what can you do about it?

The bottom line is that all you can do is REDUCE EXPOSURE time by getting down and staying out of the environment, INCREASE DISTANCE (like you'll have a choice), and INCREASE SHIELD thickness. Get into a hole, a sewer, a ditch, a pipe, under a bridge, in the water, behind a building, in a basement, whatever you have at the time. Cover your eyes and nose and mouth.

Wait for the blast, wait for the shock wave to pass, and stay the heck down, as it's going to come right back past you again. Once it does, and the stuff has stopped flying for a minute, then seek better shelter so you don't get the fallout landing on you like ash from a forest fire or volcanic eruption, which will follow shortly after.

A quick note here on "Dirty Bombs." These are made by some yahoo who gets hold of nuclear materials—maybe waste, maybe bi-products—and then use some conventional explosives to spread it around. The end result is the same—if you survive the blast and burns, mind the radiation, make your post-apocalyptic assessment, and make your survival strategy accordingly. The good news is, the direct impact from this type of blast is very low. Most likely it will affect less than a one-mile area in immediate terms.

There's lots of info, lots of factors, lots of math and science involved if you want to know more about the hard facts and figures. I have simply provided general guidelines to give you a sense of things for planning and reacting. Since you won't likely know or care about the actual math in the aftermath of an actual nuclear hit, I figure that an overview will be useful enough for most survivors. That said, when it comes to nukes, that's about all you can do, what you can expect, and what it all might mean to you. After that, welcome to the survivor's world.

And just so you know the rules: Uncle Sam does reserve the right to use first-strike nukes if it is determined vital to save the nation.

BIOLOGICAL weapons are, to my mind, by far the worst of the three (NBC). These are the bacterial attacks such as anthrax, and the viral attacks such as Ebola. These have been around since early man—using fungal matter as poisons for assassins; herbals as poisons for water sources; feces as poisons for weapon tips in battle; snakes as poison "bombs" dropped onto the heads of attacking enemies; and more. These tactics have been used as recently as 2001, against the United States, by terrorists using Anthrax in mailed letters.

Most civilized nations have realized that these things can rapidly get out of control and harm everyone, regardless of which side you're on. As such, these have been restricted, as never to be used in warfare. There are a handful of countries that have refused to sign the treaty banning biological warfare, and there are a handful of these weapons that are lost—they call them "orphans"; how quaint!

The real concern about biological weapons is that they can be made by pretty much anyone. In the old days, they would launch dead cows by catapult into forts and let the anthrax kill everyone. In this way, a simple weapon could be wielded by a terrorist or renegade country.

There is no protection, only response. See the medical section and again, welcome to survivor-ville, as you're likely to be quarantined, and rightly so, for the welfare and safety of the larger population as a whole. But that doesn't change your need to take care of you and yours.

The good news is that these weapons require a sophisticated lab to produce and that is usually not available to the bad guys, unless they have renegade government backing.

The rule here is that Uncle Sam refuses to use BIO weapons at all, and most other countries agree.

CHEMICAL weapons have also been around since antiquity. Arrows dipped in snake venom or plant poison were used for hunting by cavemen, and burning sulfur to choke out fort dwellers, are two ancient examples.

The bad news is that these things are deadly in a horrid way and there ain't a lot you can do about it. They come in three main categories—Nerve Agents, Blood Agents, and Blister Agents. They do what they say on the label. Nerve agents basically make all your nerves spasm until you crush yourself to death. Blood agents make you hemorrhage every-where, inside and out, until you bleed to death. Blister agents make your skin and lungs bubble up like a melting marshmallow until they suck all the plasma out of you and into the blisters and kill you that way, very painfully.

These are dispersed primarily by dropping them into the air. They could be aerosol, which disperses very quickly and are over in a few hours. Or they could be liquid droplets, which can last awhile, like up to a week or so.

They can be colorless and odorless or could have smells like mustard, chlorine, almonds, fruit, garlic, horseradish or even geraniums! Now there are other smells and other types, but you get the point on what they are and how they might come into play.

Funny smells, unexpected choking, spasms, bleeding, etc.—look around, check the winds and move away at a perpendicular angle, cover everything you can, hold your breath and seek cover. If it's wet, give it a week to sub-side; if it's smoke, give it a few hours. The good news is that these are so hard to deliver, that again, only a government could employ them or they'd be limited to a very confined area like a few hundred meters depending on how much was dispersed. If a convoy of planes dropped bombs, then the area would be larger, but even still, it would be a relatively localized area and it would be a time of short duration.

It is of interest for some survivalists, but most NBC or U.S. Military MOPP gear masks will not stop 90% of the chemicals that are out there in the inventory. Use them if you got 'em, but don't expect those who would use such weapons to play nice and use the kind our masks protect against!

Uncle Sam's rule for chemical weapons is that the U.S. can use them, but only as a response if they are used against us first. Tear gas is consid-ered a chemical weapon in this category. But don't sweat that for survival purposes.

At the end of the day, you'll either survive the initial action or not. If you do, then it's a matter of getting where you can and doing what you can, and it will always be a matter of survival until you can get to safety or get to care. And that's where the rest of the book comes into play.

WEATHER

Weather is all around us all day, every day. It can change in an instant and go from bad to worse, from mild to extreme, and from devastating to peaceful. The thing to remember in all this, is that it will pass and you can survive it if you're not killed right away and you apply common sense and survival knowledge.

Floods, tidal waves, tornadoes, hurricanes, fires, earthquakes, volcanoes, avalanches, blizzards, heat waves, monsoons, mudslides, droughts, and famine have all been part of life on earth since the beginning and always will be around us.

The thing to understand is that just as fires and floods are actually good for the ecology in the big-picture view, these traumatic natural occurrences have their place in the life cycle of the planet. Our time and space here is very short indeed compared to the earth and the universe. We cannot spin ourselves down asking why, and resisting the occurrence.

We must simply pay attention to the signs that lead up to these things and evacuate, avoid, or otherwise prepare to engage the event. You do the best you can to avoid or survive it and, if you don't, no more soup for you!

If you do manage to survive, then many of the aspects of this book come into play. Especially the exposure to the elements, the medical care due to exposure to disease often prevalent with mass casualty scenarios, finding clean water, etc.

The amazing thing to me is the appreciation of how great nature is compared to man. No matter how great and big and strong anything we build is, nature can come along and wipe it out easily and instantly. Remember that and don't get so attached to physical things that you can't up and leave at a moment's notice of impending disaster. If you're more married to your beach condo than your wife, this book ain't for you anyway! So the rules are simple for natural disasters:

- Nothing manmade will withstand nature at its worst, so get as far away as possible.
- If getting away isn't possible, find the best manmade structure you can for protection.

- If a natural escape is near and better, go there.
- Keep calm, use your head, and hang on.
- It will pass. You'll live, or you won't.

I've seen people survive *crazy* things they never should have, and I've seen people die from the simplest things that you'd never think would've been able to kill anyone.

Once the natural challenge passes, it's then just a matter of survival and time.

Good luck!

THE TIMES WE LIVE IN

Our current times in particular present a unique dynamic never before seen in human existence. While science indicates that mass extinction has occurred before, it was most likely caused by external sources. For the first time ever, we do face challenges that could cause history to repeat itself, but the reason this time could very well be self-induced.

You see, for the first time ever, we have created technology that has allowed us to indirectly change and thereby directly impact the entire globe, climate, and atmosphere in such a way that it may have a deleterious effect. Take your pick between global warming, nuclear winter, or other manmade or man-influenced factors.

In addition, we have clearly created, through technology, sophisticated weaponry in sufficient quantities that we can wipe out life as we know it, many times over. Just see the preceding section on NBC warfare.

Finally, we have reached a near-saturation point of population-to-resource ratio. It took us all of human history to reach a population of 3 billion people in the 1970s when I was a kid. We now have a planetary population of over 6 billion—it took only 30 years to double. By the time I reach the national average old age of 80+, we will have achieved a population of 9 billion human beings on the planet.

Think about that. In the course of one human lifetime (approximately 80 years) we will have tripled our numbers on the planet from what took us at least 10 million years to reach in the first place. (That time frame is a modest estimate based on when you choose to classify us as separate from our ape-like ancestors.) Any way you slice and dice it, that's a lot of new demand on resources in a very short amount of time.

So, just factor in one more human lifetime and it doesn't take a rocket scientist to see the extreme demands that will be placed on a planet with already vastly decreasing resources. Look at any satellite imagery of the planet a few decades ago compared to now, and you will realize just how much land foliage has been cleared to make room for humans.

Likewise, the food pyramid must be considered as well. Humans on average need about 2–5 acres of land per person to sustain life. This includes the actual land space needed to sustain the vegetation that feeds the animals, plus hold those animals, all the natural resources that provide us with the things we need in life such as clothing, shelter, fuel, tools, etc. And when you consider that not all the land on the planet is useable for sustenance—such as deserts and arctic regions—it's easy to see that there's an issue here.

With this general formula for human-to-land ratio, it is easy to see how an increase in the population becomes important as that means a decrease in available acreage needed and directly reduces each person's resources. Right now, the poor nations use about two acres and the wealthier nations average about five acres used per person.

This means that simple things like food and water will inherently become less available and more important over time. At this moment, that timeline is not that distant, and in fact, is very short, relatively speaking.

Add to this the fact that the arguably most important resource on the planet, oil, is rapidly diminishing. Most estimates put 2025 as the approximate time they expect most oil reserves to begin to run out. NOTE: These are the current oil reserves. There are many that are known but exceedingly difficult to access, and there are new ones being discovered, but these might not have great yields and could be very difficult to access and be very costly as well.

For the conspiracy theorists out there, so far only petroleum-based engines can move massive quantities of food and supplies. Solar, wind, and other "alternative" fuels cannot produce enough power to be truly cost effective on a global scale. No one is hiding this technology. The nation or entity that finds a better fuel alternative will become the wealthiest person or country on the planet overnight.

For the anti-nuclear folks, I hate to say it, but the only really viable solution so far has been nuclear power. And rightfully concerning is the fact that the depleted uranium waste from nuclear fuel can be turned into a dangerous weapon.

Combine all these factors of population explosion, oil crisis, food and water shortages, and a real need by nations for these vital and ever-decreasing limited resources, and it leads to potential for conflict. At the end of the day, all politics and religion aside, most wars are fought over one simple thing—resources.

Imagine that the whole world lived on one hill and there was only one apple tree, and all the people had to feed their families off that one apple tree. Then one day, the apples begin to run out due to natural or manmade causes (including increased population). It's easy to understand how a conflict might ensue.

Business is the counter to warfare. It is simply the practice of finding ways to get those resources by barter and trade, so long as all parties feel the relationship is mutually beneficial, or at least, more tolerable than the alternative of conflict.

And speaking of conflict, I offer you two more factors for the equation that might make you find a real value and need for the survival philosophies and skills espoused in this book.

The CIA has found two interesting statistics that have been very accurate predictors of conflict. These are "Infant Mortality Rate" and "Male to Female Birth Ratios." The IMR is the number of infants under 1 year old who die out of every 1,000. The M/F BR is the number of males born over the number of females born each year in a country.

When the IMR gets too high, then people feel that their governments have failed them by letting so many conditions such as poverty, disease, famine, and inadequate health care exist that lead to the death of so many infants. When people lose their children, they lose their reason and this is the best indicator that a coup is about to happen.

When the male to female ratio gets too high, it means there are many more men than there are women. With no reason to stay home, and no prospects for a family, many men join the military to seek a better life. This means a nation has a high number of military-aged young men joining the ranks and seeking action. Just look at any bar at the end of the night—the only people fighting are those who did not find someone to take home. See where I'm going?

Don't take my word for it, do your own research. You'll easily find that the top 10 countries with the highest IMR are very easily candidates for a coup, and the top 10 countries with the highest M/FBR are very easily seen as those most likely inclined to pick a fight.

When you add all these factors together, any way you like, these facts all indicate that the study of survival, getting back to basics, and the need for learning primitive skills are all very much warranted, indeed. Again, as I said in Chapter 1, we hope for the best, but plan for the worst—and remember: hope is not a plan!

So, let's all hope that the minds and hearts of scientists, governments, and corporations find a way to balance the technology with the human factors to prevent any of these potential calamities. In the meantime, study your basic survival skills!

BUG OUT BAGS, AID BAGS, AND SURVIVAL KITS

In SF we operate on simple principles. Keep everything you absolutely need for survival on your person at all times. Everyone should have a knife, lighter, compass, and light on them every day, and everywhere they go.

Next, keep a mini-kit in your coat, or purse, or glove compartment, or desk. This has a little bit more like a condom and or Ziploc bag as a canteen, some foil for fires and signals and dressings, some longer-term fire-starters like a magnesium bar and magnifying glass, some vitamins, some meds, a sewing kit, etc. For us, these things were always on our vest or web-belt.

Then everyone in SF also had their actual go-bag—the butt-pack or extra magazine pouch or canteen pouch filled with some food, water, first aid, fire starters, signals, maps, compasses, bigger tools and or weapons/ knives, etc.

It is this three-tier system that I encourage everyone to have and live by.

It's simple, it's easy, it works, and it's useful almost daily. So always keep: O.U.T.

On-You Kit—The minimal basics.

Urgent Kit—A bit too much to have on you at all times, but always ready to grab.

Travel Bag—The real deal you'll depend on for any duration of days.

See the charts on the following pages for items to include in your kits.

HAWKE'S RECOMMENDED SURVIVAL KIT ITEMS

Backpack, medium size, easy and light
D-Ring for mounting to vehicle or aircraft or holding off ground at camp site
Lighter, large and small (2)
Magnesium bar, fire starter
Matches, waterproof, waterproof container with whistle and compass
Whistle, with compass and magnifying glass
Compass, lensatic (military or civilian)
Water-purification tabs
Iodine drops (small bottle to purify water and treat wounds)
Electrical tape
Gauze, 1+ rolls for bandages, fire starter, toilet paper, etc.
Cravat—triangular bandage, tourniquet, sling, towel, sweat/drive-on rag, head protection, and as rag for filtering muddy water or gathering dew as well as additional pressure dressing
Soap, small bar, preventive hygiene/cleanliness
Toilet paper
Water (100 ml minimum)
Ziploc bag, large (canteen or food storage)
Trash bag, large (waterproof bag or rain coat)
Multivitamin pack
Meal bar
Beef jerky
Knife, small, Swiss style, with scissors, can opener, accessories

Knife, medium, Leatherman style with pliers, screwdriver, file, saw, etc.
Knife, large, fixed blade, utilitarian style, dual blade
Machete with saw on other side
Hammer/hatchet tool for chopping
Shovel tool (handheld or fold up)
Mag light, large
Mag light, mini
Batteries, spare, same for all items
Strobe light
Signal mirror
Pen flare, laser-type
Radio (shortwave) and transmitter
GPS & SPOT-type beacon transponder/locator
Space blankets (one as shelter from sun/rain, one as sleeping bag, two double as litter)
Net/hammock (back sack, bed, trapping, fishing, etc.)
100 feet of 550 paracord
10 safety pins
Fishing kit
Sewing kit
MRE or equivalent
Water, filter, canteen, and water containers
Canteen-style metal cup
Hunting rifle, ammo, and cleaning kit
Alternative hunting items like a slingshot, bb-gun, and bow and arrows.

Now, apply these items to your car, boat, plane, home, office, and vacation home or survival shelter.

And multiply these factors by the number of family members, and increase times by the number of days you plan for. I start with 30 days, but 15 is more reasonable, and 7 is the minimal. Use 3 days at the very least.

HAWKE'S RECOMMENDED FIRST-AID KIT ITEMS

GENERAL DESCRIPTION	SPECIFIC DESCRIPTION	QUANTITY
Bandages	Sterile 4x4	Sterile 4x4 25
	Bandage, non-adherent,	Sterile 3x4 25
	Ace wraps	6
	Band aids Various sizes and shapes	15
	Triangular bandages	2
Burn, Rash, and Sting, Non-Rx Meds, Other	Acetaminophen, aspirin, pain meds, antibiotics, specialty meds, and any others you can use, including charcoals, ipecac, etc.	100
	Anti-fungal cream tube	1
	Benadryl tabs (anti-allergy, mild sleep medication)	24
	Bismuth tabs (anti-diarrhea)	12
	Chapstick	1
	Gloves for water and waterproofing	5
	Condoms, make great canteens	2
	Hydrocort cream 1% tube (for allergic skin rashes)	1
	Ibuprofen	100
	Insect sting relief tube (also for rash, sunburn)	2
	Laxative	45
	Loperamide tabs (anti-diarrhea)	12
	Motion sickness tabs	12
	Sterile gel pad, burn dressing	8
	Tick, splinter, thorn removal	1
Tape	Surgical, medical	15
	Adhesive duct	2
	Paper type	2
	Black electrical	2

GENERAL DESCRIPTION	SPECIFIC DESCRIPTION	QUANTITY
Dental Emergency Eye, Nose & Throat,	Temporary fillings and pain meds	1
	Eye pads, eye drops	4
	Nasal spray squeeze bottle	1
	Sterile eyewash	1
	Sun screen	1
	Tongue depressors (use as small splints, medication application, tinder, etc.)	15
Instruments	Applicators, sterile	20
	Thermometer	12
	Safety pins	10
	Scalpel, sterile	1
	Shears, 7.5-inch, sharp/strong enough to cut through a penny	1
	Butterfly sutures (tape)	3
	Syringe, 30cc + 18ga irrigation needle (for wound irrigation)	1
Large Open Pocket	Hot/cold pack, reusable	1
	Ice pack (chemical cold compress)	4
	Sam splint (flexible splinting)	2
Minor Wounds, Blisters	Burn bandages	16
	Alcohol swabs/pads	50
	Blist-o-ban (large) hi-tech, ultra-thin blister pads	20
	Cotton balls (10)	6
	Duoderm (blister dressing)	2
	Iodine wipes	20
	Molefoam 4 x 3.5 (pressure-point padding)	8
	Moleskin 4 x 3.5 (prevent & care for blisters)	12
	Polysporin ointment (unit dose) (broad spectrum topical antibiotic)	28

(Continued on next page)

GENERAL DESCRIPTION	SPECIFIC DESCRIPTION	QUANTITY
	Steri-strips, minor wound closure	7
	Superglue, state-of-the-art wound closure	6
	Tegaderm, lightweight transparent wound and blister dressing	5
	Vaseline tube	1
	Vionex surgical soap packets	30
Small Compartment	Blood pressure kit	1
	Cup, aluminum	1
	Sterile saline solution (wound irrigation)	1
	Stethoscope	1
	Flashlight, pen, paper	1
	Iodine wipes	20
	Molefoam 4 x 3.5 (pressure-point padding)	8
Small Pockets	CPR kit	1
	Airway J-Tubes	2
	Forceps, 4.5-inch	1
	Forceps, halstead 5-inch	1
	Retractable knife	1
	Scissors, 5.5-inch	1
Sprains	Elastic bandage, 3-inch	3
	Elastic bandage, 6-inch	3
Survival, Repellent	Insect repellent, large canister	1
	Iodide tabs in vial	1
	Survival blanket	5
	Candles	5
	Blankets	1–2
	Trauma meds for children or elderly as needed	n/a

Last Words

The concept of surviving off the land is nothing new. It's always been there and always will be. It is, however, sometimes forgotten as needs change over time. And every once in a while its study comes back into fashion, usually out of necessity. Or, it simply becomes of interest to someone because of a change or event in their life. It was that early event for me that gave the spark, and the old SF hands who fanned the flame for my studies.

And for that, I want to thank all the old timers who taught me things over the years, both in official Army schools and as mentors professionally and personally. My childhood experiences gave me the interest and enthusiasm to learn survival, but it was through men far better than me that I learned and experienced survival. So, I'd like to give credit to them for a lot of this, as I'm mostly a conduit and a funnel for it to be channelled to others. It's up to you and them, what is to be done or undone.

I'd like to thank Earl, Pete, Dave and Jeff. They are no longer with us, but they will always mean a lot—these men gave me that true survivor spirit. I'd also like to thank the men of the U.S. Army Special Forces who were my instructors, my soldiers, my leaders, and my brothers-in-arms, from whom I learned so much, in all the ways that can't be measured and that, combined, formed a lot of who I am.

I'd like to point out here that even amongst my own, I have always been a bit on the extreme side and as such, there are some who might not agree with all I've said here. In their defense, I will say that a lot of what I have learned and believe and teach here was not taught to me by them, or at least, not directly. I will also say that there are many aspects of this book that are not officially "The Green Beret Way," only because there are no tactical, sterile, stealth, or military methodologies espoused here as they are there. The reason is simple:

In Special Forces, we have a mission that is different than that of the intended reader of this book. Theirs is to do what needs be done and leave without a trace. The "Quiet Professionals," as we're often called, consider that the best mission is the one where the media never knows we were there, and for which the credit of success goes to someone else. A big difference is that while they might have little support once behind the lines, they went in with equipment, a plan, and a commitment.

For the survivor, none of these factors hold true or have relevance. You had no plan, no preparation, no supplies, no support, and no commitment to be in this situation—it merely happened. Your mission is to get back—to be seen, heard, and to make your presence known in any and every way possible. And you must do this on your own.

In this way, the very essence of this book must deviate to some degree from that of the Green Beret way; but we teach principles, and the principles here are sound.

As for my own defense, I will let you, the reader—the survivor—decide the merit of it.

I dedicate this book to my wife, Ruth, who put up with a lot in the process and to my sons, all three of them—Gabriel the newcomer, Nicholas the graduate and Anthony the father, I say thank you for the joy you've given me, and for all I learned from watching you grow. You are my motivation during the dark times and trials of life.

I thank my brothers and sisters, who lord knows, put up with a mean and rascally elder brother, especially during the hard times of youth. I thank my family and friends who have always been good and done right by me. And finally, I thank Greg Jones at Running Press, who had the vision and the belief to make this book possible, and Jay Cassell of Skyhorse who had the wisdom to keep it running.

And to all those who come after me, and carry the torch of teaching the ways of survivalin', may you do better than I could. To those who survive, you know that life itself is thanks enough, and all life is good and precious.

Never forget: "Every day above ground is a good day!"

And always remember: Never Quit!